Anne Koziolek

AF239472

Automated Improvement of Software Architecture Models for Performance and Other Quality Attributes

**The Karlsruhe Series on Software Design and Quality
Volume 7**

Chair Software Design and Quality
Faculty of Computer Science
Karlsruhe Institute of Technology

and

Software Engineering Division
Research Center for Information Technology (FZI), Karlsruhe

Editor: Prof. Dr. Ralf Reussner

Automated Improvement of Software Architecture Models for Performance and Other Quality Attributes

by
Anne Koziolek

 Scientific Publishing

Dissertation, Karlsruher Institut für Technologie (KIT)
Fakultät für Informatik
Tag der mündlichen Prüfung: 14. Juli 2011
Referent: Prof. Dr. R. Reussner

Impressum

Karlsruher Institut für Technologie (KIT)
KIT Scientific Publishing
Straße am Forum 2
D-76131 Karlsruhe
www.ksp.kit.edu

KIT – Universität des Landes Baden-Württemberg und
nationales Forschungszentrum in der Helmholtz-Gemeinschaft

KIT Scientific Publishing 2013
Print on Demand

ISSN 1867-0067
ISBN 978-3-86644-973-2

Abstract

Quality properties, such as performance or reliability, are crucial for the success of a software system and largely influenced by the software architecture. Their quantitative prediction supports systematic, goal-oriented software design and forms a base of an engineering approach to software design. Researchers have proposed numerous approaches to predict a quality property based on a software architecture models. Using such prediction techniques can lead to better design decisions than experience.

Still, it is hard to design architectures that exhibit a good *trade-off* between multiple, often conflicting quality properties and costs. Even with a given functional design, many degrees of freedom in the software architecture (e.g. component deployment or server configuration) span a large design space. At the same time, the relation between a design decision and its effects on the quality properties can be complex and can depend on other design decisions. Thus, manually exploring the design space and finding architectures with good trade-offs is laborious.

To provide support for this task, the goal of an automated method should be to find optimal trade-off candidate architectures software architects and stakeholders can analyse and use for well-informed decisions, knowing the effects and incurred trade-offs of their choices.

A number of existing approaches addresses the challenge of improving software architecture by automatically suggesting improvements. For example, rule-based approaches that only target performance improvement have been suggested. While they codify useful knowledge from the performance prediction domain, they ignore the possible trade-off with other quality attributes. Additionally, frameworks to address multi-criteria optimization of software architectures considering several degrees of freedom have been proposed. However, their support of different degrees of freedoms or of expressive quality prediction techniques is limited, thereby severely limiting the class of analysable systems.

This thesis proposes a method and tool to improve component-based software architectures (CBA) by searching the design space using meta-heuristics. The method relies on existing performance and reliability prediction methods to evaluate candidate architectures. It supports software architects in making trade-off decisions and negotiating quality requirements with a system's stakeholders. The main contributions are the following:

- First, we identify the information needs of software architects and stakeholders that can be filled with an automated method based on model-based quality prediction. Based on this, we extend a *process model* for the development of new component-based systems with our method and include a more solid process for determining appropriate quality requirements. The method provides quantitative feedback from model-based quality predictions for software architects, requirements engineers, and stakeholders to be used in architecture design and requirements analysis. Furthermore, we embed the method in other scenarios such as software evolution scenarios or capacity planning.

- Second, we provide a *framework* for multi-objective optimization of software architectures based on quality predictions. This framework is independent of the used CBA metamodel and of the analysed quality due to its flexible and extensible *degree of freedom model*. Additionally, it allows to include domain-specific knowledge in form of architectural tactics operators known from literature and operationalized in this work.

- Third, to instantiate this framework, we provide *concrete degrees of freedom for CBA* affecting performance, reliability, and costs as well as *performance and costs tactics* for the Palladio Component Model, which allows state-of-the-art quality predictions.

The method proposed in this thesis helps software architects (1) by saving significant costs for manually exploring the potentially large design space, (2) by providing a more solid process for determining appropriate quality requirements, thus providing input for well-informed trade-off decisions in the requirements analysis phase, and (3) by providing an extensible analysis framework applicable in a large class of practical scenarios. In addition to development of new systems, the method can be used in software evolution scenarios (such as adding new functionality or change the software to adapt to changing usage or to a new environment).

We have validated the accuracy and applicability of our method and evaluated the performance of our extensions of the optimization step (e.g. using tactics). This thesis describes experiments with the novel method on two complex component-based software systems, the first being a business reporting system (BRS); and the second being an industrial control system (ICS) from ABB, which consists of more than 25 components deployed on up to 8 servers and is implemented in several million lines of code. We found that the explored design space indeed provided potential for improvement and required to make trade-off decisions. Furthermore, our tool was able to closely approximate the globally optimal candidates. Additional, our extension of standard evolutionary algorithms with tactics was able to find solutions 50% to 90% faster on average.

Zusammenfassung

Die quantitative Vorhersage von Qualitätseigenschaften (wie beispielsweise Performanz i.S.v. Zeitverhalten und Ressourceneffizienz, sowie Zuverlässigkeit) für komponentenbasierte Software-Architekturen unterstützt den systematischen, zielorientierten Software-Entwurf nach Ingenieurprinzipien, indem die Eigenschaften des zu entwickelnden Artefakts schon vor der eigentlichen Erstellung abgeschätzt werden können. Forscher haben verschiedene Ansätze um quantifizierbare Qualitätseigenschaften basierend auf einem annotierten Modell einer Software-Architektur vorherzusagen vorgeschlagen (Balsamo et al. (2004) und H. Koziolek, 2010 geben einen Überblick über Ansätze für Performanz, Gokhale (2007) für Zuverlässigkeit). Die Verwendung solcher Vorhersageverfahren unterstützt das Treffen von besseren Entwurfsentscheidungen (H. Koziolek und Firus, 2005).

Doch auch mit der Verwendung solcher Verfahren ist es schwierig, Architekturen zu entwerfen die eine gute *Abwägung* zwischen den oft im Konflikt stehenden Qualitätseigenschaften aufweisen. Weiterhin sind auch die Kosten von Qualitätseigenschaften zu berücksichtigen. Selbst wenn ein funktionaler Entwurf bereits vorliegt, liegen noch viele Freiheitsgrade im Entwurf einer komponentenbasierten Software-Architektur vor (wie zum Beispiel die Verteilung von Komponenten auf verfügbare Rechner, oder die Konfiguration dieser Rechner) und spannen einen beträchtlichen Entwurfsraum auf. Dabei ist der Zusammenhang zwischen einer Entwurfsentscheidung und ihren Konsequenzen keineswegs trivial, sondern kann komplex sein und außerdem von weiteren zu treffenden Entwurfsentscheidungen abhängen. Daher ist die manuelle Suche nach optimalen Lösungen in diesem Entwurfsraum zeitaufwändig. Eine lückenhafte Durchsuchung des Entwurfsraums führt aber in der Regel zur suboptimalen Entwürfen.

Bei der Suche nach besseren Entwürfen kann sich der Software-Architekt weiterhin nicht auf die Umsetzung vorher bereits festgelegter Anforderungen (z.B. dass die Antwortzeit des Systems kürzer als eine Sekunde sein soll) konzentrieren, denn diese können im Verlauf der Entwicklung noch gegen andere Qualitätseigenschaften abgewogen werden, oder aber wegen zu unerwarteter zu hoher Kosten verworfen werden (Berntsson Svensson et al., 2011).

Um diese Aufgabe zu unterstützen, muss es das Ziel einer automatisierten Methode sein, Architekturkandidaten zu finden, die eine optimale Abwägung von Qualitätseigenschaften darstellen; die also Pareto-optimal hinsichtlich mehrerer zu optimierenden Qualitätseigenschaften sind. Diese optimalen Architekturkandidaten können dann von Software-Architekten und anderen Interessenvertretern analysiert werden und die Grundlage für Entwurfsentscheidungen sein, bei denen die Konsequenzen der einzelnen Alternativen bereits bekannt sind. So können Entscheidungen auf Basis von gesicherten Informationen anstatt von Intuition getroffen werden.

Forscher habe verschiedene Methoden vorschlagen, um den Software-Architekten bei der Suche nach optimalen Entwurfskandidaten auf Basis von modellbasierten Vorhersagen zu unterstützen. Allerdings haben diese Ansätze spezifische Stärken und Schwächen. Regel-basierte Ansätze (Xu, 2010; Trubiani, 2011) wurden für Performanzverbesserungen vorgeschlagen. Sie kapseln Domänenwissen aus dem Bereich der Performanzvorhersageverfahren als ausführbare Regeln, die angewendet werden können um die Performanzeigenschaften (z.B. den zu erwartenden Durchsatz und die Antwortzeit) von Software-Architekturen zu verbessern. Sie betrachten allerdings nicht die Auswirkungen dieser Änderungen auf andere Qualitätsattribute. Die multikriterielle Optimierung von Software-Architekturen entlang mehrerer Freiheitsgrade wird von einigen Ansätzen unterstützt (z.B. (Aleti et al., 2009a; Saxena und Karsai, 2010b). Allerdings bieten diese Ansätze entweder nicht die Möglichkeit, verschiedene Freiheitsgrade flexibel miteinander zu kombinieren (Aleti et al., 2009a), oder sie unterstützen nur vereinfachte Qualitätsvorhersagetechniken (Saxena und Karsai, 2010b).

Die vorliegende Arbeit schlägt eine automatisierte Methode vor, um komponentenbasierte Software-Architekturen basierend auf modellbasierter Qualitätsvorhersagen zu verbessern. Sie bietet damit Unterstützung für Abwägungsentscheidungen in der Anforderungsanalysephase. Die Hauptbeiträge gliedern sich in drei Gruppen:

- Die Informationsbedürfnisse von Software-Architekten und Interessensvertretern, die von einer automatisierten Methode basierend auf Qualitätsvorhersageverfahren erfüllt werden können, wurden ermittelt. Weiterhin erweitert die Arbeit ein *Prozessmodell*, um die automatisierte Verbesserungsmethode in den Entwicklungsprozess einzufügen und eine fundierte Möglichkeit, Qualitätsanforderungen zu bestimmen, zu bieten. Das Ergebnis dieser Methode ist eine Rückmeldung über die erreichbaren Qualitätseigenschaften und deren Konflikte untereinander an Software-Architekten, Anforderungsingenieure und Interessensvertreter, die diese Information in der Anforderungsanalyse und im Architekturentwurf nutzen können. Weiterhin bettet diese Arbeit die Methode auch in andere Szenarien wie zum Beispiel die Weiterentwicklung bestehender Systeme ein.

- Ein weiterer Beitrag ist ein *Rahmenwerk* für die multikriterielle Optimierung von Software-Architekturen basierend auf existierenden Qualitätsvorhersageverfahren und dem Konzept der Freiheitsgrade. Ein wichtiger Bestandteil ist eine *Modellierungssprache für Freiheitsgrade*, die unabhängig vom verwendeten Metamodell zur Modellierung der Architektur ist. Damit ist das Rahmenwerk selbst unabhängig von dem verwendeten Metamodell und den verwendeten Qualitätsvorhersageverfahren.

Der Entwurfsraum kann weiterhin basierend auf den modellierten Freiheitsgraden für ein Eingabearchitekturmodell *automatisiert instanziiert* werden, so dass der Software-Architekt nicht manuell die einzelnen Parameter der aktuellen Architektur finden muss. Zusammen mit den verfügbaren Qualitätsvorhersageverfahren instanziiert das Rahmenwerk weiterhin ein Optimierungsproblem, für das mit evolutionären Algorithmen nach annähernd optimalen Lösungen gesucht wird. Weiterhin erlaubt das Rahmenwerk, domänenspezifisches Wissen als sog. *Taktikoperatoren* einzubinden.

- Das Rahmenwerk wird in dieser Arbeit für das Palladio Komponentenmodell (PCM, (Becker et al., 2009)) *instanziiert* indem die Freiheitsgrade des PCM modelliert werden. Weiterhin werden allgemeine *Freiheitsgrade von komponentenbasierten Software-Architekturen*, die Performanz, Zuverlässigkeit und Kosten beeinflussen, metamodellunabhängig beschrieben. Schließlich enthält die Arbeit *Performanz- und Kostentaktiken* für die gezielte Verbesserung von PCM-Modellen.

Als Vorteil dieser Arbeit wird der Software-Architekt unterstützt, indem (1) Kosten für die manuelle Suche im potentiell großen Entwurfsraum durch die Automatisierung eingespart werden, (2) die Bestimmung von Qualitätsanforderungen mit einem Fundament zur Abschätzung der erreichbaren Qualitäten und Konflikte untermauert wird, welches wohlinformierte Abwägungsentscheidungen schon in der Anforderungsanalysephase ermöglicht und (3) ein flexibles und erweiterbares Rahmenwerk für die Architekturoptimierung bereitgestellt wird, dass in vielen praktischen Szenarien anwendbar ist. Die Methode kann sowohl bei der Neuentwicklung von Systemen verwendet werden als auch in Evolutionsszenarien, wie zum Beispiel dem Hinzufügen neuer Funktionalität oder der Anpassung des Systems wegen veränderter Benutzung oder einer anderweitig veränderten Systemumgebung.

Damit entwickelt die Arbeit den momentanen Stand des Wissens weiter und ist somit von Vorteil auch für Forscher im Bereich Architekturoptimierung, da sie (1) die Rolle von modellbasierter Qualitätsvorhersage im Prozess der Qualitätsanforderungsermittlung ausarbeitet, (2) die erste Methode vorstellt, die eine flexible und erweiterbare Definition des zu durchsuchenden Entwurfsraums ermöglicht und (3) die erste Methode vorstellt die domänenspezifisches Wissen mit multikriterieller Software-Architekturoptimierung verbindet. Damit liefert diese Arbeit einen weiteren Schritt zur weiteren Entwicklung von Software-Technik hin zu einer Ingenieurwissenschaft.

Um die vorgeschlagene Methode zu validieren, wurde zum einen die Genauigkeit und Anwendbarkeit der Methode untersucht und zum anderen die Effizienz- und Gütesteigerungen unserer Erweiterungen des Optimierungsschritts (u.a. durch die o.g. Taktiken) untersucht. Die vorgeschlagene Methode wurde für zwei komplexe, komponentenbasierte Systeme angewendet, zum einen für ein Geschäftsberichterstattungssystem (business reporting system, Wu und Woodside, 2004b), zum anderen für ein Prozesskontrollsystem von ABB, das die Anwendbarkeit unserer Methode im industriellen Kontext zeigt. Es zeigte sich dass der untersuchte Entwurfsraum das erwartete Potenzial für Qualitätsverbesserungen enthielt, dabei aber auch einen Konflikt zwischen den Qualitätseigenschaften so dass sie gegeneinander abgewogen werden mussten. Weiterhin konnte unser Werkzeug die global optimalen Kandidaten gut annähern. Außerdem haben unsere Erweiterung des verwendeten evolutionären Algorithmus durch Taktiken zu einer Reduzierung der Laufzeit von im Mittel 50% - 90% geführt.

Danksagungen

Viele Menschen haben mich bei der Erstellung dieser Arbeit unterstützt, ihnen möchte ich an dieser Stelle danken. Zuallererst geht der Dank an meinen Doktorvater Prof. Dr. Ralf Reussner, der zunächst während des Studiums mein Interesse an der Wissenschaft geweckt hat und mich dann während der gesamten Promotionszeit beraten und unterstützt hat. Durch seine Vermittlung wissenschaftlichen Arbeitens, sowie seine fachlichen und methodischen Ratschläge habe ich so vieles gelernt. Weiterhin ist seine Art, den Lehrstuhl zu führen und die verschiedenen Themen miteinander zu verknüpfen, Grundstein für die gute Arbeitsatmosphäre in der Gruppe. Weiterhin danke ich meinem Korreferenten, Prof. Dr. Andreas Oberweis, für seine Hinweise und Ideen, darunter insbesondere den ersten Anstoß zum bearbeiteten Thema.

Daneben möchte ich Heiko danken, der mich zuerst als Kollege, und bald als Partner und Ehemann unterstützt hat: Ohne ihn wäre diese Arbeit in so vielfacher Hinsicht nicht möglich gewesen, von seiner Betreuung während der Diplomarbeit, über die gemeinsame Arbeit an vielen Papieren, bis hin zu der perfekt gemischten, liebevollen, motivierenden und anspornenden Unterstützung beim Aufschreiben der Diss.

Weiterhin möchte ich mich aber auch bei allen Mitgliedern der Arbeitsgruppe SDQ für die tolle Arbeitsatmosphäre bedanken. Das gegenseitige Interesse an der Arbeit der Kollegen, die spannenden und konstruktiven Diskussionen, aber auch die gemeinsamen Unternehmungen haben die Promotionszeit zu einer spannenden und produktiven Zeit gemacht. Alle Kollegen haben dazu beigetragen, aber einige möchte ich besonders hervorheben: meine Bürokollegin Lucia, mit der ich eine tolle Zeit und gute Gespräche in den verschiedenen Büros hatte; Heiko und Steffen, die zu Beginn meine Diplomarbeit betreuten und mir dabei und später vieles beibrachten; und die von mir betreuten Studenten Philipp Merkle, Tom Beyer, Timo Rohrberg, Atanas Dimitrov und Qais Noorshams, für die Unterstützung bei Implementierungsarbeiten und die Mitarbeit in Publikationen.

Next to the SDQ group, I would also like to thank the other researchers that I was lucky to work with. First of all Catia Trubiani, with whom I had a close collaboration and many interesting discussions, but also great fun during our time in L'Aquila and Karlsruhe. Also, many thanks to Vittorio Cortellessa, Raffaela Mirandola, Danilo Ardagna, Murray Woodside, and Dorina Petriu, who invited me to spend some time at their research groups, where I learned a lot and got to know great people. Grazie!

Ein Dank der ganz anderen, besonderen Art geht an meine Eltern. Alles, was ich bisher erreicht habe, geht auf sie zurück und wäre ohne sie nicht möglich gewesen. Ich kann mich sehr glücklich schätzen.

Contents

Abstract   i

Zusammenfassung   v

Danksagungen   xi

1. Introduction   1
   1.1. Motivation   1
   1.2. Problem   6
   1.3. Existing Solutions   9
   1.4. Contributions   10
   1.5. Outline   16

I. Foundations and Related Work   21

2. Component-based Software Architectures and Quality   23
   2.1. Component-based Software Architecture   23
      2.1.1. Definitions   24
      2.1.2. Component-based Software Development Process   30
   2.2. Quality of Software Architectures   32
      2.2.1. Quality Attributes of Software Architecture . . .   33
      2.2.2. Quantitative Quality Properties   37
   2.3. Modelling Concepts   42
      2.3.1. Models and Metamodels   43
      2.3.2. Essential Meta Object Facility   46

	2.4.	Model-based Quality Prediction	49
		2.4.1. General Concepts	49
		2.4.2. Performance	51
		2.4.3. Other Quality Attributes	54
		2.4.4. Quality Completions	56
		2.4.5. Integration in the CB Development Process	58
	2.5.	Palladio Component Model	59
		2.5.1. Example PCM Model	60
		2.5.2. PCM Metamodel	64
		2.5.3. Performance Analysis	65
		2.5.4. Reliability Analysis	66
		2.5.5. Cost Model	67
	2.6.	Other CBA Models With Predictive Capabilities	70
		2.6.1. CBML	70
		2.6.2. ROBOCOP	72
3.	**Multi-Criteria Optimization**		75
	3.1.	Optimization	75
	3.2.	Handling Multiple Criteria	77
		3.2.1. Preference Articulation	78
		3.2.1.1. A Priori Preference Articulation	78
		3.2.1.2. A Posteriori Preference Articulation	79
		3.2.1.3. Interactive Preference Articulation	80
		3.2.2. Pareto Optimality	80
	3.3.	Classical Methods	83
	3.4.	Multi-objective Metaheuristics	84
	3.5.	Evolutionary Algorithms	86
		3.5.1. Basic Algorithm	86
		3.5.2. Reproduction	88
		3.5.2.1. Mutation	88
		3.5.2.2. Crossover	89

	3.5.3.	Selection	91
	3.5.4.	Elitism	95
	3.5.5.	Comparing Multi-objective Evolutionary Optimization Techniques	96
		3.5.5.1. Pareto Dominance Ranking	97
		3.5.5.2. Coverage Indicator	98
		3.5.5.3. Hyper-volume Indicator	98
		3.5.5.4. Other Methods	100

4. Related Work 101

4.1. Supporting Software Architects to Improve CBA 101

    4.1.1. Scope of this Survey 102

    4.1.2. Criteria for Automated Improvement Support Comparison 104

        4.1.2.1. Addressed Improvement Problem . . . 104

        4.1.2.2. Solution Approach 107

        4.1.2.3. Flexibility 108

    4.1.3. Performance Improvement Methods 110

    4.1.4. Improvement Methods for Multiple Quality Attributes 120

    4.1.5. Summary 133

4.2. Problem-specific Knowledge in Metaheuristics 135

II. Automated Architecture Improvement 139

5. Supporting the Architect to Improve Component-based Architecture Models 141

5.1. Goal of Automated Improvement Support 141

5.2. Process 146

    5.2.1. Component-based Development Process with Quality Exploration 146

	5.2.2.	Quality Analysis Workflow	147
	5.2.3.	Architecture Exploration Workflow	150
	5.2.4.	Decision Making	152
5.3.	Model-based Improvement		154
5.4.	Scenarios		156
5.5.	Assumptions and Limitations		162
5.6.	Summary		163

6. Formalization of the Design Space 165

6.1.	Requirements for Automated Improvement		166
6.2.	Overview and PCM Example		169
	6.2.1.	Valid Changes in the Example	169
	6.2.2.	Illustration of Change Constraints	171
	6.2.3.	Degree of Freedom Examples in the PCM	172
	6.2.4.	Degrees of Freedom Instances in the Example	173
	6.2.5.	Design Space of the Example	174
6.3.	Degrees of Freedom		178
	6.3.1.	Change Definitions	178
		6.3.1.1. Change	178
		6.3.1.2. Change with Valid Models	180
		6.3.1.3. Valid Change	180
		6.3.1.4. Change Types	181
		6.3.1.5. Functionally Equivalent Change Types	182
		6.3.1.6. Change Type that Affects Quality Attributes	183
		6.3.1.7. Indivisible Change Types	184
		6.3.1.8. Primary Changeable Elements	188
		6.3.1.9. Change Groups	190
		6.3.1.10. Summary	191

6.3.2. Degree of Freedom Definitions 193

6.3.2.1. Required Information for Enriched
Change Type Description 194

6.3.2.2. Degree of Freedom 197

6.3.2.3. Degree of Freedom Instance 199

6.3.2.4. DoFIs represent DoF 202

6.3.2.5. Result 204

6.3.3. Degrees of Freedom in EMOF 206

6.4. Design Space 213

6.4.1. Derive Degree of Freedom Instances for a System 213

6.4.2. Unconstrained Design Space 219

6.4.3. Constraints 224

6.4.4. Discussion of Other Representations of the
Design Space 226

6.5. Assumptions and Limitations 227

6.5.1. Assumptions 228

6.5.2. Limitations 229

6.6. Summary 230

**7. Degrees of Freedom in Component-based Software
Architecture Models** 231

7.1. Degree of Freedom Description Schema 232

7.2. Software-related Degrees of Freedom 235

7.2.1. Selection of Components 235

7.2.2. Non-functional Component Configuration
Parameters 237

7.2.3. Passive Resources Multiplicity 240

7.2.4. Priorities 243

7.3. Deployment-related Degrees of Freedom 244

7.3.1. Allocation 245

7.3.2. Allocation with Replication 249

7.3.3.   Server Replication   253

7.3.4.   Resource Selection   256

7.3.5.   Resource Property Change   258

7.3.6.   Further Configuration of the Software Stack . . .   260

7.3.7.   Quality Completion Configuration   263

7.4.   Custom Degrees of Freedom   266

7.4.1.   Metamodel-specific Degrees of Freedom   267

7.4.2.   System-specific Degrees of Freedom   268

7.5.   Limitations   270

7.6.   Summary   272

8.   Optimization   273

8.1.   Optimization Problem   273

8.1.1.   Formalization of the Optimization Problem . . .   274

8.1.2.   Properties of the Optimization Problem   277

8.1.3.   Applicable Optimization Techniques   281

8.2.   Evolutionary Optimization   286

8.2.1.   Outline   286

8.2.2.   Candidate Representation   291

8.2.3.   Candidate Evaluation   294

8.2.3.1.   Quality Function Definition   295

8.2.3.2.   Candidate Evaluation during the Search   297

8.2.4.   Candidate Reproduction   299

8.2.4.1.   Reproduction Operators   300

8.2.4.2.   Design Space Constraints   301

8.2.5.   Candidate Selection   302

8.2.5.1.   Basic Selection Strategy   302

8.2.5.2.   Considering Quality Requirements in
Selection   303

8.2.6.   Stop Criteria   307

8.3.   Informed Quality Improvement   308

     8.3.1.   Improvement Tactics   308

           8.3.1.1.   Scope   309

           8.3.1.2.   Performance Tactics   310

           8.3.1.3.   Reliability Tactics   320

           8.3.1.4.   Cost Tactics   322

     8.3.2.   Tactics Operators   324

     8.3.3.   Intensification using Tactics   328

     8.3.4.   Starting Population Heuristics   329

           8.3.4.1.   Hybrid Optimization   330

           8.3.4.2.   Allocation Schemes Starting Population   331

8.4.   CBA Optimization Framework   332

8.5.   Discussion   336

     8.5.1.   Influences on Optimization Performance   336

           8.5.1.1.   Complexity of Optimization Problems .   337

           8.5.1.2.   Complexity of Software Architecture

                     Optimization Problems   340

     8.5.2.   Assumptions   342

     8.5.3.   Limitations   344

           8.5.3.1.   General Limitations   344

           8.5.3.2.   Current Limitations of Tactics   345

8.6.   Summary   345

III. Validation and Conclusion   347

9.   Validation   349

9.1.   Validation Goals and Derived Evaluation Questions . . .   350

     9.1.1.   Validity of the Automated Improvement Method   350

           9.1.1.1.   Validation Levels for Model-based

                     Quality Improvement Approaches . . .   351

9.1.1.2. Derived Validation Questions for
Accuracy 353

9.1.1.3. Derived Validation Questions for
Applicability 356

9.1.1.4. Out of Scope Validation Activities . . . 358

9.1.2. Validation of the Optimization Step 360

9.1.2.1. Performance Assessment for
Multi-objective Optimization 360

9.1.2.2. Derived Validation Questions 362

9.1.2.3. Out of Scope Validation Activities . . . 363

9.2. Tool Implementation 364

9.2.1. PerOpteryx Architecture 365

9.2.2. Degree of Freedom Instances in PerOpteryx . . . 367

9.3. Case Study Systems 369

9.3.1. Business Reporting System 369

9.3.2. ABB Process Control System 374

9.4. Improving CBA based on Model-based Quality Prediction 376

9.4.1. Model Accuracy 377

9.4.1.1. Existing Model Accuracy Studies for
the PCM 377

9.4.1.2. Allocation Validation Study 380

9.4.1.3. Results for Question Q1.1 386

9.4.2. Approximating the True Pareto Front 386

9.4.2.1. Experiment Set-up 387

9.4.2.2. Results for Question Q1.2 387

9.4.3. Design Space 391

9.4.3.1. Business Reporting System 392

9.4.3.2. ABB System 400

9.4.3.3. Results for Question Q1.3 401

9.5.   Validation of the Optimization Step 402

    9.5.1.   Comparing Optimization Techniques 402

        9.5.1.1.   Coverage Indicator 403

        9.5.1.2.   Hyper-volume Indicator 404

        9.5.1.3.   Combination of Quality Metrics 405

        9.5.1.4.   Time Metrics 407

        9.5.1.5.   Summary 407

    9.5.2.   Tactics 408

        9.5.2.1.   Business Reporting System 409

        9.5.2.2.   ABB System 415

        9.5.2.3.   Results for Question Q2.1 418

    9.5.3.   Intensification Phase 419

        9.5.3.1.   Experiment Set-up 419

        9.5.3.2.   Results for Question Q2.2 420

    9.5.4.   Quality Requirements Effect 421

        9.5.4.1.   Experiment Set-up 421

        9.5.4.2.   Results 422

        9.5.4.3.   Results for Question Q2.3 428

9.6.   Summary 429

10. Conclusion 431

10.1. Summary 431

10.2. Benefits 433

10.3. Assumptions and Limitations 436

10.4. Future Work 439

    10.4.1. Short Term Future Work 439

    10.4.2. Long Term Future Work 443

Appendix 449

A.   Palladio Component Model 449

    A.1.   Key for PCM Diagrams 449

    A.2.   Mapping of PCM Concepts to General Concepts 450

A.3.   Inheritance Hierarchy of Components 450

A.4.   RDSEFF Metamodel Elements 454

A.5.   Resource Repository 455

A.6.   OCL Constraint for Valid AllocationContexts . . 455

B.   Degrees of Freedom and Design Space Appendix 463

B.1.   Notes on Changes 463

B.2.   Proof for Design Space Definition 464

B.3.   Candidate Transformation Function T 466

C.   Degree of Freedom Definitions for PCM 468

C.1.   Component Selection 468

C.2.   Non-functional Component Configuration
        Parameters 474

C.3.   Passive Resources Multiplicity 475

C.4.   Priorities 476

C.5.   Allocation 476

C.6.   Allocation with Replication 480

C.7.   Server Replication 483

C.8.   Resource Selection 484

C.9.   Resource Property Change 487

C.10.   Quality Completion Configuration 489

C.11.   Subsystem Selection in the PCM 491

D.   Quality of Service Modelling Language QML 495

E.   OCL in EMOF 497

F.   Notational Conventions 501

List of Figures 503

List of Tables 511

Bibliography 513

Index 551

1. Introduction

The complexity of software systems has been growing since the advent of programming. To cope with complexity and the further constraints of practical software development, software engineering strives to apply "a systematic, disciplined, quantifiable approach" (IEEE Std 610.12-1990, 1990) to develop software. The name software engineering suggests that properties from classical engineering shall be applied. Engineers, in general, design and build artefacts based on theories and methods, while working under financial and organizational constraints (Sommerville, 2004, p.7).

This thesis is a step towards adopting engineering principles in software engineering. The remainder of this chapter motivates our work. Section 1.1 motivates the need for automated improvement of software architecture models, and Section 1.2 describes the underlying challenges in detail. Shortcomings of existing approaches are discussed in Section 1.3. Section 1.4 lists the proposed scientific contributions of this work. Finally, an outline is provided in Section 1.5.

1.1. Motivation

Engineering Principles   Two principles of engineering disciplines are that (1) engineers are able to predict and reason on properties of the developed artefacts during design, i.e. by using an abstract representation of the artefact (*prediction*) and (2) that systems are systematically constructed from more elementary components, which can be developed independently (*composition*).

A classical example for the first principle is statics in civil engineering: Bridges are built after calculations and simulations based on statics theory suggest that they will endure expected load. The ability to predict properties and reason on an artefact on an abstract level makes projects more amenable to planning and avoids late detection of problems. Note that the models may be approximations: For example, the detailed motion of air along air plane wings cannot be exactly determined, but only approximated.

An example for the second principle can be drawn from construction engineering: For buildings, the design is separated into concerns: While architects and structural engineers design the structural features of buildings such as walls and roof, other aspects are covered by specialists such as heating specialists, electrical engineers, and plumbing engineers. The independent development of building blocks allows to produce results faster and more efficiently due to abstraction and division of labour.

Problems due to late Quality Attribute Consideration   As software is intangible, systems are complex, and software engineering is a relatively new discipline, realizing large, software-intensive projects is challenging and risky. The list of failed or challenged software projects is long (Glass, 1998), and a number of recently challenged projects (i.e. projects that were significantly delayed or significantly over budget) can be partially traced back to problems with *software architecture and quality attributes* such as performance or reliability, i.e. quality problems that originate from the high-level organization of systems. Prominent examples concerning performance are provided by Schmietendorf and Scholz (2001) and H. Koziolek, 2008: The automated baggage handling systems at Denver airport and Heathrow airport, and SAP's Business by Design project.

Baggage handling systems: The initial problems with the baggage handling system caused the airport to open 16 month later than scheduled, almost $2 billion over budget and without an automated baggage system. Here, the system was planned to serve one terminal first, but later should serve all terminals of the airport (Montealegre and Keil, 2000). The system was not able to cope with this increased demand, i.e. it was not scalable enough. Similar problems in smaller scale occurred in Heathrow's newly built Terminal 5 in 2008: the number of messages generated by the baggage system was to high for the system (Charette, 2008), so that during the first weeks of operation, 23000 bags were lost and more than 500 flights were cancelled, causing losses of £16 millions (Thomson, 2008). The number of passengers of the operating carrier British Airways dropped by 220000 in the month afterwards, which is mostly contributed to the baggage handling problems (Robertson, 2008).

SAP's Business by Design is an ERP solution targeting medium-sized enterprises. In contrast to previous solutions, Business by Design is a software-as-a-service solution: the application is hosted by SAP (or a specialized provider) and enterprises rent it, paying per use or per user. The project was announced in 2007 (Briegleb, 2008), planned to be launched at the beginning of 2008 (Briegleb, 2007), and planned to win 10000 customers by 2010 leading to $1 billion sales (Storm, 2008).

However, performance problems delayed the start of the project: An early implementation was significantly slower than SAP's standard solution, and was only able to handle 10 concurrent users instead of the desired 1000 users (Briegleb, 2007). As a result, the project start was delayed until mid 2010 (Eriksdotter, 2010). At the beginning of 2011, Business by Design has 400 customers (CIO Wirtschaftsnachrichten, 2011). The costs of this delay are not known, but can expected to be high due to the large planned project volume.

In all cases, the lack of predicted quality properties (here performance) lead to high losses, both financially and in reputation, and shows the need to adopt the engineering principles in software engineering. Furthermore, quality properties need to be considered early in a software project life cycle.

Problems of Early Quality Requirement Specification   While an early consideration of quality attributes is desirable, collecting *quality requirements* early from stakeholders often leads to a long wish list of quality properties because the effects of quality demands for software are not well understood. In other engineering disciplines, it is common understanding that demanding a high-speed train will lead to higher costs than demanding a local train with maximum speed of 70 km/h. The consequences of demanding a software system that answers requests within 100 microseconds, is available 365 days a year, and secured against any type of conceivable attack, however, are not necessarily known to stakeholders. Fulfilling all requirements from such a list may lead to an expensive and over-engineered solution. The costs of quality requirements is difficult to assess at an early development stage, so that quality requirements, even if stated, are often dismissed later (Berntsson Svensson et al., 2011, p.9). Thus, while quality attributes need to be considered early, the actual quality requirements must be questioned and negotiated during the software development process.

Software Architecture and Quality Prediction   New methodologies realizing the two engineering principles of prediction and composition have been continuously introduced in software engineering to cope with the increased complexity. In the early days of software development, high-level languages and abstract data types enabled programmers to reason about their programs on a more abstract level than individual machine instructions (Garlan and Shaw, 1994). To cope with the complexity of today's large software systems, *software architecture* (Taylor et al., 2009) provides a high-level abstraction for reasoning about a software system.

Furthermore, to achieve composability of software building blocks, *software components* (Szyperski et al., 2002) strive to provide sufficient information for third party usage via interfaces, while encapsulating internal behaviour and complexity. Furthermore, a goal of the resulting *component-based software architecture* (CBA) is to make properties of software systems more predictable due to well-defined composition of components.

Quality properties considered at the level of (component-based) software architecture are performance, reliability, maintainability, costs, or security. Experienced software architects know styles and tactics to improve quality properties of a software architecture (Bass et al., 2003). Using analysis methods such as the Architecture Trade-off Analysis Method (ATAM) (Clements et al., 2001), software architects can analyse effects of design decisions on quality attributes based on informal estimations, and try to uncover trade-offs and conflicts among different quality attributes.

In recent years, many researchers have proposed to encode architectural design decisions into software architecture models (e.g., using architecture description languages or UML) (Taylor et al., 2009) thus enabling automated reasoning. Performance and reliability are considered important quality attributes in practice (Berntsson Svensson et al., 2011, p.5), so that a number of approaches evaluate architecture models for performance (Balsamo et al., 2004), (H. Koziolek, 2010) in terms of expected response times, throughputs and resource utilizations; or for reliability (Goseva-Popstojanova and Trivedi, 2001; Immonen and Niemelä, 2008) in terms of probability of failure on demand. This systematic support can lead to better decisions than experience (Martens et al., 2011). The reasoning is founded on theories for different quality attributes, such as queueing theory for performance prediction or Markov models for reliability prediction.

Support for Interpretation of Results   As a major challenge in this area, most evaluation tools are only able to determine the quality attribute values (e.g. 5 sec response time) for a given architectural model. Interpretation of prediction results, problem identification, and improvement of the software architecture are manual tasks in current practice (Woodside et al.,

5

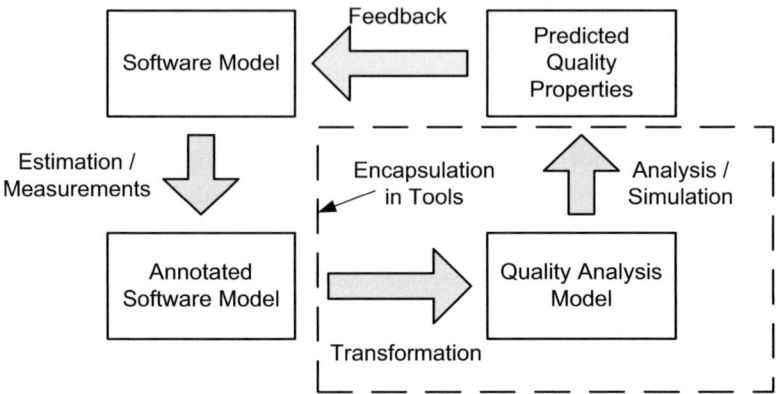

Figure 1.1.: Traditional Model-based Quality Prediction Process (adapted from (H. Koziolek, 2008))

2007). Automation is desirable, because the manual tasks (i) require rich architectural experience, (ii) are laborious and therefore cost-intensive, and (iii) are error-prone due to the overwhelmingly complex design space for humans (Bass et al., 2003). Furthermore, isolated improvement of a single quality attribute can result in degradation of other quality attributes, which is hard to determine and quantify manually.

1.2. Problem

Model-based quality prediction helps software architects to build high-quality software systems by enabling them to analyse a software architecture model for its quality properties, both for newly designed systems (i.e. without an implementation) or systems that are being evolved, redesigned, or brought into a new environment. Figure 1.1 shows the prediction process.

However, only the steps from an annotated software architecture model to a quality analysis model (e.g. queueing networks for performance) and its analysis is supported by automated methods (indicated by the dashed box). The software architect then has to interpret the prediction results manually, map them back to the software architecture level, and make design decisions. These manual *feedback* tasks are difficult and time-consuming and should be supported better (Woodside et al., 2007).

Furthermore, the feedback provided by model-based prediction is not only relevant for the software architect, but also should provide information for the *requirements engineering phase*: The quality properties achievable by the current software architecture needs to be fed back into the requirements analysis phase, providing an input for negations about quality preferences, quality requirements, and resulting costs, and thus enabling well-informed trade-off decisions. Thus, support of the feedback task should also drive the quality requirements analysis process.

Three main challenges arise for supporting this feedback task and providing input for quality requirements analysis.

Trade-off Decisions: A single software quality attribute cannot be considered in isolation, because improving a system with respect to one software quality attribute may have an effect on other software quality attributes (Bass et al., 2003, p.73). Often, architecture design decisions imply a trade-off between software quality attributes, i.e. there is a conflict of quality attributes for this decision. For example, security and reliability may conflict for architectural decisions regarding data storage: While a system is secure if it offers few places that keep sensitive data, such an organization may lead to single points of failure and decreased reliability (ibid., p.73). Similarly, many architectural decisions made to improve software quality attributes have potential to conflict with performance (ibid. p.74) due to additional required calculation and with costs due to increased development effort. Thus, when designing an architecture, trade-off decisions must be made.

As a result, automated improvement approaches need to consider several quality attributes and provide input for trade-off decisions made by the software architect and stakeholders. At the same time, automated improvement approaches should be extendable to consider any quantitatively analysable quality properties the software architect is interested in.

Flexible Degrees of Freedom: To automatically improve software architectures, changes of the software architecture must be explored. For different quality attributes, different sets of decisions are relevant, although these sets may also overlap. For example, the component deployment, the selection of components, and the server and middleware configuration (such as server speed, communication settings and load balancing) are *degrees of freedom* affecting performance and reliability properties. None of these degrees can be considered separately, they have to be considered in combination to accurately predict system quality.

To support architects in improving software architectures with respect to any quantifiable and predictable quality property, a flexible and extendible formulation of the design space to be explore is required.

Efficient Exploration and Optimization: The design space to be considered may be large, so that a full exploration is not feasible for non-trivial problems. Due to possibly time-consuming quality analyses (e.g. queueing network simulation), the optimization problem cannot solved exactly in other ways. For example, for sophisticated performance prediction approaches, such as the Palladio Component Model (Becker et al., 2009) or Layered Queueing Networks (Franks et al., 2009), performance properties cannot be determined with closed formulas; instead, simulation or approximation algorithms are necessary. In addition, the design decision space is discrete and combinatorial. We cannot assume any function properties we can exploit for optimization (such as continuity or differentiability) of the quality analyses.

At the same time, finding the exact globally Pareto-optimal solutions is not necessarily required, an approximation found in reasonable time is often enough to solve a given architectural design decision problem. Thus, an efficient technique to find near-optimal architecture models is required.

1.3. Existing Solutions

In software engineering (and in other engineering disciplines), automated *search-based* approaches have been applied to numerous problems to help software developers to come up with improved and better solutions (Harman, 2007). *Optimization* is a special case of search in which solutions that are best with respect to an objective function are sought. Searching better or even optimal *designs* is called *design space exploration*. Design space exploration can be used to support the feedback task: A software tool searches for improved software architecture models and proposes them to the software architect as feedback.

For performance, some approaches address the challenge of automating the improvement of architectures. Rule-based approaches (Performance Booster (Xu, 2010), PANDA (Trubiani, 2011)) codify knowledge from the performance domain into processable rules, to detect causes for performance problems in software models and suggest or automatically apply mitigation rules. However, these approaches are limited to performance prediction and to changes for which rules are available. Thus, they cannot provide input for trade-off decisions in the requirements analysis phase. In this work, we thus propose a novel combination of performance domain knowledge as applied by these approaches with more flexible metaheuristic optimization approaches.

9

Specialized performance deployment optimization approaches (Planner2 (Zheng and Woodside, 2003), the method by Sharma and Jalote (2008), CERAS Deployment Optimization (Li et al., 2009)) apply custom optimization algorithms to the component deployment problem. While the optimization algorithms are efficient, they are limited to deployment problems and to performance, and also do not provide trade-off support.

For reliability, numerous optimization approaches have been suggested (Kuo and Wan, 2007). However, they consider limited degrees of freedom, e.g. only redundancy, too.

Furthermore, metaheuristic-based approaches (e.g. ArcheOpterix (Aleti et al., 2009a), GDSE (Saxena and Karsai, 2010b)) have been suggested that address optimization of multiple quality properties. ArcheOpterix provides Pareto-optimal solutions as the output, thus enabling trade-off decisions. However, they are either fixed to explore certain degrees of freedom (such as allocation or service selection), or do not support the software architect in defining the relevant design space, thus requiring a large effort to adopt the method for new design problems. A more detailed discussion of existing approaches is provided in Chapter 4.

1.4. Contributions

The contribution of this thesis is an automated method to improve component-based software architectures based on model-based quality predictions, thus providing support for trade-off decisions in the requirements analysis phase.

Figure 1.2 shows the high-level process: Our method automatically identifies the design space that is opened up by the properties of CBA and relevant quality criteria and determines the optimal candidates using model-based quality prediction techniques.

The output of our method is a set of optimal trade-off architecture candidates (i.e. Pareto-optimal candidates) in the identified design space for

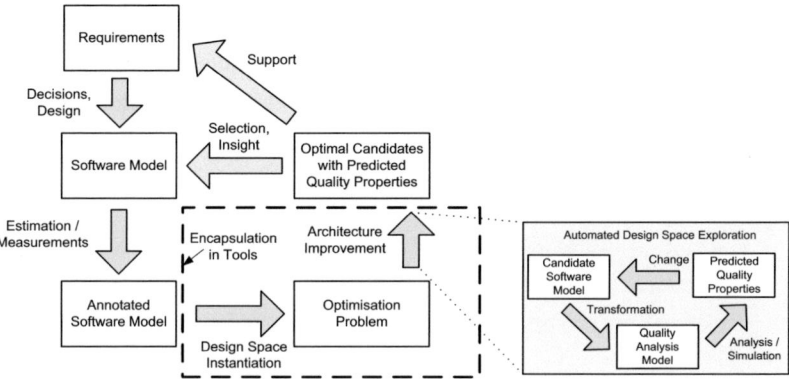

Figure 1.2.: Model-based Architecture Improvement Process with Feedback into Requirements Engineering

the considered multiple quality criteria. This set provides a basis for well-informed trade-off decisions: It enables software architects and stakeholders to negotiate requirements based on quantitative information about the current system architecture and its potential. In an iterative development process, the Pareto-optimal candidates thus can be used as a basis for decisions in the requirements engineering phase, so that the effects of decisions is known when making them.

This contribution has three main aspects:

- First, we identify the information need of software architects and stakeholders that can be filled with an automated method based on model-based quality prediction. We extend a *process model* for development of new component-based systems with our method but also embed the method in other scenarios such as evolution scenarios. As a result, quantitative feedback is provided for software architects, requirements engineers, and stakeholders to be used in architecture design and requirements analysis.

- Second, we provide a *framework* for multi-objective optimization of software architectures based on quality predictions and the notion of degrees of freedom. This framework is independent of the used CBA metamodel and quality analysed, but still allows including domain-specific knowledge in form of tactics operators.

- Third, to *instantiate this framework*, we provide concrete degrees of freedom for CBA affecting performance, reliability, and costs as well as performance and costs tactics for the Palladio Component Model.

In the following, we discuss the different aspects of the contribution in more detail.

Process

We analyse the decision support needs of software architects and stakeholders when using model-based quality prediction and embed the automated improvement method into the software development process and life cycle. Chapter 5 describes this aspect in detail. The contributions of this work in this aspect are the following:

Decision Support Needs in Requirements Analysis and Architecture Design:

Starting from the assumption that a component-based architecture model and quality analyses are available, we discuss how software architects, requirements engineers, and stakeholders can be supported by an automated improvement method. Because quality requirements should be subject to negotiation also in the architecture design phase, we cannot assume fixed requirements. Instead, software architects, requirements engineers, and stakeholders require *input for well-informed trade-off decisions* in the requirements analysis phase (Section 5.1).

Quality-Exploration enhanced Component-based Development Process:

We extend the component-based development process by Cheesman and Daniels (2000) and H. Koziolek and Happe, 2006 to include an *automated architecture exploration workflow* in the quality analysis step, which provides Pareto-optimal candidates for the considered design space. Additionally, we extend the process to incorporate the use of the newly achieved information for decision making in different phases (Section 5.2).

Architecture Exploration Scenarios:

Automated architecture exploration is not restricted to the development of new systems. We discuss the required input information of the automated architecture exploration. Based on this, we provide additional *scenarios* where automated architecture exploration can provide valuable information for software architects and stakeholders as a basis for decisions. For example, changing functional requirements, changing system environment, or changing usage are stimuli for architecture evolution and architecture exploration (Section 5.4).

Framework

To fulfil the identified need for an automated architecture exploration, we provide an automated CBA improvement framework based on multi-objective optimization with the following contributions:

Degree of Freedom Model:

To support the exploration of different types of design decisions, we provide a formal, generic, flexible, and extendible *formulation of the design space* for optimizing CBA models for a number of quality properties. We propose a novel *metamodel for describing degrees of freedom* (DoF) of any CBA metamodel that uses EMOF (Object Manage-

13

ment Group (OMG), 2006a) as meta-metamodelling language. This design space formulation is generic as it is independent of the used CBA metamodel. It is flexible as different degrees of freedom (e.g. component allocation and component selection) can be combined for a system at hand. It is extendible as additional degrees of freedom can be defined for a CBA metamodel or even custom for a specific software system at hand (Chapter 6).

Automated Design Space Instantiation:

Given a CBA model and a set of degrees of freedom of the CBA metamodel, we provide a method to derive the degrees of freedom instances of the input model automatically. The degrees of freedom instances span a *design space*, for which an optimization problem is automatically formulated. The software architect can review the found degree of freedom instances and add constraints, but does not have to specify the complete design space manually (Section 6.4.1).

Generic Multi-objective Optimization Framework for CBA:

For multi-objective optimization, we describe a *CBA optimization framework*, which is independent of the used CBA metamodel an quality prediction techniques, and builds upon standard multi-objective optimization frameworks. Given an input CBA model, a set of degrees of freedom for the underlying CBA metamodel, and a set of quality prediction adaptors that make quality prediction techniques for instanced of the CBA metamodel available to the framework, the framework can automatically instantiate the above described design space and explore it using standard metaheuristic optimization algorithms such as evolutionary algorithms. Any quality prediction technique on the given CBA metamodel can be plugged into the framework by providing an adaptor, so any combination of quality criteria for which prediction techniques exist can be considered (Sections 8.1, 8.2, and 8.4).

Integration of Domain-specific Knowledge:

Metaheuristic optimization techniques (i.e. approximate optimization techniques that do not make any assumption about the function to be analysed) treat the function to be optimized as a black-box. However, domain-specific knowledge how to improve quality attributes is available, e.g. in the form of architectural tactics (Bass et al., 2003) or performance patterns. For example, to improve reliability redundancy could be introduced. To improve performance, the load should be uniformly spread to processing nodes.

To integrate this knowledge in an evolutionary algorithm, we propose *quality tactics operators*. The use of tactics operators can make the time-consuming optimization more efficient and lead to 50% - 90% faster optimization for our test problems. Additionally, for some types of design spaces, we propose two techniques to generate starting populations (a hybrid with analytic optimization and an allocation scheme heuristic).

Framework Instantiation

To instantiate this framework, we provide concrete degrees of freedom for CBA and tactics for the Palladio Component Model.

Identification of Degrees of Freedom for CBA:

we present a list of degrees of freedom that could be available in any CBA metamodel in general, i.e. that are based on common principles of component-based software architecture or of software systems in general. The list focusses on performance, reliability, and costs. For each identified degree, we provide a definition in the Palladio Component Model (Becker et al., 2009), the Component-Based Modeling Language (Wu and Woodside, 2004b) or the ROBOCOP component model (ROBOCOP consortium, 2003) (Chapter 7).

Performance Tactics:

We codify a number of performance tactics as tactics operators for the Palladio Component Model, which make use of well-known performance domain knowledge and principles, focussing on bottleneck removal. Additionally, as some of these tactics lead to higher costs, we also provide inverse costs tactics which can be applied in places of the system where enough capacity is available (Section 8.3.1).

1.5. Outline

The thesis is structured into three main parts. Part I lays the foundations on which the work is build and discusses related work. It is organized as follows.

Chapter 2 lays the foundations concerning software architecture and quality attributes. Section 2.1 presents basics and definitions on component-based software architecture and the component-based development process on which this thesis is built. Section 2.2 discusses quality of software architecture and introduces the related terms used in this thesis. Section 2.3 introduces basic concepts regarding modelling and meta-modelling. Section 2.4 presents foundations of model-based quality prediction techniques. As an example of one CBA metamodel and quality prediction technique, Section 2.5 presents the Palladio Component Model which is used in examples throughout the thesis and in our case studies. Finally, Section 2.6 describes two other CBA metamodels which are used throughout the thesis to show the metamodel-independence of this work.

Chapter 3 introduces required knowledge on multi-criteria optimization. Section 3.1 briefly describes basic terms for optimization in general. Then, Section 3.2 discusses how multiple, conflicting criteria can be handled in optimization. Section 3.3 briefly discusses classical approaches to multi-objective optimization and their limitations, which make them not applicable in this work. Then, Section 3.4 describe metaheuristic multi-objective optimization, which make no assumptions on the search problem, thus can be used for any optimization problem, and are used in this thesis. In particular, the subclass of evolutionary algorithms is used, which are described in Section 3.5.

Chapter 4 discusses related work in two sections. The main Section 4.1 discussed related approaches that target to automatically improve software architecture models (or similar abstract software models which could be used at the software architecture level). Then, the shorter Section 4.2 describes the use of domain-specific knowledge in optimization to distinguish our tactics operators.

Part II contains the contributions of this thesis and is organized as follows.

Chapter 5 analyses how the software architect and other stakeholders can be supported by an automated method to improve a CBA model. In Section 5.1 discusses the goals and requirements of such an automated method. Section 5.2 presents our extension of the quality-driven development process (H. Koziolek and Happe, 2006) which in turn extends the component-based development process by Cheesman and Daniels (2000). Then, the relation between the representation of the software architecture as a model and the actual software system is discussed in Section 5.3. Section 5.4 presents development and evolution scenarios in which our method can be used. Section 5.5 discusses assumptions and limitations of our method. Finally, Section 5.6 concludes.

Chapter 6 describes how CBA can be changed automatically to achieve better quality. It formalizes a design space that can be automatically searched. Section 6.1 describes the requirements that automated changes have to adhere to to enable an automated search. Section 6.2

17

illustrates the topics addressed in this chapter on a PCM example model. The following sections describe the concepts formally and in detail. Section 6.3 defines how the architecture can be changed automatically to affect quality attributes, formalizing the concept of a *degree of freedom* to describe such variation options. Then, Section 6.4 describes the resulting space of architecture candidate models reachable by automated improvement. Finally, Section 6.5 lists limitations of this method and Section 6.6 summarizes.

Chapter 7 describes which degrees of freedom are available in CBA models, independent of the used CBA metamodel. Section 7.2 presents degrees of freedom found in the application layer software. Section 7.3 describes degrees of freedom in the deployment. Finally, we discuss how additional degrees of freedom, which are not generic for CBA, might be available in specific metamodels or specific systems in Section 7.4. Section 7.5 discusses the limitations of our method, and Section 7.6 concludes the chapter.

Chapter 8 then describes the optimization technique we developed to find optimal CBA models in the design space introduced in Chapter 6. Section 8.1 describes the optimization problem and discusses the applicable optimization techniques. Section 8.2 presents how evolutionary optimization is applied to the problem. Section 8.3 presents our extension to evolutionary optimization that allows to include more domain-specific knowledge as tactics operators. Section 8.4 presents the architecture for a CBA optimization framework that automates the described optimization method while being independent of the used CBA metamodel. Finally, Section 8.5 discusses additional aspects and concludes the chapter.

Finally, part III presents the validation of this work and concludes.

Chapter 9 describes the validation of our method, which is structured into two main goals: (1) To assess the validity of the automated improvement method in terms of the accuracy of the results and the applicability of the method and (2) to evaluate the performance of the optimization step quantitatively. First, Section 9.1 describes the evaluation goals in more detail and derives questions for both goals. Section 9.2 presents the used implementation of the optimization framework. Section 9.3 presents the three case study systems. Then, Section 9.4 described the results for the validity of our automated improvement approach and Section 9.5 describes the quantitative evaluation of the optimization step's performance.

Chapter 10 concludes by summarizing the contributions and the conducted validations (Section 10.1), highlighting the benefits achieved by our method (Section 10.2), pointing to assumptions and limitations discussed throughout this work (Section 10.3), and outlining future research efforts and ideas (Section 10.4).

Part I.

Foundations and Related Work

2. Component-based Software Architectures and Quality

This chapter describes the foundations on which this thesis is built and introduces the used terminology. Section 2.1 introduces component-based software architecture (CBA) and presents the terms and views used in this thesis. Section 2.2 describes how software architecture influences quality attributes, and how quality attributes are considered during software architecture design. To set the foundations for modelling aspects, Section 2.3 briefly introduces modelling and meta-modelling. Quantitative quality attributes can be predicted based on architecture models, which is presented in Section 2.4. Then, Section 2.5 describes the Palladio Component Model (PCM), which is used in this thesis to predict quality properties of CBA. Other available CBA modelling techniques are described in Section 2.6. Finally, Section 3 describes the basics of multi-criteria optimization, which are used to improve CBA models in this work.

2.1. Component-based Software Architecture

This section presents foundations on component-based software architecture. Section 2.1.1 present definitions for software architecture, components, and respective models. Section 2.1.2 describes a development process for developing component-based systems based on an architecture specification.

2.1.1. Definitions

Numerous definitions for software architecture have been formulated; and the research community has not finally agreed on a common wording. A general definition, which is used in the remainder of this work, emphasizes design decisions:

Definition 2.1 Software Architecture (Taylor et al., 2009, p.58)

A software system's architecture is the set of principal design decisions made about the system.

Interestingly, what is a principal design decision depends on the system goal. Examples named by Taylor et al. (2009, p.58) are the structure of the system, important decisions on functional behaviour, the interaction of components, and non-functional properties.

This definition only mentions the core concept of design decision. It is independent of the question how these design decisions are formulated, and thus includes intangible software architectures that are not documented. Thus, this definition separates between the software architecture and its representation in documentation. In contrast, other definitions of software architecture, such as by Perry and Wolf (1992) and the IEEE standard (IEEE Std. 1471-2000, 2000), already describe how these design decisions are captured. Additionally, other definitions emphasize the static structure of the system (system building blocks (Perry and Wolf, 1992), organization of the system as a set of components (IEEE Std. 1471-2000, 2000)).

An important subset of design decisions refer to the structure of the system, i.e., its decomposition into building blocks. To manage complexity of software systems, architects apply the principles of encapsulation, abstraction and modularity (Taylor et al., 2009) to structure the system. The resulting building blocks are called software component: "A *software component* is an architectural entity that (1) encapsulates a subset of the system's functionality and/or data, (2) restricts access to that subset via an explicitly defined interface, and (3) has explicitly defined dependencies on its required execution context" (Taylor et al., 2009, p.69).

Researchers have strived to extend the notion of a software component so that the composition of systems from independently developed components becomes possible. Szyperski et al. (2002) has identified the following characteristics of a software component that can be independently developed and reused, stressing the composability and reuse by third parties:

Definition 2.2 Software Component (Szyperski et al., 2002, p.41)

A software component is a unit of composition with contractually specified interfaces and explicit context dependencies only. A software component can be deployed independently and is subject to composition by third parties.

The contractually specified interfaces define the services that a component provides to its environment. The component can only be accessed using these provided interfaces. Interfaces specify a contract between offering component and the users in the environment and contain all information that users can rely on when interacting with the component.

To be reusable in by third parties, a component needs to make its dependencies explicit. First, dependencies include required interfaces: the component needs to specify which interfaces needs to be provided by other components in its environment. Second, dependencies specify additional dependencies to the execution environment, such as the required platform or required resources.

As a result, a component can be independently deployed and will provide its services in an environment that provides the required context capabilities (required interfaces and platform). A component is furthermore a unit of deployment, which means it cannot be deployed partially (Szyperski et al., 2002, p.36) and thus keeps its internals hidden at all times. Thus, the component can be used by third parties based on the interface and dependency information only to compose a system.

In the following, I mainly use the terms of the PCM to describe the elements of component-based architectures. The elements described, however, mainly match the elements described used by other authors. I give the terms used by other authors where applicable, in particular of Taylor et al. (2009).

To form a system, components are instantiated and connected to each other. The required capabilities of every component need to be provided, i.e. the required interface of a component needs to be connected to another component that offers this interface as a provided interface.

Definition 2.3 Component Assembly

A *component assembly* defines how a set of components is instantiated and connected to each other. A valid component assembly connects all instantiated required interfaces of the used components to instantiated provided interfaces of other used components. A *connector* connects a required interface of one component to the provided interface of another component.

Component assembly is called configuration by Taylor et al. (2009).

A system created by connecting hundreds of components, however, is confusing. Thus, a hierarchical decomposition into subsystems and composed components is required to structure the system and manage the complexity.

Definition 2.4 Component Composition and Composed Structure

Component composition is the act of hierarchically structuring the system by encapsulating a component assembly into one architectural element, called composed structure. Component composition can be either black box (composed component) or white box (subsystem). The result of a black-box composition is a component (see Def. 2.2).

Component composition or composed structure in this sense is not defined by Taylor et al. (2009) explicitly. They, however, also identify the necessity to structure a large system into subsystems as a unit of analysis (Taylor et al., 2009, p.304). In contrast to the definition of a composed structure here, their notion of a subsystem does not require any encapsulation and resulting explicit interface specification at the subsystem level.

A software architecture that is structured based on software components and connectors is called a component-based software architecture in the following.

Definition 2.5 Component-based Software Architecture (CBA)

A component-based software architecture is a software architecture whose principal design decisions regarding the structure of the systems are made by structuring the system as a set of software components. The system is thus described as a composition of components.

To express (component-based) software architectures, architects have to describe the architecture in some type of artefact. These artefacts can be ranging from natural language descriptions over UML models to formal architectural description languages such as Rapide (Luckham et al., 1995) or the Palladio Component Model (Becker et al., 2009).

Definition 2.6 Architecture Model (Taylor et al., 2009, p.75)

An architecture model is an artefact that captures some or all of the design decisions that compromise a system's architecture.

An architecture model is a *formal architecture model* if it is based on a formally defined language, e.g. defined by a metamodel (cf. Section 2.3).

For appropriately describing component-based software architectures, we define component-based architecture models to be formal models describing component-based architectures. Models of single component, just like components, can be independently created and composed to form a component-based architecture model. Thus, a component model can be delivered together with a component and be reused by third parties when composing an architectural model.

Definition 2.7 Component-based Architecture Model (CBA Model)

A component-based architecture model is a formal architecture model that uses software components as the main entity to describe the design decisions: (1) software component are explicit model entities which encapsulate internal decisions and provide information on interfaces and dependencies, (2) the model of a component can be reused in any CBA model, (3) structural design decisions are expressed as a composition and assembly of software components, only making use of the provided interfaces and context dependencies of the component models, and (4) other design decisions are described in relation to the composition or to the components (e.g. by annotating components, connectors, or assemblies).

For example, control flow is described by specifying the control flow of single components, so that the overall system's behaviour emerges as an consequence of combining several components. For example, Service Effect Specifications (SEFF) describe component behaviour in the PCM. A SEFF is an abstraction of the component C's control flow describing calls to required components if one of C's services is called.

In contrast, in UML models, system behaviour is often described only by sequence diagrams, which mix interaction between components with component-internal behaviour, and thus directly define the overall system's behaviour for a given use case. Such a model is not considered a CBA model in this work.

A CBA model is thus restricted to design decisions that can be expressed in terms of software components and annotations to them. Internal decisions of components are usually not considered when working with the

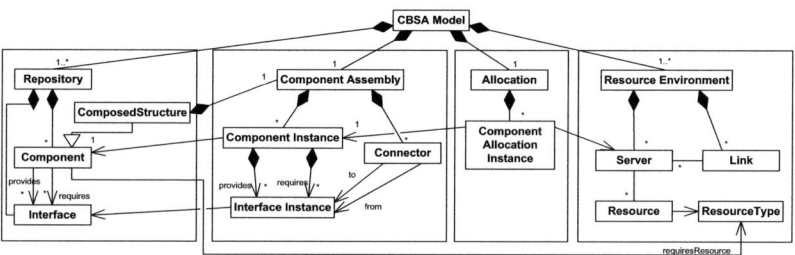

Figure 2.1.: Main CBA Concepts

CBA, because components may be provided by third parties. The focus of this model are structural design decisions, while other types of decisions (e.g. behaviour, interaction, non-functional properties) are annotated(?) to the structural elements. Some types of design decisions, such as non-existence decisions (Kruchten, 2004) (e.g. the system does not use remote procedure calls), cannot be expressed with a CBA model, and need to be represented with other types of models.

Figure 2.1 shows the main concepts in CBA models required for the purpose of this work. The concepts are modelled differently in different CBA metamodels. For example, an association may be represented by an additional association class, or a class in our figure may be represented by just an association in a concrete CBA metamodel. Additionally, multiplicities may be different, and concrete CBA models may contain more details on other aspects of the CBS (e.g. a more detailed model or the resource environment, distinguishing for example hardware servers from virtual machines as suggested by Hauck et al. (2009)).

An interface in our terminology is a definition of access to a subset of functionality, as described in definition 2.2. In other CBA metamodels, terms like service or port could be used here, too. All three terms have the common notion of defining the access to the components functionality, although the meaning may differ in detail.

As components offer access to functionality via interfaces, their dependency to other components' functionality is expressed as a dependency to interfaces, too. The interface itself serves as the contract which both parties adhere to. Additionally, components have dependencies to other system resources, such as hardware resources, operating system, or middleware resources.

Concrete component metamodels may contain information as described above. Our definition of CBA models only states the minimum requirements for such models, but allows any extensions to it. For example, different communication styles and dynamic change of connectors are emphasized by the SOFA 2.0 component model (Bures et al., 2006). Still, SOFA 2.0 shares the main concepts described above. Thus, our automated improvement method can be applied to SOFA 2.0 models as well.

In the remainder of this thesis, we refer to concepts of CBA using the terms described in this chapter and the property names are used as shown in Figure 2.1. If no property name is given in the figure, the name defaults to the referenced type (e.g. ComponentInstance.component to refer to the Component from a Component Instance).

2.1.2. Component-based Software Development Process

The development of component-based systems is unique in its "combination of top-down and bottom-up that component orientation demands" (Szyperski et al., 2002, p.458). Several development processes have been suggested to reflect these unique properties. Cheesman and Daniels (2000, Chapter 2) have proposed such a process based in the Rational Unified Process (RUP), which we present below.

Figure 2.2 shows the development process. Boxes represent workflows. They are connected by thick grey arrows indicating change of activity and thin black arrows that show the flow of information in the form of artefacts. As it can be observed from the directions of the thick arrows, the order of

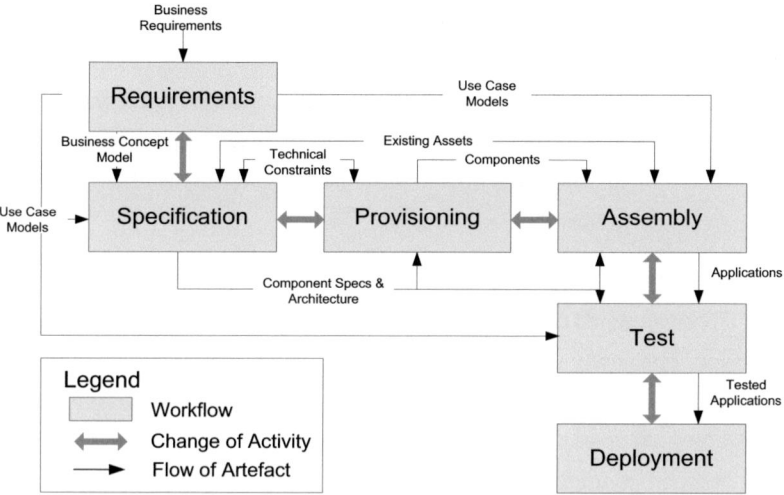

Figure 2.2.: Component-based Development Process (from Cheesman and Daniels (2000))

the workflow steps is not fixed, i.e. the process is not a waterfall model. Instead, the actors can freely change from one workflow to the other, reflecting the iterative nature of RUP.

The process contains the following steps:

Requirements: In the first step, the functional business requirements of the customers are analysed in this workflow. The outcome is a business concept model that models the relevant concepts of the system's domain and a use case model that described interactions of users with the system. Together with these use cases, quality requirements may be specified. For example, a quality requirement might describe that a use case should support a number of simultaneous users and respond within a specified time on average.

Specification: In this phase, the CBA is designed based on the business concept models and the use case models. Software architects model

31

the overall architecture by first identifying business interfaces and system interfaces and then creating component specifications. Existing components should be taken into account. If technical constraints are encountered in later phases of the process, these can be also considered in the specification step. The output of this step are component specifications and the CBA.

Provisioning: In this step, components are purchased from third-parties if components matching the specification already exist, or implemented. For newly implemented components, the designed interface specifications are input for component developers to provide conforming component implementations. The output of this step are implemented components.

Assembly: In this step, the components are assembled according to the CBA model. The output of this step is the complete deployable application, including artefacts that define the wiring of components, such as EJB deployment descriptors.

Test: The complete application can now be tested according to the use case models, using test environments.

Deployment: In the deployment step, the application is installed in its target environment.

2.2. Quality of Software Architectures

The software architecture of a system is critical to achieve quality, thus, quality should be considered when designing software architecture (Bass et al., 2003, p.73). Section 2.2.1 describes the quality attributes relevant at an architecture level. Then, Section 2.2.2 describes how to quantify quality attributes and presents the related terms.

2.2.1. Quality Attributes of Software Architecture

Developing high quality software products is a goal in many development projects. However, quality is a highly subjective term and depends on the goals and perceptions of stakeholders. To better reason on software product quality, software quality models have been suggested to describe and measure software quality (e.g. (ISO/IEC 9126-1:2001(E), 2001), by Boehm et al. (1976), or by McCall et al. (1977), see (Falcone, 2010) for a discussion and comparison).

Software quality attributes (also called quality characteristics) are characteristics which provide the basis for evaluating quality of software systems (adapted from (Falcone, 2010, p.81)). Examples for software quality attributes of software systems are reliability, usability, and performance.

Software quality attributes are one of the influence factors to take into account when designing a software architecture (Bass et al., 2003, p.73), (Posch et al., 2004, p.75). Relevant software quality attributes when designing software architecture are reliability, modifiability, performance, security, testability, and usability (Bass et al., 2003, Sec.4.4). For some software quality attributes, quantitative quality metrics are available to assess the level of quality achieved by a software system.

Performance: Performance is concerned with the timing behaviour and resource efficiency of the system. Important performance measures are response time of system services, resource utilization, and throughput (Jain, 1991). More comprehensive measures also take the time needed by users to accomplish tasks into account (Smith and Williams, 2002b), i.e. the duration of providing input for the system and waiting for the system response. Such measures can be considered the response time of usage scenarios, taking the user actions into account, too.

Reliability: Reliability is the capability of a system to provide functionality as expected for a specified period of time in the intended execution context. It is for example measured as the *probability of failure on demand* (POFOD). The notion of availability is closely related and focusses on the fraction of time that the system is available to serve requests (Bass et al., 2003, p.73). For example, one may require that a system is available 360 days a year.

Modifiability: Modifiability is concerned with the costs of changing the software system, e.g. if new functionality should be added or if corrective changes are made (ibid., p.80 et seqq.).

Security: Security is the capability of the system to resit unauthorized usage, i.e. to protect sensitive data and services so that only authorized users can access them (ibid., p.85).

Testability: Testability describes how well the software can be tested to detect faults (ibid., p.88). Measures for testability are how effective given tests can discover faults, or how much effort has to be made to achieve a certain test coverage (ibid., p.89).

Usability: Usability describes how easy users can work with the system and accomplish their tasks (ibid., p.90). For example, the ability to undo incorrect inputs easily makes a system more usable, and at the same time has consequences for the system's architecture.

Depending on the goals of the system to be developed, additional software quality attributes may be relevant, such as portability or interoperability.

Thereby, single software quality attributes cannot be considered in isolation, because improving a system with respect to one software quality attribute has an effect on other software quality attribute (ibid., p.73). Often, software quality attributes conflict: For example, security and reliability often negatively influence each other: While a system is secure if it offers few places that keep sensitive data, such an organization may lead to single points of failure and decreased reliability (ibid., p.73). Furthermore, almost all software quality attributes conflict with performance (ibid., p.74).

Additionally, economic considerations are a major driver of software development (ibid., p.307). *Business quality attributes* are, for example, costs, monetary benefit, and time-to-market (ibid., p.95).

Costs: Costs are the main quality to trade-off against the software quality attributes named above. What types of costs need to be considered depends on the organizational context: Usually, the direct development costs have to be considered. Additional costs are maintenance costs, hardware procurement costs, operating costs, or licensing costs.

Monetary benefit: The benefit to be achieved by the developed software system can be quantified and compared to the expected costs, to calculate the return-of-investment.

Time-to-market: Development time may be important if a new type of system is developed that is supposed to capture a share of an emerging new market. This quality can also be translated in monetary benefits.

We denote software quality attributes and business quality attributes together as *quality attributes*.

To achieve a software system with high quality for the relevant quality attributes, methods have been suggested to design software architectures based on identified relevant quality attributes. For example, Attribute-Driven Design (ADD) (Bass et al., 2003, p.155 et seqq.) is a recursive decomposition process to identify the structural organization of a software architecture driven by relevant quality attributes. The system is structured based on known architectural tactics and architectural patterns. The result is a high-level organization of the system, which is refined in further architecture design steps. However, even a well-designed software architecture is no guarantee that the resulting software system will indeed have the envisioned qualities. Instead, it provides only a foundation to be able to achieve these qualities. More decisions are made throughout the further design and implementation of the software system that may deteriorate the qualities.

After an initial version software architecture has been designed (using ADD for the initial steps or other methods), it can be used to analyse what qualities can be achieved when realizing the system. Evaluating the quality attributes early can help to identify wrong decisions, which are expensive to revert later in the process. Early architecture evaluation is reported to save costs later in development processes (ibid., p.263).

Several software architecture evaluation methods have been suggested to evaluate a software architecture with respect to quality attributes (a survey is provided by Dobrica and Niemelä (2002)). A widespread method that has been used in numerous industrial case studies (H. Koziolek, 2011) is the Architecture Trade-off Analysis Method (ATAM) (Clements et al., 2001), which focusses on identifying software quality attributes relevant for different stakeholders, the quality metrics to assess them, and associated risks and sensitive points in the architecture; as well as on discussing the current architectural decisions. In the process of architecture evaluation, the conflicts and trade-offs among software quality attributes can be uncovered, and their resolution can be negotiated among stakeholders (Bass et al., 2003, p.264).

A more quantitative approach to trade-off resolution is the Costs Benefit Analysis Method (CBAM) (Bass et al., 2003, ch.12), which strives to provide decision making support by quantifying the utility of achieved software qualities and compare them to the expected costs, thus enabling return-of-investment calculations. CBAM can be used after ATAM to decide whether certain architectural decisions to achieve quality actually pay off. To do so, the effect of architecture decisions on quality attributes has to be estimated. By calculating the costs and utility for each quality attribute, these are also traded off against each other.

However, ATAM and CBAM are high-level architecture evaluation methods and focus on discovering relevant quality attributes, their trade-offs and associated risk. They are based on manual estimations of the effects of design decisions on quality properties. As such they can be combined with methods focussing on evaluating certain quality attributes in more detail by using quantitative *model-based quality prediction techniques* based on formal models of the software architecture (Dobrica and Niemelä, 2002, p.650).

For a given software architecture design problem at hand, software architects have to select the appropriate methods to use from the available set of approaches. The use of quantitative quality prediction techniques can be a result of risk analysis: If a set of quality attributes are identified to be crucial for the system, it can be worthwhile to study them in more detail using quantitative prediction techniques. The approach presented in this thesis supports architecture decisions where quantifiable quality attributes have been identified as important.

Before discussing quantitative model-based quality prediction techniques in Section 2.4, we introduce the notion of quantitative quality properties of software systems in the next section and general foundations on modelling in Section 2.3.

2.2.2. Quantitative Quality Properties

Figure 2.3 illustrates the terms to describe quantitative qualities in this thesis. The concepts are related to the terms used in the Quality of Service Modelling Language (QML) (Frølund and Koistinen, 1998) (cf. comparison in Appendix D), however, we use names from the context of software architectures (e.g. as introduced in the previous section and as used by Böhme and Reussner (2008b) and Bass et al. (2003)).

As described in the previous section, quality attributes are characteristics of software systems. However, quality attributes are abstract notions of quality, and do not directly provide means to quantify the quality of a sys-

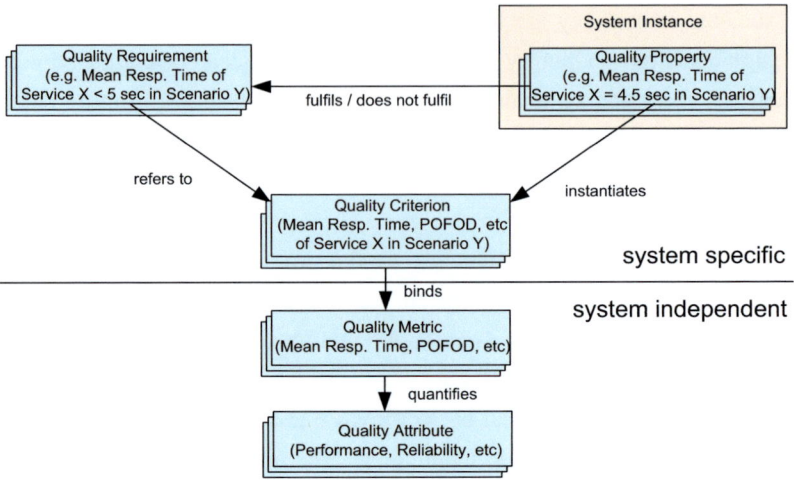

Figure 2.3.: Software Quality Terms

tem. To quantify quality attributes, *quality metrics* such as mean response time or POFOD have been introduced.

Definition 2.8 Quality Metric (adapted from (Böhme and Reussner, 2008a))

A *quality metric qm* is a precisely defined method which is used to associate an element e of an (ordered) set $\mathcal{V}_{qm}^*$ to a system S.

Different research areas for quality attributes have proposed different quality metrics to describe their quality attribute. We describe some important quality metrics in table 2.1.

The same quality metric can be relevant in multiple places when evaluating an software system. For example, the mean response times of the three most important services of a system can be considered three separate criteria. Additionally, the same quality metric can be relevant in multiple scenarios relevant for the system. For example, the response time of a service at normal workload conditions may be considered as well as the

Quality attribute	Quality metric	Description
Performance	Response time	Time interval between sending a request to a system and receiving a response. Smaller values are preferable.
	Utilization	Ratio of the time that a resource is busy (e.g. processing requests or being held) to the total elapsed time in a period of time. High utilization leads to long waiting time, while low utilization is a indicator for oversized resources. Thus, a targeted nominal values needs to be specified.
	Throughput	Rate in which a system handles requests, measured in requests (or tasks or other units of work) per time unit. Higher values are usually preferable.
Reliability	Probability of failure on demand (POFOD)	Probability that a request to a service of the system or an interaction with the system will fail, i.e. will not provide the expected result. Lower values are preferable.
Costs	Component procurement costs	Sum of the costs of all bough third-party components. Lower values are preferable.
	Initial CBA costs	Sum of component costs (development or procurement) and hardware procurement costs. Lower values are preferable.

Table 2.1.: Example Quality Metrics

response time of this service at peak workload times, leading to two quality criteria based on which the quality of the system is judged. A *scenario* defines a number of environment conditions under which the quality metric is to be collected, e.g. workload conditions for performance metrics or types change requests for modifiability metrics. Thus, we define a *quality criterion* as the collection of a quality metric for a place in the software system in a certain scenario. While a quality metric only defines how to quantify, a quality criterion binds a quality metric to a concrete element of software system.

Definition 2.9 Quality Criterion

A *quality criterion q* collects a quality metric *qm* at a defined place in a system *S* in a defined scenario. Thus, a quality criterion is defined specifically for a system *S*. It can be collected for different *instances* of *S*, e.g. different versions of *S* over time, or different configurations of *S* for different customers. Let *instances*(*S*) denote the set of all instances of *S*, and let *m*(*q*) denote the quality metric on which *q* is defined. Then, a quality criterion can be considered a function

$$q : instances(S) \rightarrow \mathcal{V}^*_{m(q)}$$

We deliberately do not restrict the notion of a system instance to certain interpretations, e.g. system versions over time, execution environment, or product configurations on product lines. What sensible system instances to consider are depends on the development project. For specialized software such as process control systems (see also our case study in Section 9.3.2), it may be sensible to consider each version of the system deployed for a customer's plant as one system instance. For mass software which is sold to millions of customers, it may be more useful to consider different editions of the system—for example the premium and the standard edition—as different instances, and reason on them assuming a certain minimum execution environment of the end users. Furthermore, the notion of system instance and scenario may overlap: While a certain workload condition may be considered a scenario for which a quality criterion is defined in one case, in other cases the system under different workload conditions may be considered different system instances which are judged based on a workload-independent quality criterion.

In the following, we just speak of the mean response time or the POFOD of a software system if there is only one relevant quality criterion for these quality metrics.

For quality criteria, requirements can be specified which state which values have to be achieved to satisfy the stakeholder's needs for this quality. For example, a quality requirement may state that a service of a system must respond faster than 5 seconds in the given scenario. Thus, a quality requirement adds a value to achieve to a quality criterion. All values better than the requirement equally satisfy the stakeholders needs.

Definition 2.10 Quality Requirement

A *quality requirement r* defines a value which satisfies a quality criterion q. If the value is achieved by a system instance, the quality criterion is satisfied. Values better than the required values all have equal utility for the stakeholders. Formally, a quality requirement is a tuple of a quality criterion and a value from the respective quality metric's domain:

$$r = (q, v) \text{ with } v \in \mathcal{V}^*_{m(q)}$$

This notion of a quality criterion and quality requirement are related to quality attribute scenarios (QAS) of ATAM (Bass et al., 2003, p.75). A QAS defines which quality metric to collect at which place in the system (called artefact in QAS) in which scenario (called stimulus and environment in QAS), and defines which value of the metric is required to be observed for this scenario (called response measure in QAS). Thus, a QAS, in our terminology, is the combination of a quality criterion and a quality requirement for it.

Quality requirements are strict concepts, defining that there is no need to further improve a quality beyond the stated values. However, it is not clear whether stakeholders can make such precise and absolute definitions about their preferences (cf. discussion in Section 5.1). Thus, we also introduce the notion of a quality bound, which also defines a value for a quality criterion which must be achieved, but does not state whether values better than the systems are of equal utility. Thus, improvement beyond the bounds may be desirable as well.

Definition 2.11 Quality Bound

A *quality bound* b defines a value to minimally achieve for a quality criterion q. Further improvement of the value beyond the quality bound may or may not be desirable. Formally, a quality bound is a tuple of a quality criterion and a value from the respective quality metric's domain:

$$b = (q, v) \text{ with } v \in \mathcal{V}^*_{m(q)}$$

Finally, a system instance has a certain value for the quality criteria. For example, a service X of a version of the system deployed at customer Y has a mean response time of 5 seconds when called with a defined workload. We denote this value as a quality property.

Definition 2.12 Quality Property

A *quality property* is a value that a system instance has for a quality criterion q. Let s be a system instance. Then, the quality property is the function value of q:

$$q(s)$$

2.3. Modelling Concepts

Before discussing model-based quality prediction in the next section, this section introduces the basic concepts of modelling and meta-modelling which enable to describe formal models of software architectures Section 2.3.1 describes basic concepts of modelling and meta-modelling. Then, Section 2.3.2 presents the Essential Meta Object Facility (EMOF) (Object

Management Group (OMG), 2006a) as an example for a meta-metamodel which can be used to define CBA metamodels. .

2.3.1. Models and Metamodels

Definition 2.13 Formal Model (from (Becker, 2008b) based on (Stachowiak, 1973))

A *formal model* is formal representation of entities and relationships in the real world (abstraction) with a certain correspondence (isomorphism) for a certain purpose (pragmatics).

In the remainder of this work, we denote formal models by the term *model*, too. Metamodels formally describe the set of models for a particular modelling domain:

Definition 2.14 Metamodel (adapted from (Stahl and Völter, 2006, p.85))

A *metamodel* is a formal model that describes the possible models for a domain by defining the constructs of a modelling language and their relationships (abstract syntax) as well as constraints and modelling rules (static semantics).

By that, a metamodel defines the abstract syntax and the static semantics of a modelling language, but not the concrete syntax (Stahl and Völter, 2006, p.85). Figure 2.4 shows the relations between real world, model, and metamodel.

A metamodel is a formal model itself, describing the entities and relationships of models in the target domain. Thus, its structure can again be described by a metamodel, leading to a hierarchy of arbitrarily many meta-levels. The meta-relationship here is relative to a currently considered model. Models that are two meta-levels away from the currently considered model are called meta-metamodel.

43

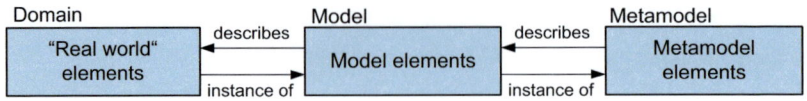

Figure 2.4.: Relationship between Real World, Model, and Metamodel from (Stahl and Völter, 2006, p.86)

Models that are described by a metamodel are called instances of the metamodel. We distinguish several levels: First, models that match to the structure prescribed by the metamodel by the abstract syntax *structurally conform to* the metamodel. Additionally, models which structurally conform to the metamodel and fulfil the static semantics *conform to* the metamodel.

To simplify reasoning on models in the remainder of this work, we introduce the following relation symbols and names. We write $M \lhd MM$ if a model M structurally conforms to a metamodel MM. We use the relation $M \blacktriangleleft MM$ if a model M conforms to a metamodel MM . Furthermore, a model M is a set of model elements, where each model element $e \in M$ is an instance of a meta-class mc of M's metamodel MM, denoted by the relation e instanceOf $mc : \forall M \lhd MM : \forall e \in M : \exists mc \in MM : e$ instanceOf mc. The index at the end of this work (p. 550) lists the used symbols and relations for quick reference.

Metamodels for software architectures often only describe the static semantics of models in the target domain. Additional semantics, e.g. dynamic semantics, of the target domain are often not captured formally by the metamodel (Becker, 2008b). Instead, the additional semantics may be annotated to the metamodel using natural language or by defining a mapping to a model which has more semantics; or they are simply a mutual agreement between the metamodel users. We call models that conform to the metamodel and fulfil the relevant additional semantics *valid model instances*.

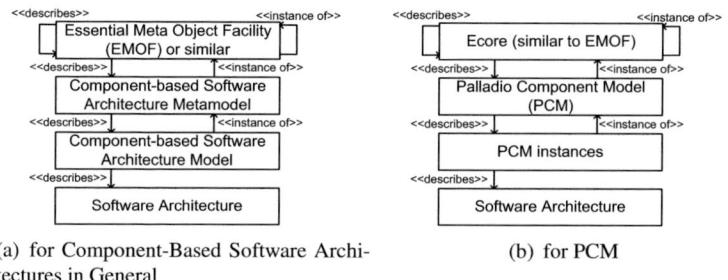

(a) for Component-Based Software Architectures in General

(b) for PCM

Figure 2.5.: General Modelling Schemata

While static semantics can be easily checked automatically for a meta-model, there are often no means to check dynamic semantics based only a on given model and its metamodel, without additional information (such as a mapping to a formal system) (Becker, 2008b, p.28). Often, whether a model instance is a valid model instance can only be checked by human interpretation or by transforming the model into other formalisms (for example simulation code or formal mathematical models for analyses) where the violation of the semantics are uncovered.

To give an example for static semantics, the PCM metamodel (cf. Section 2.5) prescribes that in a valid model, each component of a system need to be allocated to a server. Otherwise, the model is invalid, and cannot be transformed into quality models for analysis.

Additionally, to give an example for dynamic semantics, for each variable characterization used in for example an internal action, the variable needs to have a value assigned when evaluating the characterization. This semantics are not expressed in the PCM metamodel, but are checked when transforming the model into quality models such as Layered Queueing Networks (LQNs). If no variable assignment is available, an error occurs.

In the context of this thesis, our modelling focus is a CBA. The meta-modelling levels for this setting are shown in Figure 2.5(a) and, as an example, for the PCM in Figure 2.5(b). The metamodel level is a *software*

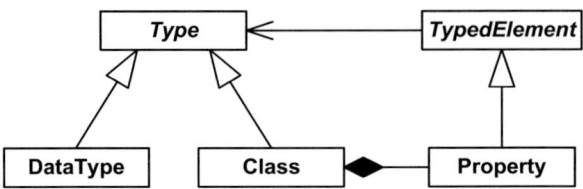

Figure 2.6.: Excerpt from EMOF

architecture metamodel, describing the concepts used to model software architectures. For example, the PCM is a software architecture metamodel. The meta-metamodel level is a model to describe metamodels. For example, the Essential Meta Object Facility (EMOF) (Object Management Group (OMG), 2006a) is such a meta-metamodel which describes, among others, UML models. It is independent of the target domain to model software architectures. EMOF describes itself, so no more meta-levels are required.

2.3.2. Essential Meta Object Facility

In this section, we describe the Essential Meta Object Facility (EMOF) (Object Management Group (OMG), 2006a) as an example of a meta-metamodel for software architectures. We use EMOF throughout the thesis as a meta-metamodelling language. EMOF is chosen because it is a widespread meta-metamodelling language (in its full form MOF it is the metamodel of UML) and has extensive tool support.

Figure 2.6 shows the aspects of EMOF relevant in this section again. The attributes of the classes as well as details of the associations are omitted here, see (Object Management Group (OMG), 2006a,d) for the detailed specification of the metamodel.

Concepts in a metamodel are modelled using Classes[1]. Each Class is of a certain Type and contains a set of Properties. Properties are Ty-

---

[1] For better readability, the name of (meta)metamodel elements is inflected for plural forms, e.g. one MOF Property, several MOF Properties.

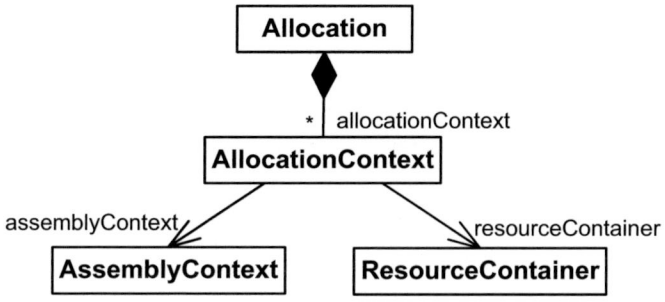

Figure 2.7.: Excerpt of PCM: Allocation

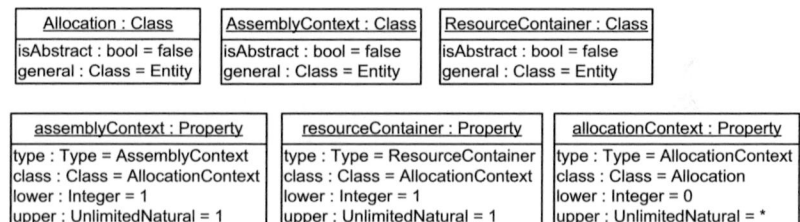

Figure 2.8.: Allocation Excerpt of PCM shown as an Instance of EMOF

pedElements, that means they have a Type. The Type of a Property can be a DataType such as primitive types of enumerations, or a Class. With Properties, associations as well as attributes of Classes can be modelled. Properties have additional properties which are not shown here, such as cardinality and whether they are composite.

As an example, consider the excerpt of the PCM in Figure 2.7. An AssemblyContext is the place holder of a component in a System. A ResourceContainer represents a server. An AllocationContext maps a component to a server by referencing an AssemblyContext and a ResourceContainer. The Allocation contains AllocationContexts for all components in the System.

While Figure 2.7 shows the excerpt of the PCM metamodel in UML graphical syntax, Figure 2.8 shows the same concepts as instances of the

MOF meta-metamodel. The excerpt contains four Classes (described above). Three Properties connect the concepts to each other. For example, the Property assemblyContexts defines the association between AllocationContext and AssemblyContexts that defines which component is allocated by this AllocationContext.

To reason on EMOF-based models (i.e. instances of EMOF, and instances thereof), we introduce some further terms. As described in the previous section, models consist of model elements. In EMOF, relevant model elements are instances of Classes and instances of Properties. Properties model attributes and relationships of Classes. Thus, in instances of instances of EMOF, the descendants of Properties have values. For example, instances of the assemblyContext Property shown in Figure 2.8 refer to concrete AssemblyContext in PCM model instances. To reason on these values, we refer to Properties of Classes using a dot-notation, so for example, for an AllocationContext A, A.assemblyContext refers to the instance of AssemblyContext referenced by the Property instance's instance.

For a model M, let $v_m(M)$ denote the value of the model element m in M. For example, in a model M, let A be an instance of Allocation context, which refers to an instance of AssemblyContext C as the component instance to deploy. Then, $v_{A.\text{assemblyContext}}(M) = C$.

Thus, we can compare the values of properties two models M and M' which contain some shared model elements. For example, two versions V_1 and V_2 of architecture models can be compared, i.e. two models. In model V_1, the AllocationContext A refers to server1 as A.resourceContainer. In model V_2, A.resourceContainer refers to server2. Then, we can say that $v_{A.\text{assemblyContext}}(V_1) \neq v_{A.\text{assemblyContext}}(V_2)$.

If the model M does not contain the model element m, the function v_m is undefined and comparisons with it always evaluate to false. If a model element is a containment association, the equality also checks for equality of the contained model elements.

In the following, for a more comprehensive presentation, we additionally assume that all model elements are connected, i.e. that for any two model elements m and m' in a model, we can either navigate from m to m' or from m' to m using the above described dot-notation.

To define static semantics, the Object Constraint Language (OCL) (Object Management Group (OMG), 2006b) can be used for EMOF-based metamodels.

2.4. Model-based Quality Prediction

Quantitative quality prediction techniques allow to evaluate software architecture models (or, more generally, other models of software) for their quantitative quality properties. In this section, we focus on component-based techniques in particular. Section 2.4.1 describes the general concepts of quality prediction. The next two sections briefly describe basics of quality prediction for performance (Section 2.4.2) and other quality attributes (Section 2.4.3). Section 2.4.4 describes the concept of quality completions, which help to bridge the gap between abstract software architecture models and quality-relevant, but low-level details of the software systems. Finally, Section 2.4.5 presents the inclusion of quantitative quality prediction into the component-based development process.

2.4.1. General Concepts

Figure 2.9 shows the main concepts: When using quantitative quality prediction techniques, the software system (lower left corner) may be already implemented or only exist as a design so far. If the software system is already implemented, it *has* certain *quality properties* (lower right corner). If it is still in the design phase, it does not have quality properties yet. Only after the system design will be realized in an implementation, it *will have* quality properties. These quality properties, of course, do not only depend

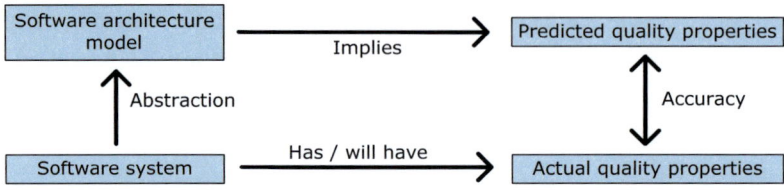

Figure 2.9.: Model-based Quantitative Quality Prediction

on the design but are also influenced by the decisions made during implementation.

When modelling the software architecture of the software system (upper left corner), we abstract from the system in its whole complexity. Depending on the software architecture metamodel, different aspects of the system can be reflected in the model. For example, in the PCM, an abstract specification of the behaviour is modelled (cf. Section 2.5). Aspects that cannot be expressed in the modelling language are left out. For example, variable assignments and component state cannot be modelled in the PCM. Additionally, for a concrete software system at hand, the modeller decides how to abstract from the software system in the model. For example, even though the PCM allows to model passive resources, the modeller may decide not to model the detailed locking behaviour of a database system.

As a result, the abstraction of the model depends on both the metamodel capabilities and the modellers decisions how to abstract.

Based on the model of the software architecture, quality properties can be *predicted* (upper right corner) for the software system. Thus, we say that the model *implies* the *predicted quality properties*. If the software architecture model reflects the software system well enough for a given quality property, and if the quality prediction method (for example a queueing network analysis for performance) is sound and valid for this model, the quality can be accurately predicted, i.e. the implied predicted quality property value is the same than or similar to the actual quality property of the system.

Quality prediction techniques thus allow to evaluate architecture models to predict the quality properties of the (possibly to be implemented) system. We can express the evaluation as a function on the models:

Definition 2.15 Quality evaluation function

The quality evaluation for a quality criterion q can be expressed as a *quality evaluation function* from the set $VM := \{M' \,|\, M' \blacktriangleleft MM\}$ of model instances conforming to M's metamodel MM to the set of possible values of q's quality metric $m(q)$, denoted $\mathcal{V}_{m(q)}^*$.

$$\Phi_q^* : VM \to \mathcal{V}_{m(q)}^*$$

Then, $\Phi_q^*(M)$ denotes the evaluated value of a quality criterion q for an architectural model $M \in MM$.

For example, when evaluating the quality metric mean response time (*mrt*), $\mathcal{V}_{mrt}^* = \mathbb{R}_+$. For a specific candidate a, the *mrt* in seconds for an offered service s (denoted $q = mrt_s$ here) might evaluate to $\Phi_{mrt_s}^*(a) = 5$ sec. When evaluating the probability of failure on demand (*pofod*), $\mathcal{V}_{pofod_s}^* = [0, 1]$. For example, for an offered service S of a specific candidate a, $\Phi_{pofod_s}^*$ could evaluate to $\Phi_{pofod_s}^*(a) = 0.005$.

2.4.2. Performance

Early methods for performance modelling of computer systems are hardware-focusses methods (H. Koziolek, 2008, p.30 et seqq.), which model a system based on the used resources such as CPUs and hard disks. Example modelling techniques are queueing networks, stochastic Petri nets, or Markov chains (Bernardo and Hillston, 2007). Requests to the resources are abstractly modelled. In particular, control flow within the software is not in the focus (H. Koziolek, 2008, p.37).

Software Performance Engineering (SPE) (Smith, 1990; Smith and Williams, 2002b) shifts the focus to the software behaviour, leading to mixed software/hardware models. The driving scenario is the evaluation of software designs for performance early in the software life cycle, to avoid expensive redesign due to performance flaws later. Furthermore, the whole development process should be accompanied by SPE, so that drifts from the initially predicted behaviour can be detected and countered quickly.

Since SPE, numerous methods to model and analyse software designs (and software architectures) have been developed, a survey is presented by Balsamo et al. (2004).

In early SPE methods, such as by (Smith and Williams, 2002b), the performance relevant properties of software designs are captured in specialized software performance models, which focus on the performance-relevant aspects only. However, two manual tasks make the use of such methods difficult: First, the software performance models need to be created in addition to software design models (e.g. in UML (Object Management Group (OMG), 2005)). During the evolution of the design, they need to be kept corresponding to each other. Second, results on the software performance model level need to be mapped back to the software design to make decisions.

To encounter the gap between design and performance model, automated transformation approaches have been suggested which allow to directly annotate a software design model (e.g. a UML model) with performance-relevant information (e.g. using the UML MARTE profile (Object Management Group (OMG), 2006c)) and then automatically transform the design model in a performance model for analysis. Thus, the performance aspects are closer to the design and easier to maintain during the development process. Additionally, the results of analyses can be mapped back to the design, e.g. also using MARTE annotations.

However, SPE methods require a white-box view of the software system and thus are not applicable to component-based systems if components are provided by third-parties.

For component-based software, approaches have been suggested to enable performance prediction for component-based systems based on performance specification of individual components. Surveys on existing methods is provided by Becker et al. (2006), (H. Koziolek, 2010), and Crnković et al. (2010). The main features, as identified by (H. Koziolek, 2010), are

Schedulable resource demands: Accesses of components to different types of active resources, such as CPUs or hard disks need to be reflected by the models, because the contention and resulting waiting times on the resource level is the main influencing factor for performance analysis. To enable prediction across different platforms, the resource demands need to be specified in a platform independent way, e.g. by modelling the used byte code instructions (Krogmann et al., 2010).

Passive resource demands: In addition to active resources, additional passive resources such as semaphores or thread pools may be available at the software level and lead to waiting times. Thus, the access of components to such limited passive resources need to be modelled.

Control flow: Because the order of requests to active and passive resources can affect the resource contention, the internal control flow within components should be reflected by component performance specifications.

Required service calls: Because the final assembly of components into a system is unknown when specifying a component performance specification, the calls to other required components need to be modelled explicitly so that the overall performance model can be derived by composing the component performance specifications.

Parameter dependencies: As the usage context of components is also unknown when specifying component performance models, any parameter that affects the performance of a component (e.g. the amount of processed data) must be explicitly modelled and the performance specification of the component needs to be parametric.

Internal state: Similarly to the usage parameters, the state of a component may affect the performance relevant properties and should be modelled in these cases.

The last four properties are not only relevant for performance prediction for component-based systems, but also for other quality attributes such as reliability. Only if a component quality specification is parametrized and encapsulates the inner performance relevant properties, it can be composed to system performance models without the need to adopt it to other parts of the system.

2.4.3. Other Quality Attributes

We briefly present techniques for the three other quality attributes that have quantitative prediction techniques based on architecture models in the following.

Reliability prediction on the software architecture level has been studied since the mid 1990s (Gokhale, 2007). Surveys are presented by Goseva-Popstojanova and Trivedi (2001), Gokhale (2007), and Immonen and Niemelä (2008). The targeted quality metrics to predict are, for example, the POFOD. However, compared to performance, reliability prediction techniques are more difficult to use because their predictions cannot be validated by measurements during the course of a software development project.

For security, quantitative evaluation is difficult (Grunske and Joyce, 2008). Still, a number of techniques has been presented. Grunske and Joyce

(2008) provide a survey on quantitative security prediction techniques, especially focussing on techniques applicable for component-based systems, for which similar considerations that for performance (i.e. parametrization with respect to usage and hardware) are of particular importance. For example, their own technique evaluated the risk of security breaches (the quality metric) based on estimated attack probabilities and modular attack trees for the components of the system. Thus, while quantitative security prediction is still in an early research stage, techniques such as presented by Grunske and Joyce (2008) can be used to evaluate a CBA model for security properties.

Approaches to predict costs of a software architecture differ from the above, because costs is a business quality attribute, which is also related to the development process and organizations involved in creating the architecture, thus taking a more broad view on the system and its surroundings.

Costs estimation approaches are usually concerned with predicting the costs of a software project. Example methods are COCOMO II (Constructive Cost Model, (Boehm et al., 2000)) and its relatives (Boehm and Valerdi, 2008). The estimation of the relevant parameters is the crucial aspect in these methods. Numerous surveys on costs estimation techniques for software development projects are available, for example (Briand et al., 1999),(Jørgensen, 2007) and (Boehm and Valerdi, 2008, p.78). However, the accuracy of costs estimation for newly developed systems is limited and costs estimation are often based on experience only in practice (Berntsson Svensson et al., 2011, p.8).

Calculating the overall costs of a software architecture based on the estimated costs of its constituent, i.e. components (bought or developed in-house), middleware, and hardware, is then more straightforward: Usually, the costs for the overall system is the sum of costs of its parts. Costs models of the overall system can become more complex if particular licensing models are used (such as pay-per-use for externally hosted components, i.e. services, which make the costs dependent on the usage) or if more complex contracts with the vendors of third-party components are available (such as a quantity discounts if several components are bought from the same vendor). Still, these relations can be straightforwardly represented by a mathematical function, which may be project- or organization-specific.

2.4.4. Quality Completions

By definition, a CBA model is an abstraction of the modelled software architecture. However, for performance, low-level details of the system implementation also affect the performance properties of the later system. For example, in distributed systems, the choice of third-party communication middleware may have a large impact on the response time and scalability of the system. While the architecture in this case should reflect that a third-party communication middleware is used, it is impractical to include low-level performance-relevant detail of the communication middleware itself in the architecture model.

To include such detail in a non-intrusive way, *performance completions* (Woodside et al., 2002) have been suggested to weave relevant low-level detail into the performance model before performance analysis, thus keeping the architectural model unchanged. The concrete messaging mechanisms used by a communication middleware (e.g. that each message is confirmed by an acknowledge message on the middleware level) can be included in the performance model without having to consider them at the software architecture level (e.g. here we only model that the sender component sends a message). Technically, performance completions can be realized as model transformations (Becker, 2008b; Kapova and Reussner, 2010; Kapova, 2011). Annotations to the software architecture model mark the places where low-level details should be added. If the considered low-level aspects provide configuration options (such as communication middleware offers configuration regarding message size, reliability of deliveries, etc.), the chosen configuration can be reflected by the annotations.

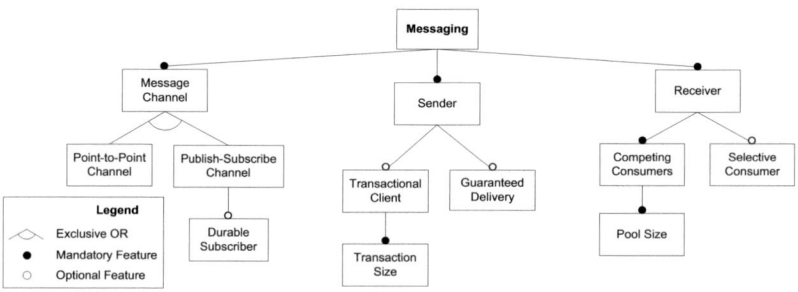

Figure 2.10.: Example Feature Model for Messaging Configuration from (Happe et al., 2010)

Feature models and feature configuration (Czarnecki and Eisenecker, 2000) as general often-used models for describing configurability. Feature models describe the possible configurations for the considered aspect (e.g. communication middleware) as a tree of features that can be selected. The performance effect of each feature can be captured by model transformation fragments. Then, the software architecture can be annotated by a feature configuration, which describes the selected features. For performance prediction, the transformation fragments of the selected features are combined to one model transformation when executing the performance completion (Kapova and Reussner, 2010; Kapova, 2011). Figure 2.10 shows an example feature model describing different performance-relevant options to configure a message-oriented middleware, as used by Happe et al. (2010) and Kapova and Becker (2010).

Other low level details which can be handled by completions are the performance impact of application servers, e.g. to consider the effect of different thread pool configurations (Kapova, 2011). Similarly, low-level aspects important for other quality attributes than performance (e.g. reliability) could be modelled by the completion mechanism as well, leading to the general concept of *quality completions*.

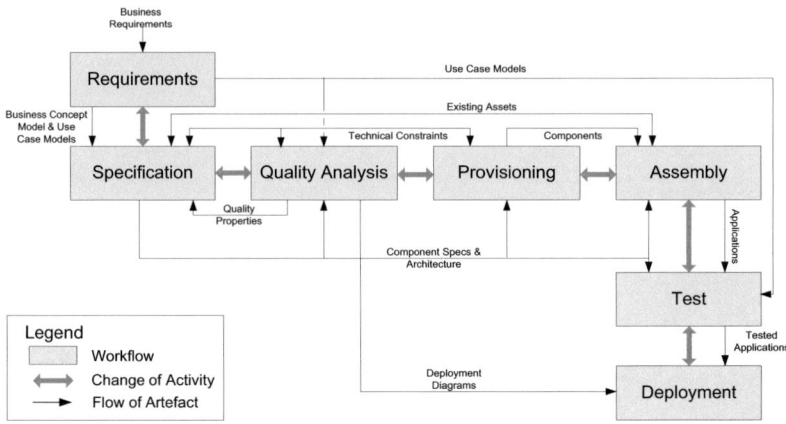

Figure 2.11.: Quality-driven Component-based Development Process by H. Koziolek and Happe, 2006

2.4.5. Integration in the CB Development Process

Prediction of quantitative quality properties can be included in the CB development process as proposed by H. Koziolek and Happe, 2006 and shown in Figure 2.11 (we adjusted the names of workflows and artefacts to match the terminology used in this work, cf. Section 2.2.1). Compared to the basic CB development process by Cheesman and Daniels (cf. Figure 2.2), a new workflow *Quality Analysis* has been introduced in which the created specifications are analysed for their quality properties.

The inputs of the quality analysis workflow are component specifications, the CBA specification, and use case models, which also contain informal information on quality requirements. The output of the quality analysis steps are the predicted quality properties. If the quality properties do not match the quality requirements, the specification in the specification workflow needs to be updated.

Figure 2.12 shows the internals of the quality analysis step. Several developer roles are involved. To enable quality prediction, deployers provide additional models for the resource environment, including its quality prop-

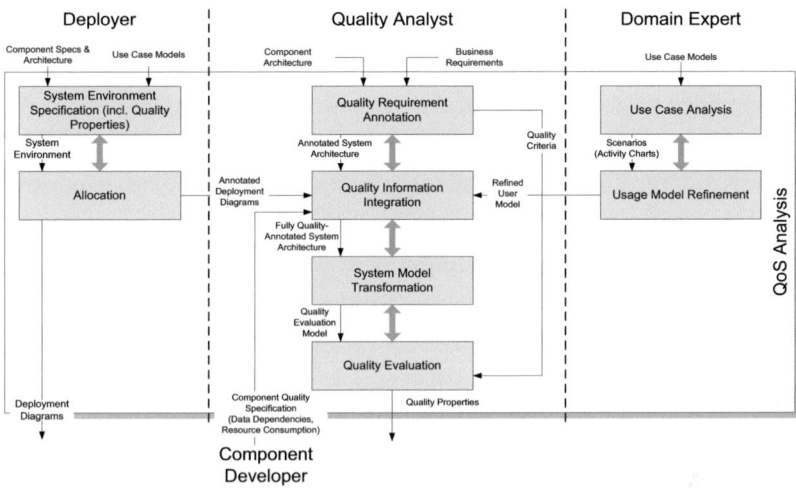

Figure 2.12.: Quality Analysis Step by H. Koziolek and Happe, 2006

erties. Domain experts estimate quality relevant properties of the use cases models and thus refines them into usage models suitable for quality prediction. Then, the quality analyst (this role is often assumed by the software architect) integrated all information (including the information on quality requirements from the requirements workflow) into one model and uses quality prediction approaches to predict the quality properties of the design (first transforming the CBA into a suitable quality model such as queueing networks, and then analysing the quality).

2.5. Palladio Component Model

The Palladio Component Model (PCM, (Becker et al., 2009; Reussner et al., 2011)) is a metamodel for component-based software architectures and also provides a set of analysis tools for performance, reliability, and costs evaluation.

The PCM is specifically designed for component-based systems and strictly separates parametrized component performance models from the composition models and resource models, also providing configuration options of the models. Thus, the PCM naturally supports many architectural degrees of freedom (e.g., substituting components, changing component allocation, etc.).

Section 2.5.1 describe an example PCM model, which is used as a running example throughout this thesis. Section 2.5.2 presents the main concepts of the PCM metamodel relevant for this thesis, and relates them to the general CBA concepts described in Section 2.1.1. The next three sections 2.5.3, 2.5.4, and 2.5.5 describe the quality analyses available for the PCM for performance, reliability, and costs, respectively.

2.5.1. Example PCM Model

Consider the minimal PCM model example in Fig. 2.13, which is realized using the Ecore-based PCM metamodel and visualized here in UML-like diagrams for quick comprehension (the key for the diagram is shown in Figures A.1 and A.2 in the appendix, p. 449). The architecture model specified by the software architect consists of three connected software components C1 - C3 deployed on three different hardware nodes. The software components contain cost annotations, while the hardware nodes contain annotations for performance (processing rates), reliability (mean time to failure (MTTF), mean time to repair (MTTR)), and cost (fixed and variable cost in an abstract cost unit).

The example system used here is a Business Trip Management system with booking functionality. Users are administrative employees that plan and book journeys. They either plan the journey for an employee and book it (80% of all cases), or they only check the journeys efficiency and order a reimbursement for an employee that has booked himself (20% of all cases). The system is intentionally kept very simple here, because it meant to convey the PCM concepts quickly, and is not meant to be an example of practical component-based design.

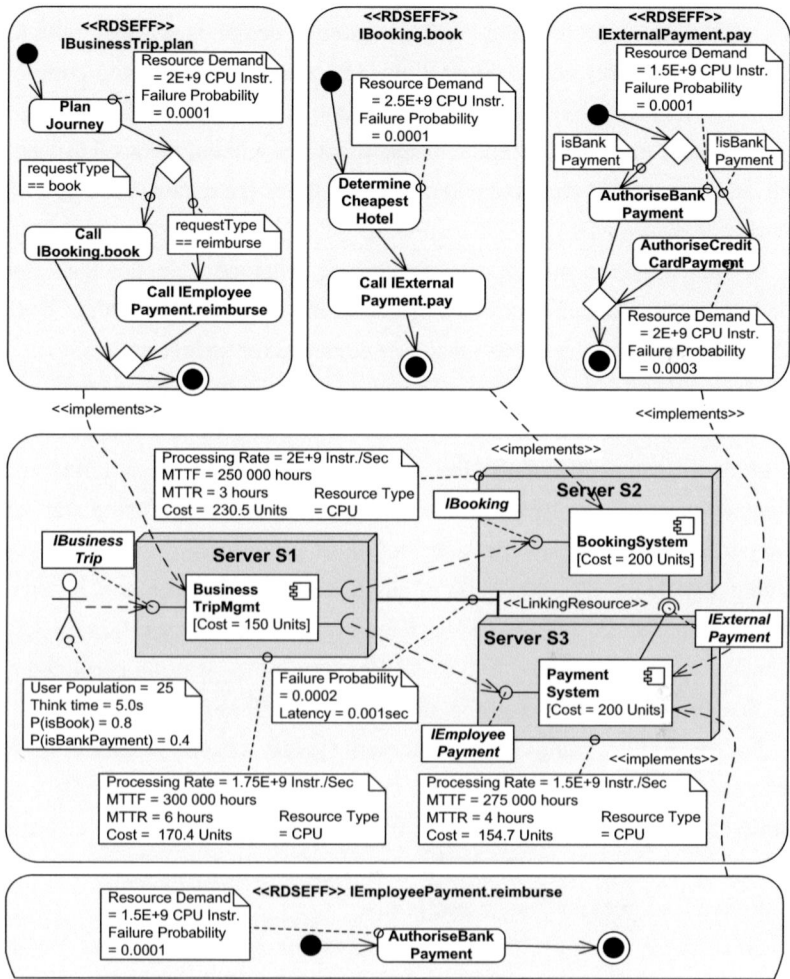

Figure 2.13.: Simple Example PCM Model: Business Trip Booking System

For each software component service, the component developers provide an abstract behavioural description called service effect specification (SEFF). SEFFs model the abstract control flow through a component service in terms of internal actions (i.e., resource demands accessing the underlying hardware) and external calls (i.e., accessing connected components). Modelling each component behaviour with separate SEFFs enables us to quickly exchange component specifications without the need to manually change system-wide behaviour specifications (as required in e.g. UML sequence diagrams).

For performance annotations, component developers can use the extended resource-demanding service effect specifications (RDSEFFs). Using RDSEFFs, developers specify resource demands for their components (e.g., in terms of CPU instructions to be executed), which, during analysis, are divided by the processing rate of the modelled resource environment to determine the actual execution time demanded from the processors. Resource demands can be specified as distribution functions, either using standard functions such as exponential distribution or gamma distribution, or by defining a stepwise approximation of any distribution function, e.g. based on measurement data. Figure 2.14(a) shows an example for a single resource demand specification, and Figure 2.14(b) shows the resulting predicted response time distribution for a request to the overall system.

For reliability, component developers specify failure probabilities for component internal actions, which can be determined for example using software reliability growth models (Musa et al., 1987), or code coverage metrics during testing. The PCM also supports hard disc drive rates and software resources such as thread pools.

A software architect composes component specifications by various component developers into an application model. With an additional usage model describing user arrival rates (open workload) or user population and think time (closed workload) of the system, and an additional model of the resource environment and the allocation of components to resources,

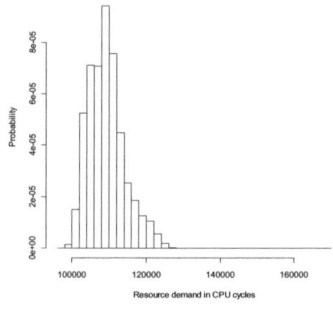
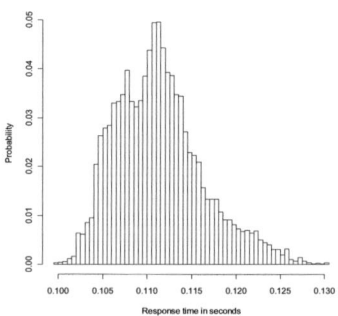

(a) Example Resource Demand
    Distribution

(b) Example Resulting Response Time
    Distribution

Figure 2.14.: Examples for Arbitrary Distribution Functions (Gouvêa et al., 2011)

the model is complete and can be transformed into analytical or simulation-based models for quality analyses.

For the PCM, we briefly explain the existing analysis methods for performance and reliability in the following sections. For each architectural candidate, we evaluate the quality property (e.g. "response time 5 sec") for each quality criterion (e.g. criterion "response time of service *s*").

The predicted quality properties for the example shown in Fig. 2.13 are depicted in Tab. 2.2. Although the example in Fig. 2.13 is simple, it is not obvious on how to change the architecture model efficiently to improve the quality properties. For example, the software architect could increase the processing rate of server S1, which would result in better performance but higher cost. The software architect could also change the component allocation ($3^3 = 27$ possibilities) or incorporate other component specifications with different QoS attributes.

The design space even for such a simple example is huge. Manually checking the possible design alternatives in a trial-and-error approach is laborious and error-prone. The software architect cannot easily create design

63

Quality Criterion	Metric	Value
Performance	Avg. Resp. Time	4.6 sec
	Utilization S1	42 %
	Utilization S2	37 %
	Utilization S3	10 %
Reliability	POFOD	7.36E-4
Cost	Overall Cost	54 units

Table 2.2.: Quality Property Prediction Results

alternatives that are even locally optimal for all quality criteria, and finding global optima is practically impossible because it requires modelling each alternative. In practice this situation is often mitigated by over-provisioning (i.e., incorporating fast and expensive hardware resources), which can lead to unnecessary high cost.

2.5.2. PCM Metamodel

Figure 2.15 shows the excerpt[2] of the PCM metamodel that corresponds to the general CBA concepts shown in Figure 2.1. The mapping of concepts is described in detail in Appendix A.2. The excerpts of the metamodel for RDSEFFs is shown in Appendix A.4.

Note that the PCM metamodel is actually specified in Ecore (Steinberg et al., 2008), which is another meta-metamodelling language in the context of the Eclipse Modelling Tools (EMF). Ecore and EMOF are very similar (Steinberg et al., 2008, Sec. 2.6.2) or even "effectively equivalent" (Merks, 2007) and EMF provides means to serialize in memory models as both Ecore models and EMOF models (Steinberg et al., 2008). Thus, we do not

---

[2]The property names in the PCM are usually named like the referenced type. For example, AllocationContext.assemblyContext refers to the AssemblyContext to deploy. These default names are left out of Figure 2.15. For simplicity, we have left the complex inheritance hierarchy out of Figure 2.15. Thus, the figure does not accurately reflect which abstract class introduces which properties for the concepts. Appendix A.3 shows more details on the inheritance hierarchy of components and composed structures.

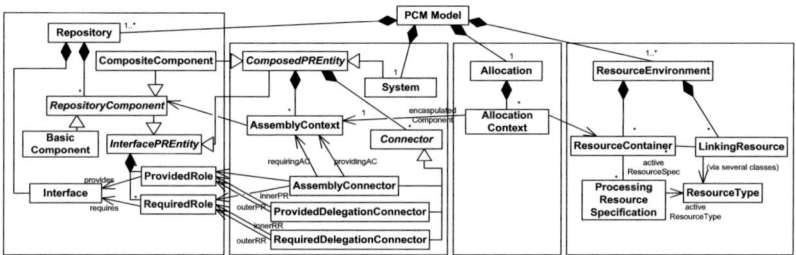

Figure 2.15.: Excerpt of the PCM Metamodel

make a distinction between Ecore and EMOF in this work and use EMOF to describe metamodels (including the PCM).

There is no defined root model element in the PCM. An architecture is described for analysis using an allocation model (which refers to the other model parts, see associations in Figure 2.15) and a usage mode (not shown here). Thus, the repository is unaware of systems using it, and systems are unaware of allocations using it, so that different CBA models can use a shared repository or system.

2.5.3. Performance Analysis

For performance analysis, the PCM supports a transformation into a discrete-event simulation (SimuCom (Becker et al., 2009)) or LQNs to derive response times, throughputs, and resource utilizations.

SimuCom is based on model-to-code transformations and the SSJ simulation framework (L'Ecuyer and Buist, 2005). It is in the class of extended queueing networks: The resources of the PCM are mapped to queueing stations, which an be governed by different scheduling strategies. The discrete-event simulation executes the modelled control flow of the system and issues requests to the queueing stations for each resource demand. For resource demand distributions, a sample is drawn from the distribution each time the resource demand is evaluated. Thus, SimuCom allows analysing models containing resource demands specified as arbitrary distribution functions, but can be time-consuming to derive stable results. The resulting performance data is a detailed log of events occurring during the simulation (calls and resource demands), from which any performance measure can be derived.

The transformation PCM2LQN (H. Koziolek and Reussner, 2008) generates a Layered Queueing Network (LQN, (Franks et al., 2009), cf. Section 2.6.1) instance from a PCM instance. Similarly to SimuCom, the control flow is retained and mapped to LQN activities. Components are mapped to LQN tasks and resources are mapped to LQN processors, which are the queueing stations in the analysis. Several scheduling strategies are supported. Resource demands in LQNs are simplified to mean values and variance. The LQN solver (Franks et al., 2009) provides a heuristic performance analysis using mean value analysis (Reiser and Lavenberg, 1980) and can often quickly produce results. However, some control flow constructs such as arbitrary passive resources cannot be used. Additionally, an LQN simulator is available, which supports all LQN constructs including passive resources.

2.5.4. Reliability Analysis

For reliability analysis, the PCM supports a transformation into absorbing discrete time Markov chains (DTMC) (Brosch et al., 2010, 2011a) or a reliability simulation to derive the probability of failure on demand (POFOD) for an usage scenario.

The control flow of the system is mapped to a Markov chain. For each RDSEFF action has a software failure rate, a transition to a failure state is generated with the respective probability. For internal actions, the availability of the hardware is also considered. Then, the probability to reach the success state is calculated using standard techniques, taking into account the PCM control flow actions. For example, the probability for a failure in a sequence of internal actions is the product of each individual failure probability.

The failure rates of the resources are defined as mean-to-failure and mean-time-to-repair values for servers and failure probabilities for linking resources. Then, the above calculations are executed for each possible hardware state (a faster approximative solution can also skip hardware states with low probability).

2.5.5. Cost Model

Reducing costs is a major interest in software development and thus need also to be taken into account when designing software architectures. For finding the best software architecture for a given software development project, one needs to trade off quality attribute improvements and costs. Thus, it is important to take into account costs and cost savings that architectural design options induce in later development stages.

Costs arise in multiple phases of the software development life cycle, and are caused by multiple activities. Costs that are affected by the software architecture are component cost, system cost, and hardware cost. To assess the total cost of ownership, a cost model has to take development costs, but also later costs such as maintenance into account.

Component cost arise in various life cycle stages. First of all, components need to be provisioned. This results in development costs for components that are developed in-house and procurement costs for buying or licensing third-party components. Possibly, third-party components first need to be adapted to the system, also causing development costs which depend on how well the component as-is suits the system as well as how understandable and usable its interfaces are. In later life cycles, components induce testing costs, and maintenance costs or licensing / support costs. Different components with different quality attributes may result to different cost. For example, developing a high-performance component with highly optimized algorithms might be more expensive than using a standard component off the shelf.

System costs are costs that are related to the overall system and cannot be attributed to single components. These costs arise when assembling the system and when selecting and preparing the required middleware (such as application servers, operating systems and messaging systems). Again, options of different quality might result in different cost. For example, a highly reliable messaging system might require more initial set-up cost or licensing costs than a simpler solution.

Hardware costs arise from the procurement of hardware to deploy the system. This includes costs for servers as well as for infrastructure such as network. In addition, the operation of the system in terms of operating costs such as hardware maintenance and energy costs can be taken into account, if these costs will be attributed to the developing organization, too. Today's IT services offer many different deployment options, from acquiring servers in an own computer centre up to deploying a system at a third-party infrastructure provided, e.g. in a cloud. Depending on the resource demands and resource efficiency of the software system, a different amount of hardware needs to be acquired and paid for.

To include the cost dimension in this work, we realized a simple cost annotation model that allows to express the cost differences of different design options and to assess the cost differences between architectural candidates. The model allows to annotate the software architecture with costs estimations. Similar to other costs optimization approaches, such as by Cortellessa et al. (2008), it does not provide means to estimate the costs, as this is a different research field. The advantage of the independent costs annotation model is that it can either be created based on rough estimations, or it can be created based on results from more sophisticated cost estimation approaches, such as COCOMO II (Boehm et al., 2000) and its relatives (Boehm and Valerdi, 2008), or project- or organization-specific approaches.

The used cost model allows to assign costs to components and to hardware. It distinguishes initial costs and operating costs, so that the software architecture effects to the total cost of ownership can be assessed. Users can either calculate total costs for example calculating the present value of the costs based on a assumed interest rate, or they can treat the two types of costs as separate criteria to improve and to trade off. Thus, component costs reflect all relevant costs induced by that component's implementation and later life cycle phases. Different options for a component can be modelled as different available components, and then be annotated with component costs.

Hardware costs annotate servers and / or processing resources. Here, selection of fixed hardware entities can be annotated with fixed costs each. For example, a server of type A with certain reliability and performance properties properties costs 1000€, while a server of type B with different properties costs 1500€. Alternatively, a cost function can be specified to map parameters of the hardware to a price, to reflect a wider range of options. For example, a costs function can map clock speed of CPUs to costs based on the price tables of CPU producers. Again, the model allows to specify both initial costs and operation costs.

For cost analysis, we have developed a PCM cost solver for this work. It relies on a static analysis of a PCM model instance annotated with the presented costs model. It calculates the cost for each component and resource based on the annotations specified in the PCM instance and then adds these cost to derive the overall expected cost for the architecture. If a server specified in the model is not used, i.e. no components are allocated to it, its cost do not add to the overall cost.

The costs model and costs solver are simple, because the main challenge of cost prediction is the estimation of costs, which we assume given. If the initial costs and operating costs of the single parts of the architecture are known, it is straightforward to calculate the overall costs.

2.6. Other CBA Models With Predictive Capabilities

Two other component models that support performance prediction are CBML and ROBOCOP, which are presented in the following. A survey on other component-models that can be used for performance prediction has been presented by H. Koziolek, 2010. For methods for other quality attributes, refer to the surveys mentioned in Section 2.4.3.

2.6.1. CBML

The Component-Based Modeling Language (CBML, (Wu and Woodside, 2004b; Wu, 2003)) is a component model based on Layered Queueing Networks (LQN) (Franks et al., 2009).

Before describing the component-based extensions of CBML, we give a brief overview on LQNs in the following. The goal of LQNs is to capture the software-related effects for performance analysis. In particular, it has been observed that layered systems may introduce additional queueing delays if a limited number of threads to process requests are available on each layer and block while the layer is waiting for responses of lower layers (Franks et al., 2009).

Figure 2.16(a) shows a small example LQN. The four parallelogram represent LQN Tasks, which represent software processes forming the layers. The layering of tasks is not strict: the Database task is accessed by both the DataReporting task and the Application task. A task can provide a set of services, called entries. An entry can have a fine-grained behaviour model consisting of a graph of activities, as shows for Entry1. Resource demands are given in brackets, other numbers denote call probabilities. Tasks are deployed by mapping them to Processors, shown as circles.

CBML extends LQN and adds the possibility to specify reusable components. Figure 2.17 shows the CBML metamodel and Figure 2.16(b) shows such a component. The component offers three services, called inPorts, Entry4 to Entry6 in the example. Each inPort is delegated to an

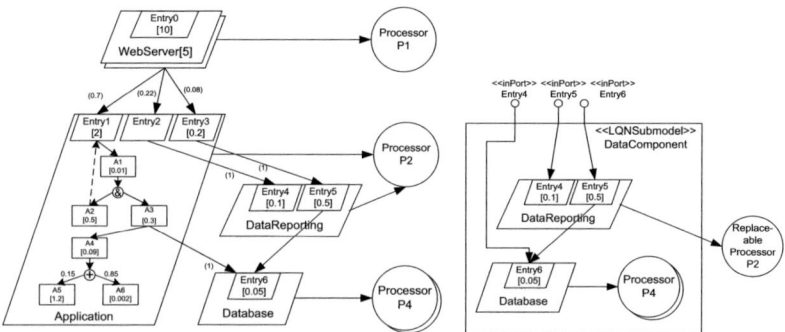

(a) Example LQN Model (adapted from (H. Koziolek and Reussner, 2008))

(b) Example CBML Component

Figure 2.16.: Example LQN and CBML Models

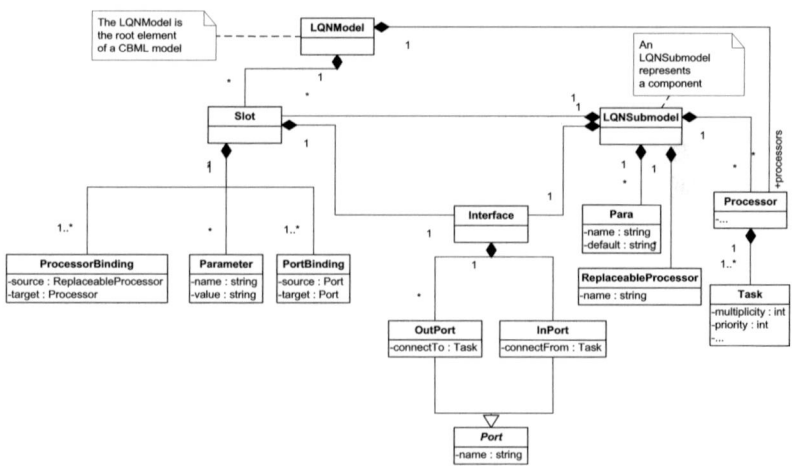

Figure 2.17.: Excerpt of the CBML Metamodel, Extracted from the XML Schema

71

internal entry. OutPorts (not shown in the example) can analogously be used to model control flow leaving the component. Components can specify dedicated processors (processor P2 in the example) or replaceable processors.

Both system and allocation is modelled by a set of Slots. Each Slot corresponds to a component instance, but also defines how its component is connected to other components in the system (connectors) and the deployment of its component (component allocation instance).

For performance analysis, CBML models are transformed into plain LQNs by resolving the bindings. For example, the LQN model shown in Figure 2.16(a) could be the resulting LQN model of a CBML input model containing Figure 2.16(b) and additional components for the WebServer and Application task.

2.6.2. ROBOCOP

ROBOCOP (ROBOCOP consortium, 2003; Bondarev and Chaudron, 2006; Bondarev et al., 2006, 2007) is a component model primarily targeting the automotive domain. With the component model, a development environment, a set of quality analyses, and a specification for ROBOCOP runtime environments are provided.

The ROBOCOP metamodel is not defined explicitly as a metamodel, so we extracted it from the grammar, natural language description and figures in the publications and project deliverables. Figure 2.18 shows the resulting metamodel[3].

Components are modelled with the so-named meta-class Component (Bondarev and Chaudron, 2006). A ResourceModel and a Behaviour-Model describe non-functional aspects of a component (Bondarev et al.,

---

[3]Note that we have not optimized the model for readability, but rather reproduce the concepts as accurately as possible to keep resemblance to the ROBOCOP publications, using the names from the grammar where appropriate. If the concepts were modelled anew using a metamodel, some aspects could be represented more elegantly.

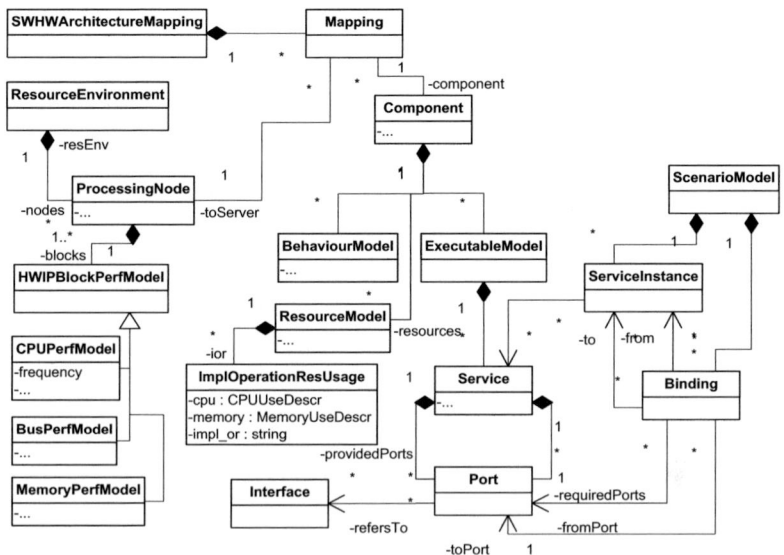

Figure 2.18.: Excerpt of the ROBOCOP Metamodel, Extracted from Natural Language Description and Graphics (Bondarev et al., 2004; Bondarev and Chaudron, 2006) as well as the ROBOCOP IDL (ROBOCOP consortium, 2003)

2007), while an ExecutableModel contains the implementation of the component (Bondarev and Chaudron, 2006). The implementation of components is realized as Services, which are comparable to public classes in object-oriented programming (Bondarev and Chaudron, 2006).

A Service defines a set of provided Ports and a set of required Ports (ROBOCOP consortium, 2003, A.2.3, p.214), which are equivalent to ProvidedRoles and RequiredRoles, respectively, in the PCM. Each port refers to an Interface (ROBOCOP consortium, 2003, ibid.).

For performance properties, the resource usage of a component is defined in the ResourceModel described in Bondarev and Chaudron (2006). For each operation the component implements (referenced as ior for implemented operation resource usage), CPU usage and memory usage can be defined, or can remain undefined if the component does not require one of the two resource types. Here, we abstract from the details of this specification by using the types CPUUseDescr and MemoryUseDescr as a place holder for the concrete resource usage description, because the details are not relevant in this work (see (Bondarev and Chaudron, 2006) for details).

The assembly of components is realized by a ScenarioModel (Bondarev et al., 2004). The ScenarioModel instantiates Services as ServiceInstances. A Binding connects two components by binding a provided Port to a required Port and by referring to the respective ServiceInstances that contain the Ports to make the references unique.

The allocation of component to servers is realized by a SW/HW architecture mapping (SWHWArchitectureMapping (Bondarev et al., 2006)). It maps a a Component to a ProcessingNode. Note that the roles were not named in the available ROBOCOP documentation, so we added our own names to be able to refer to metamodel properties later. Interestingly, components are directly mapped to servers and component instances (service instances in ROBOCOP) are not considered in the mapping. This is a difference to the general CBA metamodel described in Section 2.1 and leads to the limitation that different component instances cannot be mapped separately to their own server nodes in ROBOCOP.

The quality properties of the different hardware resources (HW IP blocks) of a server are defined as separate models. In case of performance, a HWIPBlockPerfModel models the performance properties of a hardware IP block. Hardware IP blocks can be CPUs, memory, or bus blocks. For each, quality properties are defined to allow performance analysis together with the component performance properties. As we do not require further details on the ROBOCOP performance analyses in this work, we do not give further detail on these model elements (see (Bondarev and Chaudron, 2006) for details).

3. Multi-Criteria Optimization

To find the best software architecture in a development context can be understood an optimization problem with multiple quality criteria to consider. This section lays the foundations for multi-criteria optimization and introduces the terms and concepts required to understand the remainder of the thesis.

Section 3.1 briefly lays foundations for optimization in general. Then, Section 3.2 describes how to deal with multiple, possibly conflicting criteria when solving optimization problems. Section 3.3 briefly describes classical methods and their limitation before Section 3.4 provides a overview on Pareto-based approximative metaheuristic techniques. As a particular metaheuristic technique used in this work, Section 3.5 presents multi-objective evolutionary algorithms.

3.1. Optimization

Optimization is the procedure of determining the best solution in a given context.

The available solutions are mathematically characterized as a set of decisions D, each of which has a set of possible alternative choices $A_d, d \in D$. Then, a single solution can be characterized as a vector x in the *decision space* $\mathcal{O} = \Pi_{d \in D} A_d$. The vector x is called decision vector. If values in A_d are (mostly) discrete, the problem is also named a *combinatorial optimization problem*.

What solutions is best is defined by an objective function on D which is to be minimized or maximized. In case of single-objective optimization, the objective function assigns scalar values (e.g. real numbers) to each decision vector, for example $f : \mathcal{O} \to \mathbb{R}$. In case of multi-objective optimization discussed in the next section, the objective function is a vector-valued function mapping each x to a vector of values.

Possibly, additional constraints can be defined which have to be fulfilled by decision vectors in order to be viable alternatives. Let *constraints* denote a set of constraints, where each constraint is defined as a predicate on the vector x.

An optimization problem (here for minimization of a single-objective function) can then be written formally as :

$$\min_{x \in \mathcal{O}} f(x) \text{ subject to } \forall P \in constraints : P(x)$$

The domain of f is the *objective space*. The image of all viable alternatives in $\mathcal{O}$ (i.e. all x that fulfil the constraints) is the set of achievable values in the given optimization problem.

The concept optimization is related to search and design space exploration as follows. Search algorithms find an object with certain properties in a set of objects. Thus, they can be used for optimization: The goal of such optimizing search algorithms is to find the optimal objects as defined by an objective unction in a set of objects, i.e. in the decision space. Search-based optimization techniques use search to find the optimal solutions (or an approximation thereof).

The term design space exploration is used in embedded system design and denotes the (often multi-criteria) optimization of embedded system designs. In particular, the term denotes the "process of systematically altering design parameters [to achieve better quality of the design]" (Gries, 2003, p.5). For example, the number of parallel gates in a circuit can be increased, which improves performance at the expense of area (Gries, 2003, p.5).

3.2. Handling Multiple Criteria

When optimizing real-world problems, multiple criteria are often of interest. As discussed in Section 2.2.1, multiple criteria are relevant for quality of software architectures. In decision making theory, three methods to handle problems with multiple criteria (i.e., in our case, quality criteria) have been identified based on when decision makers have to articulate their preferences for solutions (cf. van Veldhuizen and Lamont (2000), and Branke et al. (2008)): *a priori*, *a posteriori*, and *interactive* preference articulation.

- First model the preferences for each criterion, then create a scalar objective function and use single-objective optimization (a priori method)

- Find the optimal trade-off solutions (Pareto-optimal solutions, cf. Section 3.2.2) and then decide (a posteriori method)

- Interactively articulate preferences (interactive method)

Note that we distinguish multi-criteria optimization problems and multi-objective optimization problems in this work. In *multi-criteria optimization problems*, multiple criteria are relevant in the real world problem. They may be solved by using single-objective optimization (mapping all criteria to one scalar objective function based on preferences) or multi-objective optimization (using the criteria (or a representation thereof) directly as the vector-valued objective function). This distinction is not common in the literature[1]

Section 3.2.1 describes the three types of handling multi-criteria problems in more detail and discusses their advantages and disadvantages. Sec-

---

[1]In the literature, e.g. (Deb, 2001), multi-objective refers to both the solved-real world problem and the solution technique. In that terminology, multi-objective problems (i.e. multi-criteria problems) can be converted to single-objective problems. We find our terminology more useful as it is more precise.

tion 3.2.2 then defines Pareto-optimality to define optimal solutions in multi-objective problems.

3.2.1. Preference Articulation

We present the three methods when to articulate preferences in the following, giving examples for quality of software architecture to better relate the concepts to our goal.

3.2.1.1. A Priori Preference Articulation

In the preference-based method or *a priori method*, the preferences of the decision maker are elicited and captured in a preference model that allows to rank solutions. Using a-priori preferences, a multi-criteria problem can be mapped to a single-objective optimization problem by defining a scalar objective function based on the preference model. For example, a simple preference model could state that performance is more important than costs for a given software architecture, so that an architecture candidate is preferable to another one if its has lower costs.

A more complex preference model for quality properties could assign utility values to different quality property values and then compare architecture candidates based on the overall utility. For example, let us assume that the software architect (together with the stakeholders) agrees that a response time of 5 seconds for a given service of the system has a utility of 0.5 while a response time of 2 seconds has a utility of 1. At the same time, a POFOD for this service of 0.99 has a utility of 0.3, a POFOD of 0.995 a utility of 0.7 and a POFOD of 0.999 a utility of 1. At the same time, the software architect and the stakeholders agree that both quality properties are equally important. Then, an architectural candidate with POFOD 0.99 and response time 2 seconds has a overall utility of 1.3 and a second candidate with POFOD 0.995 and response time 5 seconds has a utility of 1.2.

In this scenario, one would deduce that the first candidate is better under this preference model.

The problem of this approach is that finding such a preference model is difficult (Deb, 2001, p.6)(Miettinen, 2008, p.3, p.19). The decision maker(s) may not have enough information to accurately model their preferences (van Veldhuizen and Lamont, 1998, p.50). Furthermore, preference models may depend on what trade-offs are reachable. If the expectations of the decision maker about the achievable quality properties are too pessimistic or too optimistic when modelling the preferences, the preference model may be wrong for the actual decision making situation (Miettinen, 2008, p.18). Furthermore, if several stakeholders are involved in the decision making, creating a preference model that reflects all stakeholders preferences and appropriately weights them is even more difficult.

3.2.1.2. A Posteriori Preference Articulation

In the *a posteriori method*, no preferences are assumed before the search, so that two solutions can only be ranked with respect to each other if one is objectively better, i.e. better in all objectives. If one solution is better in one objective and the other solution is better in another objective, these two solutions are incomparable. In this method, an automated search supporting the decision maker cannot rank such solutions, so that the goal of the search is to find the set of Pareto-optimal solutions (see next Section 3.2.2). The result is a multi-objective optimization problem.

A posteriori methods usually have a higher computational effort than a priori methods, because the full approximation of the Pareto front needs to be found instead of only a single solution. Their advantage, however, is that decision makers do not have to create a preference model in advance, but instead can select a suitable solution from the automatically found Pareto-optimal set. Thus, this method also provides more insight into the trade-offs of the given problem. For example, an experiment by Corner and Buchanan

(1997) showed that decision making using an a priori method was both assessed to be more difficult and to require more effort than decision making using an a posteriori method.

3.2.1.3. Interactive Preference Articulation

The third method is an intermediate solution in which an automated search process and the decision maker interact: While the search progressed, the decision maker reviews the currently available solutions and interactively modifies the preference model. Interactive methods usually build on top of a posteriori methods in that they start with presenting a Pareto-optimal solution to the decision maker (Miettinen et al., 2008b, p.28), based on which the decision maker can start to model his preferences. Thus, every a posteriori method can be extended to become an interactive method.

3.2.2. Pareto Optimality

Recall that in a multi-objective optimization problem, the objective function is vector-valued, i.e. $f(x) = \langle f_1(x), \ldots, f_n(x) \rangle$ for n objectives. Each objective function component f_i could be optimal when minimized or maximized. Usually, the criteria conflict with each other, which means that there is no single solution which is optimal with respect to all individual objective function components (otherwise, one could reduce the problem to one of the criteria, leading to a single-objective problem). Thus, there is mostly no single objectively optimal solution to a multi-objective optimization problem. Instead, the task of multi-objective optimization is to find all solutions with optimal trade-offs between the objectives, so that the decision maker can choose one solution in the subsequent preference articulation phase.

The concept of Pareto-optimality and Pareto-dominance define such optimal trade-off solutions. The concepts are illustrated in Figure 3.1 and defined in the following.

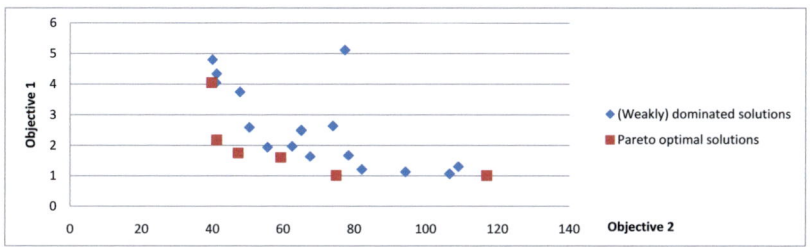

Figure 3.1.: Example for Pareto Optimal Solutions

First of all, it is necessary to define when a solution is better than another. First, let $f_i(x) \leq_i f_i(y)$ denote that x is equal to or better than y with respect to the i-th objective function component. An objective relation independent on preferences is Pareto-dominance, which imposes a strict partial order[2] on the decision space (cf. (Deb, 2005) and (Knowles et al., 2006)):

Definition 3.1 Pareto dominance and non-dominance (from Noorshams (2010) based on Knowles et al. (2006, p.4))

A solution $x \in \mathcal{O}$ *Pareto-dominates* (or short: *dominates*) a solution $y \in \mathcal{O}$ denoted by $x \prec y$ if

$$f(x) \neq f(y) \wedge \forall i : f_i(x) \leq_i f_i(y) \tag{3.1}$$

A solution x is *non-Pareto-dominated* (or short: *non-dominated*) by y if

$$y \not\prec x \tag{3.2}$$

As a result, a solution a is better than another solution b if $a \prec b$, whereas incomparable solutions are non-dominated (w.r.t. each other). A weaker comparison of solutions is done by the notion of weak Pareto dominance,

---

[2]The Pareto-dominance relation is asymmetric and transitive (Deb, 2005, p.29 et seq.).

which drops the asymmetry property and is reflexive instead, i.e. two equal solutions are considered to weakly Pareto dominate each other, too:

Definition 3.2 Weak Pareto dominance (based on Knowles et al. (2006, p.4))

A solution $x \in \mathcal{O}$ *weakly Pareto-dominates* (or short: *weakly dominates*) a solution $y \in \mathcal{O}$ denoted by $x \preceq y$ if

$$\forall i : f_i(x) \leq_i f_i(y) \tag{3.3}$$

Based on Pareto-dominance, optimality can be defined as follows:

Definition 3.3 Pareto optimality (from Noorshams (2010) based on Deb (2005))

A solution $x \in \mathcal{O}$ is *Pareto-optimal* (or short: *optimal*) w.r.t. a set $\mathcal{C} \subseteq \mathcal{O}$ if

$$\forall y \in \mathcal{C} : y \not\prec x \tag{3.4}$$

A solution x is *globally Pareto-optimal* (or short: *globally optimal*) if x is Pareto-optimal w.r.t. the entire feasible search space $\mathcal{O}$. The set of all non-dominated, (globally) optimal solutions is called the *Pareto-set*. The by F mapped Pareto-set is called the *Pareto-front*.

The notion of Pareto-dominance can also be applied to sets of solutions as follows:

Definition 3.4 (Weak) Pareto dominance of sets (based on Knowles (2006))

For a dominance relation $rel \in \{\prec, \preceq\}$ and for two sets of solution vectors $A, B \subseteq \mathcal{O}$, we define the dominance relations for two sets as

$$A \ rel \ B \Leftrightarrow \forall y \in B : \exists x \in A : x \ rel \ y$$

Figure 3.1 above illustrates the terms of this section assuming minimization of the objectives. The red squared results are the Pareto-optimal solutions, they form the Pareto front. The blue diamond-shaped solutions are (weakly) dominated by the optimal solutions.

The multi-objective optimization problem can thus be defined as follows. Let $\overset{\prec}{\min}$ denote the optimization with respect to Pareto-dominance, i.e. the best elements are the Pareto-optimal solutions. Then, the optimization problem is

$$\overset{\prec}{\min_{x \in \mathcal{O}}} f(x) \ \text{ subject to } \forall P \in \mathit{constraints} : P(x)$$

3.3. Classical Methods

In this section we provide a some classical methods to solve multi-objective optimization problems. Several methods are based on scalarizing the objective function, of which we present the two most common ones (Ehrgott, 2005, p.98) in the following.

In the weighted sum method (cf. (Deb, 2001, Sec.3.1)), the objective function components are combined by a weighted sum. Then, the weights are systematically varied: For each assignment of the weight, the resulting single-objective problems. Graphically, this can be pictured as sampling the Pareto front with tangents (cf. Figure 3.1). The disadvantage of this method is that the tangents skip non-convex parts of the Pareto front, i.e. dents towards in the case of minimization problems. For example, the Pareto-optimal solution at (59, 1.6) could not be detected.

The ε-constraint method mitigates this problem. Here, all but one objective function components are transformed into constraints of the optimization problem. Then, a single-objective technique can be used to determine the best solution with respect to this objective while fulfilling the constraints in the other objectives. The front can be sampled by varying the constraint values. For our example in Figure 3.1, one could optimize objective 1 subject to objective 2 being smaller than an ε_2 value, and successively vary ε_2 from 120 down to 0. Afterwards, the same can be repeated for optimizing objective 2 with constraints on objective 1.

For optimization problems where these sub-problems can be efficiently solved, e.g. using linear programming, these scalarizing methods can quickly produce results. However, if the sub-problems themselves have to be solved by metaheuristics as well (e.g. single-objective evolutionary optimization), a multi-objective metaheuristic is expected to be more efficient as it can make use of all information found during the search, while a sub-problem optimization is reset for each sub-problem.

Other classical optimization techniques such as lexicographic optimization (Ehrgott, 2005, p.128) or different varieties of goal programming (weighted, min-max, cf. (Deb, 2001, Sec.36)) require additional preference information (priorities of objectives and reference point, respectively), and thus are not further discussed here.

For quality prediction of software architecture, however, the quality analysis which is used as objective function can be arbitrarily complex. For example, for performance, only models with strong assumptions can be expressed as closed formulas. For others, approximate numerical or even simulative solutions are required (Jain, 1991).

3.4. Multi-objective Metaheuristics

Metaheuristics are approximate high-level search-based optimization strategies that are independent of the optimization problem, i.e. they make no assumptions on the objective function properties but treat the objective function as a black box (Blum and Roli, 2003). Often, metaheuristics are non-deterministic.

Two main types of metaheuristic have been suggested (Blum and Roli, 2003):

Trajectory methods (or local describe a trajectory in the search space: They start at one (possibly random) solution in the search space. A successor solution is found based on the current solution and the metaheuristic's method. For example, steepest ascent hill climbing explore the neighbourhood of the current solution and pick the best solution from the neighbourhood. The neighbourhood of a solution can be differently defined: For example a neighbour solution could be to vary a single decision, i.e. one component of the decision vector x, by one step. This process is repeated until no better solution is found in the neighbourhood, which means that a local optimum has been reached. More sophisticated trajectory methods are simulated annealing (which also allows downward moves to escape local optima), tabu search, and variable neighbourhood search (Blum and Roli, 2003). Because trajectory methods always handle one current solution, they tend to be better suited for single-objective optimization and less for multi-objective optimization where the goal is to find a set of solutions.

Population-based methods, however, operate on a set of current solutions, manipulate this set in each iteration of the search, and generate multiple result solutions in one run (Deb, 2001, p.7). Thus, most population-based methods are suited to handle multi-objective optimization problems. Furthermore, candidate evaluation within one population can be parallelized. Most classical methods, only update a single solution at a time (are not population-based) and thus cannot take advantage of parallel candidate evaluation (Deb, 2001, p.83).

The most popular method are evolutionary algorithms, which are detailed in the next Section 3.5. Other population-based methods are ant colony optimization and particle swarm optimization (Blum and Roli, 2003). All three have multi-objective versions.

Successful metaheuristics balance two goals during the search, *intensification* and *diversification*. Yagiura and Ibaraki (2001) provide a concise definition: "Intensification is to search carefully and intensively around

85

good solutions found in the past search [...]. Diversification, on the contrary, is to guide the search to unvisited regions" (Yagiura and Ibaraki, 2001, p.24).

3.5. Evolutionary Algorithms

Evolutionary algorithms are a class of population-based metaheuristics inspired by the biological process of evolution and have been initially proposed by Holland (1975). The guiding principle is to create new offspring based on a current population of candidates, and then select the fittest to survive and mate. Evolutionary algorithms have been particularly successful for hard multi-objective optimization problems (Deb, 2001). Due to their suitability for the optimization problem tackled in this work (discussed in more detail after the problem is defined, in Section 8.1.3), we present them here in more detail.

Section 3.5.1 describes the basic algorithm, which is described specifically for our problem in more detail later in Section 8.2. Section 3.5.2 then gives an overview on the standard reproduction operators, followed by an overview on selection strategies described in Section 3.5.3. To ensure that the search does not loose already found good solutions, the concept of elitism has been suggested and is discussed in Section 3.5.4. Finally, Section 3.5.5 describes how the performance of different evolutionary optimization techniques can be compared to assess the utility of new algorithms or extensions.

3.5.1. Basic Algorithm

Figure 3.2 shows the basic evolutionary algorithm. The three parameters are the population size n, the number of parents per iteration μ, and the number of offspring per iteration λ. The input to the process are n usually randomly generated solutions.

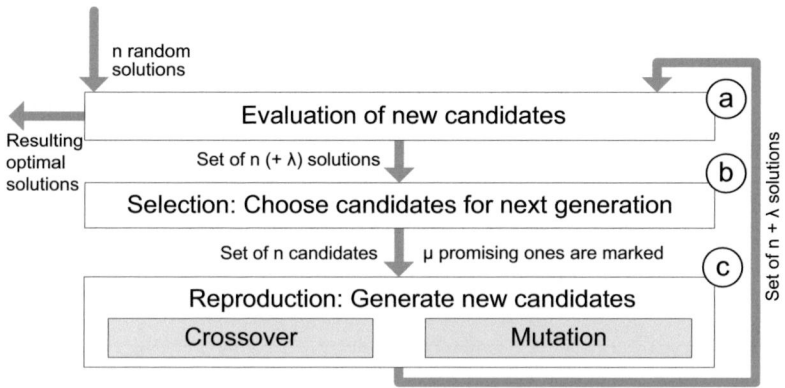

Figure 3.2.: Basic Evolutionary Algorithm

In the first step (a), each yet unevaluated solution is *evaluated*, i.e. the objective function components are calculated. The evaluated solutions (n in the first iteration $n + \lambda$ in the subsequent iterations) are fed into the next step.

In the *selection* step (b), two inner selection steps take place. First, the population is again reduced to n solutions by removing the worst ones (not in the first iteration). Second, μ solutions are selected to be the "parents" of the this iteration.

In the *reproduction* step (c), λ new solutions are generated based on the selected parents. The resulting set of $n + \lambda$ solutions are input to the evaluation step.

The process is repeated until a stop condition is fulfilled after evaluation. The Pareto-optimal solutions found so far are determined and form the result set.

The next two sections provide more detail on the reproduction (Section 3.5.2) and selection step (Section 3.5.3).

3.5.2. Reproduction

The two goals of the candidate reproduction step are to move the search to new, yet unevaluated, and preferably better candidate vectors (Blum and Roli, 2003). Reproduction operators take one or several candidates as an input (*input candidates*) to generate *new candidates* based on them.

The two standard operators for evolutionary algorithm are crossover and mutation. Usually, for each pair of candidates to generate new candidates from, the operators to apply are chosen randomly. A common configuration is that the probability of a crossover is determined by a configuration parameter called *crossover rate*. Additionally, the candidate (resulting from the crossover or unchanged) is mutated. The operator selection can be become more complex if additional operators are applied.

The number of candidates to generate with these operators, also called number of offspring, is configurable parameter λ.

3.5.2.1. Mutation

The driving idea of mutation operators is that more good candidates (and potentially superior ones) can be found in the neighbourhood of a given input candidate. Thus, a mutation operator creates a candidate that is similar to the input candidate. Usually, mutation operators take a single input candidate.

There are different options to implement mutation operators. They vary in the ways single genes are changed, and how the genes to change are selected.

Regarding the mutation of a single gene, some mutation operators make use of an order on the value range of a dimension, and only apply a small change to each gene. This method is useful for degrees of freedom with a notion of similar values for a single dimension (e.g. for real-values dimension, such as a continuous processing rate degree, the distance can be used). Then, the similarity of the resulting genome to the input candidate's genome is achieved by the small distances between an input gene and a resulting gene. Not all dimensions have a useful distance measure, either because they have no order at all, or also because single elements in the order differ too much from each other. Here, mutation operators randomly choose a different value from the value domain of a dimension.

Regarding the mutation of the complete genome, the mutation operator selects a number of genes to mutate. One option is to statically decide how many genes are mutated as described above per application of the mutation step (e.g only one gene is mutated, or all genes are mutated). Alternatively, the number of genes to mutate can be determined probabilistically. Here, often a mutation rate is specified that defines the probability to mutate each gene. An often chosen value for the mutation rate is the inverse of the genome length (Aguirre and Tanaka, 2005), so that the expected number of mutated genes is 1 per mutation, but also more or fewer genes can be varied. The benefit of probabilistic mutation is that more candidates are possible as the outcome of a mutation. Local optima can be overcome if two genes are varied at once. At the same time, little mutation is also possible so that the good candidates are not disrupted.

3.5.2.2. Crossover

Crossover operators (also called recombination operators) combine two or more input candidate (the parents) to form new candidates (the offspring). The driving idea is that the advantageous properties of promising parents may lead to even better offspring when combined. The new candidates are likely to be superior than a random candidate (Deb, 2001, p.93).

Again, there are different options for crossover operators. The simplest case is the one-point crossover. Here, the genome of two parents is cut at a random point, and new candidates are created by recombining the resulting pieces (the front part from one parent, and the back part from the other parent, cf. Fig.3.3(a)). For genomes with a fixed length, the random point needs to be the same in both parents in order to achieve offspring genomes with the same length. An extension of the one-point crossover is the use of several cut points. Fig. 3.3(b) shows a two-point crossover, for example. The number of cut points can also be randomly varied during the optimization run.

The cutting of the genomes at several, but few point results in a higher probability for genes that are close to each other on the genome to stay together in the offspring (also called *linkage* (Luke, 2009, p.36)). For example, in a one-point crossover, the start gene and end gene in an array genome are always separated, whereas two neighbouring genes are only separated if the cut point is placed between them. If the genome can be structured into blocks of genes in a meaningful way to better reflect the properties of the search space, few-point crossover operators can make use of this structural knowledge.

If no relation between neighbouring genes is given in the search space, using such a crossover operator might introduce unnecessary bias that impedes the search. The uniform crossover operator (Sywerda, 1989) (cf. Fig 3.3(c)) randomly chooses which parent's gene to copy for each gene of the offspring. Thus, in this work the uniform crossover has been used. Spears and DeJong (1991) provide a more detailed discussion of the advantages and disadvantages of this operator.

As an extension to the process, a hybrid method could be devised that uses different crossover strategies for several parts of the genome, e.g. for several degree of freedom types. Additionally, similarly to the mutation operators, the crossover strategy could also be varied over time, focussing more on diversification or intensification, depending on the state of the search. A more detailed overview on additional crossover operators is provided by Deb (2001, p.111 et seqq.), including crossover operators that can be used for genomes with varying length, and crossover operators that do not just choose one of the parents' value for the offspring, but combine

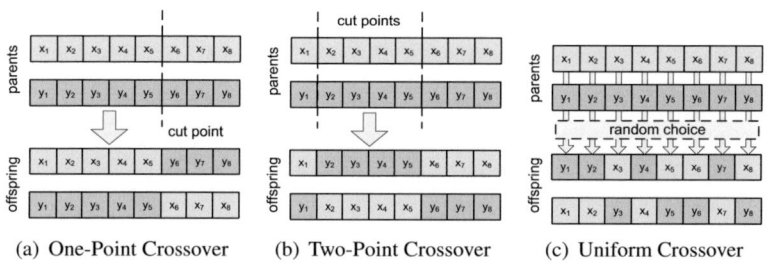

Figure 3.3.: Different Crossover Operators (adapted from (Luke, 2009))

the values themselves (e.g. by taking the mean of both parents' values) (Deb and Goyal, 1996).

3.5.3. Selection

The goal of candidate selection is to select promising solutions for reproduction and to remove the worst solutions from the current population, so that the search can focus on promising candidates.

As we are considering a multi-objective problem, it is not straightforward what the most promising and the worst candidates are. On the one hand, promising candidates have good quality properties, but in the face of conflicting objectives, the measure of good quality properties is not obvious. On the other hand, promising candidates should be the basis for a successful continuation of the search. Here, a diversity of candidates is advantageous to achieve a good approximation of the true Pareto-front.

Selection strategies are concerned with measuring usefulness of candidates for the search so that promising candidates can be used for reproduction and the worst candidates can be discarded.

Different selection strategies have been suggested in the literature. Initial approaches to multi-objective evolutionary optimization use weighting of the objectives (possibly varying weights in the course of the optimization) to assign the candidates a usefulness measure and select the most useful one. However, such approaches do not reflect the goal of multi-objective optimization to find a Pareto-front well (Deb, 2001, p.173). Thus, newer approaches assess the usefulness of a candidate based on Pareto-domination (suggested by Goldberg (1989)). While the earliest of such approaches (e.g. (Fonseca and Fleming, 1993; Srinivas and Deb, 1994)) still considered both the objective values and the Pareto-domination and thus, their performance depend on the shape of the Pareto front (Deb, 2001, p.206,222). Recent approaches only consider Pareto-domination and are discussed in the following.

Pareto-dominance does not impose a total order on candidates in a population. Only if a candidate A is better in one and at least equal in all other quality properties than another candidate B, A dominates B and is objectively superior. To compare candidates that do not dominate one another, additional measures that are independent of the absolute objective values are introduced.

Two popular measures for how well a candidate performs with respect to Pareto-dominance are the Pareto rank (suggested in the Non-Sorting Genetic Algorithm NSGA (Srinivas and Deb, 1994)) and Pareto strength (suggested in the Strength Pareto Evolutionary Algorithm SPEA (Zitzler and Thiele, 1999)).

The Pareto-rank (Deb, 2001, p.210 et seq.) of a candidate is a measure of how "close" a candidate is to the Pareto-front. The candidates of the current Pareto-front are assigned the lowest and best rank of one. Then, all candidates of the Pareto-front are removed and the Pareto-front of the remaining candidates is calculated. The now non-dominated candidates are assigned a rank of two and then are removed. This approach is continued until all candidates have been assigned a rank.

The Pareto strength measure (in its revised form described in Zitzler et al. (2002a)) is based on the number of dominating candidates. The raw strength of a candidate c is the ratio of candidates in the population that c dominates. Then, the sum of the raw strength values of all candidates dominating c is calculated and determines c's Pareto strength value. The smaller the Pareto strength value, the better the candidate is.

Still, candidates can have the same Pareto rank or Pareto strength, as it is a discrete measure. To discriminate between two candidates with the same Pareto rank or Pareto strength, density measures to favour candidates in objective space areas with low candidate density have been suggested.

The density measure "crowding distance" is used in NSGA-II (Deb, 2001, p.248 et seq.). For a candidate A, the crowding distance is the average distance between the neighbouring candidates of A along the objectives. The higher the crowding distance, the lower is the density of that region and the better is candidate A. In SPEA2, the density of candidates is calculated as the inverse of the distance to the k-th nearest neighbour of a candidate.

Together, the Pareto rank / Pareto strength and the density measure impose a fine-grained order that discriminates most candidates, called *fitness*. The fitness assignment in NSGA-II (using Pareto rank and crowding distance), for example, is the following. Let $\prec$ denote Pareto-dominance (cf. Section 3.2.2) and for a candidate c, let $r(c)$ denote the Pareto rank of c and $d(c)$ denote the crowding distance of c. A candidate c's fitness $f(c)$ is determined so that $f(c) > f(c')$ if

- c' is dominated by c, or

- c' is not dominated by c nor does c' dominate c and c' has a higher Pareto rank than c, or

- c' is not dominated by c nor does c' dominate c and c' has the same Pareto rank, and c''s crowding distance d is smaller.

Formally, this means

$$
\begin{aligned}
f(c) > f(c') \quad &\Leftrightarrow \quad c \prec c'' \\
&\vee \quad c \not\prec c' \wedge c' \not\prec c \wedge r(c') > r(c) \\
&\vee \quad c \not\prec c' \wedge c' \not\prec c \wedge r(c') = r(c) \wedge d(c') < d(c)
\end{aligned}
$$

Based on the fitness, candidates are selected for reproduction. In some approaches, unfit candidates are also selected for deletion, whereas other approaches just delete the complete parent population and only keep the new candidates.

A problem of both fitness measures is that they may lead to circular preference of solutions, which may lead to circular behaviour of the algorithms and hinders convergence (Zitzler et al., 2010, p.62). New approaches for fitness assignment have been suggested that overcome these problems (Zitzler et al., 2010; López-Ibáñez et al., 2011).

A popular selection strategy for selecting a set of solutions from the population based on their fitness is the tournament selection. This strategy has been shown to be superior to other selection strategies (Deb, 2001, p.89). In tournament selection, candidates are pairwise compared and the winner of each pair is selected. The number of rounds that a candidate has to win in order to be selected can be configured and steers how selective the tournament is. Other selection methods degenerate when one candidate in the population is much better than others, leading to a reduced diversity in the population (scaling problem (Deb, 2001, p.92)).

There are more differences in detail in different selection here, the reader is referred to Deb (2001) and the experiments comparing the effects of different aspects by Laumanns et al. (2001). The parameters of the search need to be carefully set, because they steer how well the algorithm can converge to the front by determining the relation of exploration of new candidates and preservation of current good solutions.

3.5.4. Elitism

Elitism is an extension to multi-objective evolutionary algorithm which has been introduced by Rudolph (2001).

Elite solutions are optimal with respect to all previously evaluated solutions. Elitist evolutionary algorithms preserve elite solutions, i.e. they ensure that elite solutions are always carried over into the next generation in the selection phase (Deb, 2001).

Elitist evolutionary algorithms supposedly converge faster than the basic algorithm (Deb, 2001, p.235), which has been demonstrated in experiments by Zitzler and Thiele (1999); Zitzler et al. (2000), van Veldhuizen (1999) and Knowles and Corne (2000), which are summarized by Deb (2001, p.375). For example, Zitzler et al. (2000) have compared basic versions of existing algorithms with elitist versions and found that the elitist version was almost always superior to the basic version (with respect to their coverage indicator, which is briefly described in Section 3.5.5). Furthermore, Rudolph and Agapie (2000) have proven that their formulations of a elite-preserving multi-objective evolutionary algorithms converge towards the globally Pareto-optimal solutions (other algorithm versions are covered in an earlier and later publication).

Often, however, a bounded archive for elite solutions is used, where some elite solutions are deleted if the archive is full to ensure a maximum memory consumption. More recent convergence proofs are also available for elitist evolutionary algorithms with bounded archives (López-Ibáñez et al., 2011) if their strategy to delete solutions from the archive fulfils some properties. However, these proofs do not hold for the two famous elitist evolutionary algorithms NSGA-II (Deb et al., 2000) and SPEA2 (Zitzler et al., 2002a), both using bounded archives, too.

3.5.5. Comparing Multi-objective Evolutionary Optimization Techniques

The performance of an optimization approach is typically measured by assessing the quality of the solutions and the time needed to generate the solutions (Zitzler et al., 2008). Compared to the straightforward assessment of single-criteria optimization approaches and exact methods, performance assessment of multi-criteria evolutionary optimization faces two main challenges (Zitzler et al., 2008): First, the evolutionary optimization is a stochastic process. Each run can create a different result. Thus, for each optimization approach and example problem, the outcome is random variable, and each concrete run is a sample from that distribution. As a result, the performance of an algorithm cannot be assessed based on a single run for a given problem. Second, the result is a Pareto-front where each candidate has multiple values, one for each objective, so we cannot directly use the objectives as a metric for quality. Thus, we require additional quality metrics based on the objective values to assess the quality of the Pareto front.

To address the first problem, when comparing multi-objective optimization techniques, all experiments should be replicated several times so that we obtain a set of resulting Pareto-fronts and can estimate the underlying random variable.

To address the second problem, several quality metrics and indicators have been suggested. We present the which quality metrics and indicators used in this work in the following.

First, the Pareto dominance relation can be used as a quality metric to test whether the result sets produced by one optimization approach A dominates the results from another approach B. For a number of runs created by each approach, we can compare each pair of runs from A and B and rank the runs according to how many other fronts they dominate. If the Pareto fronts created by A have statistically significant better ranks than the results created by B, we can objectively say that one algorithm is better (Zitzler et al., 2008, p.389). Section 3.5.5.1 below presents more detail on this method.

However, we do not always obtain such a clear result. Two Pareto fronts are incomparable if one front is better in one region of the objective space and another one in another region. To assess such cases, several quality indicators have been proposed (Zitzler et al., 2002b, 2008) that use additional preference information to calculate a quality indicator for a Pareto front (unary quality indicator) or for a pair or Pareto fronts to compare (binary quality indicator), and thus can be used for comparison and statistical tests. Sections 3.5.5.2 and 3.5.5.3 thus present two quality indicators, the coverage indicator and the hyper-volume measure. Finally, Section 3.5.5.4 briefly describes other indicators not used in this work.

3.5.5.1. Pareto Dominance Ranking

Pareto dominance ranking (Zitzler et al., 2008) is a method to compare the outcome of a set of runs for two optimization approaches (or settings) S and T. Recall that for two Pareto fronts P_1 and P_2, $P_1 \preceq P_2$ denotes that all candidates in P_2 are weakly dominated by at least one candidate in P_1 and that P_1 and P_2 are not equal (cf. Section 3).

Then, for each optimization approach S and T, we perform a set of runs $\{S_r \,|\, r = 0, \ldots, n\}$ and $\{T_r \,|\, r = 0, \ldots, n\}$. We select a certain iteration i to compare the results at. Then, each run has produced a Pareto front $P(S_r^i)$ or $P(T_r^i)$. We can now compare all $P(S_r^i)$ with all $P(T_r^i)$ and assign a rank to each front similar to the Pareto rank used in NSGA-II as follows (adapted from Knowles et al. (2006)):

$$rank(P(S_r^i)) = \left| \left\{ P \,\middle|\, P \in \{P(T_r^i) \,|\, r = 0, \ldots, n\} \wedge P(S_r^i) \preceq P \wedge P \npreceq P(S_r^i) \right\} \right|$$

and vice versa for T. The lower the rank, the better $P(S_r^i)$ is with respect to the runs created by T. The result of the ranking is a rank value for each run of each setting. We can then compare whether the ranks of the runs one of the optimization approaches S or T is statistically significantly smaller (thus better) than the ranks of the runs of the other one.

If a significant difference is detected, the optimization approach with the better ranks can be deemed the better one for the given problem. However, the dominance ranking method does not provide information of how much better the approach is. To quantitatively assess the difference, we additionally use the quality indicators presented below. Additionally, if fronts of the runs are often incomparable, the no significant result can be determined and we can only resort to the quality indicators for comparison.

We use the Performance Assessment Tools (Knowles et al., 2006) provided with the PISA optimization framework (Bleuler et al., 2003) to calculate the Pareto Dominance Ranks and perform the statistical tests.

3.5.5.2. Coverage Indicator

The original coverage indicator $\mathscr{C}(P_1, P_2)$ has been proposed by Zitzler and Thiele (1999) and is a useful measure to compare two optimization runs' resulting Pareto fronts P_1 and P_2 independent of the scaling of the objectives. The coverage indicator compares how many candidates in A are non-dominated by candidates in B and vice versa. The additional preference information here is that the number of non-dominated candidates is relevant.

3.5.5.3. Hyper-volume Indicator

The hyper-volume, also called size of the dominated space (Zitzler and Thiele, 1999), measures the volume (in the three dimensional case) of the objective space weakly dominated by a Pareto front. For minimization problems, this measure requires a reference point to define the upper bounds of this volume. Figure 3.4(a) visualizes the hyper-volume of a Pareto front "front 1" and a reference point z as a grey area. The reference

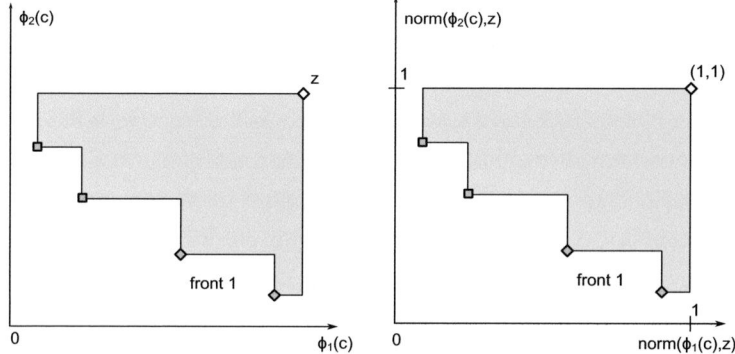

(a) Example of the Hyper-volume of a Pareto Front

(b) Example of the Hyper-volume of a Normalized Pareto Front

Figure 3.4.: Hyper-volume Examples

point is usually set to the maximum values encountered in all compared optimization runs.

Because the scale of the objectives can be very different (e.g. POFOD ranges from 0, ..., 1, while costs is orders of magnitude larger), the objective values are normalized using the reference point before determining the hyper-volume. The values of each objective are normalized so that the reference point has the value 1 for each objective[3]. The normalization uses the metric d_q defined for each quality criterion.

Figure 3.4(b), for example, shows a normalized front. The theoretically maximally achievable hyper-volume is 1; however, this value is only reached if one candidate has the value 0 in all objectives and thus is the only single candidate in the Pareto front. For a point o in the objective space, let $norm(o,z)$ denote the normalized objectives values with respect to a reference point z. As a result of the normalization, we cannot compare the absolute volumes across different settings.

---

[3]We assume here that all objective values are positive, so that the point of origin is unchanged. However, one could as well add a second minimal reference point z' and normalize the front so that z' lies at point $(0, \ldots, 0)$

Let the function $hvolume(P,z)$ denote the normalized hyper-volume enclosed by the front P and the reference point z in the objective space $\Pi_{q \in Q} V_q$ as shown in grey in Figure 3.4(b). Mathematically, a hyper-rectangle is constructed for each candidate c in the front with the opposite corners $norm(\Phi(c),z)$ and $(1, \ldots, 1)$. Then, the union of these hyper-rectangles is determined and its hyper-volume is measured. For example, the volume for a Pareto front with a single candidate having the normalized objective values $(0.5, 0.3, 0.6)$ and the reference point $(1,1,1)$ is $(1 - 0.5)(1 - 0.3)(1 - 0.6) = 0.14$. In other words, $hvolume(P,z)$ measures the size of the dominated objective space with respect to the metrics $d_q, q \in Q$. Then, we can compare two Pareto fronts by comparing their hyper-volumes.

3.5.5.4. Other Methods

Another proposed method how to assess and compare optimization approaches is to calculate the so-called empirical attainment function for each optimization approach. However, while this method looses less information and keeps the multi-dimensionality of the results (Zitzler et al., 2008), it is only practically applicable to two objectives and does not provide a single measure how to compare two optimization approaches. Thus, we do not consider empirical attainment functions in this work.

Additionally, we decided not to use other quality indicators that require additional utility information like the R indicator (Zitzler et al., 2008), because we want to impose as little preference information as possible (cf. Section 5.1).

4. Related Work

This chapter surveys related work to out method and is divided into two aspects. First, we discuss other methods that share the goal of our method, i.e. that target to support the software architect in improving a component-based software architecture based on model-based quality prediction in Section 4.1. As a focus of this work is performance improvement, we consider methods that improve either performance or performance combined with other quality attributes.

Second, we relate our tactics-based new heuristic operators to existing work in the field of evolutionary algorithms in Section 4.2.

4.1. Supporting Software Architects to Improve CBA

Numerous model-based quality prediction methods allow the software architect to model a software architecture and evaluate a single or several quality attributes. We have presented some of these methods in Section 2.4, and refer to the mentioned surveys for more detail. Most of these methods, however, do not explicitly support the software architect or quality analyst in changing the software model based on the evaluation results. Still, prediction methods that target CBA can be used as quality predictors in the improvement approach presented in this work.

In this section, we present methods that build on or extend model-based quality prediction methods to help the software architect to improve a software architecture at hand, i.e. that explicitly support the task of interpreting model-based prediction results and finding better architectures.

For some methods, we provide several references in the following: Both one of the early works as well as the most recent paper. Thus, we obtain a better understanding of when a method was initially proposed as well as the most recent status.

This section is organized as follows. First, Section 4.1.2 discussed the criteria to compare related methods. Then, Section 4.1.3 described improvement methods that target performance, or performance combined with costs. Section 4.1.4 then discussed methods that, like our method, target several quality attributes including performance. Finally, Section 4.1.5 concludes the findings and highlights gaps in the related works.

4.1.1. Scope of this Survey

We focus on methods that are applicable at the software architecture level, and thus exclude more low-level improvement approaches that for example optimize code (e.g. for parallel execution, or when compiling). Some of the methods presented in the following are more general and do not specifically target component-based systems or do not specifically target software architecture, but are applicable at this level as well.

Because all architecture models have some notion of components, we broaden our survey beyond the requirements of CBS (cf. Section 2.1) to consider methods striving to improve any notion of software architecture. Thus, we use the term "software architecture" instead of CBA in the following.

Additionally, we focus on software performance prediction. Thus, we only consider approaches that improve performance as one of the considered quality attributes, or that can be readily extended to consider performance (such as the ArcheOpteryx method, see below). The main other research area concerned with architecture optimization is reliability optimization, where redundancy of components and component deployment are the main considered degrees of freedom to improve an architecture's reliability. Kuo and Wan (2007) provide a survey on such methods.

Two other prominent domains in which automated improvement and optimization is used are the design of embedded systems and the self-adaptation of systems (often service-oriented ones) at runtime.

For the first area of embedded systems, Gries (2003) and Grunske et al. (2006) provide a survey. Design space exploration frameworks like the ones suggested by Künzli et al. (2005); Künzli (2006) have been developed for this domain. However, the degrees of freedom and quality properties in these domains are more homogeneous and better understood, and the frameworks are tailored to them, so that the frameworks are at the same time not readily applicable to software architecture optimization as considered in this work. On the other hand, completely generic multi-objective optimization frameworks like PISA (Bleuler et al., 2003) and Opt4J (Lukasiewycz et al., 2010) have been developed in this context, and can be used for the problem of software architecture optimization as well (cf. Chapter 8).

In the second area of self-adaptive systems, methods have different goals. A survey of existing approaches and research challenges is given by Cheng et al. (2009). First, it is often more important that the methods deliver quick responses to reconfiguration requests instead of providing optimal ones. After all, the optimization must not consume more resources that the adaptation saves. Second, a self-adaptive system is already in a certain state when considering adaptation. Thus, the goal is not to find an globally optimal state to change to without consideration of the current state, but also to find a near good state. Finally and most importantly, self-adaptive systems have to decide autonomously for a new configuration that satisfies the requirements of the environment, while the goal of this work is to provide interpretation and decision support.

Considering all quality attributes and also other domains such as the design of embedded systems, a large number of optimization approaches have been suggested. We are currently working on a broader review considering more that 200 papers in this broader domain by Aleti et al. (2013). For the broad scope of software engineering task in general, Harman (2007); Harman et al. (2009) has coined the term search-based software engineering.

4.1.2. Criteria for Automated Improvement Support Comparison

In the following sections, we compare the related work with respect on three aspects, namely the targeted improvement problem (Section 4.1.2.1), the applied solution (Section 4.1.2.2), and the flexibility of a method to be extended in the future (Section 4.1.2.3). We first introduce each aspect with a short outline of its criteria, and then describe the criteria in detail, arguing which properties are desirable for each criterion to achieve a useful and expressive architecture improvement support.

4.1.2.1. Addressed Improvement Problem

First, the *improvement problem addressed* by the method is considered. These characteristics determine for which improvement problems an approach can be used. The main properties here are (P.1) the addressed quality attributes and quality criteria, (P.2) which architecture properties are considered to be varied to improve these quality attributes (e.g. component deployment, server configuration), and (P.3) the goal of the improvement (e.g. single improvement step, optimize utility, multi-criteria optimization). Additional properties regarding the problem are (P.4) whether the problem is formulated on the design level (e.g. using an architectural model) or on the quality analysis model level (e.g. queueing networks) and (P.5) whether additional architectural constraints can be considered.

P.1 **Quality Attribute (Criteria):** The addressed quality attribute(s) and the quality criteria considered to assess these attributes (in parenthesis), if applicable. The more quality attributes and criteria can be considered, the better support an approach can give to software architects in general. Still, for special architecture design cases where only few quality properties are of crucial interest and others are known to be of minor interest, methods that target these quality attributes only are just as useful.

P.2 **Changed architecture properties:** The properties of the architecture that are changed by the method to improve the quality attributes. Here, we name those (in case studies or described explicitly). These properties correspond to our concept of change types and degrees of freedom. However, because the architecture properties cannot necessarily independently varied as we define our notion of degrees of freedom, we use this more neutral term here. Here, the more architecture properties can be considered, the better support an approach can give to software architects in general. Again, in scenarios where only few architecture properties are open for change, methods that target a limited set of properties can be just as useful (see also Section 5.4 for a discussion of architecture improvement scenarios).

P.3 **Improvement goal:** The goal of the improvement methods differ: Some target to satisfy given requirements, other target to find optimal solutions with respect to an objective function. The underlying difference are the assumed preferences of the software architect and how much is assumed to be known about them. As described in Section 3.2.1, the three types of preference articulation are a priori, a posteriori, and interactive.

A notable subtypes of a priori preference in the context of architecture improvement are quality requirements. A quality requirement means that software architects and stakeholders agree on a value that has to be achieved for the respective quality property. Thus, quality requirements are a form of preference model, which can be understood as assigning a utility of 1 to each candidate meeting all quality requirements and a utility of 0 to all others.

As we have discussed in Section 3.2.1, a priori preference articulation is difficult. In both cases (utility functions or quality requirements), it is questionable whether stakeholders can reliably agree on such a preference model before knowing the available optimal trade-off candidates (We discuss this aspect in more detail in Section 5.1).

P.4 Design Level? Solutions automatically found for problems on the design level (e.g. based on UML models or other architecture modelling languages) can be more easily understood and realized by software architects than solutions found on lower level of abstraction, e.g. on the queueing network level. In the latter case, solutions need to manually mapped back to the design level. Furthermore, it is not necessarily clear whether a solution found on the lower level is feasible on the design level. Thus, architecture improvement on the design level is more desirable.

P.5 Architectural Constraints: Finally, if the problem is defined on the design level, additional architecture constraints specified by the software architect can be included in the improvement, to ensure that all found solutions are actually feasible. To give some examples, software architects may restrict the number of components to the number of available development teams, they may restrict the number of servers available to deploy the system, or they may exclude certain combination of changes. Here, the most flexibility is achieved by allowing arbitrary constraints formulated by the software architect. However, if methods only address certain changeable architecture properties, sophisticated architecture constraints are not required.

4.1.2.2. Solution Approach

Second, the *solution approach* to the problem is discussed. These characteristics determine how well a method can solve the posed problem, and also show the assumptions and simplifications a method makes in order to efficiently solve the problem. A relevant property is (S.1) the used quality model, which determines the expressiveness and validity of the predictions. The used optimization or improvement technique (S.2) described which actual optimization or improvement algorithms are used to find better solutions. Finally, we check whether and how domain-specific knowledge (S.3) is integrated into the method.

S.1 **Quality model:** We survey what quality prediction model is used. In particular, the composition of quality properties from properties of single architecture elements is of interest. Here, simplified models assume aggregation functions, e.g. that a quality property of the system is the sum of quality properties of architecture elements, such as components. While such a simplified models can be useful for some quality attributes (such as costs), other quality attributes are emerging properties of the system (e.g. performance or reliability) and their simplified handling requires strong assumptions. Thus, more expressive quality models are desirable in general. However, in particular domains such as service-oriented systems where the performance of one service is independent of the performance of another, such assumptions are more realistic. Thus, depending on the domain of software architectures considered, less expressive quality can enable more efficient optimization approaches at the cost of being limited to that domain. In the table, we name the concrete quality models used in presented case studies in parenthesis.

S.2 **Optimization / Improvement technique:** Here, we name the optimization or improvement algorithm used to solve the improvement problem of each method. Based on the formulated problem and the chosen quality model, different optimization techniques are feasible (cf. Section 3.5). The choice influences the performance of the method, i.e. how good found solutions are and how computationally expensive a method is. All methods described in this work do not guarantee to deliver the globally optimal solution due to the complexity of the problem. The more restricted the problem is (limited choice of quality attributes, limited changed architecture properties), the more efficient optimization approaches are used.

S.3 **Domain-specific Rules / Tactics:** Because one contribution of this work is the integration of domain-specific knowledge as tactics operators into the improvement process, we survey the use of domain-specific knowledge in other methods. In this property, we do not consider the domain-specific problem formulation in all optimization problems, such as the encoding of the genome in evolutionary algorithms. We only consider domain-specific rule that integrate knowledge in addition to the objective function. Regarding the integration of domain-specific knowledge in optimization techniques in general, Section4.2 surveys related work.

4.1.2.3. Flexibility

Third, we survey the *flexibility and extensibility* of each method. If a method is strictly limited to the current quality attributes, it can only be used to support the software architect for these and cannot be extended to consider additional quality attributes and concerns, potentially particular for the developing organization. The most flexibility is provided by a framework approach that (F.1) allows to plug-in arbitrary quantitative quality prediction techniques, that (F.2) explores to change the architecture in any way desired by the software architect, and that (F.3) allows to study architectures described in different modelling languages.

However, flexibility comes at the price of efficiency, because methods that are limited to certain quality attributes can make simplifications and thus achieve more efficient optimization techniques. Still, we believe that for an automated method that should support a software architect in the improvement task, flexibility is more important, because (a) the methods are automated and thus the additional effort is machine effort and cheap and (b) each particular architecture design problem may be faced with special constraints and requirements, so that the assumptions of limited methods may not hold in many cases.

F.1 **QA extendable?:** Here, we check whether additional quality attributes (QA) can be integrated into the method if quantitative model-based prediction approaches are available. Different levels achievable here are that (1) the method is restricted to the considered quality attributes, (2) the method can be extended to quality attributes with the same assumptions on quality composition (see S.1 above), or (3) the method can be extended for any new quantitative model-based quality prediction technique, thus enabling trade-off between any relevant quantitatively-analysable quality attributes.

F.2 **Changed architecture properties extendable?:** Here, we survey whether a method can be extended to cover more additional change-able architecture properties. The most flexibility is provided by an approach that additionally lets software architects model the possible changes for their specific architecture improvement problem. In the table, we only provide a simplified classification, more details on the requirements for such flexibility in an automated approach are described in Section 6.1.

F.3 **Metamodel / Quality model independent?:** First, in different organizations, different architecture modelling languages might be used. Training of developers and possibly used other available analysis techniques or code generation prevent the software architect to freely choose the architecture modelling language as needed by the improvement method. While model transformations can be used to translate from one to the other, information may get lost if the two models do not have the same level of detail. Thus, it is desirable for a method to be applicable to any architecture modelling language. On the other hand, the available changeable architecture properties depend on the architecture modelling language, thus, certain assumptions about the architecture modelling language have to be made.

Second, different quality models may be appropriate for different types of systems. Additionally, depending on the available input data and training of the developers, using a certain quality model may be beneficial. Thus, it is desirable if different quality models can be used by an improvement method.

Both aspects are related because a model transformation from the architecture modelling language to the quality modelling language needs to be available in order to analyse an architecture.

4.1.3. Performance Improvement Methods

In this section, we discuss related approaches that improve or optimize performance, possibly combined with costs optimization or costs constraints. We do not consider methods to improve only costs of a software architecture without considering other quality attributes, because such methods focus more on the economic and organizational context of a project than on the software architecture.

Tables 4.2 to 4.3 show an overview of all surveyed method improving performance only or performance and costs as quality attributes. In the tables, we refer to the methods by their name, the last name of first author of the first paper describing the method, the year of the first publication and the year of the most recent publication. The entries of the table, however, are based on the most recent status of the method. Refer to the detailed description of each method in this section for the references.

As described above, we focus here on methods that improve a software architecture (or, more generally, high-level software design) based on performance models and performance predictions. The methods considered provide interpretation support and automatically suggest new architecture candidates. Thus, we exclude monitoring-based approaches like (Parsons and Murphy, 2008) that only provide feedback on potential problems without suggesting solutions, manual approaches such as Cortellessa and Frittella (2007), or approaches that only target to present the available information to the software architect for an easier result interpretation and decision making, such as (Bondarev et al., 2007) or (Krogmann et al., 2009).

Planner2 The Planner2 (Zheng and Woodside, 2003) methods improves the deployment of a software architecture in order to meet soft deadlines, i.e. requirements that a certain percentage of requests must fulfil the defined response time deadline.

The considered quality attribute is performance, in particular percentiles of response time (e.g. the response time that 90% of requests achieve). Two properties of the architecture are changed: The deployment of tasks to servers (where the tasks can be interpreted as components in the software architecture) and the change of priorities of tasks. The goal of the optimization is the satisfaction of the above-mentioned soft deadlines. The method operates on the performance model level, not on the design level. No architectural constraints are discussed.

The used performance model are Layered Queueing Networks (LQNs), which are expressive. To optimize deployment and priorities, a problem-specific, approximative algorithm is used which makes use of the detailed performance results of the LQN evaluation, such as utilization of servers. Thus, the algorithm is based on domain-specific rules.

Approach	P.1 Quality Attribute (Criteria)	P.2 Changed architecture properties	P.3 Improvement goal	P.4 Design Level?	P.5 Architectural Constraints
Planner2 (Zheng 2003)	Performance (response time percentile)	Deployment, priorities	Satisfy requirements	✗	✗
OPEDo (Buchholz 2006–2009)	Performance (any measure)	Resource demand, number of resources, resource speed, buffer space	Optimize utility function (arithmetic expression of result measures)	✗	✗
PANDA (Cortellessa 2007–2011)	Performance (response time, throughput)	Split components, deployment, scheduling	Satisfy requirements	✓	✗
Performance Booster (Xu 2008–2009)	Performance (mean response time, throughput), costs of changes	Deployment, change resource demands, introduce concurrency, change interaction among processes	Optimize or satisfy requirements	✗	✗
Deploying Components For Performance (Sharma 2008)	Performance (throughput)	Component deployment	Optimize	✗	✗
CERAS Deployment Optimization (Li 2009)	Performance (throughput), costs	Deployment	Optimize one quality subject to requirements of the other	✗	✗
SLA-Driven Planning Framework (Li 2010)	Performance (mean response time), costs (including power costs)	Number of threads, number of cores, resource speed	Multi-criteria optimization	✗	✗

Table 4.1.: Problem Criteria for Performance Improvement Methods

Approach	S.1 Quality model	S.2 Optimization / improvement approach	S.3 Domain-specific rules / tactics
Planner2 (Zheng 2003)	Performance model (LQN)	Problem-specific algorithm	✓
OPEDo (Buchholz 2006–2009)	Discrete-event simulation analysis (JMT, OMNeT++)	Metaheuristics (Evolutionary Algorithm, Kriging-models, Random, Local searches)	✗
PANDA (Cortellessa 2007–2011)	Performance model (LQN or EQN)	one improvement step, or hill climbing	✓
Performance Booster (Xu 2008–2009)	Performance model (LQN), cumulated costs of changes	rule-based; hill climbing or steepest ascent hill climbing	✓
Deploying Components For Performance (Sharma 2008)	Performance model (DTMC)	Problem-specific algorithm (similar to greedy bin packing)	✓
CERAS Deployment Optimization (Li 2009)	Performance model (LQN), costs based on resource usage	Solution of multiple linear programming problems	✗
SLA-Driven Planning Framework (Li 2010)	Performance Model (Simple QN), Power model	Multi-objective Evolutionary Algorithm (SMS-EMOA)	✗

Table 4.2.: Solution Criteria for Performance Improvement Methods

Approach	F.1 Quality attributes extendable?	F.2 Changed architecture properties extendable?	F.3 Metamodel / Quality model independent?
Planner2 (Zheng 2003)	✗	✗	✗ / ✗
OPEDo (Buchholz 2006–2009)	✗	Any simulation model parameter	✓ / ✓
PANDA (Cortellessa 2007–2011)	✗	any performance antipattern solution as rules	✓ / ✓
Performance Booster (Xu 2008–2009)	✗	any rule on LQN	✗ / ✗
Deploying Components For Performance (Sharma 2008)	✗	✗	✗ / ✗
CERAS Deployment Optimization (Li 2009)	✗	✗	✗ / ✓
SLA-Driven Planning Framework (Li 2010)	✗	✗	✗ / ✗

Table 4.3.: Flexibility Criteria for Performance Improvement Methods

The method is restricted to LQNs and cannot be extended to other quality attributes, due to the specialized optimization algorithm. For the same reason, the changeable architectural properties are fixed.

The main difference to our method is that Planner2 is a highly specialized method to solve this particular problem, but it is not extendible to help the software architect for other types of decisions.

OPEDo The OPEDo tool (Buchholz and Kemper, 2006; Arns et al., 2009) has been developed to optimize discrete event systems that are analysed with simulation methods. Any performance result measure from the simulation can be optimized.

In the application of OPEDo, changed architecture properties were change of resource demand, change of number of resources, change of resource speed, and change of buffer sizes. In general, the tool can be used to vary any parameter of a simulation model.

The goal of the improvement is to optimize a utility function, which the user defines as an arithmetic combination of result values. The user directly handles the simulation model, thus, the method does not target the design level. No architectural constraints are available, because the model to optimize is a black box, only exposing the parameters to vary.

The tool is configurable and can be used to optimize models for different simulation engines, such as the mean value analysis of the Java Modelling Tools (Bertoli et al., 2009) or OMNeT++ (Varga and Hornig, 2008). Different metaheuristics, such as evolutionary algorithms or local search) are used to solve the optimization problem. No domain-specific rule are available.

While several result values from the simulation can be aggregated to form a utility function, only one evaluation approach seems to be connected to the tool, so that only one simulation for performance can be executed per candidate. Thus, we classified OPEDo to be a performance-only improvement method.

The simulation engines are connected to the OPEDo tool by simulation-engine-specific adaptors, that provide the OPEDo tool with the configurable parameters and result values. Users configure which parameters to vary. However, the tool can only vary a single parameter per optimization variable in the model. Thus, degrees of freedom that require adjustment of several model elements are not supported (e.g. component selection in the PCM, cf. Section 7.2.1).

Additionally, there is not necessarily a mapping of these parameters to design decisions, e.g. whether it is possible to vary the demanded time of a component. Thus, any model parameter can be optimized, and users have to select the right parameters manually for their problem.

The focus of OPEDo is to provide several optimization techniques and a graphical user interface. The question of how a model at hand is connected to the optimization is simplified and solved using parameters. Thus, the method is limited to Here, our notion of degrees of freedom and the automatically derived design space for quality improvement could complement the OPEDo tool and could be integrated as a so-called "black box model".

Thus, the main difference to our method is that OPEDo is limited to simulation approaches and only allows to search design spaces spanned by single parameters in the simulation models. The mapping to design spaces the software architect faces is not necessarily clear.

PANDA The PANDA method (Performance Antipatterns aNd FeeDback in Software Architectures, (Cortellessa and Frittella, 2007; Cortellessa et al., 2009; Trubiani, 2011)) is concerned with detecting software performance antipatterns in design models and suggesting solutions to the software architect. For antipatterns where an automated solution is possible, an automated search can independently search for optimal solutions.

The targeted quality attribute is performance and different criteria such as response time and throughput can be considered. When antipatterns are detected and solution strategies are available, refactoring action change the architecture model. Currently, automated refactoring actions are the splitting of components, the change of component deployment, and the change of scheduling.

The goal of the approach is to remove antipatterns until performance requirements are fulfilled. No architectural constraints are considered.

The used performance model has to be expressive to collect enough information for antipattern detection. Used performance models were LQNs and different variants of EQNs (among them the SimuCom simulator (Becker et al., 2009)). The improvement is done step-wise as feedback to the software architect, or applying several antipattern solutions in a hill climb or exhaustive search. The antipattern rules can be considered domain-specific rules.

The method is inherently limited to performance. It is, however, independent of the used software architecture metamodel. So far, it has been applied to UML (Cortellessa et al., 2010a) and, in joint work, to the PCM (Trubiani and A. Koziolek, 2011). The antipattern rules need to be manually specified again for each target metamodel, based on a metamodel-independent description.

As a stand-alone, automated method, PANDA is limited to those architecture changes for which rules exist and automated solution is possible. The method cannot explore regions of the design space for which no domain-knowledge has been codified. Additionally, it is limited to performance.

PANDA can, however, also be combined with our method, as shown by Trubiani and A. Koziolek, 2011. In this study, the antipattern detection and solution has been implemented for the PCM using our framework. The solution of antipattern for the PCM has been realized as directed changes of degrees of freedom, i.e. as tactics operators. Using this combination, the antipattern detection and solution can thus also be used when improving a software architecture for several quality attributes. Then, the search can both efficiently explore regions of the design space where domain-knowledge in form of antipatterns (and other tactics, cf. Section 8.3) is available, but also use the exploratory power of stochastic search methods like evolutionary algorithms.

Performance Booster Performance Booster (Xu, 2008, 2010) is a method to configuration and design improvements on the performance model level. Based on a LQN model, performance problems (e.g., bottlenecks, long paths) are identified in a first step. Then, mitigation rules are applied. The improved quality attribute is performance (in terms of response time or throughput), while constraints on the number of changes can be defined as maximum cumulated change costs.

To mitigate the detected performance problems, several changes can be applied to the performance model: the deployment of tasks (i.e. components) is changed, resource demands are reduced, concurrency is introduced, or the interaction among processes is changed.

The goal of the improvement is to satisfy given requirements, or to optimize a single performance criterion. As the method operates on the LQN level, found changes need to be manually mapped back to the design model, and may even not be feasible on the design level. No architecture constraints are supported.

Like for PANDA, the used performance model has to be expressive to collect enough information to detect performance problems. The method has been applied to LQNs only, but the rules could be rewritten for other performance models with similar expressiveness. Based on the performance prediction results, Performance Booster tries to apply the performance problem rules.

Two types of rules are distinguished, namely rules for design changes and for configuration changes. Design changes are associated with some cost, because they cannot readily be achieved for the real system. while configuration changes are considered to be free. Thus, the method always applies as many configuration changes as possible before using a design change, to keep the expected costs low. An upper limited for the costs (i.e. the amount of design changes) can be given.

Some of the suggested design changes require changing the implementation of components, which is not desired when dealing with black box components. As the approach suggests changes on the level of LQNs, it might not only be costly, but infeasible to map suggested solutions back to the design. For example, it might be impossible to speed-up a certain component implementation to reach a certain service time because of inherent algorithmic complexity.

As a method, Performance Booster is limited to improving performance criteria. The set of rules can be extended, if performance domain knowledge is available, so that more architectural properties are changed.

Compared to our method, Performance Booster shares the limitations of PANDA. Similarly, its rules can be integrated in our method as tactics, so that the available performance domain knowledge is used.

Deploying Components For Performance   Sharma et al. have presented a method for deploying components for performance (Sharma and Jalote, 2008). The considered performance criterion is throughput, and the only considered change of the architecture is component deployment. The goal of the method is to optimize a system's throughput.

The used performance model are Discrete Time Markov Chains (DTMC). A problem-specific algorithm, similar to a greedy bin packing approach, deploys the components one by one (e.g. based on their resource demand, in descending order) to the available servers. The underlying performance knowledge is that the load should be evenly spread in the system. However, communication overhead is not considered, although it can have a significant impact on the performance of a distributed system.

The method is only applicable to deployment optimization to improve performance, which is the main limitation compared to our method.

CERAS Deployment Optimization The CERAS (Centre for Research in Adaptive Systems) Deployment Optimization (Li et al., 2009; Litoiu et al., 2010) targets to cost-optimally deploy a set of services in a cloud computing environment while fulfilling performance (throughput) requirements. The method works on the LQN level and thus not directly on a design level. Still, the mapping back to the design level is comparably straightforward, because only the deployment is changed. No architectural constraints are considered.

The method requires a performance model that considers resource contention among services, which is important to consider if several services share the same server. Costs are determined based on the predicted server load.

To find the cost-optimal deployment, the method uses an iterative approach: A simplified model is optimized using efficient linear programming. Then, for the found optimal model, the correct queueing delays are determined using an LQN. The queueing delays are integrated in the simplified model, which is solved again. These steps are repeated until the models converge.

We consider the method to be quality model independent, because the queueing delays could be derived by other performance prediction techniques as well. Still, the method is limited to performance and costs, and to changing the deployment, which is the main limitation compared to our method.

SLA-Driven Planning Framework The SLA-driven planning framework (Li et al., 2010a) targets to size and optimize enterprise applications with service-level agreements (SLAs), in particular an SAP ERP system. The target quality attributes are performance (in terms of mean response time) and costs (in terms of procurement costs of the hardware and power costs for operating the system). The considered sizing options are to change the number of cores and the resource speed. Additionally, the optimal number of thread is determined.

The goal of the method is to find Pareto-optimal sizing options of an enterprise application so that a human decision maker can assess the achievable service-level agreements and the associated costs. The method does not work on a design level model and no architectural constraints are considered.

The performance model is a simple queuing model (queueing network with finite capacity regions). A multi-objective evolutionary algorithm (SMS-EMOA (Beume et al., 2007)) is used and no domain-specific rules are considered.

The method is specific to performance and the used three-tiered performance model. Thus, it is tailored towards enterprise applications and not readily transferable to other types of software architectures.

4.1.4. Improvement Methods for Multiple Quality Attributes

In this section, we discuss related approaches that improve or optimize several quality attributes other than only performance and costs. Tables 4.4 to 4.6 give an overview on the surveyed methods improving several quality attributes. In the tables, we refer to the methods by their name, the last name of first author of the first paper describing the method, the year of the first publication and the year of the most recent publication. The entries of the table, however, are based on the most recent status of the method. Refer to the detailed description of each method in this section for the references.

AgFlow AgFlow is a quality-of-service aware middleware for web service composition (Zeng et al., 2003, 2004, 2008) and includes optimization capabilities to select an optimal set of web services to optimize a weighting utility function on different quality properties of the service composition. Currently, performance (response time and response time variance), reliability (POFOD), availability (probability that a service is able to accept a

Approach	P.1 Quality Attribute (Criteria)	P.2 Changed architecture properties	P.3 Improvement goal	P.4 Design Level?	P.5 Architectural Constraints
AgFlow (Zeng 2003–2008)	Performance (mean response time, response time variance), reliability (POFOD), availability (service accessible), costs, reputation	(Web) service selection	Optimize utility function (simple additive weighting of objectives)	✓	✗
QoS-aware Service Composition (Canfora 2005–2008)	Performance (mean response time), costs, availability, reliability	(Web) service selection	Satisfy requirements, or optimize a single criterion subject to requirements	✓	✗
ArchE (Bachmann 2005–2008)	Modifiability (costs), performance (schedulability)	Change of responsibilities	Satisfy requirements	✓	✗
ArcheOpterix (Grunske 2006–2011)	Reliability, performance (communication overhead), energy, costs	Component deployment, redundancy allocation	Multi-criteria optimization	✓	✓
SASSY (Menascé 2008–2010)	Performance (response time, throughput), availability, security	Service selection, architectural patterns	Optimize utility function (any)	✓	✗
PETUT-MOO (Maswar 2007–2010)	Performance (utilization, latency, schedulability), availability, costs	Replicate components, remove idle processors, replace software components, increase or decrease bus capacity	Multi-criteria optimization	✓	✗
Generic Design Space Exploration Framework (Saxena 2010)	Performance (utilization, worst-case execution time), costs	Product line configuration	Optimize a single criterion	✓	✓

Table 4.4.: Problem Criteria for Improvement Methods for Multiple Quality Attributes

121

Approach	S.1 Quality model	S.2 Optimization / improvement approach	S.3 Domain-specific rules / tactics
AgFlow (Zeng 2003–2008)	Linear aggregation function of individual service properties	Linear Integer Programming	✗
QoS-aware Service Composition (Canfora 2005–2008)	Aggregation function of individual services properties	Evolutionary Algorithm	✗
ArchE (Bachmann 2005–2008)	Modifiability analysis (impact analysis), real-time performance model (RMA)	rule-based, focus on one improvement step and interaction	for modifiability
ArcheOpterix (Grunske 2006–2011)	Hardware/software reliability model, DTMC, Markov reward model for energy, communication overhead function	Multi-objective Evolutionary Algorithm (NSGA, MOGA), Multi-objective Ant Colony (P-ACO), own hybrid (hAGO)	✗
SASSY (Menascé 2008–2010)	Aggregation function of individual services properties	Hybrid (heuristic service selection, hill climbing)	heuristic neighbourhood filtering
PETUT-MOO (Maswar 2007–2010)	Performance Model (e.g. LQN, RMA), Sum of costs	Multi-objective Evolutionary Algorithms (e.g. SPEA-2)	✗
Generic Design Space Exploration Framework (Saxena 2010)	Arithmetic function on architecture elements' properties	Constraint satisfaction solver	✗

Table 4.5.: Solution Criteria for Improvement Methods for Multiple Quality Attributes

request), and reputation (based on a user-defined ranking) are considered as quality criteria.

The considered quality properties of the individual web services have to be known, e.g. based on monitoring data. These quality properties are assumed to be fixed and independent from any selection choices. Then, the quality properties of the composed service is derived based on a linear aggregation function for each quality criterion. The used utility function defines weights for each quality criterion. No domain-specific rules are used.

Approach	F.1 Quality attributes extendable?	F.2 Changed architecture properties extendable?	F.3 Metamodel / Quality model independent?
AgFlow (Zeng 2003–2008)	Any linear aggregation function	✗	✗ / (✓)
QoS-aware Service Composition (Canfora 2005–2008)	Any aggregation function	✗	✗ / (✓)
ArchE (Bachmann 2005–2008)	✓	Any modification rule	✗ / ✓
ArcheOpterix (Grunske 2006–2011)	✓	Can be problem-specifically implemented	✓ / ✓
SASSY (Menascé 2008–2010)	Any aggregation function	Any architectural patterns with composition function	✗ / (✓)
PETUT-MOO (Maswar 2007–2010)	✓	Any model refactorings as transformations	(✓) / ✓
Generic Design Space Exploration Framework (Saxena 2010)	Any aggregation function	Configuration options and constraints can be metamodel-specifically defined	✓ / (✓)

Table 4.6.: Flexibility Criteria for Improvement Methods for Multiple Quality Attributes

Based on the linear utility function, the linear quality evaluation functions and binary variables to select services, a linear programming problem is defined and solved using standard techniques.

Additional quality properties could be integrated, if linear composition functions can be specified, or the functions can be linearized. Only service selection is supported. Thus, the approach is dependent on the used metamodel (it is not mentioned how it could be extended to other metamodels describing service-oriented systems, and it cannot be extended to other CBA metamodels). Due to the limitation to linear quality composition functions, it is only partially independent of the used quality model.

Compared to our method, the main limitation of AgFlow is the restriction to service selection and linear quality aggregation functions based in independent and fixed service quality properties.

QoS-aware Service Composition   Canfora et al. have suggested QoS-aware Service Composition (Canfora et al., 2005, 2008) to optimize web service compositions for a quality attribute of interest while satisfying a number of other quality attributes. Currently, performance (mean response time), costs, availability, and reliability (as defined above for Ag-Flow) are supported.

Like AgFlow, the quality properties of the individual services are assumed to be known and fixed. Then, in contrast to AgFlow, any aggregation function can be used to describe the quality properties of the composed service: The assumption for linearity is dropped. The resulting optimization problem becomes more difficult, so that evolutionary algorithms are used to solve it.

Concerning extensibility to additional, possibly application-specific quality attributes, the method allow for users to define their own quality functions. These functions can aggregate quality properties of individual services.

Only service selection is supported. Thus, like AgFlow, the approach is limited to service-oriented metamodels. Due to the assumption of an aggregation function for quality properties, the method is only partially independent of the used quality model.

Compared to our method, the main limitation of Canfora's method is the restriction to service selection and quality aggregation functions based in independent and fixed service quality properties.

More works on service selection   In addition to these two initial methods, more work in this direction has been presented. The additional methods share the limitation that (1) they are limited to service selection as a degree of freedom and that (2) they use simple quality composition formulas for calculating the quality properties of a composed service based on the known quality properties of individual services.

Instead of using expressive quality models, these approaches rather focus on quickly finding approximate solutions so that they can be used to adapt service-oriented systems at runtime.

ArchE The ArchE framework (Bachmann et al., 2005; McGregor et al., 2007; Díaz Pace et al., 2008) assists the software architect during the design to create architectures that meet quality requirements. It helps to create architectural models, collects requirements (in form of scenarios), collects the information needed to analyse the quality attributes for the requirements, provides the evaluation tools for modifiability or performance analysis, and suggests modifiability improvements based on rules. Currently, modifiability and performance are supported quality attributes.

The used model is a preliminary architecture which assigns functionality to building blocks in the architecture. Such a mapping is called responsibility. The changeable architecture properties are the change of responsibilities (e.g. adding or splitting responsibilities). The goal of the improvement is to satisfy given requirements. No architectural constraints are considered.

The quality model for modifiability is impact analysis (Bohner and Arnold, 1996) based on the responsibility model. For performance analysis, rate monotonic analysis (RMA) (Klein et al., 1993) is used.

The current architecture is changed by applying rules that codify architectural tactics (Bass et al., 2003). Currently, only rules for improving modifiability have been realized. It is also planned to add rules that modify parameters of the performance model (Díaz Pace et al., 2008).

However, ArchE focusses on interaction with the user when improving the architecture. Although ArchE also provides a multi-step mode where a number of tactics is applied in a hill-climbing or exhaustive search fashion, the focus is on suggesting a single improvement to the user and have the user review this suggestion before continuing. The intent of ArchE is not to automatically provide an optimal solution (Díaz Pace et al., 2008, p.187). Consequently, the method does not focus on the feasibility of suggestions.

For example, the moving of functionality to improve modifiability is suggested, but whether such moves are possible cannot be checked due to the limited expressiveness of the models. Additionally, the performance effects of such changes must be manually estimated.

ArchE allows to plug-in in any quality prediction technique (Díaz Pace et al., 2008) as quality reasoning frameworks. These reasoning frameworks are additionally supposed to apply domain-specific knowledge and propose changed architectures. Thus, both the considered quality attributes and the used quality models can be changed.

The architecture description is fixed to be in the form of so-called quality attribute scenarios. Thus, is is unclear how changes proposed by one quality reasoning framework can be propagated so that the effects on other quality properties are considered.

As a result, compared to our work, ArchE does not search the whole design space, but advances step-wise based on rules with user-interaction. The architecture model is not component-based, consequently, degrees of freedom as presented later in this paper cannot be readily identified and the combination of suggestions by different quality reasoning frameworks can only be partially automated.

ArcheOpterix ArcheOpterix (Grunske, 2006; Aleti et al., 2009a,b; Meedeniya et al., 2010) is a generic framework to optimize software architectures modelled as AADL models (Architecture Analysis and Description Language (Feiler et al., 2006)). Several optimization problems have already been solved with this method. Optimized quality attributes include reliability (Meedeniya et al., 2010; Meedeniya et al., 2011a), performance (Aleti et al., 2009a,b), and energy (Meedeniya et al., 2010).

Currently, the addresses changeable architecture properties are component deployment (Aleti et al., 2009a,b) and redundancy allocation (Grunske, 2006; Meedeniya et al., 2010), which is the combination of changing the number of used servers and replicating the components onto the additional ones to improve reliability. The goal of the improvement is to find the Pareto-optimal architecture candidates, i.e. multi-criteria optimization.

Architectural constraints can be defined in ArcheOpterix, examples are memory constraints, localization constraints, and co-localization constraints (Aleti et al., 2009b).

Different quality models have been used in different ArcheOpterix applications. For energy prediction, a Markov reward model has been created (Meedeniya et al., 2010). Reliability is modelled with their own hardware/software reliability model (Meedeniya et al., 2011a), using a Discrete Time Markov Chain (DTMC) (Meedeniya et al., 2010), or with a formula for data transmission reliability (Aleti et al., 2009a). The performance model is simpler and considers only communication overhead (Aleti et al., 2009a).

As optimization techniques, several metaheuristics have been used. A new hybrid optimization algorithm combining a first phase of ant colony optimization and a second phase of evolutionary algorithms (hAGO) is suggested by Aleti et al. (2009b) and compared empirically to an ant-colony algorithm (P-ACO (Doerner et al., 2004)) and an evolutionary algorithm (MOGA (Fonseca and Fleming, 1993)). NSGA is used by Meedeniya et al. (2010). These optimization techniques are generic and do not use further domain-specific knowledge.

Due to its framework character, ArcheOpterix is extendible to any other quality attributes for which quantitative prediction for AADL models is available. Quality prediction techniques can be plugged in as "Attribute Evaluators". The attribute evaluators receive information about the architecture candidate to evaluate via a metamodel-independent interface.

The core of the framework is an architecture analysis module in which the optimization problem at hand is defined independent of the metamodel. However, the optimization problem to solve has to be defined by implementing a new architecture analysis module as a set of Java classes. Thus, the changed architecture properties are defined anew for each problem at hand.

Thus, the framework (as of version 2.1 [1]) is currently limited to the studied deployment problems. No support for degrees of freedom that appear in multiple problems is given yet. Thus, the software architect has to be familiar with how to describe optimization problem definition and how to implement these as ArcheOpterix modules.

As such, the ArcheOpterix framework is closest to our method in goal and capabilities. The main difference is that ArcheOpterix does not yet provide a way to model the architecture properties to change (neither conceptually nor in the tool). To use the framework for new architecture improvement problems, the implementation has to be changed.

SASSY Menascé et al. (Menascé et al., 2008, 2010a,b) generate service-oriented architectures that satisfy quality requirements. The considered quality criteria are performance (response time, throughput), availability, and a simple security representation. In addition to service selection, more architecture properties can be changed by introducing architectural patterns such as load balancing or redundancy.

The goal of the method is to optimize a user-defined utility function defined on the quality criteria. No architectural constraints are available. The quality models are similar to the ones used by Canfora et al. (see above): Individual service quality properties can be aggregated to composed quality properties.

To solve the resulting optimization problem, SASSY uses its own hybrid algorithm. The optimization in SASSY is separated into two phases, service selection optimization and pattern application: First, the optimal services are selected for a randomly generated architecture using the algorithms described by Menascé et al. (2010a) which apply branch-and-bound principles. Then, SASSY generates a number of new candidates in

---

[1]available at http://mercury.it.swin.edu.au/g_archeopterix/downloads/ArcheOpterix_2.1.zip

the architectural patterns neighbourhood of the current solution by applying one architectural pattern each. The best resulting candidate is chosen and again fed into the optimal service selection optimization. The current candidate is such changed until no more improvements are possible. Then, the procedure is re-initialized with another random architecture and repeated, until a maximum number of evaluations have been spent or the user stops the search.

During this search, the neighbourhood of the hill-climbing is filtered by a heuristic: Only the k service selections that have been worst so far (contributed least to the overall utility) are improved by architectural patterns that target the problematic quality properties. This heuristic is similar to our tactics

First, the k quality properties with the lowest numeric contribution to the utility are determined. Then, architectural patterns are only applied to components that are involved in exhibiting this quality property. For example, the two services that exchange sensitive data are relevant for a security property, or all services that together provide one service of the composed system are relevant for the execution time of this composed service. This information is directly available from the definition of the relevant quality properties. Only patterns that are known to improve the quality attribute of the problematic quality property are chosen.

Thus, while this heuristic makes use of the domain-specific knowledge about which pattern is expected to improve which quality criterion, Still, for the purpose of (web)service-oriented systems (where services are provided by independent service providers, which excludes the hardware environment with its difficult contention effects), such heuristics capture all relevant domain knowledge. The simple and abstract models of quality criteria used in this service-oriented scenario do not provide more detailed information that could be leveraged by tactics.

SASSY can be extended to consider additional quality properties and additional architectural patterns. However, only quality properties for which the quality of the composed service can be expressed as a function of the individual services and the effect of the considered architectural patterns are supported. For example, performance cannot be considered in a scenario where services are hosted locally and have contention effects. Similarly, only architectural patterns that can be expressed in the service composition workflow and for which the effect on quality composition is known can be used.

Like AgFlow and Canfora's method, the approach is limited to service-oriented metamodels. Due to the assumption of an aggregation function for quality properties, the method is only partially independent of the used quality model.

Compared to our method, the main limitation of SASSY method is the restriction to service-oriented systems and quality aggregation functions based in independent and fixed service quality properties.

PETUT-MOO The PETUT-MOO tool (Performance-Enhancing Tool using UML Transformations and Multi-objective Optimizations, (Maswar et al., 2007; Li et al., 2010b)) is a model-driven framework to improve a software architecture modelled in UML using model refactorings.

The targeted quality attributes are performance (utilization and latency) and costs, but the authors emphasize that any quality prediction technique could be considered. The currently discussed changes of the architecture are to replicate components, to remove idle processors, to replace software components, and to increase or decrease bus capacity. The goal of the improvement is to find the Pareto-optimal architecture candidates, i.e. multi-criteria optimization. Architectural constraints are not discussed.

The quality models used or describes in the publications are different performance models (e.g. LQN, RMA) and a costs model that sums up costs of parts. The predictions are made using the ROBOCOP environment (ROBOCOP consortium, 2003). For optimization, the method uses the PISA framework (Bleuler et al., 2003) and thus can apply a number of optimization techniques such as SPEA2 (Zitzler et al., 2002a). No domain-specific rules are used.

The tool is independent of the considered quality attributes, any quality prediction technique based on UML can be plugged in. Additional architecture refactoring transformations can be integrated in the method, thus, different architecture properties can be studies. However, it is not clear whether the combination of transformations necessarily results in a design space with valid candidates, because transformations might have conflicting effects in general (as discussed by Kapova and Becker (2010) for a similar issue when applying model completions). Furthermore, it is not clear how the architecture transformations are translated into genes in the evolutionary algorithms.

The architecture refactoring transformations are UML-specific at this time, but it seems that they could as well be defined for other metamodels, thus we categorize the method as partially metamodel independent.

The main limitation compared to our method is that the combination of changes to form the design space is not considered, as there is no definition of how the model transformations interact. Additionally, the publications only describe the approach so far. Only a very brief example is described without providing details on the optimization (Li et al., 2010b). The tool is not available online. Thus, it remains unclear whether the method is already realized or rather a proposal for a future method.

Generic Design Space Exploration Framework   The recently suggested Generic Design Space Exploration Framework (GDSE) (Saxena and Karsai, 2010b,a) is motivated from the embedded systems domain, but targets to provide a general, domain-independent framework using model-driven techniques. The framework can be used for any design-level metamodel by extending the metamodel and thus marking the relevant classes and properties for optimization.

Only one example application of the framework has been described so far. The considered quality attributes were performance (utilization and worst-case execution time) as well as costs. The changed architecture properties was the configuration of a product line architecture. The improvement goal was to optimize one of the considered quality criteria.

The quality model, however, is simple: The user can define an arithmetic function over any architecture properties. For example, the utilization of a processor can thus be described as a function on the properties of the tasks deployed to this processor. Then, as the relation between architecture properties and quality properties is a simple function, the resulting optimization problem can be mapped to a constraint satisfaction problem and be solved by standard solvers. Domain-specific tactics are not used.

The considered quality attributes are extendable and can be modelled by the user. However, more complex quality evaluation functions than expressible by an arithmetic function are not supported (Saxena and Karsai, 2010b, p.1947), (e.g. values retrieved by simulation or approximative algorithms).

The set of changed architecture properties can be extended by extending the target design metamodel by using an abstract template language, and thus defining design alternatives and constraints in the target domain. However, the model can only reflect discrete design decisions, such as feature configuration, and does not seem to support more complex changes in the models, e.g. including changes of connectors. The original model is never changed (as it would be required to feed it in prediction approaches), on the contrary, the design space formulation as a constraint satisfaction problem is extracted and fed into standard solvers. Thus, the design alternative model of GDSE would have to be substantially changed to enable prediction of more complex quality attributes.

The main limitations compared to our method are that (1) the modelling language to define design alternatives inherently does not support complex quality prediction techniques and (2) the design alternatives seem to be limited to configuration problems, so that more complex changes of the architecture cannot be considered.

4.1.5. Summary

To summarize, we observe that the surveyed methods vary in scope and focus. In the following, we summarize the main findings and motivate the need for a more comprehensive approach.

The first category of methods improving performance (possibly in combination with costs, described in Section 4.1.3) provide specialized solutions for removing performance problems. However, they lack the combination with other quality attributes. Architecture decisions that improve performance are particularly known to conflict with almost any other quality attribute (Bass et al., 2003, p.74). Thus, a method that also considers other quality attributes and thus highlights trade-off is expected to be more beneficial to the software architect.

The second category of methods that consider performance combined with other quality attributes (in addition to costs, described in Section 4.1.4) has a diverse set of methods.

AgFlow, the QoS-aware Service Composition, and SASSY specifically target web-service-oriented system. They use the assumption that services have independent quality properties to achieve efficient optimization techniques. However, their application is limited to architectures where their assumption holds. Note that this is not the case in any service-oriented architecture, as the CERAS method shows: As soon as two services are deployed together on the same server, their performance properties may be affected by the resource demand of the other server.

The focus of ArchE is more on the interaction with the method user. Although a multi-step mode is available, the method often requires user input to decide how a change will affect other quality attributes. Thus, the method is useful if the architecture models are in an early stage and much estimation of the user is required.

ArcheOpterix, PETUT-MOO, and GDSE are methods that share the goals of this work: They all have framework-character and target a flexible approach to architecture (or design) improvement. However, each of them has limitations. The main ones are:

ArcheOpterix does not provide models to define the changeable architecture properties, but requires the user to write an architecture analysis module in Java for each new combination of changeable architecture properties and quality attributes. The interaction between the different framework parts with respect to architecture changes and their effect on quality properties is not well-defined.

PETUT-MOO is an initial proposal for an optimization approach. It is unclear how the different architecture transformations can be combined to form the design space. Still, the flexibility of model transformations to describe architecture changes is promising and could be integrated into our method in future work.

While GDSE has a sound foundation in model-driven techniques, it is severely limited by the definable quality functions. Because the optimization problem formulation as a constraint satisfaction problem depends on the simplicity, the method cannot easily be extended to more powerful quality prediction techniques.

Interestingly, none of the framework methods integrates domain-specific knowledge, while this is common for methods that only improve performance.

As a result, we observe that none of the surveyed methods fulfils the criteria for automated improvement support discussed in Section 4.1.2. Open issues are the insufficient combination of expressive quality predictions and a simple-to-use but flexible optimization problem definition. Because this combination of properties leads to difficult optimization problems (cf. Chapter 9), even for metaheuristics, the integration of domain-specific knowledge is desirable.

4.2. Problem-specific Knowledge in Metaheuristics

In the field of metaheuristic search techniques (Coello Coello et al., 2010) and evolutionary algorithms in particular, problem-specific knowledge, including domain specific knowledge, can be integrated into a metaheuristic in several ways (Grefenstette, 1987; Cheng et al., 1999). First, the problem representation itself contains knowledge about the domain. For example, genetic encoding can be chosen so that only feasible solutions are constructed.

Second, the initial population may be constructed instead of being randomly generated by considering domain-specific knowledge (Grefenstette, 1987). Third, the performance of the search can be enhanced by problem-specific knowledge, discussed in the following.

For some metaheuristic techniques, neighbourhoods can define how the search can advance. Here, knowledge about the problem can help to design a neighbourhood with a smooth fitness landscape, in which metaheuristics can search efficiently.

Usually, the starting population of an evolutionary algorithm is randomly chosen. Here, start population heuristics can be used to already start with a population that has above-average fitness (Grefenstette, 1987).

In evolutionary techniques, heuristic operators can be defined that contain problem-specific knowledge. For example, Cheng et al. (1999) present a heuristic crossover operator based on a problem-specific neighbourhood definition. Grefenstette (1987) present two heuristic crossover operators for the travelling salesman problem. While previous crossover operators for this problem only ensured that the resulting path is valid, the heuristic crossover operators also take the costs of edges into account when merging two parent solutions into an offspring solution. However, these heuristic operators are defined based on static properties of the search problem (neighbourhood, edge costs).

Pillay and Banzhaf (2010) have suggested a heuristic mutation operator for the examination timetabling problem which is concerned with planning the dates for a set of examinations so that the enrolled students do not overlap. In their mutation operator, only examinations that are in conflict with others are re-planned, and each re-planned examination is scheduled to a time slot with lowest costs. Costs are a proximity measure for examinations with the same students and prefers well-spaced examination for each student to leave time for preparation. Thus, this heuristic mutation operator uses more than static properties of the search problem, because it also takes into account additional metrics (here costs). However, the proposed heuristic mutation operator is the only mutation used in the examination timetabling optimization and it is not combined with traditional mutation operator. Thus, the approach may suffer drawbacks of rule-based approaches that parts of the search space are not reached.

In performance prediction (and quality prediction in general), often *more* information than the quality criterion to optimize is generated by a quality evaluation, too. For example, a performance evaluation does not only result in response time and/or throughput values for a given architecture, but also provide additional measures like the utilization of servers or the frequency of communication between computing node or components. Experienced software architects intuitively know styles and tactics to improve quality attributes of a software architecture (Bass et al., 2003). Some of these tactics can be codified into processable rules to improve a software architecture, as realized in the rule-based quality improvement methods (e.g. (Xu, 2010)) presented in the previous section.

In addition to static problem properties (such as edge costs) and the predicted quality property (e.g. mean response time), the tactics consider additional information from the quality evaluation (e.g. resource utilization).

This information is not available in the optimization problem definition per se, but it can only be obtained by candidate evaluation.

In this work, we suggest the use of this detailed problem-specific knowledge in a new tactics operator (presented in Section 8.3). This type of heuristic operator is always problem-specific (e.g. for performance prediction), but can be plugged into an evolutionary optimization algorithm and thus be combined with the standard, randomized evolutionary operators. To the best of our knowledge, tactics operators for quality improvement and the resulting hybrid optimization has not been described before.

Part II.

Automated Architecture Improvement

5. Supporting the Architect to Improve Component-based Architecture Models

In this chapter, we discuss how the software architect and other stakeholders can be supported by an automated method to improve a CBA model. The benefit such assistance is reduced effort due to the partial automation of the design space exploration task. Additionally, it has been recognized that automated, search-based approaches can help to produce unexpected, but valuable solutions that humans would have overlooked because of bias (Harman, 2007, Sec.7.3), because of time constraints, or because of limited insight into the problem.

In Section 5.1, we discuss the goals and requirements of such an automated method. Section 5.2 presents our extension of the quality-driven development process (H. Koziolek and Happe, 2006) which in turn extends the component-based development process by Cheesman and Daniels (2000). Then, the relation between the representation of the software architecture as a model and the actual software system is discussed in Section 5.3. In Section 5.4, we present development and evolution scenarios in which our method can be used. Section 5.5 discusses assumptions and limitations of our method. Finally, Section 5.6 concludes.

5.1. Goal of Automated Improvement Support

The goal of this work is to provide software architects with an automated method that supports them to improve a given CBA based on quality predictions and to determine optimal trade-offs. We assume that the software architect has identified a set of quality properties that are relevant for the software system and that a subset of these quality properties can be quantitatively analysed. Additionally, we assume that an initial software architecture model with the required quality annotations is already available, so that this subset of quality properties can be predicted. Then, the software architect requires assistance in making use of the prediction results to improve the architecture.

Usually, several quality properties, such as performance, reliability, security, or costs, are relevant for a software architecture. These quality properties may be conflicting, as discussed in Section 2.2.1. Achieving good performance can be costly due to more expensive hardware or more development and maintenance effort for highly optimized or parallelized components. Similar trade-offs exist between other quality properties (Bass et al., 2003, p.73). Usually, there is no architecture for a given software system that delivers optimal values for all quality properties, e.g. that allows the system to have good performance, be highly reliable and secure as well as maintainable and portable while having low costs of development and operation.

Different stakeholders of the software system may have different preferences for quality properties: While performance is important for users, maintainability is relevant for developers and costs matter for managers. When designing an architecture, the software architect and requirements engineers have to trade-off these quality properties (including costs) against each other while considering the preferences of all stakeholders and negotiating with them.

For an automated improvement process, however, we require a clear definition of how to compare and judge software architecture models, so that the automated method can search for improved architecture candidates. An order on candidates needs to be introduced, which automatically leads to the definition of the optimal candidates.

As presented in Section 3.2.1, there are three methods of how to handle multiple conflicting criteria in optimization: the a priori method, in which preferences are articulated before the search so that any two candidates can be compared; the a posteriori search where no information about the preferences among criteria is modelled before the search, so that the goal of the search is to find Pareto-optimal candidates; and an interactive approach focussing on the elicitation of user preferences using intermediate search results.

As described in Section 3.2.1, modelling preferences is difficult. Thus, we believe it is not appropriate to assume that software architects can reliably specify their preferences before the search, especially because several stakeholders may be involved. Indeed, in the context of the cost-benefit analysis method (CBAM), researchers noted that "eliciting the utility characteristics from the stakeholders can be a long and tedious process" (Bass et al., 2003, p.311). Still, utility curves are collected in CBAM and cost-benefit calculations are done with them, even though it is recognized that the captured utility values are "rough approximations" (Bass et al., 2003, p.311). Furthermore, an automatically determined set of Pareto-optimal candidates could be useful in discussion and agreement among stakeholders, as these candidates objectively and quantitatively show the available optimal options and thus are a basis for well-informed trade-off decisions.

Some methods to support software architects in improving the design assume that quality requirements are available, i.e. that the software architect and stakeholders agree on certain values that have to be achieved for each quality property (e.g. (Bachmann et al., 2005), cf. Chapter 4). Quality requirements are another form of preference model, which can be understood as assigning a utility of 1 to each candidate meeting all quality requirements and a utility of 0 to all others.

In line with the argumentation above, the difficulty here is to find and agree upon the required values. It is certainly possible to ask each stakeholder for required values for e.g. performance and reliability, resulting in for example statements that the system should respond within a second and be available 364 days of the year. However, it is questionable whether trade-offs among the quality properties are sufficiently considered in such an approach: If a system that satisfies the above stated requirements costs millions, while the relaxation of of the quality properties by few percent saves a significant amount of costs, stakeholders may want to reconsider their requirements. Thus, also the quality requirements are subject the actually achievable quality properties. This fact is recognized in methods like ATAM, where architecture evaluation meetings are supposed to "uncover conflicts and trade-offs [between previously stated quality requirements], and provide a forum for their negotiated resolution" (Bass et al., 2003, p.264). As a result, quality requirement values should not be used to guide an automated search, because the final requirements may actually depend on the outcome of the search.

While it is difficult for stakeholders and architects to specify their full preferences, they may indeed know that certain values for quality properties are unacceptable. Here, the question is not which quality properties are desired for a system, but which quality properties are certainly unacceptable. For example, a project may have a fixed upper limit for budget or user representatives may state that a response time of the system of more than 15 seconds on average is unacceptable. While this information is not enough to rank all possible solutions in an automated search, it provides *partial preference information* that can still be used within an a posteriori method.

For the problem of improving software architectures for their quality properties, the a posteriori method is thus more useful than the a priori method. First, no tedious preference modelling is required. Second, the insights into the existing trade-offs can be used in negotiations with stakeholders. Knowing the properties of the problem, the software architect, requirements engineers, and the stakeholders can agree on how to resolve the conflicts and trade-offs among quality properties. Partial preference information can be used to guide the search and focus on relevant regions of the Pareto front (cf. Section 8.2.5.2).

We expect no benefits from an interactive method over the a posteriori method in this work: First of all, quality predictions can be time consuming and thus the rate of candidate evaluation is relatively slow. As a result, the software architect cannot be constantly interacting with the method, but has to wait for new results, which we expect to be a tiring process. Additionally, if the software architect is not the only decision maker but needs to get feedback from multiple other stakeholders, the interaction loop becomes even longer. Thus, it seems to be more beneficial to first automatically collect all Pareto-optimal solutions and use these, e.g. in a meeting with stakeholders, to select the best architecture candidate or to agree on further manual changes of the architecture. Still, if these expectations are not fulfilled, an a posteriori method can be extended to become an interactive method, too.

Note that the above argumentation does not apply to all types of software systems or software-intensive systems. In some domains with real-time constraints and safety considerations, quality requirements are given and strict, be it because of physical constraints (e.g. the time to inflate an air bag after impact) or legal constraints (e.g. safety requirements in air planes). In such situations, quality requirement values are given and are not subject to trade-offs as described above. An automated improvement method could translate these requirements into constraints, while searching for candidates with good trade-offs in other quality properties no strict requirements are available for.

As a result of this discussion, we observe that an automated, search-based approach to support the software architect to improve a given software architecture for quality properties should apply the a posteriori method. Unless strict quality requirements are externally imposed, all quality properties are subject to trade-off and negotiation. Thus, the goal of such an automated method is to find the Pareto-optimal solutions, i.e. the candidates with optimal trade-offs.

5.2. Process

This section presents the component-based development process with quality exploration, which is an extension of the quality-driven CB development process. Section 5.2.1 presents the extension of the overall quality-driven CB development process. Section 5.2.2 described the extension of the quality analysis workflow and Section 5.2.3 presents the new Architecture Exploration workflow. Finally, Section 5.2.4 describes the use of the exploration results for decision making in both the specification workflow and requirements workflow.

5.2.1. Component-based Development Process with Quality Exploration

The original process by H. Koziolek and Happe, 2006 is shown in Figure 2.11, Section 2.4.5, which in turn extends the CB development process by Cheesman and Daniels (2000) (Figure 2.2, Section 2.1). However, the quality-driven CB development process does not account for automated support for improving the CBA based on the insight gained from quality prediction. Thus, we extend the quality analysis step in their process and the flow of artefacts to include our method.

Figure 5.1 shows the resulting component-based development process with quality exploration. Our extension (marked bold) changes the outputs of the quality analysis workflow: the step does not only provide predicted quality properties for the input specification as in the original method, but also provides the set of *optimal candidates with quality properties*. The candidates are optimal with respect to the considered quality criteria and degrees of freedom. This information can be used in both the specification and the requirements workflow for *decision making*, which is explained in more detail in Section 5.2.4 below.

Additionally, the use case models contain only *quality criteria* (and possible upper quality bounds), but not final quality requirements like in the

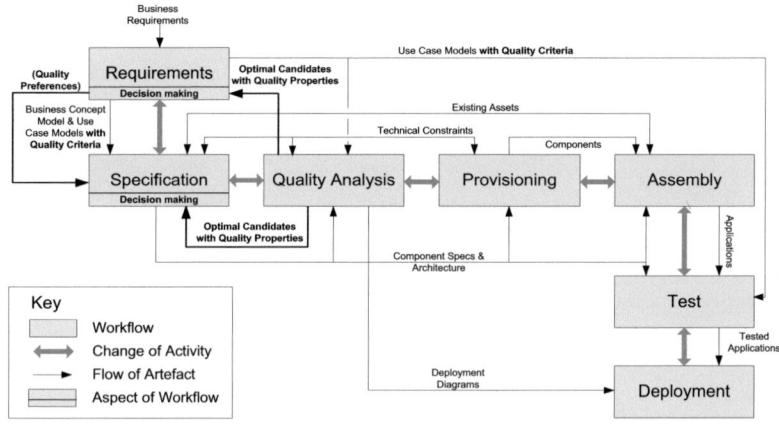

Figure 5.1.: Component-based Development Process with Quality Exploration (based on (H. Koziolek and Happe, 2006))

original process: We assume that stakeholders should not be forced to model their full preferences for quality criteria in advance, but instead should be supported to make well-informed trade-off decisions (cf. Section 5.1). Only after at least one iteration of quality analysis (thus marked with parentheses), stakeholders can decide on *quality preferences* based on the available trade-offs.

5.2.2. Quality Analysis Workflow

Figure 5.2 shows our extension of the quality analysis workflow. All workflows in the middle of the figure are updated. Note that, in contrast to (H. Koziolek and Happe, 2006), we assume in this work that these tasks are executed by the software architect instead of a specialized quality analyst role, because the workflow now contains making design decisions and negotiating with stakeholders, too. Still, it is possible that software architect delegates part of these tasks to a specialized quality analyst. The workflows of the deployer and the domain expert remain unchanged.

147

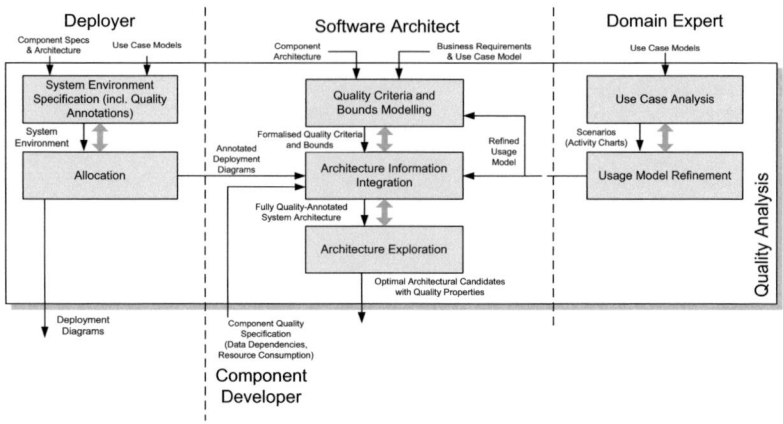

Figure 5.2.: Quality Analysis Step in Component-based Development Process (based on (H. Koziolek and Happe, 2006))

In the first workflow *Quality Criteria and Bounds Modelling*, software architects formalize the quality criteria that are relevant and that should be considered in the following workflows. The relevant quality criteria are collected from the use case models (e.g. duration of a use case, i.e. the cumulated response times of the involved services). Additional quality criteria may be added (e.g. the costs criteria or maintainability criteria which are not captured in use cases). For some few quality criteria, unacceptable values may be known (cf. Section 5.1), so that the software architect can also specify them as quality bounds. Then, the quality criteria and quality bounds are annotated to the architecture and to the refined usage model using our extension of the Quality of service Modelling Language (QML) (Frølund and Koistinen, 1998), cf. Section 8.2.5.2 and Appendix D. The resulting quality model (referencing the CBA) is transferred to the next workflow.

In the *Architecture Information Integration* workflow, all information from the other developer roles is integrated to form the fully quality-annotated architecture model. If information is missing, the software architect

148

has to estimate it or trigger other developer roles to provide this information. The resulting model can be a complete PCM instance, for example, as shown in Figure 2.13 in Section 2.5. In general, the resulting model contains the component architecture (e.g. a PCM system model and PCM allocation model), component quality specification (e.g. PCM SEFFs), an environment model (e.g. a PCM resource environment model), a usage model (e.g. a PCM usage model) and quality criteria and bounds (e.g. annotated to the PCM using QML).

The resulting fully quality-annotated architecture is input to the *Architecture Exploration* workflow. The goal of this workflow is to identify possibilities how to improve the CBA. It thus has two aspects: First the identification of possible changes of the CBA, i.e. the identification of *design space* (or a part thereof), and second the search for improved or even optimal solutions in this design space, i.e. the *optimization*. In this work, this workflow is implemented by an *Automated Architecture Exploration* workflow (explained in detail below in Section 5.2.3) that automatically identifies the design space that is opened up by the properties of CBA and searches this design space for improved solutions. Additionally, the software architect may manually explore the design space in this workflow, either for quality criteria that are not quantifiable or not analysable, or for design aspects that cannot be analysed automatically. For example, manual architecture exploration is conducted in ATAM (cf. Section 2.2.1), too, which could be combined with the method and process described in this work (so that our method provides automated exploration of parts of the design space and quantitative data to be used within ATAM). The outcome of the architecture exploration workflow is a set of candidates that are Pareto-optimal with respect to the relevant analysable quality criteria.

The result of the quality analysis workflow is thus a set of Pareto-optimal architecture candidates with quality properties. Additionally, all other evaluated candidates with quality properties are available for inspec-

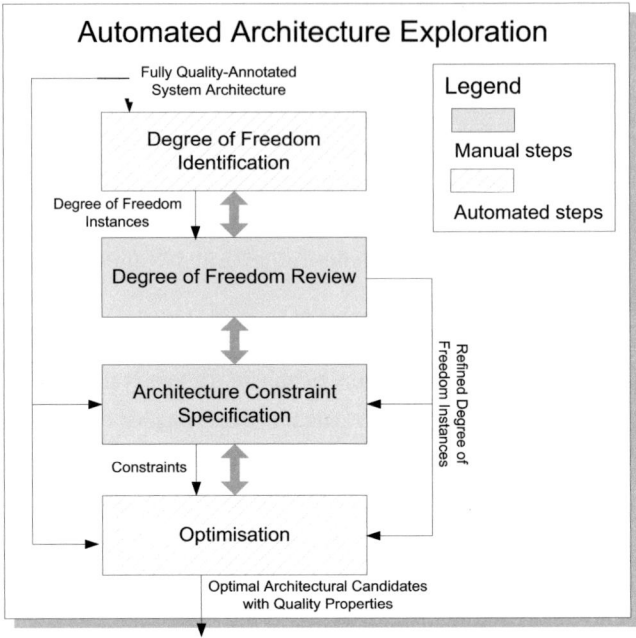

Figure 5.3.: Automated Architecture Exploration Workflow

tion if needed (not shown in the figure because the optimal candidates are the main result).

5.2.3. Architecture Exploration Workflow

Figure 5.3 shows the implementation of the Architecture Exploration workflow with our *Automated Architecture Exploration*. The input to this workflow is the fully quality-annotated architecture, including quality criteria and bounds. The presented workflow has manual steps (shown in grey) and automated steps (shown in white with grey pattern).

In the first step *Degree of Freedom Identification*, the degrees of freedom are automatically identified for the given software architecture based on the principles of component-based architectures and the used CBA metamodel.

For example, components can be allocated to different servers (allocation degree of freedom) and components can be replaced by other components that offer the same interfaces and require no more interfaces than available in the system (component selection degree of freedom). The notion of degrees of freedom is explained in more detail in Chapter 6. These degrees of freedom span the design space that can be searched automatically later.

In the second step *Degree of Freedom Review*, the found degrees of freedom are reviewed by the software architect. The software architect can remove degrees of freedom that should not be explored or add custom, system-specific degrees of freedom. Additionally, the software architect can add information to the architecture models about available options in e.g. the hardware environment (alternatively available servers) or the component architecture (e.g. available alternative component implementations), and then rerun the degree of freedom identification so that additional degrees of freedom can be identified. Furthermore, the software architect can configure the found degrees of freedom, and for example specify the range of CPU speeds that should be explored.

In the third step *Architecture Constraint Specification*, the software architect may define additional constraints for the design space. For example, considering our PCM example model from Figure 2.13, an additional constraint could be that BusinessTripMgmt and BookingSystem must not be deployed on the same server because of e.g. conflicting system library version requirements. Another reason for additional constraints could be quality criteria that are not analysable and thus have to be considered by the software architect. For example, the software architect might want to separate two components handling critical data to separate servers so that in case of a attack to one server, only one of the component is compromised. We assume, however, that few constraints on the degrees of freedom are required in this step (cf. Section 8.2.2).

Finally, the forth step *Optimization* runs an optimization tool to find the Pareto-optimal candidates when varying the software architecture along the degrees of freedom. The result is a set of Pareto-optimal architectural candidates with their quality properties. Because the optimization cannot guarantee globally optimal results for complex quality properties (cf. Section 8.1.3), the resulting set is an approximation thereof.

Note that while we assume here that one initial software architecture model is given, it is also possible that the software architect already starts with several architecture candidates.

The first three steps of this workflow are described in Chapter 6 in more detail, while the last step is described in Chapter 8.

5.2.4. Decision Making

Based on the Pareto-optimal candidates found in the architecture exploration, decisions are made in the specification workflow or the requirements workflow. In the specification workflow, the software architect makes decisions based on the found results. In the requirements workflow, all or a subset of the stakeholders make decisions, possibly guided by the software architect or by specialized requirements engineers. In the following, we refer to both groups as *decision makers*.

The decision maker review the found set of Pareto-optimal candidates. Based on the optimal candidates, the decision makers negotiate to agree on the best trade-off candidate for the given situation and the (implicit) preferences. The effect of demands by stakeholder groups (e.g. for fast response times, or a maintainable architecture) becomes quantifiable in terms of costs and effect on other quality properties. While we expect this task to be simpler than modelling preferences from scratch (see Section 5.1), selecting such a final candidate from the set is still difficult (Branke et al., 2008) and subject to multi-criteria decision making research (Belton and Stewart, 2002). For example, the Analytic Hierarchical Process (Saaty, 1980) has been used to decide for an architecture alternative out of many (Zhu et al., 2005).

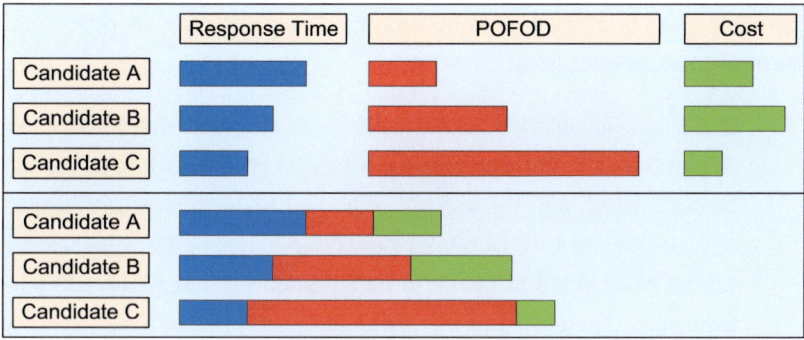

Figure 5.4.: Value Chart Example by Rohrberg (2010) for Result Analysis and Decision Making Workflow (The bars in the upper part reflect the utility of achieved quality properties as defined in a utility function. The width of each column in the upper part can be changed interactively by the user to reflect the weights of objectives, and the ranking in the lower part of the figure changes accordingly.)

For our architecture exploration method, decision making support based on multi-attribute value theory (Keeney, 2003, Chapter 3) for this phase has been investigated by Rohrberg (2010), who also provides a graphical visualization of results. Results can be explored for two objectives using Pareto front diagrams (cf. Figure 3.1, page 81) and for any number of objectives using Value Charts ((Carenini and Loyd, 2004) as shown in Figure 5.4). Value Charts also provide decision making support by allowing to model preferences in form of utility functions and observe the change of resulting overall utility of all candidates when changing weights of objectives.

In the best case, the decision makers choose one of the resulting architecture candidates to be realized, and updates the system architecture accordingly. Then, the architect can proceed to the later phases of the CB development process (Provisioning, Assembly, Testing, Deployment).

Alternatively, the analysis of the found trade-offs and the properties of the optimal architecture candidates leads to new insights, for example that two quality criteria are more in conflict than expected. These insights can stimulate more high-level decisions in both the specification workflow and the requirements workflow:

- In the specification workflow, insights can stimulate more high-level design changes. For example, the use or other architecture styles can be considered, e.g. the use of a pipe and filter architecture instead of a blackboard-centred architecture (Garlan and Shaw, 1994), if the central blackboard turns out to be a bottleneck with respect to performance. The results of the exploration can provide hints here, for example because the main difference of candidates along the Pareto-front is the configuration of the server that holds the blackboard component or mechanism.

- In the requirements workflow, insights can stimulate re-negotiations of the expectations of the system. For example, functional requirements may be revised to make the system less complex (for example, the scope of the system or the level of automation could be reduced). In the worst case, the project is cancelled because its realization turns out to be too risky or expensive.

In summary, the architecture exploration results enable decision makers to decide based on quantitative information about the system in form of the available optimal solutions and the resulting trade-offs. Thus, the process makes the effect of demands predictable in terms of their effect on other quality properties, including costs.

5.3. Model-based Improvement

In this section, we consider how a model-based architecture optimization approach relates to the targeted task of improving a given software system for its quality properties. Figure 5.5 visualizes the relation between the targeted task (lower part) and the model-based optimization, building upon the model-based prediction concepts shown in Figure 2.9, page 50.

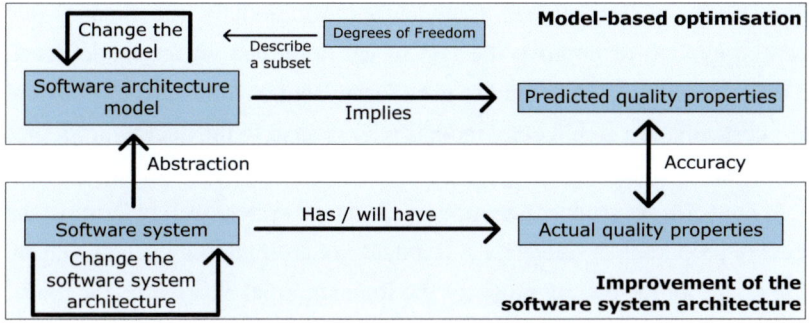

Figure 5.5.: Model-based Software Architecture Optimization

The starting point of the improvement process is a *software system* to improve, shown in the lower left corner. Improving the quality properties of the system means to change the software system in some way. In this work, we are concerned with *changes of the software architecture*, which is a subset of all possible changes. Such changes may affect the quality properties the system has (in case of an implemented system) or will have (in case of a system design without implementation).

To reason on the software system, the *software architecture model* is an abstraction capturing the details relevant for quality analyses. A (not necessarily strict) subset of the possible changes can be reflected on the model level as *changes of the software model*. In this work, we focus on the improvement of quality properties only. Changes to the functionality are excluded. Thus, the optimization on the model level is restricted to changes that are known to not affect the functionality of the system. These changes are described by *degrees of freedom*. Different degrees of freedom in combination span the search space in which our optimization method searches for good software architecture models (more details on the problem formulation in Chapter 6 and on the optimization method in Chapter 8).

In this work, we present a method to improve the software system on the model level. The quality properties to consider are predicted based

155

on a model of the software architecture. Additionally, the changes that can be applied to improve the system are described on the model level. Then, an optimization problem can be formulated on the model level to find the best software architecture models with respect to the quality properties reachable by these changes.

If the software architecture model reflects the system well in terms of the quality properties of interest, i.e. if it does not abstract away details that are important for the quality property, the found optimal changes on the model level correspond to optimal choices on the actual system level for those changes that can be reflected in the models. Of course, changes that cannot be reflected on the model level cannot be considered.

5.4. Scenarios

In addition to the inclusion in a CB development process as presented in Section 5.2, the automated architecture exploration can be used in other scenarios during software development and software evolution. In this section, we discuss these different application scenarios.

The automated architecture exploration can be applied in any process that fulfils the preconditions to apply our method, which are the following:

Architecture Models: The CBA must be described by an architectural model that conforms to a CBA metamodel. The described aspects include components, the static structure, and their deployment to hardware nodes.

Usage Information: Information about the targeted usage of the system must be available. Because many quality properties such as performance and reliability, but also security, safety, and energy-consumption, depend on how the system is used, this information has to be provided in a usage model.

Quality Annotations: The above models must be annotated with quality annotations so that the models can be transformed into analysis method of the respective quality property. Then, the analysis models can be evaluated and the quality properties of the software architecture can be predicted.

Stimulus for Exploration: For a newly designed system, the stimulus for architecture exploration is the development project itself. For an already implemented and possibly running system, some additional stimulus must be present to cause new architecture exploration. We discuss the possible stimuli below.

Stimuli that cause architecture exploration can be any of the following and possibly more. The first four scenarios are concerned with software evolution, while the two last ones are additional types of analyses which can be conducted at any development or evolution time.

Changed requirements: Over time, software systems evolve. Causes of software evolution are changed functional requirements or changed perception of quality criteria and the subsequent change of preference and trade-off decisions. For example, system users may demand a new functionality, which is new functional requirement. Another example is that users get used to quickly responding systems due to their use of other systems, so that it could be beneficial to improve the previously sufficient response time of the system.

Changing hardware or middleware: A second driver of software evolution is changed technical environment. For example, new hardware, new operating systems, or new middleware may be available. The need to adopt new technology can stem from licensing or maintenance problems or from the expectation of reduced costs or better quality properties. Then, the quality analysis step of the CB development process has to be repeated to predict the effects on quality properties, possibly inducing further changes of the design. In this scenario, the architecture exploration could explore different allocation options and could be analysed by systems deployers.

Changing usage: The usage of a system might change over time or may be predicted to change. For example, the workload of a web-based system may increase or decrease over time; or it may even change dramatically when events such as Christmas shopping or acquisition of other companies with a resulting higher number of internal system users. Here, the first step is to predict whether and how the quality properties of the system will be affected by the usage changes. If the quality properties are predicted to be affected, the software architect may want to update the system design. New architecture exploration can result in different optimal architecture candidates, e.g. an updated allocation of components to servers. To continue the example, a web-based system with increased load could be allocated to more servers, while and decreasing load can be encountered by consolidating servers. Possibly, the software architect also considers higher-level changes of the architecture and revisits the specification phase.

Deployment in a new environment: An existing system could be deployed at a new site. For example, an enterprise resource planning system could be deployed at a new customer. The new customer may use the system differently or even require adjustments of the system (both is likely to be the case for enterprise resource planning systems). Then, the automated architecture exploration can result in better configuration of the system or unveil the need to more deeply change the system's design in order to cope with the new situation. This situation can be a combination of the three scenarios "Changed requirements", "Changed hardware", and "Changing usage" described above.

Capacity planning: For performance, the number of users as well as their input parameters can have an effect on the overall performance of the system (Menascé et al., 2004, p.101). These values need to be included in the usage specification, as described above. At the same time, it can be studied how the optimal CBA changes along changing number of users or other usage model parameters to study the scalability and robustness of the system. To do so, these usage model parameters can be considered degrees of freedom and objective at once, so that the scalability of the system at hand in relation to other degrees of freedom can be studied.

Exploration of high-level design decisions: The architecture exploration can also be used when manually studying more high-level design options, for example concerning architectural styles, which cannot be mapped to our degrees of freedom. In these cases, the automated architecture exploration can be applied separately to each high-level design alternatives to determine the potential of each. Thus, each design alternative can be compared "at its best" without manually tuning the degrees of freedom (Zheng and Woodside, 2003).

While in a new development, many degrees of freedom are available (from the software level, such as component selection, to the deployment level, such as used middleware, hardware selection and allocation of components to servers, cf. Chapter 7), the degrees of freedom are usually more limited for existing systems. We give some examples in the following:

1. In a system the components are already implemented or bought for, software architects usually do not consider to exchange or reimplement certain components. Still, even this can be considered under special circumstances, if the quality of the existing components is not sufficient or the environment or other factors of the system have

changed so much that the existing components are not useful any more.

2. If a system is already installed on procured servers, the allocation may be limited to these servers or an extension of these servers instead of freely choosing more resources.

3. If developers are already familiar with certain middleware techniques, these should not be changed any more.

On the other hand, systems that are built to be flexible, such as service-oriented systems that use external pay-per-use services or systems running in virtualized environments (cloud computing), retain many degrees of freedom during their life cycle.

The architecture exploration as proposed in this work could even encompass more aspects than the CBA architecture if these aspects are contained in a common (CBA) model of the system and if they can be quantitatively and automatically analysed: For example, our method could be integrated with business process modelling to achieve a concurrent engineering approach (Paech et al., 2009). Given an integrated metamodel that covers both quality properties of the IT system and the business processes, degrees of freedom can be identified and our method can be directly applied to optimize response time of both IT system and human activities together.

Furthermore, if models for the utility and development costs of functionality (e.g. in form of components) are available, the architecture optimization can even be used to study trade-offs between functional properties and quality attributes. For example, a software architect may ask whether it is better to sacrifice some convenience functionality to achieve better performance. For all functionality aspects, costs are a trade-off (as the implementation of the functionality results in development costs or procurement costs to buy and adapt the components). Thus, as costs are usually also in conflict with other quality attributes, we observe that functionality decisions and quality decision can be interconnected as well. The design space identification aspect of the architecture exploration, however, is expected to be manual.

Note, however, that due to the planned interaction with the software architect, our method is probably not applicable as-is for the runtime adaptation of autonomous software systems. In such scenarios, the preferences as well as the available degrees of freedom must be unambiguously modelled beforehand, so that the system can autonomously execute optimization algorithms to cope with changed situations. Because these requirements differ from the requirements studied in this work (cf. Section 5.1), we do not consider autonomous system optimization further. In our work, the software architect (or another role, such as the system deployer in the "changed hardware" scenario) is the ultimate decision maker, and the automated exploration method's task is to provide decision support.

Our method can, however, support a software architect in designing such adaptive, autonomous systems. If quality prediction approaches are available that predict the adaptive system's quality properties in different envisioned situations, these quality properties can be used to make trade-off decisions for architectural aspects that are fixed at design time. For example, an adaptive system could be designed which can autonomously deploy its components to one to three servers, depending on the workload. Then, the software architect may face the question of which third party component to buy to realize a functionality. The architectural model could be analysed for the envisioned workloads could be analysed for quality properties, and the potential trade-offs of different available third-party can be studied. Furthermore, the choice of adaptation rules or adaptation policies could be a variable for the improvement. In all these sketched cases, the expected system workload must be known to make quality predictions.

To summarize, architecture exploration can be applied by software architects regardless of whether a system is already implemented or not. Especially for performance predictions, quality predictions for implemented systems can even be more accurate because the quality models can be built from measurements of the system.

5.5. Assumptions and Limitations

The assumptions of our method as presented in this chapter are the following:

Relevant quality criteria known: We assume that the software architect, together with other stakeholders, has already identified the relevant quality criteria (cf. Section 5.1). If new quantitatively analysable quality criteria become relevant after the architecture exploration step, this step should be repeated to account for them.

Available models: We assume that the software architect has a model of the CBA annotated with information to predict the relevant quality properties (cf. Section 5.1). The techniques how to obtain such quality annotations depends on the quality criterion (cf. e.g. (Jain, 1991; Menascé et al., 2004) for performance, (Gokhale, 2007) for an overview regarding reliability, or (Boehm et al., 2000) for costs).

Because this assumption is fundamental to our work, we discuss the need for modelling as motivated in Section 1.1, its costs, and its benefits in more detail in Section 10.3.

A limitation of our method is the following:

Qualitative quality attributes: Our method is restricted to quality attributes that can be quantitatively assessed and automatically analysed based on models. Quality attributes such as security, usability, and portability are difficult to capture in architecture models and no quantitative models are available at this time. Thus, they cannot be considered in our automated method yet. These qualities have to be considered manually by the software architect. As soon as quantitative prediction methods for these quality attributes, they can be integrated in our method.

Furthermore, our method inherits all assumptions and limitations of the underlying quality prediction techniques (e.g. for the PCM, see (Becker et al., 2009) for performance and (H. Koziolek and Brosch, 2009) for reliability). Assumptions and limitations of our formulation of the degrees of freedom and the design space as well as the applied optimization technique are discussed separately in Sections 6.5 and 8.5 in the respective chapters.

5.6. Summary

In this chapter, we discuss how software architects can be supported by an automated method that helps them to interpret quality prediction results, map them back to the software architecture level and make design decision based on them to improve the quality properties of the software system (feedback tasks).

The contributions of this chapter are

- Analysis of the possible automated decision support to help software architects with the feedback tasks: We identify the need for a method that requires no initial preference articulation (a posteriori method).

- Integration of automated architecture exploration in the CB development process.

The benefit of assistance with this task is reduced effort due to the partial automation of the design space exploration task and possibly new insights that would not be found manually.

6. Formalization of the Design Space

As described in the previous chapter, the starting point for an automated model-based architecture improvement is a software architecture model and a set of quality attributes of interest.

To improve an input software architecture model automatically, we require a formulation of how an automated method can *change* this input model in order to find improved variants. We define the *design space* of the input software architecture model as the set of all architecture models reachable from the input software architecture model by an automated improvement method. Thus, the leading question of this chapter is:

> How can the design space be formalized so that a software
> tool can automatically search it for architectural models with
> improved quality attributes of interest?

In this chapter, we identify what changes are possible and relevant with respect to this question. The resulting set of possible architecture models, or *architectural candidate models*, is input to the automated search for the best architecture models using multi-objective optimization described in the next chapter.

The concepts described in this chapter are applicable to any component-based software architecture model. Thus, we describe them independently of any metamodel using only the properties of CBA as presented in Section 2.1. Additionally, we give examples for the three CBA metamodels PCM, ROBOCOP, and CBML when presenting the types of changes that make up the design space for CBA in Chapter 7. Partially, the concepts can be transferred software architecture models in general, too, if the software architecture metamodel unambiguously models different aspects of software architectures with different metamodel elements.

The remainder of this chapter is organized as follows. Section 6.1 describes the requirements that automated changes have to adhere to to enable an automated search. In section 6.2 we first illustrate the topics addressed in this chapter on a PCM example model, revisiting the constraints described above and giving an intuitive description of the core ideas. In the following sections, the concepts are then described formally and in detail. In section 6.3, we define how the architecture can be changed automatically to affect quality attributes, and we formalize the concept of a *degree of freedom* to describe such variation options. Then, Section 6.4 describes the resulting space of architecture candidate models reachable by automated improvement. Finally, Section 6.5 lists limitations of this method and Section 6.6 summarizes.

In the next Chapter 7, we then discuss what degrees of freedom are inherent to component-based architecture models, and list relevant degrees for performance, reliability, and costs.

6.1. Requirements for Automated Improvement

The goal of an automated improvement process is to find meaningful design alternatives that can be realized in the system at hand. Thus, the automated process cannot change the CBA model arbitrarily but must adhere to a set of constraints to ensure that the results are meaningful. Based on the discussion in the previous chapter, we have identified four constraints that describe the allowed changes.

First, the considered changes must be relevant for the considered quality attributes to have potential to improve quality properties. For example, the allocation of components to servers is relevant for performance and can also be relevant for costs if the number of needed servers is varied (cf. Section 7.3.1). To give a counterexample, the names of components are irrelevant for performance, thus, their change is irrelevant for automated performance improvement.

C1 Changes must capture relevant influence factors on quality properties.

Second, we are only interested in changes of the architecture model that conform to the metamodel. This means that the changed architecture model must conform to the metamodel as described in Section 2.3. This is reflected in constraint C2:

C2 After changing the architecture model, the result must be a model conforming to the architecture metamodel.

Third, we want to address changes that affect the quality attributes of the system, but not its intended functionality. For example, we do not want to replace a component *A* that realizes accounting functionality in the system with a faster component *B* that just stores the passed information without processing it. Additionally, the system described by the model must be realizable. For example, we cannot change the model by dividing the resource demand of an internal action representing a highly optimized search algorithm, if the resource demand of the search algorithm in the real system cannot be optimized further. These two aspects are related, because the reduction of the resource demand in this case could only be achieved by limiting the functionality of the search algorithm by e.g. searching only half of the data. This is reflected in constraint C3:

C3 The functional behaviour described by the software architecture model must remain unchanged and the system must be realizable.

If two software architecture models provide the same functionality, we call them *functionally-equivalent*.

Because the architecture model abstracts from the actual system and its implementation, the models do not necessarily contain enough information to decide automatically for any change whether it changes functionality or not. For example, the automated improvement method Performance Booster (Xu, 2010) contains a rule that suggests to reduce the resource demand of an LQN software task to improve performance. Such a change leads to a conforming model, because only the resource demand parameter—a double value in LQN—is changed in the suggested new model. However, we cannot decide automatically whether the changed software task can still provide the same functionality with this reduced effort, because information on the used algorithms and the resulting functionality is not contained in the LQN model. In this example, only humans can interpret the suggested new model with reduced resource demand and decide whether it is functionally-equivalent to the initial model. Furthermore, even if the architectural model contained a specification of the functional semantics, the resulting problem would be undecidable in general.

However, in an automated improvement process, it is infeasible to ask the human designer to decide the fulfilment of constraint C3 manually for every change that fulfils constraint C2. Thus, as a forth constraint, which change fulfil constraint C3 must be described on the metamodel level, so that these description can be reused automatically when assessing model instances. As a result, we exclude changes of the architecture model that *may* lead to changes of the functional behaviour of the system in automated improvement. We only use changes we know not to affect functionality, because the metamodel semantics prescribe it. Then, no human designer needs to provide additional information during the improvement process.

C4 Which changes fulfil constraint C3 must be described on the metamodel level. If a change may affect functionality, it is excluded.

Note that this constraint does not exclude to extend a software architecture model by introducing annotations that provide additional information to decide constraint C3, so that more changes can be considered in the automated improvement.

6.2. Overview and PCM Example

To illustrate the concepts of this chapter, we discuss them informally for an example architecture model in this section. Consider the example model shown in Figure 2.13 in Section 2.5, page 61. For the following discussion, let us assume that we are interested in improving performance (mean response time) and reliability (probability of failure on demand) of calling the IBusinessTripMgmt.plan service as well as costs of the system. This section illustrates what can be changed in this example architecture in an automated improvement method. The concepts are described formally and in detail in the next sections 6.3 and 6.4.

6.2.1. Valid Changes in the Example

Valid changes keep the architecture model valid and do not change functionality.

In the example model, the allocation of components can be changed. If we move component PaymentSystem to server S2, we do not affect the functionality of the system (as this is encapsulated inside PaymentSystem and BookingSystem as SEFFs, which remain unchanged), but we affect the quality attributes: The system becomes cheaper, because one server less is required, while the performance of the system may worsen, because components PaymentSystem and BookingSystem now compete for server S2's processing resources.

Additionally, we can change the server configuration in the example model. The system's functionality does not depend on the chosen hardware. Thus, other processors can be used in all three servers. For example, faster and more expensive processors (e.g. 2.5GHz with costs 884 units) could be bought, which may additionally have a higher reliability. This change affects performance, reliability, and costs of the architecture model.

Finally, some of the architecture's components may offer standard functionality for which other implementations (i.e. other components) are available. In the PCM, components offer the same functionality if they provide the same interfaces. In this example, let us assume a fourth available component QuickBooking also offers the IBooking interface as shown in Figure 6.1. Then, BookingSystem can be replaced by QuickBooking without changing the functionality of the system. Because QuickBooking has less resource demand, is more reliable, but is also more expensive than BookingSystem in this example, the resulting architecture model has a lower response time, lower probability of failure on demand, but higher costs.

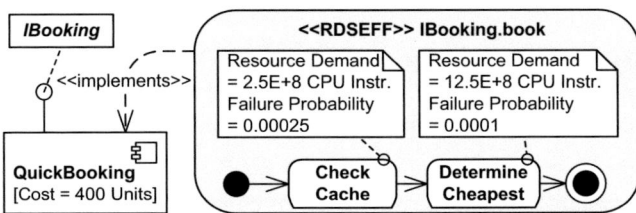

Figure 6.1.: Alternative Implementation of the IBooking interface

More changes may be possible, such as adding load balancing capabilities or replicating servers for increased reliability. Note that we are only interested in changes that actually have a potential to affect the quality attributes of interest. To give a counter example, in a scenario where performance and reliability are studied, the change of a name of a component in the PCM does not change the system's functionality (because names are not used for references, they are labels) and the resulting model is valid, as long as the name is not empty. Still, even though this change fulfils the constraints, it is not interesting here, because it does not affect performance or reliability. If maintainability was one of the quality attributes of interest, however, the name might be of interest, because it affects the understandability of the architecture.

6.2.2. Illustration of Change Constraints

To illustrate invalid changes, we revisit the constraints described in the introduction of this chapter with respect to this example.

Constraint C1 requires that a change is relevant for the considered quality attributes. Assuming that performance and costs are relevant here, the names of components as well as any other names are irrelevant. Constraint C2 requires that changes result in a well-formed model with respect to the metamodel. For example, a change that removes component BookingSystem from the model is not of interest. The resulting model would be invalid because component BusinessTripMgmt's requirement of a component implementing interface IBooking would not be satisfied.

Constraint C3 requires that the functional behaviour of the described system remains unchanged. For example, changes to the behaviour specification of components may affect functionality. If we remove the internal action DetermineCheapestHotel of BookingSystem to reduce the resource demand of this component, this could mean that the component does not determine the cheapest hotel any more, but picks a hotel randomly. Even if we simply change the order of the internal actions of BookingSystem.book, this can lead to a change of functionality: For example, if we move DetermineCheapestHotel after the external call to IPayment.pay, this could change the component's behaviour from sending the cheapest hotel information to the PaymentSystem to sending any hotel information, thus making the PaymentSystem pay a different one than the booked ones.

Constraint C4 requires that we describe functional-equivalence on the metamodel level. To continue the example, the behaviour specifications in the PCM cannot be modified automatically as is, because there may be changes that change functionality, as sketched above. Thus, we have to exclude changes that remove internal actions from the behaviour specification in the PCM in general (unless we can define a subset of changes removing internal actions on the metamodel level that can be guaranteed to not change functionality).

As a result, we see that for example removing components without substitution, or changes of the behaviour specification are no valid changes in the PCM, and thus cannot be exploited by an automated improvement process.

6.2.3. Degree of Freedom Examples in the PCM

As we have seen from the example, whether a given change (here: removing an internal actions, or reallocating a component) may or may not affect functionality can be determined from the semantics of the PCM metamodel. These semantics are not formally described in the PCM metamodel, they are part of the interpretation of metamodel elements. Thus, the constraint whether functional behaviour may be affected by a change must be manually interpreted in relation to the metamodel's semantics.

A metamodel, however, describes all possible conforming model instances. Thus, from analysing functionality effects on the metamodel level, we cannot only conclude that a specific change at hand (e.g. moving component BookingSystem to server S3) is valid, but also that this type of change is valid in general (e.g. the allocation of components can be changed in general). We can analyse the metamodel semantics and determine types of changes that do not affect functionality. We call such types of changes *degrees of freedom* (DoF) of a metamodel.

As we see in this example, the PCM metamodel offers at least three such DoF: (1) changing component allocation, (2), changing resources of servers (here the processors), and (3) exchanging components which offer the same interfaces. As the metamodel semantics need to be considered, a DoF definition is specific to the CBA metamodel at hand. Still, the concept of DoFs can be applied to any CBA metamodel: The DoF metamodel for EMOF that we present in Section 6.3.3 can be used to model DoF of any EMOF-based CBA metamodel.

In Chapter 7, we discuss the degrees of freedom of the PCM in detail and define them formally. Here, we proceed with this intuitive notion to illustrate how to apply degrees of freedom to an architecture model at hand, and how the design space of possible changes for that architecture model is defined by them.

6.2.4. Degrees of Freedom Instances in the Example

Based on the degrees of freedom of a metamodel, i.e. the notion what can be automatically changed in model instances of this metamodel, a set of changes that could be applied to a specific system at hand can be derived. We group the changes according to which model elements are changed, because mostly, such changes can then be considered independently from each other. For example, there are several options of how to change the allocation of BusinessTripMgmt in our example and there are several independent options of how to change the allocation of BookingSystem. Different types of changes are independent, too: We can replace the component BookingSystem by the component QuickBooking regardless of its allocation (i.e. of the allocation of its AssemblyContext). At the same time, changes within the group are mutually exclusive: We cannot allocate BusinessTripMgmt to both server S1 and server S2 in this system. We call such groups of changes on a set of model elements in a specific system at hand *degree of freedom instances* (DoFI) or simply degree of freedom. The seven degree of freedom instances here are

1. Allocation of BusinessTripMgmt

2. Allocation of BookingSystem

173

3. Allocation of `PaymentSystem`

4. Select processor for S1

5. Select processor for S2

6. Select processor for S3

7. Select component to provide functionality of `IBooking`

For each such degree of freedom instance, several options on how to change the system may exist. For example, component `BusinessTripMgmt` could be relocated to S2 or S3. Including the initial architecture model, three options on how to allocate `BusinessTripMgmt` exist in this example. Thus, the degree of freedom instance has three *design options* available. For the resource selection degree (here processors), the number of design options depends on how many different processor types are available for the given software system. Let us assume that in this example, 13 different processor types $\{P_1, ..., P_{13}\}$ are available with different processing rates (from 1GHz to 4GHz in equidistant steps), failure probabilities, and costs. Then, 13 options exists for each resource selection degree of freedom instance in this example. Finally, assuming only the one possible replacement for `BookingSystem` as described above, the degree of freedom instance to select a component to realize `IBooking`'s functionality has two design options, namely `BookingSystem` and `QuickBooking`. Table 6.1 lists all degrees of freedom for the example and their design option sets, denoted *designOptions*.

6.2.5. Design Space of the Example

Together, the degree of freedom instances define a set of possible architecture models. Each of these possible architecture models is defined by choosing one design option for each DoFI. We call such a possible architecture model an *architectural candidate model* or just *candidate model*.

Degree of freedom	Degree of freedom instance d	Design option set $designOptions_d$
Allocation	of BusinessTrip-Mgmt	$\{S1, S2, S3\}$
	of BookingSystem	$\{S1, S2, S3\}$
	of PaymentSystem	$\{S1, S2, S3\}$
Resource Selection	of CPU Server$_1$	$\{P_1, ..., P_{13}\}$
	of CPU Server$_2$	$\{P_1, ..., P_{13}\}$
	of CPU Server$_3$	$\{P_1, ..., P_{13}\}$
Component Selection	Alternatives for IBooking	$\{$BookingSystem, QuickBooking$\}$

Table 6.1.: Degrees of Freedom in the Example

The set of all possible candidate models is the set of all possible combinations of the design options.

The size of this set is the product of all design option set sizes. For n DoFIs $d_1, ..., d_n$, we have n design option sets

$$designOptions_{d_1}, ..., designOptions_{d_n}$$

Then, the size of the design space is

$$\left|designOptions_{d_1}\right| \cdot ... \cdot \left|designOptions_{d_n}\right|$$

In our example model, we get

$$|\{S1, S2, S3\}|^3 \cdot |\{P_1, ..., P_{13}\}|^3 \cdot |\{BookingSystem, QuickBooking\}|$$
$$= 3^3 \cdot 13^3 \cdot 2 = 118638$$

architecture candidate models defined by the DoFI.

We call this set of possible architecture models the *design space*. Figure 6.2 visualizes the design space as a seven-dimensional space.

Each candidate model in the design space can be characterized with respect to the DoFI by the set of chosen design options, i.e. as a point in this space. The initial architecture model (i.e. the initial candidate model) can

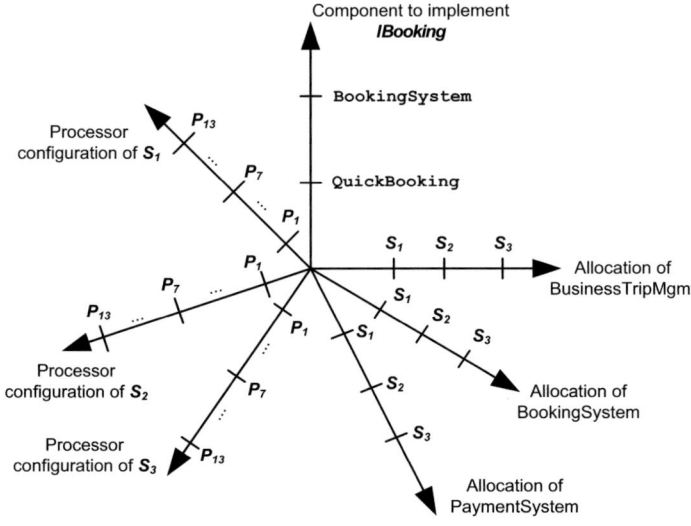

Figure 6.2.: Visualization of the Seven-dimensional Design Space of the Example

be characterized as shown in Table 6.2. Another candidate model, shown in Figure 6.3, can be characterized as shown in Table 6.2. Compared to the initial candidate model, we have changed the allocation of BusinessTrip-Mgmt, and chose a different processor for S2. Using the quality analyses described in Sections 2.4 and 2.5, we obtain different response time, probability of failure on demand and costs.

In many cases, the options of DoFI are independent, as in our example. However, in some cases, design options of DoFI may conflict with each other. For example, two components may have conflicting operating system requirements so that they cannot be deployed on the same server. Such interactions between DoFI and their design option sets can be detected by checking the constraints of the metamodel again.

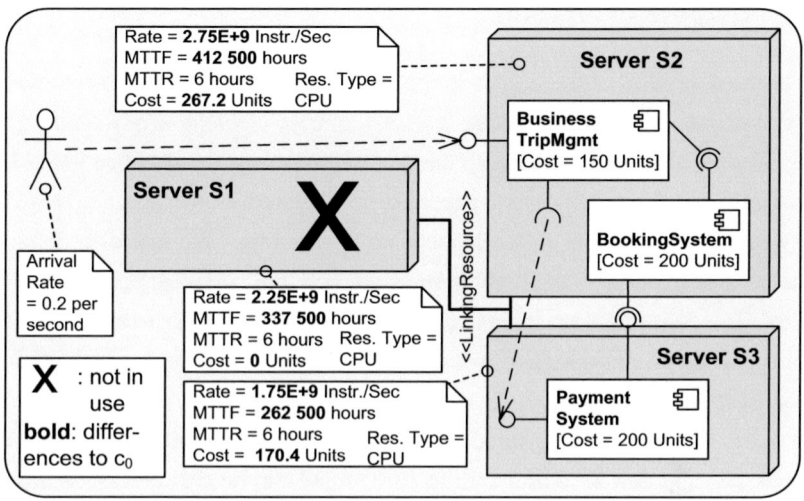

Figure 6.3.: A Architectural Candidate Model in the Example

Degree of freedom	Degree of freedom instance	Initial Candidate Model	Candidate Model of Fig. 6.3
Component allocation	of BusinessTrip-Mgmt	S1	S2
	of BookingSystem	S2	S2
	of PaymentSystem	S3	S3
Resource Selection	of CPU $Server_1$	$P_4 = 1.75$GHz	$P_6 = 2.25$ GHz
	of CPU $Server_2$	$P_5 = 2$GHz	$P_8 = 2.75$ GHz
	of CPU $Server_3$	$P_3 = 1.5$ GHz	$P_4 = 1.75$ GHz
Component Selection	Alternatives for IBooking	Booking-System	Booking-System
Quality Analysis Results			
Response time		7.3 sec	6.8 sec
POFOD		1.14E-3	7.95E-4
Costs		1078.55 units	1294.85 units

Table 6.2.: Choices for two Architectural Candidate Models

6.3. Degrees of Freedom

For the definition of the design space that can be explored in an automated improvement method, we define the core concept of a *degree of freedom* of a software architecture model in this section. Then, in the next Section 6.4, we can formulate the design space to be explored as the space spanned by the combination of different degrees of freedom. We formally define degrees of freedom using natural language and logic predicates in this section. The definitions are independent of any concrete CBA metamodel, but only reason on properties of metamodels in general and CBA metamodels (cf. Section 2.1).

As described in the introduction of this chapter, our goal in this chapter is to describe how an initial architecture model can be changed automatically to achieve better quality properties. Thus, we first provide descriptive definitions for *changes* and sets of changes in Section 6.3.1. Then, we define *degrees of freedom* as rules to produce such sets of changes in Section 6.3.2.

6.3.1. Change Definitions

This section provides preparatory definitions and terms to enable us to reason about model changes and their properties when defining degrees of freedom in the next section 6.3.2. We first define how to describe a *change* of a model. Additionally, we make some preparatory definitions about classes of changes, in particular the distinction of *change types*. Then, we introduce predicates describing that change types fulfil the constraints C1, C2, C3 and C4 informally described in the introduction of this chapter.

6.3.1.1. Change

First, let us define how to describe changes of models. For the purpose of defining the design space, we are not interested in how model changes are realized technically. The important aspect of changing a model is that a change results in a new model with potentially different quality properties. Thus, we define a change solely as a pair of an initial model M and a result model M'. The relevant properties of changes are the model elements that are updated and the new values these model elements take.

Definition 6.1 Change

A model *change c* is some operation on a model M that leads to a new model M' that is different than M, i.e. $M' \neq M$. For this work and the following definitions, it is sufficient to describe a change as the pair of *initial model M* and *result model M'* and write $c = (M, M')$. Alternatively, we write $M \xmapsto{c} M'$.

Recall from Section 2.3.2 that we refer to the value of a model element m in a model M as $v_m(M)$. To be able to describe the differences of M and M', we refer to the set of model elements that have been changed as *updated*$(c) \subseteq M$ with

$$updated(c) := \left\{ m \in M \,\middle|\, v_m(M) \neq v_m(M') \right\}$$

For example, consider the following changes of our example model (Figure 2.13, page 61).

- The processing rate of server S1 (modelled as a parameter of the server's CPU called ProcessingRe-sourceSpecification.processing-Rate) is changed to 2.5GHz. Then, the changed model element is CPU.processingRate: *updated*$(c) = \{$ CPU.processingRate$\}$. The old value of this model element is $v_{CPU.processingRate}(M) = 1.75$GHz and the new value is $v_{CPU.processingRate}(M')$.

- We can move component BookingSystem from server S2 to server S3. The model element that describes BookingSystem's allocation

AllocationContext.resourceContainer has been updated. Let the allocation context of BookingSystem be called AL-BkSys. Then, $updated(c) = \{$ AL-BkSys.resourceContainer$\}$. The old value of this model element is $v_{AL-BkSys.resourceContainer}(M) = 1.75\text{GHz}$ and the new value is $v_{AL-BkSys.resourceContainer}(M')$.

6.3.1.2. Change with Valid Models

For an automated improvement, we are interested only in valid model instances as defined in Section 2.3, which is reflected by constraint C2. Recall from Section 2.3.1 that the relation $M \blacktriangleleft MM$ expresses that a model M conforms to a software architecture metamodel MM, i.e. that M structurally conforms to MM (i.e. $M \in MM$) and that M fulfils the static semantics of MM. Then, we define a change to *have conforming models* if it both models conform to the metamodel.

Definition 6.2 Change with Conforming Models

A change $c = (M, M')$ for a metamodel MM *has conforming models* (written as *hasConformingModels(c,MM)*) if both the source model M and the result model M' are valid instances of MM:

$$hasConformingModels(c,MM) :\Leftrightarrow M \blacktriangleleft MM \wedge M' \blacktriangleleft MM$$

Our example model (Figure 2.13, page 61) is a valid model. If we remove component PaymentSystem without replacing it with something else, however, the result model is invalid because the required interfaces of BusinessTripMgmt and BookingSystem remain unbound.

6.3.1.3. Valid Change

In addition to having valid models, we require changes to not change functionality and result in a realizable architecture model in an automated quality improvement method, which is reflected by constraint C3. Let us define a predicate $valid(c,MM)$ to express that a change has conforming models, that it does not change the functionality of the CBA, and that the described result model is realizable (cf. Section 6.1).

Definition 6.3 Valid Change

A change $c = (M,M')$ for a metamodel MM is *valid* (written as $valid(c,MM)$) if it has conforming models and if it does not change the functionality of the described CBA:

$$valid(c,MM) :\Leftrightarrow hasConformingModels(c,MM)$$
$$\land M' \text{ is functionally equivalent to } M$$
$$\land M' \text{ is realizable}$$

In our example model (Figure 2.13, page 61), moving the internal action DetermineCheapestHotel in BookingSystem.book after the call to the IExternalPayment interface is a change with valid models, but not a valid change, because the functionality is not retained. Similarly, reducing the resource demand of the internal action DetermineCheapestHotel by 90% is a valid model, but probably not a valid change, if we assume that the algorithm is already rather efficiently implemented or estimated to be efficient.

6.3.1.4. Change Types

Because a metamodel defines all possible model instances, it can be used as a reference to describe changes on any model instance. Each model element is an instance of a metamodel element. Thus, changes can be classified according to which metamodel element describes the model elements they update:

Definition 6.4 Change Type

A *change type ct* defines a set of metamodel elements *changeable*(*ct*) ⊆ *MM*. Then, all changes *c* that have valid models and that only change instances of metamodel elements in *changeable*(*ct*) are of the change type *ct*. Let *C* denote the set of all possible changes in models described by *MM*, i.e. $C = (MM \times MM) \setminus \{(M,M) \,|\, M \in MM\}$. Then,

$$
ct := \left\{ c \in C \;\middle|\; \begin{array}{l} hasConformingModels(c,MM) \\ \wedge\; \forall e \in updated(c) : \exists m \in changeable(ct) : e \text{ instanceOf } m \end{array} \right\}
$$

For example, the allocation of components is a change type in the PCM. Let us denote this change type with *alloc*. The set *changeable*(*alloc*) contains the metamodel element that maps components to servers; in the PCM it is AllocationContext.resourceContainer: *changeable*(*alloc*) = {AllocationContext.resourceContainer}.

With the definitions above, all changes of a change type by construction fulfil constraint C2 "After changing the architecture model, the result must be a model conforming to the architecture metamodel" informally described in the introduction of this chapter. Let us additionally define predicates for change types that fulfil the constraint C3 "The functional behaviour described by the software architecture model must remain unchanged and the system must be realizable". These predicates reason on the metamodel level, so they adhere to constraint C4 "Which changes fulfil constraint C3 must be described on the metamodel level. If a change may affect functionality, it is excluded".

6.3.1.5. Functionally Equivalent Change Types

As discussed in Section 6.1, automated quality improvement must not change the functionality of the described CBA and must result in realizable models (constraint C3). Additionally, which changes fulfil this constraint must be described on the metamodel level, so that humans are not involved during the improvement process (constraint C4). Thus, we define a predicate *funcEquiv(ct,MM)* for functional equivalent change types that express that all changes of that change type are functionally-equivalent and realizable:

Definition 6.5 Functionally Equivalent Change Type

A change type ct for a software architecture metamodel MM is called *functionally equivalent* (written as *funcEquiv(ct,MM)*) if every change $c \in ct$ is a valid change:

$$funcEquiv(ct,MM) :\Leftrightarrow$$

$$\forall c \in ct : valid(c,MM)$$

Because changes in ct have valid models by definition, this effectively requires that for every change $c = (M,M') \in ct$ that M' is functionally equivalent to M and realizable based on the semantics of the metamodel MM.

Because the predicate is defined on the metamodel level for all valid models and because it reasons on all possible changes of ct, reasoning on functionally equivalent changes types fulfils constraint C4.

For example, in the PCM, we can vary the processing rates of server resources without affecting the system's functionality. The change type *procRate* with the changeable element *changeable(procRate)* = { ProcessingResourceSpecification.processingRate} is functionally-equivalent in the PCM: *funcEquiv(procRate,PCM)*.

6.3.1.6. Change Type that Affects Quality Attributes

For automated quality improvement, only changes that affect quality attributes of software architecture models are relevant, as described with constraint C1. We define the predicate *affects(ct,Q)* to express that changes of a change type ct potentially affect a quality attribute Q.

Definition 6.6 Change Type that Affects a Quality Attribute

A change type ct for a software architecture metamodel MM *potentially affects* a quality attribute Q (written *affects*(ct,Q)) if there exists at least one possible model instance M, at least one change c that is an instance of ct, and at least one quality criterion qc that measures Q so that if c is applied to M, the resulting new model instance M' has a different quality property than M:

$$affects(ct,Q) :\Leftrightarrow$$
$$\exists qc \in \text{measures}(Q)\ \exists M \blacktriangleleft MM\ \exists (M,M') = c\ \text{instanceOf}\ ct :$$
$$qc(M) \neq qc(M')$$

For example, changing the allocation of components (change type *alloc* above) or changing the processing rate of resources (change type *procRate* above) may affect performance. Thus, with P denoting the quality attribute performance, it holds that *affects*$(alloc,P)$ and *affects*$(procRate,P)$. In contrast, changing the names of components does not affect any quality attribute that can be automatically analysed for PCM models. Thus, if we denote the change type that changes a component name by *name*, we can write $\neg$*affects*$(name,P)$.

6.3.1.7. Indivisible Change Types

For the automated improvement as sketched before, we are interested in the degrees of freedom in the architecture models that span the design space to search. Thus, we are interested in those change types that—in combination—can characterize the design space.

First, it is useful to exclude trivial changes that do not affect quality attributes, such as the change of a label, from the change types to consider to focus on relevant changes for the automated improvement. We have introduced the predicate *affects*(ct,Q) for these relevant changes.

Additionally, we want to consider "small", i.e. indivisible, change types that can then be combined explicitly to create larger changes. In an indivisible change type, all metamodel elements contribute to the quality property effect (1). Additionally, an indivisible change type is not separable in several functionally-equivalent change types that together can produce changes with the same quality effects (2).

Let us consider two simple examples for divisible change types. As a counter example for (1), consider an example change type *allocAndLabel* that contains the change of allocation of components and the change of component names with *changeable(allocAndLabel)* = {AllocationContext.resourceContainer, RepositoryComponent.entityName}. Let us assume that we only consider the quality attributes performance and reliability in this example. Then, the component name has no effect to both quality attributes. Thus, this change type is divisible, because we can as well remove the metamodel element RepositoryComponent.entityName from the changeable elements and directly use the change type *alloc* as described above.

As a counter example for (2), consider a change type *allocAndPR* that contains the change of allocation of components and the change of resources' processing rates with *changeable(allocAndPR)* = {AllocationContext.resourceContainer, ProcessingResourceSpecification.processingRate}. This change type is divisible, because we can as well consider two different change types "allocation of components" *alloc* and "change of processing rate" *procRate* described above. Thus, to characterize the design space, we use only *alloc* and *procRate* and do not consider the change type *allocAndPR*.

The two change types *alloc* and *procRate* are indivisible change types with respect to performance, because they affect performance and they cannot be divided. In this case, they cannot be divided because they only contain one changeable metamodel element.

As an example for a indivisible change type with multiple changeable metamodel elements, consider the selection of components in the PCM as change type *compSelec*. An example is given for the Business Trip Management system (Figure 2.13, page 61) where we assume that an alternative component that can replace the BookingSystem component is available (cf. Figure 6.1, page 170). To replace the BookingSystem component by the alternative QuickBooking component in the PCM, several model elements have to be updated: First, the AssemblyContext.encapsulated-Component is changed to point to QuickBooking instead of Booking-System. Additionally, the connectors in the system have to be updated to refer to the provided and required roles of QuickBooking instead of BookingSystem. Thus, the changeable elements for this component selection are *changeable(compSelec)* = {AssemblyContext.encapsulated-Component, AssemblyConnector.providedRole, AssemblyConnector.requiredRole} (for simplicity, we do not discuss the delegation connectors, here, see Section C.1.1 for a complete description of this change type). This change type is indivisible, because changing only a subset of the changeable elements in a valid PCM model leads to either invalid models or does not affect quality. For example, changing only the encapsulated component of the AssemblyContext or only the connectors leads to invalid models.

For the automated improvement, we want to consider these as-"small"-as-possible, i.e. indivisible, change types like *compSelec*, *alloc* and *procRate*, to be able to define the design space as a space spanned by the combination of such change types.

To define indivisible change types, let $c_1 \circ \ldots \circ c_n$ denote a sequence of changes where change c_i, $1 < i \leq n$, is applied to the result model of change c_{i-1}, and c_1 is applied to the initial model. We then write $M \xrightarrow{c_1 \circ \ldots \circ c_n} M'$ to denote that the sequence of changes $c_1 \circ \ldots \circ c_n$ has the initial model M, which is at the same time the initial model of c_1, and the result model M', which is at the same time the the result model of c_n.

Definition 6.7 Indivisible Change Type

A change type ct for a software architecture metamodel MM is *indivisible* with respect to a quality attribute Q (written as *indivisible*(ct,MM,Q)) if all updated elements contribute to the quality property effect or ensure either validity or functional equivalence and if the change type is not separable into several change types. This means that the change type is functionally-equivalent and affects quality attribute Q (6.2), that there does not exist a subset ct' of the changeable metamodel elements that form a functionally-equivalent change type by itself with the same quality effects (6.3) and that there do not exist two subsets of changeable metamodel elements ct' and ct'' (6.4) that do not contain each other as subsets (6.5), that form functionally-equivalent change types (6.7), and that contain changes which can produce any change of ct when combined (6.6):

$$indivisible(ct,MM,Q) \tag{6.1}$$

$$:\Leftrightarrow funcEquiv(ct,MM) \land affects(ct,Q) \tag{6.2}$$

$$\land\, (\exists qc \in measures(Q) : \neg\exists ct' : changeable(ct') \subset changeable(ct)$$

$$\land funcEquiv(ct',MM)$$

$$\land \forall c = (M,M') \in ct\ \exists c' = (M,M'') \in ct' : qc(M') = qc(M'')) \tag{6.3}$$

$$\land\, (\neg\exists ct',ct'' : changeable(ct') \subset changeable(ct)$$

$$\land changeable(ct'') \subset changeable(ct) \tag{6.4}$$

$$\land changeable(ct') \not\subseteq changeable(ct'')$$

$$\land changeable(ct'') \not\subseteq changeable(ct') \tag{6.5}$$

$$\land \forall c \in ct : \exists c' \in ct', c'' \in ct'' : M \xrightarrow{c' \circ c''} M' \lor M \xrightarrow{c'' \circ c'} M' \tag{6.6}$$

$$\land funcEquiv(ct',MM) \land funcEquiv(ct'',MM)) \tag{6.7}$$

Minimal change types are the analogues to degree of freedoms, which will be defined in the next subsection. In our experience (cf. Chapter 7), indivisible change types mostly have only one metamodel element in the set of changeable elements *changeable*. Well-designed CBA metamodels should separate concerns and thus, changing one non-functional aspect of the system should result in changing only a single model element, which is instance of a single metamodel element. Changes that affect multiple model elements are thus often divisible into a sequence of smaller changes that are of indivisible change types (see most degrees of freedom for CBA in Chapter 7).

6.3.1.8. Primary Changeable Elements

Sometimes several model elements need to be changed to ensure the consistency of the model, however, although the changes describes just one conceptually indivisible change in the system. For example, if a component is replaced in the PCM, one needs to update the reference to the component in the system (AssemblyContext.encapsulatedComponent) but also the connectors connecting the component to the rest of the system, because they need to refer to the roles of the new component (i.e. they define which interfaces provided or required by the new component are connected to which other interfaces of the other components in the system). Still, the change of connectors are determined by the change of components and offer no further valid possibilities: For one change of the component in AssemblyContext.encapsulatedComponent, there is only one valid way how to change the connectors. Thus, we observe that there is one primary element to change in the set *changeable* in this case, while the changes of the other elements are a consequence of that primary element's change.

In both cases described above, if any two changes of an indivisible change type have the same new values in the instances of the primary changeable elements, then they are the same change (i.e. the other changed model elements get the same new values, too). We formally describe this condition with the predicate *hasPrimaryChangeable(ct)* in the following.

Let *updated(c,e)* denote the subset of changed model elements in *c* that are instances of metamodel element *e*.

$$updated(c,e) := \{m \mid m \in updated(c) \land m \text{ instanceOf } e \}$$

Recall that $v_m(M')$ denotes the value of the model element *m* in model *M*. Then, we define the predicate *hasPrimaryChangeable(ct)* as:

Definition 6.8 Change Type has Primary Changeable Element

A change type *ct* has a primary changeable element *primaryChangeable(ct)* $\in$ *changeable(ct)* if the new values of instances of *primaryChangeable(ct)* define the new values of all other changed metamodel elements. That means that if two changes have the same new values for all instances of *primaryChangeable(ct)*, then they also have the same values for all other instances of the other

$$hasPrimaryChangeable(ct)$$
$$:\Leftrightarrow \exists p \in changeable(ct) \; \forall c = (M,M') \in ct, c' = (N,N') :$$
$$updated(c,p) = updated(c',p) \rightarrow$$
$$($$
$$\forall e \in updated(c,p) : v_e(M') = v_e(N')$$
$$\rightarrow$$
$$\forall e' \in updated(c) \cup updated(c') : v_{e'}(M') = v_{e'}(N')$$
$$)$$

If there are several such *p* in *changeable(ct)*, fixing any of them to one value uniquely defines the values of the other. We refer to any fixed of these *p* as *primaryChangeable(ct)* in the following.

The predicate is trivially fulfilled for all change types that have a changeable elements set of size 1.

In general, there may be additional cases where several model element are changed without one being the primary element as defined above. As metamodels may have an arbitrary topology of meta-model elements, a metamodel could require to change any number of model elements in order to realize one conceptual change (e.g. the allocation of a component) that does affect the functionality of the system. However, we exclude such metamodels here and assume in the following that every indivisible change type has a primary changeable element, so $\forall ct : indivisible(ct,MM,Q) \rightarrow hasPrimaryChangeable(ct)$.

Then, the changes of an indivisible change type can always be described in terms of one primary changeable metamodel element. For the possible additional other changeable elements, the instance's new value can be unambiguously derived from the values of the primary element's instances. We assume that this condition is fulfilled in real-world metamodels, however, we cannot prove this assumption. Still, the assumption is not vital for the method presented in this work: To remove this assumption, the notion of degrees of freedom in the following could be extended to support virtual model elements that reflect the conceptual changes of an indivisible change type and are equipped with additional rules that map a change of this single virtual model element to a set of model elements.

6.3.1.9. Change Groups

For a given architecture model at hand that describes a concrete system, the instances of changeable metamodel elements need to be identified to determine the automatically achievable changes. To reason on the changes available for a given architecture model and on their combination, we can further group changes of a change type based on which model element (i.e. which instance of the primary changeable metamodel elements of ct) are changed. These groups are the analogues to degree of freedom instances defined in the next subsection. We call such groups *change groups*.

Definition 6.9 Change Group

A change group cg is a subset of an indivisible change type ct and contains changes that change the same primary model element in a model M. A change group cg defines the changed model element $primaryChanged(cg) \in M$ that is an instances of its change type ct's primary changeable element $primaryChangeable(ct)$. Then, we say that all changes $c \in ct$ that change $primaryChanged(cg)$ but that do not change other instances of $primaryChangeable(ct)$ are in the change group cg. Let ct be an indivisible change type with changeable elements $changeable(ct)$. Let $primaryChanged(cg) \in M$ be the model element to group the changes for, with $primaryChanged(cg)$ instanceOf $primaryChangeable(ct)$. Then, the change group cg is defined as

$$
cg := \left\{ c \left| \begin{array}{l} c \in ct \\ \land\, primaryChanged(cg) \in updated(c) \\ \land\, \neg(\exists ce \in updated(c) : \\ \quad (ce \neq primaryChanged(cg) \\ \quad\quad \land\, ce \text{ instanceOf } primaryChangeable(ct))) \end{array} \right. \right\}
$$

6.3.1.10. Summary

In this section, we define a set of terms and predicates that allow us to reason on changes of architectural models. In a simplified summary, the following terms have been defined:

Change: A change c is a pair of initial model M and result model M' written as $c = (M, M')$ or as $M \xmapsto{c} M'$.

Change with Conforming Models: A change has conforming models if both the source model M and the result model M' are valid instances of MM. This is written as $hasConformingModels(c, MM)$.

Valid Change: A change is valid if it has conforming models and if it does not change the functionality of the described CBA.

Change Type: A change type is a class of changes updating model elements that are instances of the same set of metamodel elements. Only changes with valid models are considered.

Functionally Equivalent Change Type: A change type ct for a software architecture metamodel MM is functionally equivalent (written as $funcEquiv(ct,MM)$), if all its changes do not change the functionality of their initial models.

Change Type that Affects a Quality Attribute: A change type ct for a software architecture metamodel MM potentially affects a quality attribute Q (written $affects(ct,Q)$) if there exists at least one change $c \in ct$ that changes the quality attribute as measured with any available metric.

Indivisible Change Type: A change type is indivisible if it is functionally-equivalent and affects a quality attribute and if no subsets of its changeable metamodel elements are change types of their own that can produce equivalent changes in combination.

Primary Changeable Element: The value of instances a primary changeable element of a change type ct define the new values of all other changed metamodel elements of ct.

Change Group: A change group is a subset of an indivisible change type. A change group contains changes that change the same primary model element.

Now, equipped with these terms and definitions, we proceed to the information required to automatically instantiate and explore the design space for automated quality improvement.

6.3.2. Degree of Freedom Definitions

In this section, we describe rules of how an automated method can produce changes that adhere to the three constraints C2, C3, and C4. To fulfil the forth constraint C1, each rule additionally contains the information which quality attribute is potentially affected.

For an automated improvement, it is impractical to enumerate all valid changes of a given system to be improved, because the number of valid changes is too large for reasonably large CBA models. Instead, to enable the use of a larger set of optimization techniques, such as metaheuristics, we need an explicit definition of all software architecture models reachable by any combination of valid changes—the design space—without enumerating all changes. In addition to the definition how to apply a single change, we need information of how multiple changes can be combined and what the results are.

As we cannot ask the human designer to evaluate each change whether its models are functionally equivalent, we have to restrict the design space to the changes of functional-equivalent change types, i.e. we include only changes for which we can decide the functional equivalence of their models on the metamodel level. Additionally, we exclude any changes that do not affect the quality attributes of interest. Thus, our design space is all software architecture models reachable by any combination of changes from indivisible change types.

We define this design space by creating an enriched description of indivisible change type that can automatically *produce* any candidate from the design space of a given architecture model. In the following, we discuss the required information to support this operationalization in an automated improvement process, resulting in the definition of degrees of freedom.

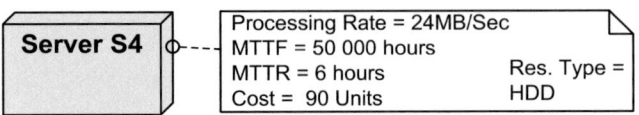

Figure 6.4.: An Additional Server with only Hard Disc Drive

6.3.2.1. Required Information for Enriched Change Type Description

As described above, from the metamodel and its static semantics, we can decide whether a change has conforming models by checking the resulting model of a change. To continue with the example, component Booking-System can be allocated from server S2 to server S3, because the resulting model is valid. However, component BookingSystem cannot be allocated to a storage server S4 shown in Figure 6.4, because the resulting model would be invalid as S4 does not offer the required CPU resource.

While we can determine whether a change is valid from the static semantics, we cannot readily determine the list of valid changes for a given software architecture model without applying the change and checking the resulting model for validity. This list, however, is required in an effective automated improvement process that can produce valid changes without checking the result models.

Thus, for effective automated improvement of software architecture models, we need an enriched description of an indivisible change type ct that contains all required information to produce its valid changes $c \in ct$. Such a description should only refer to the metamodel and should be independent of the concrete system to improve so that it has to be defined only once (in this work for the PCM) and can be reused for any improvement of model instances of that metamodel.

The required information, explained in detail in the following, is

1. which model elements in the architecture model at hand are changed together ($changeable(ct)$ and $primaryChangeable(ct)$),

2. rules that describe the new values that these model elements can take, thus describing all possible changes $c \in ct$, and

3. additional information for the interaction of changes.

Elements that are changed together   We identify the model elements that can be changed independently of the system at hand by defining their metamodel elements (*changeable elements*). One of these metamodel elements is identified as the *primary changeable element*.

Selection rules define which model elements can be selected to be changed. Often, all instances of the primary changeable element in the model can be changed, so this is the default selection rule. Sometimes, only a subset can be changed. In particular, if instances of multiple metamodel elements are changed together, the change of the primary changeable element's instance defines the choice of the other changeable element's instances. For example, in the PCM, if a component is replaced, the AssemblyContext is changed to instantiate the new component in this place in the system and the AssemblyConnectors connecting this Assembly-Context have to be updated accordingly. In such cases, we need rules that describe which instances of the other changeable elements must be changed to get a valid change.

Each instance of the primary changeable element selected by the rules is the primary changed element of a change group.

Rules that describe the values   *Value rules* describe the values changed model elements can take. Value rules describe the possible values of changed model elements statically and independent of other changes that are applied to the architecture model. A set of values is defined for the primary changed element. Additional rules define which values the other changeable elements instances take depending on the value of the primary changeable element's instance. In our example, such a rule needs to state

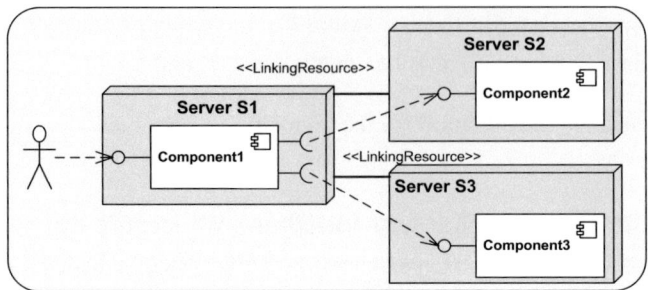

Figure 6.5.: Simple Example with Partially Connected Servers

that all servers offering the required resources are valid values to change the allocation of the component to.

Interaction of changes   In some cases, however, the set of allowed values for a model element depends on changes applied to other model elements of the architecture model, i.e. changes interact with each other. There are two types of change interactions: First, for two model elements that are changed, some combinations of values from their sets of possible values may produce invalid models. Second, changes may add or remove model elements and thus restrict the applicability of other changes.

Concerning the combination of values that lead to invalid models, let us look at an example. Consider the simplified system shown in Figure 6.5. Component1 communicates with Component2 and Component3, all of which are allocated to different servers. Server S1 is connected to server S2 with one LinkingResource and to server S3 with another one. In this case, we cannot allocate Component1 to server S3, because it could not communicate with Component2. We can, however, combine the three changes that (a) we allocate Component1 to server S3, (b) we allocate Component2 to server S1, and we (c) allocate Component3 to server S1, too. In this case, all possible values for the allocation of all three components are all three servers. To decide whether a specific combination of changes is valid, we have to additionally validate the result model of the changes and check the metamodel constraint that defines that communicating components have to be allocated to servers that are connected.

In general, we check a subset of the metamodel's constraints again to decide whether a result model is valid. If interactions are seldom compared to the number of independent changes, this does not strongly affect the effectiveness of the improvement. As a result, the enriched description should refer to those metamodel constraints that may be violated by produced candidate models, so that not all metamodel constraints have to be validated for every produced model. We refer to these metamodel constraints as *interaction constraints*.

Finally, the second type of change interaction is that changes may also add new model elements or remove elements. In that case, if one change is applied to a model and adds a new model element, new instances of primary changeable model elements may be available, or existing instances may be removed. Thus, we explicitly specify which type of model elements may be added or removed by the production rules. We add a list of *added elements* to the description that names the metamodel elements of which instances may be added or removed.

Table 6.3 summarizes the discussed information.

6.3.2.2. Degree of Freedom

An enriched description of an indivisible change type as discussed above can produce any valid changes of this change type. We call this enriched description a *degree of freedom*:

Information	Description
Changeable elements	The set of changeable metamodel elements *changeable*(*ct*) of the change type
Primary changeable element	The primary changeable metamodel element *primaryChangeable*(*ct*) ∈ *changeable*(*ct*) of the change type
Selection rules	Rules to select the model elements to change for each changeable metamodel element in *changeable*(*ct*)
Value rules	Rules to define the values that the selected model elements can take
Interaction constraints	A set of metamodel constraints that may be violated by the selection and value rules because of interactions with other changes
Added elements	A list of metamodel elements this change type may add instances of

Table 6.3.: Required Information to Produce Changes

Definition 6.10 Degree of Freedom (DoF)

A *degree of freedom* of a software architecture metamodel *MM* with respect to a quality property *Q* consists of information and rules to produce the changes of an indivisible change type *ct*. A DoF contains the following information to produce these changes:

- The set of changeable elements *changeable*(*ct*) ⊂ *MM*.
- The primary changeable element *primaryChangeable*(*ct*) ∈ *changeable*(*ct*).
- For each changeable element:
  - Selection rules (optional, the default is: all instances of *changeable*(*ct*) in the model at hand)
  - Values rules
- Interaction constraints (optional)
- Added elements (optional)

Examples for DoF are the DoF that produce the change types *alloc*, and *compSelec* in the PCM shown in table 6.4. The rules are described informally here, they are defined formally in Chapter 7 in Sections 7.3.1 and 7.2.1.

The DoFs of a metamodel need to be determined manually, because metamodels usually do not include a formal specification of functional equivalence of two models. If they contained such information, this information could be used to extract the possible DoF automatically. However, no metamodel to describe component-based software architecture is known today that offers such specification, so we do not further discuss this automated extraction and require that DoFs are manually determined by analysing the metamodel static semantics.

6.3.2.3. Degree of Freedom Instance

DoF allow to produce all changes of a change type for any software architecture model that is an instance of a CBA metamodel. For improving a concrete software architecture model at hand, however, we are only interested in changes that lead us to other models in the design space of this model. Thus, we are interested in a representation of these changes that relate to this given software architecture model.

An intermediate step of determining all possible changes for a given model at hand is to consider *degree of freedom instances* (DoFI). DoFI can be considered instances of a DoF for a given CBA model at hand: While a DoF defines generic change types such as "allocation of software components", a DoFI instantiates a change type in a model at hand and for example describes the "allocation of the BusinessTripMgmt component".

The resulting representation of the design space on the model level—as opposed to the metamodel level—additionally allows software architects to manually modify the design space as desired and thus adjust the automated improvement process to their needs (cf. Section 6.3.3).

199

DoF information	in component allocation DoF *alloc*	in component selection DoF *compSelec*
Changeable elements	*changeable(alloc)* = {AllocationContext.resourceContainer}	*changeable(compSelec)* = {AssemblyContext.encapsulatedComponent, AssemblyConnector.providedRole, AssemblyConnector.requiredRole}
Primary changeable element	*primaryChangeable(alloc)* = AllocationContext.resourceContainer	*primaryChangeable(compSelec)* = AssemblyContext.encapsulatedComponent
Selection rules	All instances of AllocationContext	All instances of AssemblyContext
Value rules	All servers that offer the resources that the reallocated component requires and that provide linking resources to all communication partners of the component.	All components that provide all interfaces of the component to be replaced and that require no more interfaces that the component to be replaced.
Interaction constraints	none	none
Added elements	none	If one of the new components to use is a composite component, new inner components are available.

Table 6.4.: Example DoF

200

In Section 6.3.1.9, we have observed that changes of a change type can be further grouped according to which model elements they affect in a concrete CBA model at hand (change groups). As these model elements can often be varied independently, we use this grouping on the enriched description level:

Definition 6.11 Degree of Freedom Instance (DoFI)

A *degree of freedom instance d* of a software architecture model *SM* with respect to DoF *G* with change type ct_G is a rule for producing changes of a change group cg_d. It consists of

- the primary model element to be changed (*primaryChanged(d)* = *primaryChanged(cg)*) which is an instance of its *G*'s primary changeable element *primaryChangeable(ct_G)* and

- the the possible values that this element can take (called *design option set* and written as the set *designOptions(d)*) determined by the DoF's value rules for these elements.

The values for the other changeable elements *changeable(ct_G)* can be derived with *G*'s value rules.

With this definition, a DoFI can produce all changes of a change group. Moreover, the DoFI may produce *more* changes than contained in the associated change group, by producing changes that are not valid.

As an example, consider again the simple system with Component1, Component2, and Component3 shown in Figure 6.5. The relevant DoFI for our example here is the allocation of Component1 with the possible values {S1, S2, S3}. This DoFI can produce the change that we allocate Component1 to server S3. The resulting model is invalid, because the components could not communicate with each other. Thus, only when excluding the invalid changes from the set of produced candidate models with the interaction constraints, the set of produced changes equals the set of changes in the change group. Still, there changes where Component1 can be allocated to server S3, e.g. if all other components are also allocated to that server, so S3 is in the design option set of the DoFI.

Thus, the set of changes produced by a DoFI needs to be additionally restricted by the interaction constraints of its DoF to ensure that only valid changes are produced. Let the predicate *interaction*(M,G) denote that a model M fulfils the interaction constraints of the DoF G with change type ct, let *changeGroup*(cg) denote that cg is a change group, and let *changes*(d) denote the changes produced by a DoFI d. Then, we can say that when excluding the invalid changes from the set of produced candidate models with the interaction constraints, the set of produced changes equals the set of changes in a change group of ct:

$$\exists cg \subset ct : changeGroup(cg)$$
$$\wedge\, cg = \{c = (M,M') \in changes(d)\,|\,interaction(M',G)\,\}$$

Then, defining one DoFI for each model element that is instance of the DoF's changeable element is equivalent to the DoF definition itself. We show this property in the following.

6.3.2.4. DoFIs represent DoF

With a combination of changes produced by degree of freedom instances, all changes of the respective DoF in a model at hand can be produced.

Theorem 6.1. *For a model M and an indivisible change type ct produced by DoF G, a set of DoFI D can be defined which–in combination–produces an equivalent sequence of changes for all changes of ct. Not all DoFI are necessarily instantiated on M directly, they may as well be instantiated in an intermediate model after a new model element has been added.*

Proof. For all changes $c = (M_0, M') \in ct$, a sequence of changes $c_1 \circ ... \circ c_n$ can be found where each c_j is produced by a DoFI and the sequence of changes is equivalent to the change c, i.e. $M_0 \xrightarrow{c_1 \circ ... \circ c_n} M'$.

Let P be the set of instances of the primary changeable element:

$$P = \{ p \,|\, e \in M_0 \wedge e \text{ instanceOf } primaryChangeable(ct) \}$$

We show that we can find DoFIs that can produce a set of changes (not necessarily valid ones) that are equivalent to c when applied in sequence.

Let the index set $I = \{1, ..., |P|\} \subset \mathbb{N}$ be an index set that orders the primary changeable element's instances P in any order. Let $i \in I$. Let d_i denote the $d \in D$ that changes $p_i \in P$, so that $primaryChanged(d_i) = p_i$.

Then, each d_i can produce one change c_i that assigns the value of p_i in the result model M' to p_i as follows. For this, let $N(p \leftarrow v)$ denote the result model of a change c that changes a model N by assigning the value v to the primary model element p. In c, possibly other non-primary model elements are changed (as they are unambiguously defined by the value of p, we can omit them here). Additionally, let $M_i, 0 < i \leq |I|$ denote the result model of c_i, so for example, $c_1 = (M_0, M_1)$. Then, we produce the changes as follows:

For $1 < i \leq |I|$ (if any) we produce $c_i = (M_{i-1}, M_i)$ with $M_i := M_{i-1}(p_i \leftarrow v_{p_i}(M'))$. There is such a c_i because the value $v_{p_i}(M')$ is in the set of all possible values produced by the DoF G (otherwise c itself could not have used it). c_i is not necessarily a valid change. If c_i adds a new model element (or several ones) to the model M_{i-1} which is instance of $primaryChangeable(ct)$, we collect this set of new model elements in a new set A_i.

$$A_i = \{ e \,|\, e \in M_i M_{i-1} \wedge e \text{ instanceOf } primaryChangeable(ct) \}$$

After a pass through all instances of the primary changeable element in M, we have collected more instances of the primary changeable element in the sets A_i if changes have added model elements of that type. Thus, we need to repeat the following assignments until all instances have been handled. Because models are finite, this repetition always stops. Let $A :=$ $\bigcup_{1 \leq j \leq |I|} A_j$ be the set of collected elements.

Let n be the number of changes we have created to far. M_n is the resulting model of the last change. Then, with $1 \leq k \leq |A|$ we create additional changes $c_{n+1}, ..., c_{n+|A|}$ as $c_{n+k} = (M_{n+k}, M_{n+k}(a_k \leftarrow v_{a_k}(M')))$. We collect possible additional added elements as

$$A_{n+k} = \{e \,|\, e \in M_{n+k} M_{n+k-1} \wedge e \text{ instanceOf } primaryChangeable(ct)\}$$

If the union $A := \bigcup_{1 \leq k \leq |A|} A_{n+k}$ is not empty after this pass, we repeat this paragraph with the new A.

As a result, the last change c_n produces the model $M_n = M'$, because all p_i have the new value $v_{p_i}(M')$ and all model elements a from the set $A_k, 1 < k \leq n$ have the new value $v_a(M')$. Thus, the sequence of changes $c_1 \circ ... \circ c_n$ is equivalent to the change c, because its changes produce the same model M' as a result.

$\square$

6.3.2.5. Result

We can apply changes produced by different DoFIs independently and thus, the combination of the DoFIs defines the design space. Within a DoFI, the changes are mutually exclusive and cannot be combined.

Then, in automated software architecture improvement, a model is varied automatically by choosing a DoFI d and varying its changed model element $changed(d)$. The model element is varied by choosing a new value for this model element from the design option set. The resulting model may be invalid which can be detected by the interaction constraints. All so created models that fulfil the interaction constraints then also fulfil the constraints C2, C3 and C4.

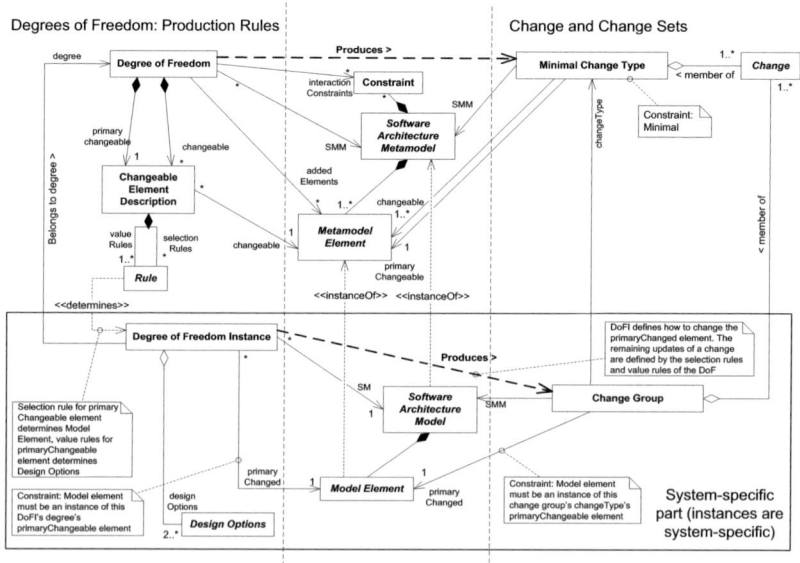

Figure 6.6.: Degree of Freedom and Change Concepts

Additionally, we can combine changes by using several DoFI at once. In that case, we can change the changed model elements of each DoFI independently by assigning them values from the respective design option set. Thus, based on a starting architecture model, all architecture models that are reachable by a combination of changes are defined. We discuss the resulting design space of possible architecture models in more detail in Section 6.4.

Figure 6.6 shows an overview of the concepts introduced in this section and the previous section. It does not show all concepts and constraints and thus does not serve as a definition itself, but rather to summarize the concepts.

Note that due to possible interactions of changes, DoF definitions may depend on each other. If a new DoF is introduced in a given set of DoF, the value rules and the interaction constraint of the DoF may have to be updated to account for possible conflicts.

Even if DoFs are only formally defined in relation to a metamodel, we describe DoFs that are common for component-based software architecture metamodels in general in Chapter 7. We describe these general DoF of CBA informally by referring to the properties of CBA (Section 2.1). Additionally, we define these DoF formally for the PCM as an example if appropriate. These general descriptions of DoF can be applied to other metamodels as well if the metamodel supports the concepts. In that case, our general description gives an orientation how to formally define the DoFs.

For a concrete system at hand, additional DoFI to be considered in the design space can also be defined ad hoc. To do so, DoF is described on the metamodel level like other DoF, defining value rules for the primary element. Then, the DoFI can be either instantiated automatically, or manually for the system at hand. The manual instantiation has the advantage that no selection rules are needed for the primary model element. Additionally, if the set of changeable elements contains more elements than just the primary one, the ad-hoc DoFI needs to specify the selection rules and value rules for the additional elements. Interaction rules and added elements need to be added if required. For system-specific degrees of freedom, a simpler modelling language could be devised as well, which allows the software architect to directly annotate a model element with design options. Such a language is subject to future work.

6.3.3. Degrees of Freedom in EMOF

In the previous sections, we have defined DoF and DoFI in general based on our definitions of changes of CBA models. This definition is independent of any used CBA metamodel or meta-metamodel.

What changes affect quality attributes and can be identified to be functionally equivalent on the metamodel level depends on the concrete CBA metamodel. Thus, DoFs need to be specified manually for each CBA metamodel. In this section, we provide a language to specify DoF and DoFI for CBA metamodels specified in EMOF. In addition to the description, we give an illustrative example. Using this language, experts for a given CBA metamodel can define the DoF for this metamodel. For the PCM, we define the DoF using this language in Chapter 7. The language is defined in form of a metamodel defined using EMOF and is called *DoF metamodel* in the following.

The selection rules and values rules are defined as OCL queries in our DoF metamodel. The OCL queries must be OCL expressions with one or several context definitions, as defined in the OCL specification (Object Management Group (OMG), 2006b, p.167) with the grammar rule 12.12.1 packageDeclarationCS.

Example: To give an example for a degree of freedom of a EMOF-based metamodel, consider the simplified metamodel for describing component allocation in Figure 6.7. The metamodel only describes allocation as a mapping from components (from a repository) to servers (from a resource environment). A valid model must map all components from the repository to servers, i.e. there must be a mapping for each component. For the sake of illustration, let us additionally assume that there are components that can only be executed on servers with a single core. These components have the property Component.singleThreaded set to true (see OCL constraint in the figure).

A possible degree of freedom (DoF-A) is the allocation of components. A second DoF (DoF-B) is to vary the number of cores of a server.

(Primary) Changeable Elements: The changeable elements *changeable*(g) are the set of elements of the metamodel whose instances can be changed. *changeable*(g) is a set of Properties of the

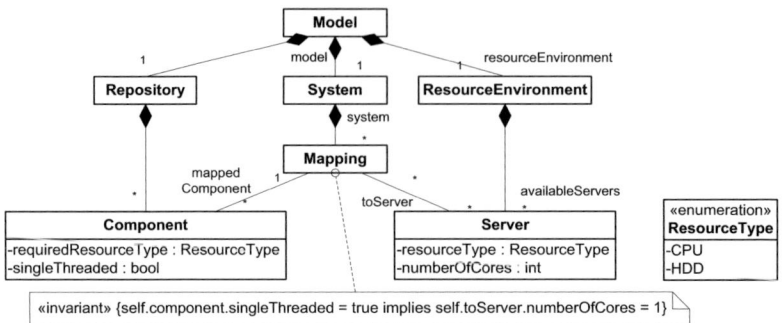

Figure 6.7.: Simple Example Metamodel Describing Allocation to Illustrate DoFs.

metamodel *MM*. Each property $p_i \in changeable(g)$ is member of a metamodel Class that we call the the changeable container of p_i *changeableContainer*(p_i) (cf. figure 2.6 in Section 2.3.2). One of the properties p_i is the primary changeable element, usually written as the first one.

For DoF-A, the Property Mapping.toServer has to be changed to change the allocation of a component. Thus, *changeable*(*DoF-A*) = {Mapping.toServer}. For DoF-B, the changed Property is Server-.numberOfCores: *changeable*(*DoF-B*) = {Server.numberOfCores}.

Selection Rules: Properties cannot be directly selected in models based on EMOF. Thus, we select the changeable container *changeable-Container*(p_i). The default selection rule selects all instances of *changeableContainer*(p_i). The DoF may specify more specific rules that constrain which instances of *changeableContainer*(p_i) can be selected. For each changeable element, this can be expressed by an OCL query *selectionRule*(p_i) selecting the instances of this Property's class *changeableContainer*(p_i). This query defines which instances of *changeableContainer*(p_i) are possible, either statically or based on another selected instance of $C_j, j < i$. In the latter case, the query is defined in the OCL context of the selected instance of C_j.

To avoid cycles, only the values of preceding Properties $p_j, j < i$ may be referenced. The selection rules for the primary element can be defined in any context. They are executed for each instance of the metamodel element in whose context they are defined and the union of the results is the set of matching model elements.

No selection rules are required for DoF-A and DoF-B; any instances of Mapping.toServer and Server.numberOfCores: can be changed:

$$selectionRule(Mapping.toServer)$$
$$= selectionRule(Server.numberOfCores) = \emptyset$$

Value Rules: For each p_i, rules describe the set of all potential new values that p_i may take in combination with any other change of the other change types for the metamodel at hand. For p_i, the description of all potential new values is an OCL query $valueRule(p_i)$ which returns a range R of possible values for Properties of Type Data-Type, or a set of model elements for Properties of Type Class. The value rules are defined in the context of the selected instance of p_i's container class.

The value rules may also refer to other changeable elements $p_j, j < i$. The restriction $j < i$ here ensures that the allowed values can be determined by one pass through all Properties. While the new values of Properties of Type Class can always be defined generically on the metamodel level, the values for Properties of Type DataType may depend on the model instance at hand. Then, a generic range is given on the metamodel level, which can be restricted on the model instance level.

In our example, a component can be mapped to all modelled servers from the resource environment, with the restriction that the server has to have a resourceType with the same value as the component's requiredResoureType. This description of possible values can be expressed with the following OCL query *valueRule(Mapping.toServer)* to select the allowed value for a Mapping.toServer Property:

```
context Mapping
def : getAvailableServers : Set ( Server ) =
self.system.model.resourceEnvironment.availableServers
  ->select(resourceType
    = self.mappedComponent.requiredResourceType)
```

For DoF-B, because Server.numberOfCores is a Property whose Type is a DataType, we need to give a range for the possible values. For the degree of freedom on the metamodel level, any number of cores could be possible, so the *valueRule(Server.numberOfCores)* defines a range $R^B = \mathbb{N}_+$. This range can be restricted later for a concrete system at hand (cf. Section 6.4.1), because no servers with e.g. a million cores exists nowadays.

Interaction Constraints: The DoF refers to the metamodel constraints that may be violated by this DoF as *interactionConstraints(g)*. In the example, DoF-A and DoF-B interact, because certain combination of values of their design option sets are invalid. A single threaded component must not be allocated to a server with multiple cores. Thus, the invariant shown in Figure 6.7 is referenced here for both DoF.

Added elements: The added elements are a set of metamodel elements of which this DoF may add new instances or remove instances. In this example, no elements are added.

Figure 6.8 shows the resulting metamodel for degrees of freedom in EMOF.

In addition to the DoF, the degree of freedom instances can also be characterized in more detail for metamodels specified in EMOF. Figure 6.9 shows the DoFI metamodel in EMOF.

All degrees of freedom instances *d* (class DegreeOfFreedom) refer to one model element that is the primary changeable element *primaryChanged(d)*.

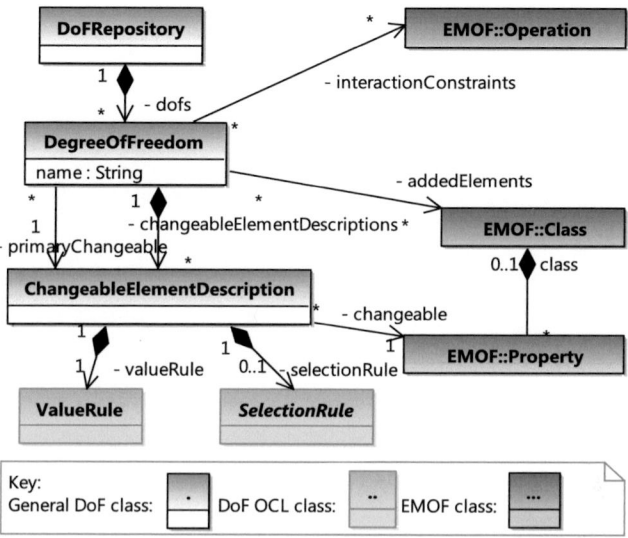

Figure 6.8.: Degrees of Freedom in EMOF

The Property that is defined in the DoF cannot be directly referenced in MOF, thus we usually refer to the model element containing the Property. Which Property is actually updated when using a degree of freedom instance needs to be separately defined. If the Property's multiplicity is larger than one, and if we want to separately vary each of the elements referenced by the Property, however, referencing the containing model element is not enough to uniquely identify the changed element. If the Property is a composition[1], we can also refer to the referenced model element or to the model element referenced by the Property. Otherwise, we need additional information to identify the changed element for the list of elements of the Property.

---

[1]A composition Property in EMOF has the attribute isComposite set to true. It defines a composition in the UML sense, i.e. the referenced model element only belongs to this one instance of the Property.

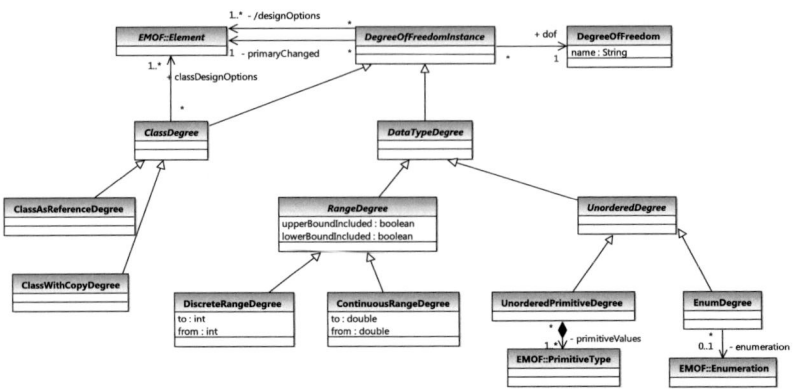

Figure 6.9.: Degree of Freedom Instance Metamodel for Models in EMOF

The degrees' design option sets is defined differently depending on the MOF Type of the possible values and is reflected by the different subclasses of DegreeOfFreedom. Leftmost, the ClassDegree models values for changeable Properties of Class: A set of model elements (here Entities) is referenced by a ClassDegree instance and form the design option set.

The other subclass of DegreeOfFreedom DataTypeDegree models degrees for Properties of Type DataType. Here, RangeDegree models design option sets that are an interval of a strictly and totally ordered DataType, specified using interval boundaries. Two example subclasses are shown by DiscreteRangeDegree (for natural numbers) and ContinuousRangeDegree (for real numbers). The RangeDegrees could be sub-classed for additional strictly and totally ordered DataType, or to allow to define several intervals of strictly and totally ordered DataType, if required.

The UnorderedDegree models unordered design option sets of a specified DataType. Here, subclasses either list a set of primitive type values or refer to an enumeration in the CBA metamodel.

To define degrees of freedom for CBA metamodels defined in other meta-metamodelling languages than EMOF or Ecore, it may be advisable to redefine the DoF metamodel for these meta-metamodelling languages. We expect this conversion to be straightforward. The model described here has also been published by A. Koziolek and Reussner, 2011.

6.4. Design Space

This section describes how the design space for a system at hand can be defined using DoF and DoFI as well as potential custom constraints. Figure 6.10 shows an informal outline of the concepts discussed in this section. We first discuss in more detail how DoFI can be derived for a particular architecture based on the DoF (Section 6.4.1). Then, we introduce our definition of the design space based on the system at hand and the DoFI (Section 6.4.2). The design space can be constrained by restrictions from the DoF and manual constraints (Section 6.4.3). Finally, we conclude this section with some additional remarks on details of the problem representation (Section 6.4.4.

6.4.1. Derive Degree of Freedom Instances for a System

The DoFI can be automatically instantiated for a given architecture model at hand. Then, before the DoFI are used in an automated improvement the software architect can review the determined DoFI and adjust them.

The input to automated instantiation of the DoFI is a architecture model which we denote here as a set of model elements M and a set of DoF, denoted G. The DoFI are instantiated by applying the selection rules of the DoF to determine the primary changed elements and by applying the value rules to determine the design option sets. Not all DoFI are instantiated in the initial model M: If a DoFI d adds elements, additional DoFIs $d_1, ..., d_n$ may be instantiated in intermediate models, i.e. d *opens up* new DoFIs. We can ignore that other DoFIs $d'_1, ..., d'_n$ may become irrelevant for an intermediate model if a model element is removed by a DoFI d' here. In both cases, the

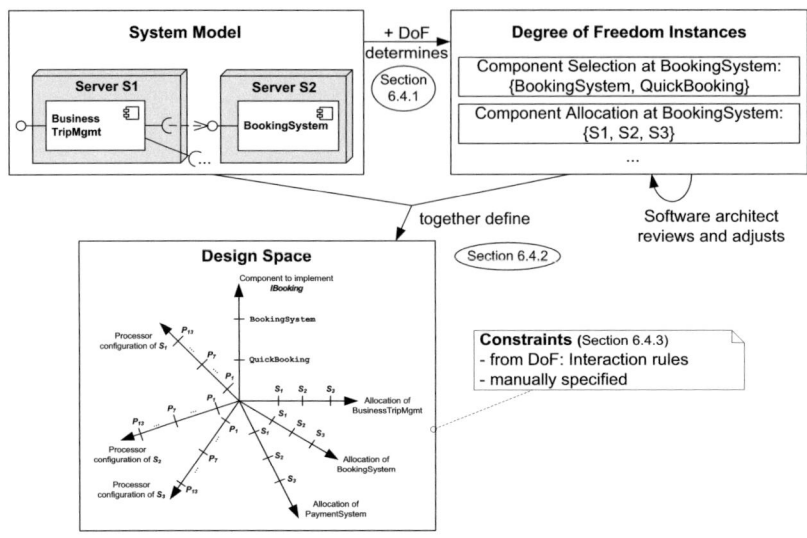

Figure 6.10.: Outline of Design Space Section (Section 6.4)

DoFIs $d_1,...,d_n$ and $d'_1,...,d'_n$ *depend* on d and d', respectively, because they have only effect if d or d', respectively, have a certain value.

The DoFI are instantiated for a architecture model at hand with the algorithm shown in Java-like pseudo code below. It uses the DoF metamodel in EMOF described in Section 6.3.3. The function query(q, M) evaluates a OCL query q in all matching instances[2] in the set of model elements M. The function getAllInstancesOf(M,MC) retrieves all instances of the meta class MC in the set of model elements M. The statement $M(p \leftarrow v)$ for a model M, an instance of a property p and a value v denotes the model transformation that property instance p is assigned the new value v. As a side remark, note when implementing this algorithm, a property instance

---

[2]Matching instances are instances of the metamodel element that is the OCL context of the selection rule, see Section 6.3.3. For example, the selection rule for the primary changeable element ProcessingResources of the Resource Selection Degree of Freedom is defined in context of an ResourceEnvironment, so it is executed for all resource environment model elements in the architecture model.

would be technically referred to by the pair metamodel property and instance of the container class.

For the sake of readability of the algorithm below, we assume that G is ordered so that if a DoF g_1 opens up new degrees of DoF g_2, g_1 precedes g_2 in G. As there are no circular dependencies in the currently considered DoF, this is sufficient. If a DoF could circularly open up new degrees of freedom of other types, then one has to repeat the algorithm until no new model elements are added.

```
1   instantiateDoFI(
2     Set M /* CBA model */,
3     Set G /* set of DoF*/ ){
4
5   // output: set of DoFI:
6   Set determinedDoFIs = new Set();
7
8   // Variable to store new model elements that are created by a DoF
9   Set addedModelElements = new Set();
10
11  for (g in G) {
12
13    Set potentialPrimaryElements; //potential primary changed elements
14
15    // select all instances of primary changeable element
16    if (g.primaryChangeable.selectionRule != null) {
17     potentialPrimaryElements
18       = query(g.primaryChangeable.selectionRule, M);
19     potentialPrimaryElements.add(query(g.primaryChangeable.selectionRule,
20       addedModelElements));
21    } else { // select all instances in model
22     potentialPrimaryElements = getAllInstancesOf(M, g.primaryChangeable
23       .changeable.class);
24     potentialPrimaryElements.add(getAllInstancesOf(
25       addedModelInstances,(g.primaryChangeable
26         .changeable.class));
27    } // end else
28
29    while (potentialPrimaryElements.size() != 0){
30
31      Set justAddedModelElements = new Set();
32
33      for (primaryElement in potentialPrimaryElements){
34
```

```
35      Set  values  =  query (g. primaryChangeable . valueRule , primaryElement );
36
37      if  ( values . size () > 1) {
38        DoFI  d = new  DoFI ();
39        d. primaryChanged  =  primaryElement ;
40        d. designOptions  =  values ;
41        determinedDoFIs . add (d );
42
43        // if g opens up new DoFI because of additions ,
44        // apply d to check for new model elements
45        if  (g. addedElements . size > 0){
46          for  (v in d. designOptions ){
47            Model  newM = M(d. primaryChanged <- v );
48            justAddedModelElements . add ( additionalElements (newM,M ));
49          } // end for
50        } // end if
51      } // end if
52    } // end for
53
54    potentialPrimaryElements . clear ();
55
56    // check if g opened up new instances of itself
57    // and if yes , instantiate them .
58    if  (justAddedModelElements . size ()>0){
59      // apply g itself again .
60      if  (g. primaryChangeable . selectionRule != null ) {
61        potentialPrimaryElements . add (
62          query (g. primaryChangeable . selectionRule , justAddedModelElements ));
63      } else {
64        potentialPrimaryElements . add ( getAllInstancesOf (
65          justAddedModelElements , g. primaryChangeable ));
66      } // end if
67    } // end if
68
69    addedModelElements . add (justAddedModelElements );
70
71  } // end while
72  } // end for g in G
73  return  determinedDoFIs ;
74  }
```

For each DoF *g*, we traverse the architecture model *M* and collect all instances of primary changeable element as follows. If there is a selection rule
for the primary changeable element, it is executed on all model instances
for which the selection rule is defined and on model elements opened up by

previous DoF (stored in the list addedModelElements). If there is no selection rule for the primary changeable element, all instances of the primary changeable element are selected.

Then, for each determined potential primary changeable element, the value rule is executed to determine all possible values. If the set of possible values is larger than one, a new DoFI is instantiated.

If the DoF g opens up new DoFIs because of added model elements, these model elements are added to the list addedModelElements so that later DoF can check them for instantiating DoFI, too. Additionally, the selection rule of the current DoF is repeated to find possible additional instantiations. The filled set of DoFI is returned at the end.

We assume here that the number of DoFI is finite, i.e. that the finite initial set of DoFI for the initial model only (transitively) opens up a finite number of new DoFI. Otherwise, the algorithm below does not terminate. For the currently considered DoF (cf. Chapter 7), the number of added DoFI is finite because new degrees are only opened up for component selection degrees and the number of available components is finite. We do not expect that meaningful DoF will produce an infinite set of DoFI for a given model. Still, we cannot exclude this case in general. To account for possibly infinite number of potentially opened DoFIs, a counter could be introduced in the algorithm below to stop instantiation after a maximum number of DoFIs is reached.

After determining all DoFI, software architects can review the DoFI. They may want to define more specific subsets of allowed values for primitive types, or to exclude values that are not wanted from design option set. Additionally, they can consider to specify and add system-specific degrees of freedom (see Section 6.3.2).

For the degrees of freedom that define a general value range such as the natural numbers, we can as well define a more restricted, system-specific set of values for a DoF before determining the DoFI. For example, the capacity of all passive resources could be restricted to values between 2 and 25 for a given system. Thus, the software architect does not need to specify the range later manually for each DoFI.

Note that the values of the other, non-primary changeable elements are not relevant for determining the design space, thus they are not considered here.

In the example in Section 6.2, the DoF to consider are the allocation of components to servers, the choice of processors, and the selection of a component type for the BookingSystem component (these degrees of freedom are formally defined for the PCM in Chapter 7). The *Allocation Degree* is instantiated once per component allocation instance. The changed element is AllocationContext.resourceContainer of the component allocation instance.

For the *Resource Selection degree*, let us assume that there is a resource repository which defines the thirteen possible processors $P_1, ..., P_{13}$. Then, the Resource Selection Degree is instantiated once per server[3]. The changed element is the ResourceContainer.activeResourceSpecifications of the respective server. The ProcessingResourceSpecification that contains the specification for the resource type for CPU is varied. Finally, the Component Selection degree is instantiated just once, because for the other components instances, no alternatives are available (thus, the design option sets would have size one). The changed element is the AssemblyContext.encapsulatedComponent of the component instance of BookingSystem.

Table 6.5 shows the DoFI for the example model. The information of the table is the same as the information of table 6.1 previously, but now in the format of DoFI, naming the primary changed element. As described before, the design space contains 118638 architecture candidate models.

---

[3]Once per server because we only consider the CPU here it would be additionally instantiated per server for each additional resource type such as hard disc drive, if these were considered

Degree of freedom	Degree of freedom instance	
	Primary Changed Element of the DoFI	Design option set of the DoFI
Allocation	AllocationContext.resourceContainer of BusinessTripMgmt	{S1, S2, S3}
	AllocationContext.resourceContainer of BookingSystem	{S1, S2, S3}
	AllocationContext.resourceContainer of PaymentSystem	{S1, S2, S3}
Resource Selection	ResourceContainer.activeResource-Specifications of Server$_1$ for CPU	$\{P_1, ..., P_{13}\}$
	ResourceContainer.activeResource-Specifications of Server$_2$ for CPU	$\{P_1, ..., P_{13}\}$
	ResourceContainer.activeResource-Specifications of Server$_3$ for CPU	$\{P_1, ..., P_{13}\}$
Component Selection	AssemblyContext.encapsulated-Component for IBooking	{Booking-System, QuickBooking}

Table 6.5.: DoFI Definitions for the Example Model

6.4.2. Unconstrained Design Space

The degrees of freedom instantiated for a given architecture model span the design space which can be searched by automated improvement methods. Note that the term design space here does not refer to the full design space of the software architecture with all decisions that are made during the course of designing it, but that it only refers to the decisions that can be explored in an automated improvement method. Although this definition of the term design space may be misinterpreted to mean all decisions related to the system design, we use this term because it has been established in related domains, such as the design space exploration for embedded systems.

The design space is the set of all software architecture candidate models produced by the changes types of a selected set of DoF for a given system at hand. Let M be a architecture model and G the set of DoF to consider.

Let D denote the set of DoFI instantiated in M, either directly after automated derivation or after the review and possible adjustment of the software architect.

Definition 6.12 Architectural Candidate Model

An *architectural candidate model* (or just *candidate model*) is a software model M' that is a result of applying a sequence of changes produced by a set of DoFI D to an initial architecture model M. The DoFI in D do not have to be instantiated on M directly, they may be instantiated on intermediate models, too. The predicate *candidateModel(M',M,D)* states that a software model M' is an architectural candidate model for an initial model M and a set of DoFI D:

$$candidateModel(M',M,D) :\Leftrightarrow$$
$$\exists c_1,...,c_n \in \{c \mid c \in changes(d), d \in D\} : M \xrightarrow{c_1 \circ ... \circ c_n} M'$$

As DoFI may produce invalid changes, an architectural candidate model is not necessarily conforming to the metamodel. Recall that $M \blacktriangleleft MM$ expresses that a candidate model M conforms to the metamodel MM (cf. Section 2.3.1).

The initial architecture model itself is an architectural candidate model, too, "produced" by applying the empty sequence. The set of architectural candidate models for a set of DoFI D and an initial architecture model M is called the unconstrained design space:

Definition 6.13 Unconstrained Design Space

The *unconstrained design space* for a set of DoFI D and an initial architecture model M is the set of architectural candidate models of D and M. We denote the unconstrained design space by

$$\mathscr{D}_{M,D} = \{M' \,|\, candidateModel(M',M,D)\,\}$$

.

Note that the unconstrained design space includes invalid candidate models, too.

An architectural candidate model can be identified by a vector of values that the primary changed elements of the DoFI in D take, because there is only one candidate model for each value assignment for the primary changed elements. We call such a vector a *candidate vector*. Candidate vectors correspond to decision vectors (cf. Section 3.1), and thus the set of all candidate vectors is the *decision space*:

Definition 6.14 Decision Space and candidate vector

The *decision space* $\mathscr{O}_{M,D}$ for a set of DoFI D and an initial architecture model M is the Cartesian product of the design option sets of the DoFI:

$$\mathscr{O}_{M,D} := designOptions(d_1) \times \ldots \times designOptions(d_{|D|})$$

A *candidate vector* or decision vector is a vector $x \in \mathscr{O}_{M,D}$.

In the following, we show that the decision space represents the design space, because each candidate model in $\mathscr{D}_{M,D}$ can be represented by a candidate vector $x \in \mathscr{O}_{M,D}$. To show this, we show two aspects:

- Each candidate vector $x \in \mathscr{O}_{M,D}$ uniquely represents a candidate model $a \in \mathscr{D}_{M,D}$, i.e. there is a function that maps each $x \in \mathscr{O}_{M,D}$ to one unique candidate model in $\mathscr{D}_{M,D}$.

- Every candidate model in $\mathscr{D}_{M,D}$ can be represented by a candidate vector $x \in \mathscr{O}_{M,D}$, i.e. this function is surjective.

Theorem 6.2. *Each $x \in \mathscr{O}_{M,D}$ represents one candidate model $a \in \mathscr{D}_{M,D}$. This means we can define a function from $\mathscr{O}_{M,D}$ to $\mathscr{D}_{M,D}$.*

Proof. We can define the following function from a candidate vector x in the decision space $\mathscr{O}_{M,D}$ to a software architecture candidate model in the design space $\mathscr{D}_{M,D}$:

$$T_{M,D} : \mathscr{O}_{M,D} \to \mathscr{D}_{M,D}$$

with

$$(v_1, ..., v_{|D|}) \mapsto$$
$$M(primaryChanged(d_1) \leftarrow v_1, ..., primaryChanged(d_{|D|}) \leftarrow v_{|D|})$$

We call T the *candidate transformation function.* Because the assignment of a value to a primary changed element $designOptions(d)$ describes a unique change, there is only one possible result model $M(designOptions(d_1) \leftarrow v_1, ..., designOptions(d_{|D|})$. Thus, $T_{M,D}$ is a function and every candidate vector represents one candidate model. □

T can be defined generically for a meta-metamodel used to described CBA metamodels. For example, an implementation of T for Java and EMF models is shown in Appendix B.3.

Next, we show that the function is surjective, i.e. that every architectural candidate model a can be produced by a vector from $\mathscr{O}_{M,D}$ with this function.

Theorem 6.3. *The function $T_{M,D}$ is surjective, i.e. every architectural candidate model can be produced by a vector from $\mathscr{O}_{M,D}$:*

$$\forall a \in \mathscr{D}_{M,D} : \exists x \in \mathscr{O}_{M,D} :$$
$$a = M(designOptions(d_1) \leftarrow v_1, ..., designOptions(d_{|D|}) \leftarrow v_{|D|})$$

The idea is that for each $d \in D$ that produced one of the changes of a, the value to which the primary changed element of d has been changed is used in the vector. For each $d' \in D$ that does not produce one of the changes of a, the value of the initial model is used. The complete proof of $T_{M,D}$ being surjective is given in the appendix B.2.

Because $T_{M,D}$ is is a function and is surjective, an additional representation of the unconstrained design space is

$$\mathscr{D}_{M,D} = \{a \,|\, \exists x \in \mathscr{O}_{M,D} : a = T_{M,D}(x)\}.$$

In our example from Section 6.2, the initial candidate model can be expressed as $(S1, S2, S3, P_4, P_5, P_3, \texttt{BookingSystem})$ with the ordering of degrees of freedom as given in Table 6.1.

Note that some of the candidate vectors in $\mathscr{O}_{M,D}$ may map to the same architectural candidate model, because some of the degree of freedom have no effect if they are opened up only for certain values of the other degrees. For example, the allocation of the inner components of a PCM subsystem are only relevant if the subsystem is used in the system (i.e. if there is not a Subsystem Selection Degree for it that has selected a different Subsystem in the current candidate model). Thus, two vectors in the design option space $\mathscr{O}_{M_e,D_e}$ for this example model M_e with example degrees D_e map to the same candidate model if their subsystem selection degree selects subsystem A and they are equal in all values except for the allocation of the inner components of a subsystem B that is an alternative for A. As a result, the function $T_{M,D}$ is not injective in general.

In addition, some of the architectural candidate models may be equivalent in terms of quality properties: They have the same quality properties, even though they are not identical. For example, the processing speed of a hardware node is only relevant if components are actually deployed to it. Otherwise, the configuration of that server has no effect on the quality attributes.

Not all candidate models in the unconstrained design space are valid candidate models. In the next subsection, we discuss how to constrain the set

$\mathscr{D}_{M,D}$ to get a representation of the feasible design space that only contains candidate models which are feasible options to improve the architecture.

6.4.3. Constraints

As discussed in the previous sections, some candidate models produced by the degree of freedoms are not valid instances of the metamodel. To describe the feasible design space for the automated improvement, we have to exclude the invalid candidate models from the unconstrained design space. One way of filtering out the invalid candidate models is to check every candidate model for conformance to the metamodel. However, the metamodel may contain many constraints, and only a few of them may be violated by our produced candidate models. For a more efficient filtering the design space, we make use of the interaction constraints which define additional conditions for the changed elements of a DoF (e.g. as described for the PCM and component allocation in presence of partially connected servers in Section 6.3.2.1, with an example model in Figure 6.5, page 196). For the PCM, most DoF do not have any interaction constraints and very few checks must be made. For metamodels with a lot of interaction constraints, it may be more efficient to check the validity of models with the metamodel constraints directly.

In addition to these interaction constraints derived from the metamodel, there may exist additional restrictions on combinations of design options for the system at hand, because the metamodel does not capture some aspects that lead to incompatibility of choices in the system itself. Such *system-specific constraints* cannot be reflected in the metamodel, but can be manually added by the software architect for an initial model M as the set *systemSpecificConstraints*(M). An example for a constraint on combinations is that BusinessTripMgmt and BookingSystem must not be deployed on the same server because of e.g. conflicting system library version requirements. Like the interaction constraints, this does not limit the design options for each degree of freedom separately, but does constrain the set of all candidate models $\mathcal{D}_{M,D}$. Combinations could also be invalid because of other non-functional properties that cannot be automatically quantitatively evaluated for the system under study, such as maintainability. Also, the software architect may predict unforeseen side effects of certain combinations that are not covered by the quality models (if rather abstract quality models are used).

Combination constraints result in a set of candidate models being infeasible. Recall that $interactionConstraints(g)$ denotes the set of interaction constraints from a DoF g. Let g_d denote the DoF that produced a DoFI d. Then, $modelConstraints(M,D) := \bigcup_{d \in D} interactionConstraints(g_d) \cup systemSpecificConstraints(M)$ denotes the set of all constraints on $\mathcal{D}_{M,D}$. Formally, we can consider the constraints in the sets as predicates that have to hold and define the feasible design space as follows:

Definition 6.15 Feasible Design Space

The feasible design space $\mathcal{F}_{M,D}$ is the subset of the unconstrained design space $\mathcal{D}_{M,D}$ that contains all candidate models that are conforming model instances and that fulfil additional system-specific constraints:

$$\mathcal{F}_{M,D} = \{a \,|\, a \in \mathcal{D}_{M,D} \land \forall P \in modelConstraints(M,D) : P(a)\}$$

where P denotes a predicate from $modelConstraints(M,D)$. For a given design space, we have a fixed set of constraints (predicates) and thus can transform this formula into first-order logic by connecting all predicates with a conjunction.

The constraints need to be formalized in a constraint language. For some modelling languages and meta-(meta-)models, specialized constraint languages already exist. As we use EMOF in this work, we use the Object Constraint Language (Object Management Group (OMG), 2006b) (OCL) for constraint specification. An interesting alternative for future work could be the recently suggested, more specialized Constraint Specification Language (Saxena and Karsai, 2010a).

6.4.4. Discussion of Other Representations of the Design Space

In this subsection, we discuss an alternative representation of the design space and argue why we have not chosen it. For this argumentation, we have to anticipate some details of later chapters to cover the whole range of arguments.

Alternatively to the presented definition of the design space as a spaced spanned by the degrees of freedom, an alternative representation could be *modelling of changes as first class entities*. Starting from an initial software architecture, each possible change of the architecture could be represented. The set of all possible change sequences would define the design space. Then, improving the architecture means finding a sequence of changes that leads to a superior software architecture model.

As discussed in Chapter 4, deterministic rules to improve the architecture cannot cover the complete search space without fully enumerating it and interesting global optima may be unreachable by them. Thus, in this work, we apply stochastic elements to overcome local optima (more detail on this choice in the next Chapter 8). When using stochastic elements, a change-based approach has several disadvantages compared to the degree of freedom approach.

First, a change-based search is biased towards architectures that are similar to the initial architecture, because they are represented by a shorter sequence of changes and thus more probably created by a stochastic search. While this can be beneficial if the software architect happens to create a good initial system, there is no reason to assume that the initial system is better than other candidate models in general. Thus, an unnecessary bias is introduced.

Second, a change-based search may create identical candidate models in one search path by applying changes that revert previous changes. Thus, detection mechanisms need to be added that complicate the search procedure. It may be difficult to capture which changes revert each other under which conditions.

Third, the representation using degrees of freedom is more flexible and allows to use and compare various search strategies. For example, the change-based search can be mimicked by using hill-climbing with a neighbourhood definition of one change in the genome.

For dependent degrees of freedom, such as component selection within a replaceable subsystem, the change-based approach does not offer advantages in terms of reducing the possible candidate models to consider. The amount of possible candidate models could only be reduced by a top-down search where the search first starts applying selection changes to components on top of the component hierarchies (e.g. subsystems) and then descends to the inner child components. However, as it is in general impossible to predict the effect of choosing a subsystem before deciding which inner components to use, this restriction would limit the search space and may lead to getting stuck in local optima.

An advantage of a change-based approach would be the more simple representation of domain knowledge during the search: Tactics can simply be included by choosing promising changes with a higher probability. However, this advantage does not outweigh the previously discussed disadvantages, especially because it is possibly to successfully include tactics into a degree-of-freedom-based search as well (see Section 8.3.1).

6.5. Assumptions and Limitations

This section discusses the assumptions and limitations of the design space formalization.

6.5.1. Assumptions

Primary Element: For the DoF definition, we assume that for each relevant type of change, a primary changeable element is available as described in Section 6.3.1.8. We assume that this condition is fulfilled in real-world metamodels, however, we cannot prove this assumption. In general, there may be additional cases where several model element are changed without one being the primary element as defined above. As metamodels may be arbitrary, a metamodel could require to change any number of model elements in order to realize one conceptual change (e.g. the allocation of a component) that does affect the functionality of the system. Still, the assumption is not vital for the method presented in this work: To remove this assumption, the notion of degrees of freedom in the following could be extended to support virtual model elements that reflect the conceptual changes of an indivisible change type and are equipped with additional rules that map a change of this single virtual model element to a set of model elements.

Connected Model Elements: As already mentioned in Section 2.3.2, a technical assumption of our approach is that all model elements are connected to each other, i.e. that we can navigate between any two model elements m_1 and m_2, either from m_1 to m_2 or m_2 to m_1. Thus, the presentation of the concepts could be simplified. Dropping this assumption would require to add additional reverse lookup capabilities.

Finite Number of DoFI is Opened up: We assume that the number of DoFI opened up by DoF is finite in practice, i.e. that the finite initial set of DoFI for the initial model only (transitively) opens up a finite number of new DoFI. For the currently identified DoF for CBA (cf. Chapter 7), the number of added DoFI is finite because new degrees are only opened up for component selection degrees and the number of available components is finite. We do not expect that meaningful DoF will produce an infinite set of DoFI for a given model. Still, we cannot exclude this case in general. To account for possibly infinite number of potentially opened DoFIs, a counter could be introduced in the DoFI instantiation algorithm to stop instantiation after a maximum number of DoFIs is reached.

6.5.2. Limitations

Partial Design Space: With our method, we can only help the software architect to consider design decisions that are expressible in the models. The most support is provided for degrees of freedom that are known to fulfil our constraints based on the metamodel alone. For these, the design space can be automatically instantiated. System-specific degrees of freedom can be expressed by modelling them on the metamodel level and then reviewing their instantiation on the model level, or instantiating them manually on the model level (cf. Section 6.3.2.5). Design decisions that cannot be expressed with the given metamodel or model cannot be considered in this work. Thus, the explored design space is usually a strict subset of the true design space the software architect is faced with. Still, automated exploration of this partial design space can reduce effort for the software architect. Additionally, they can compare more high-level design decisions by automatically exploring the partial design space of each high-level alternative, as described in Section 5.4.

One metamodel for CBA: Our approach assumes that one metamodel exists that describes a CBA and all relevant information to determine the quality attributes of interest. If several models are used to study a single software architecture, e.g. an UML model for the static structure, a loosely coupled LQN model for performance and a Markov Chain for reliability, the approach cannot be applied as is. As a solution, an artificial super-metamodel could be created that joins and references the used metamodels in one and links the different model elements. This metamodel could also support several modelling techniques for one aspect, e.g. LQN and Queueing Petri Nets for performance.

6.6. Summary

The leading question of this chapter is how software architecture models can be changed automatically. The main requirements that are identified for to realize automated variation of the model are

- C1 Changes must capture relevant influence factors on quality properties.

- C2 After changing the architecture model, the result must be a model conforming to the architecture metamodel.

- C3 The functional behaviour described by the software architecture model must remain unchanged and the system must be realizable.

- C4 Which changes fulfil constraint C3 must be described on the metamodel level. If a change may affect functionality, it is excluded.

The changes that fulfil these requirements and thus can be used in automated improvement are defined in this chapter. The main concept is a degree of freedom, which describes independent ways a given software architecture model can be varied. Using the degrees of freedom, the space of possible architectural candidate models to which a given architecture model can be changed to improve quality is spanned.

In the next Chapter 7, we present a set of DoF that are typical for CBA metamodels and can be used to improve CBA architecture automatically. Then, Chapter 8 describes our optimization method used to find the optimal trade-off candidates in the feasible design space.

7. Degrees of Freedom in Component-based Software Architecture Models

The following presents the DoF that we have identified in software architecture models and that can be automatically searched. As described in the previous chapter, DoF are required include changes which are known to affect a certain quality effect. Here, we have focussed on DoF that affect performance, costs, or reliability. For these degrees, some anticipated effects for other quality attributes are additionally listed. For the use of other quality prediction techniques, for example for security (cf. Section 2.4.3), additional degrees of freedom could be identified. In the following, we describe the DoF generically, referring only to the concepts found in CBA as described in Section 2.1 (such as components or component allocation) and concepts of software systems in general (such as scheduling priorities or semaphores). Then, the DoF is applicable for every CBA metamodel that supports to explicitly model these properties.

Together with the presentation of each degree of freedom, we discuss impacts on quality properties. If applicable, we show how the degree of freedom is modelled for the PCM, including the list changeable metamodel elements and the rules to created valid changes in OCL, and give an example. Additionally, we sketch how the degree is modelled in one other CBA model, namely CBML or ROBOCOP.

In terms of the component-based developer roles, these degrees of freedom belong to the modelling domain of the software architect and system deployer. Tables 7.1 and 7.2 show an overview of the different degrees of freedom presented in this chapter.

Section 7.2 presents degrees of freedom found in the application layer software. Section 7.3 describes degrees of freedom in the deployment. Finally, we discuss how additional degrees of freedom, which are not generic for CBA, might be available in specific metamodels or specific systems in Section 7.4. Section 7.5 discusses the limitations of our method, and Section 7.6 concludes the chapter.

7.1. Degree of Freedom Description Schema

We use the following schema to describe each degree:

Rationale: A concise rationale of the degree of freedom motivating its presence in component-based software architecture models.

Description: A description of the degree of freedom, independent of any metamodel. The description includes a definition, which is informal because a formal definition could only be achieved by referencing a concrete software architecture metamodel.

(Primary) Changeable elements: A description of the changeable model elements and the primary changeable model element, based on the component concepts described in Section 2.1.1 and shown in Figure 2.1 if applicable. If only one model element is named, it is the primary changeable element.

Quality Effects: The quality attributes that are affected by this degree of freedom, and a description of how they are affected. The quality effects anticipated here are not necessarily the final list of effects, because additional quality attributes may be specified in the future. Here, I discuss the effects on the quality attributes performance, reliability, maintainability, and costs.

Metamodel-specific definitions: The formal definition of this degree of freedom in the PCM, which names the changeable metamodel ele-

Degree of Freedom	Primary Changeable Element (in Example Metamodel)	Sec.
Software-related degrees of freedom		
Selection of components	Binding of component in system (AssemblyContext.encapsulatedComponent)	7.2.1
Non-functional Component Configuration Param	Configuration parameter of a component (AssemblyContext.configParameterUsages)	7.2.2
Passive resource multiplicity	Multiplicity of Passive Resource (PassiveResource.capacity)	7.2.3
Priorities	Model elements that represent priority ((CBML) TaskType.priority)	7.2.4
Deployment-related degrees of freedom		
Allocation	Mapping of component allocation instances to servers (AllocationContext.resourceContainer)	7.3.1
Allocation with replication	Mapping of component allocation instances to servers (AllocationContext.resourceContainer)	7.3.2
Server replication	Server multiplicity ((extended PCM) ResourceContainer.multiplicity)	7.3.3
Resource selection	Resources of a server (ResourceContainer.activeResourceSpecifications)	7.3.4
Resource Property Change	Properties of resources (ProcessingResourceSpecification.processingRate)	7.3.5
Further configuration of the SW stack	depends on *MM* (Feature Configurations)	7.3.6
Quality completion configuration		7.3.7

Table 7.1.: Software and Deployment Degrees of Freedom for CBA Overview, with Examples for Primary Changeable Elements in the PCM (Default) or Another Metamodel (Indicated)

Degree of Freedom	Primary Changeable Element (in Example Metamodel)	Sec.
Custom degrees of freedom		
Metamodel-specific degrees of freedom	any	7.4.1
For PCM: Subsystem selection	which components are allocated Allocation.allocationContexts	7.4.1
System-specific degrees of freedom	NA	7.4.2

Table 7.2.: Custom Degrees of Freedom for CBA Overview, with Examples for Primary Changeable Elements in the PCM (Default) or Another Metamodel (Indicated)

ments (Properties) and the OCL constraints for selection rules, value rules, and interaction constraints. In addition to the formal definition in the PCM, we sketch the degree of freedom definition for CBML or ROBOCOP. If the degree of freedom is not available in the PCM (such as the change of priorities degree of freedom), only another software-architecture metamodel are used. For space reasons, we provide the formal definition in Appendix C.

Example: If the degree of freedom is available in the PCM, we describe it based on an example PCM model visualized in UML instance diagrams. Otherwise, we describe an informal example.

For a better readability of the PCM-specific OCL rules for selecting valid values, we assume that the set of available Repositories of a PCM instance can be selected by the variable repositories, the System can be selected by the variable system, and the Allocation can be selected by the variable allocation. This replaces the sometimes complicated navigation from a given metamodel element to these concepts. These short cuts can be used in each PCM sub-model (e.g. Assembly model) to reach elements in the same sub-model (e.g. Assembly model) or in any referenced sub-model (e.g. Repository model, but not Allocation model), because it is always possible to navigate from any model element to any other one within a sub-model and sub-models are linked as described in in Section 2.5.2.

7.2. Software-related Degrees of Freedom

The degrees of freedom from the software architect's modelling domain are concerned with the components on the application layer, their wiring, and their configuration. This subsection presents four software-related degrees of freedom shown in table 7.1, using the schemata presented in the introduction of this section.

7.2.1. Selection of Components

Rationale: Component-based architecture models encapsulate the functionality of the system into components with well-defined provided and required interface. Thus, other components that provide the same functionality, but have different quality properties, can replace the given components in the architecture.

Description: In the following, we assume that an interface describes what functionality is offered. Thus, if two components provide the same interface, this means that they provide the same functionality and that they can both be used in the architecture to provide this interfaces.

Let A be a component instance (cf. Figure 2.1), i.e. the mapping of an instantiation of a component to a place in the architecture. Let the set $C = \{C_1, ..., C_n\}$ be the set of connectors that connect the interfaces of the component to other components in the system. Note that usually, in component models, all interfaces required by the component have to be bound to other components in the system that provide the functionality, whereas not all interfaces provided by the component need to be bound and used. Some component models tolerate unbound required interfaces (e.g. (Reussner et al., 2003)), in those cases, a more fine-grained metamodel-specific definition of what a component requires needs to be used by first determining the "active" required interfaces. Without loss of generality, we will proceed with the notion that all required (active) interfaces need to be bound.

Additionally, let R be the set of available components. This set can, for example, be the union of components from all referenced component repositories.

Then, a component $B \in R$ can be selected for this place in the architecture A (replacing the component used there before), iff (1) B provides at least all the interfaces required by the rest of the system at this place in the architecture, and (2) B requires at most the interfaces provided by the rest of the system to this place in the architecture.

Let $S \subset R$ be the available set of components that can be selected for the place A.

If at least two components exist in the models that can be selected for the place A, i.e. if $|S| \geq 2$, then there is a *component selection degree of freedom* at A with the possible values S.

Components selection according to this definition ensures that functionality is retained. Component selection may open up new component selection degrees of freedom if a component is replaced by a composed component that internally allows for additional choices.

(Primary) Changeable elements: The model elements that instantiate components in the system, i.e. ComponentInstance.component (primary element) and potentially Connectors.

Quality Effects: Component selection can affect all quality properties depending on the implementation characteristics of the chosen components. Additionally, component selection options can have different costs for development, maintenance, procurement and/or operation.

Metamodel-specific definitions: PCM and ROBOCOP definitions are provided in Appendix C.1

Example: Consider the PCM model in Figure 2.13 and the alternative component QuickBooking in Figure 6.1. Because QuickBooking offers the same interface as BookingSystem (Interface IBooking), and because QuickBooking does not require more functionality than BookingSystem (both require none), QuickBooking can replace BookingSystem. Figure 7.1(a) shows the relevant excerpts of an UML object diagram of the PCM example model, and highlights the Properties that are updated when QuickBooking is inserted in the architecture model. Figure 7.1(b) shows the resulting model after inserting QuickBooking for BookingSystem.

While the initial candidate model using BookingSystem had a POFOD of 0.0011, costs of 1079 units and response time of 7.3 sec, the new candidate model using QuickBooking has POFOD 0.0013, costs of 1279 units and mean response time of 6.2 sec: The new candidate model is faster, but at the same time less reliable and more expensive than the initial candidate model.

7.2.2. Non-functional Component Configuration Parameters

Rationale: If components provide configuration parameters that only affect the component's delivered quality, but not the functionality, their values can be varied during the search. For example, a component can have a parameter to choose from several available compression algorithms, to choose from different security levels (such as encryption key lengths), or to choose from different fault handling strategies, e.g. number of retries.

Description: A component configuration parameter (also configuration parameter in the following) is a parameter of a component that allows to configure the component when instantiating it, affecting its behaviour.

We assume that configuration parameters always take primitive data types such as integers, doubles, or Strings. Properties with other types, e.g. other metamodel elements, cannot be considered configuration parameters of a component because they express more complex relations in the architecture, e.g. define communication partners, and do not represent a local configuration of a component. Often, only a subset of the domain of

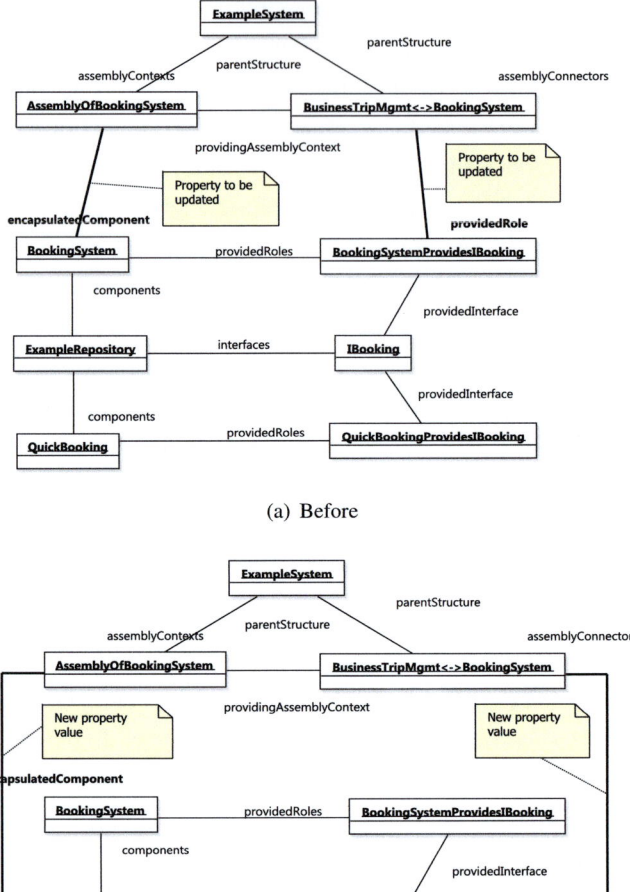

(a) Before

(b) After

Figure 7.1.: Component Selection Example for Example Model from Figures 2.13
and 6.1. The bold properties in part (a) show the Properties to be
updated. The bold Properties in part (b) show the updated values.
Note that the figures only show the necessary parts from the model, all
other Properties have been omitted.

the parameter's data type is valid. For example, the component may have a certain internal cache size as an integer parameter with implementation-dependent minimal and maximal allowed values. In this example, not every integer value is valid for the configuration parameters, but only values between the minimal and maximal value. In general, the valid values are specific to the modelled component and cannot be predefined on the metamodel level.

A non-functional component configuration parameter is a configuration parameter that does affect not the provided functionality. Let C be a component instance in the architecture and let P be a property of this component that represents a non-functional component parameter. Let V be the subset of valid values of this configuration parameter, identifiable on the instance level. Then, there is a *component configuration parameter degree of freedom* at P with the valid values V.

Note that a component configuration parameter with primitive data type is not necessarily a non-functional component configuration parameter. For example, a parameter of an accounting component could determine which taxation system is used to calculate value-added taxes. The information whether a parameter is a non-functional component configuration parameter could either be available from the metamodel (if e.g. the metamodel provides different model elements for non-functional configuration parameters and other parameters) or from annotations that the software architect uses to mark non-functional configuration parameters in model instances.

If component configuration parameters have interdependencies and are hierarchically structured, feature models (cf. Section 2.4.4) can be used to describe the possible configuration options, and a set of configuration options can be considered as one degree of freedom (cf. Section 7.3.7).

(Primary) Changeable elements: The model elements that represent non-functional component configuration parameters, or model elements that represent component parameters in general together with annotations that mark the parameter instances as not affecting functionality.

Quality Effects: Non-functional component configuration parameters can affect all quality properties except component costs and maintainability, because they might lead to any change of behaviour inside the component (as illustrated by the examples above). Component costs are not affected, because the implementation of the components remains fixed. Other costs could be affected: For example, if energy costs are considered, then a configuration that puts more load on the used resources can lead to higher energy costs.

Metamodel-specific definitions: PCM and CBML definitions are provided in Appendix C.2

Example: Assume that the component `PaymentSystem` from running example system additionally has a component parameter to configure the length of the used encryption key and that this parameter affects the resource demand of this component has when making a credit card payment, as shown in figure 7.2. The allowed values of this component parameters are 128 bit or 256 bit. Changing this component parameter does not affect the functionality of the system, but does affect performance and security.

7.2.3. Passive Resources Multiplicity

Rationale: The multiplicity of passive resources, such as thread pools or database connection pools, can be varied to find a good balance for the utilization of underlying resources. Multiplicity of mutual-exclusion locks for critical regions (which can also be modelled with passive resources with capacity of 1) must not be varied.

Description: A passive resource is a software resource that limits the concurrency in parts of the system. The basic form of a passive resource is a semaphore. Passive resources can also be used to model more complex constructs such as thread pools, database connections, or file handles. In any case, a passive resource protects some region (which can be a resource)

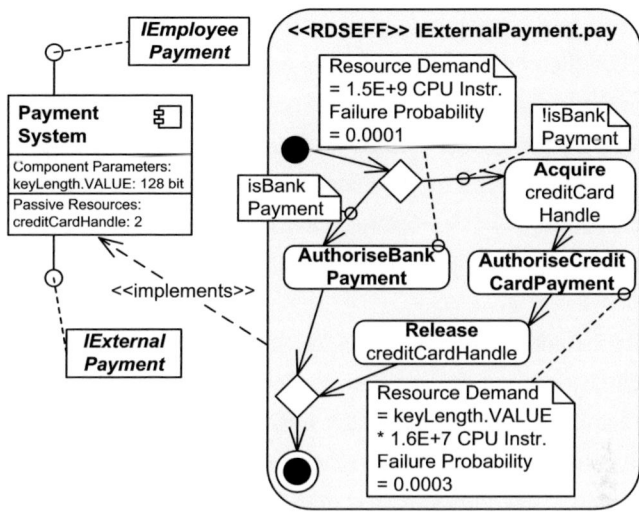

Figure 7.2.: Extended Example System with Component Parameter and Passive Resource

and limits access to it. The capacity of a passive resource specifies how many concurrent threads or processes may enter the protected region.

As a degree of freedom for automated quality improvement, passive resource capacity can be varied. However, only passive resources that do not affect functionality may be changed, such as the above-mentioned thread pools, database connections, or file handles. Passive resources that protect regions for functional reasons, e.g. to ensure data integrity, must not be changed. Usually, passive resources with functional effect have a capacity of just one, i.e. only one thread or process is allowed to enter the protected region. Passive resources with higher capacity are, in contrast, used to reuse software resources in pools or to avoid over-utilization. Thus, while such passive resources may have a maximum number (e.g. the number of file handles to a file is limited), they can be varied.

Let P be a passive resource in the architecture model with a capacity c. If $c > 1$ then there is a *passive resource multiplicity degree of freedom* at P with the value range $R = \mathbb{N}_+$. R can be restricted on the instance level.

(Primary) Changeable elements: Passive resources can be defined in several places depending on the metamodel, e.g. as part of a component, of the infrastructure, or of the resource environment. In any case, the changeable element is the model element that defines the capacity of the passive resource.

Quality Effects: This degree of freedom can affect performance, as it might increase or decrease parallelism. Performance can improve if the underlying hardware resources are well utilized, but it can also deteriorate if too much contention on load-dependent resources leads to additional overhead (e.g. context switches). Costs may be affected in special cases where the capacity of passive resources is covered by licenses. Reliability may be affected in cases where the reliability of components is dependent on the degree of parallelism inside the component (e.g. more parallel executing threads may be more susceptible to faults caused by race conditions).

Metamodel-specific definitions: PCM and CBML definitions are provided in Appendix C.3

Example: Consider the extended example system shown in figure 7.2. Let us assume that for the authorization of credit card payments, a handle for the internal credit card library is required that can only be used by one process at a time. Then, the number of available handles can be increased to allow more concurrent credit card authorizations. At the same time, more handles might lead to higher licensing cost, e.g. 30 units per handle. In the example, the AuthoriseCreditCardPayment InternalAction is protected by the PassiveResource creditCardHandle that limits how many processes can simultaneously authorize credit card payments, including the required encryption. The number of creditCardHandles is initially set to two.

Increasing the number of handles allows more concurrent transactions, which can be beneficial if the component is deployed to a multi core server.

On the other hand, more handles lead to higher licensing cost. With the given system load, the number of handles could as well be reduced to one to save licensing cost, because only few requests access the credit card authorization at the same time.

7.2.4. Priorities

Rationale: If a system offers several services simultaneously, the response times, failure probabilities, and throughputs of each service can be considered independent objectives for the automated improvement. Then, a degree of freedom of the architecture can be to prioritize requests to certain services. For example, business-relevant transactions can be assigned a higher priority than maintenance functions. Similarly, different components could be assigned priorities.

Description: Different entities of the software model (usage scenarios or components) can be assigned a priority. If a resource (both active resources or passive resources) is requested, requests from higher prioritized software entities are favoured. Different scheduling strategies to handle priorities are imaginable: Either high priority requests are directly put to the top of the queue, which may lead to starvation, or more complex scheduling schemes are used, e.g. also increasing the priority of long-waiting jobs with initial low priority to ensure liveliness.

Let S be a software entity in the architecture model with priority p and a range of possible priority levels $p_1, ..., p_n$. Then there is a *priority degree of freedom* at S with the value range $R = p_1, ..., p_n$.

(Primary) Changeable elements: Different software entities could support priorities in the architecture metamodel. The changeable elements of this degree are the model elements that represent a software entity's priority.

Quality Effects: Prioritization improves performance for the higher prioritized software entities, while deteriorating it for others. Thus, prioritization is beneficial if critical services of the system are assigned a high priority. Reliability might decrease in general if the prioritization mechanism introduces additional potential for faults. Possibly, the effort to realize prioritization can lead to additional development or procurement costs for the components or the middleware as well as to decreased maintainability due to higher complexity.

Metamodel-specific definitions: PCM and CBML definitions are provided in Appendix C.4

Example: As priority optimization is not supported in the PCM, we consider an example for a software architecture modelled using LQNs in the following. El-Sayed et al. (2001) present a protection switching software for a BLSR (Bidirectional Line Switching Ring, an optical ring configuration) from Nortel Networks. In the example, several processing nodes are connected in a ring communication with a bi-directional traffic flow between neighbouring nodes. Requests are routed for the shortest path. If a connection between two nodes is destroyed, some requests need to be rerouted the other way around the ring. When such failure occurs, all nodes should react within 50 ms and reroute traffic.

The protection software is composed of 16 software tasks that are allocated to the two processors of each node. The method presented in El-Sayed et al. (2001) then finds the optimal allocation of the node's tasks to the two processors as well as optimal priorities of each task on its processor. While the used ring topology is no longer state-of-the-art, this example nonetheless illustrates the use of priorities to influence performance.

7.3. Deployment-related Degrees of Freedom

In addition to the pure software-level view of the software architect, more degrees of freedom are available when considering the deployment of the system to hardware and infrastructure, such as application servers or virtual machines. Deployment aspects include hardware choices, mapping of components to hardware and the configuration of lower levels of the software stack. This subsection presents five deployment-related degrees of freedom shown in table 7.1, using the schemata presented in the introduction of this section.

7.3.1. Allocation

Rationale: Large systems may be distributed to several servers, each providing hardware resources such as CPU and hard disc. In component-based architectures, the allocation of components to servers can be varied.

The simple case is that one component is always allocated to a single server; this case is discussed in the following. The next degree of freedom ("Allocation with Replication") describes the more case that a component can be replicated and allocated to several servers.

Description: The allocation defines how many servers are used and which component is executed by which server by defining component allocation instances (cf. Figure 2.1), i.e. a mapping of each component instance of the architecture to a server.

Let A be the component allocation instance mapping a component instance C to a server S. An architecture model is only valid if S provides resources for all the resource types that C requires, e.g. CPU and hard disc drive. Thus, C can only be allocated to other servers that provide the required resources. Let RT_C be the set of resource types that C requires and let RT_S be the set of resource types that S provides.

Additionally, the linking resources connecting the servers, such as LAN connections, must be considered: C can only be allocated to servers that are connected to all of C's communication partners (i.e., component allocation instances that are linked to C in the architecture model) by linking resources. In particular, a linking resource must be available for the direction(s) in which the C and its communication partners send messages. Additionally, if the architecture model restricts the type of linking resource used by a communication of a component, e.g. that certain communication has to use a wireless LAN connection, then the linking resource between the two components also has to be of the correct type t_l. Because the allocation of the communication partners can change as well, this restriction cannot be statically defined for one system at hand, but must be handled with interaction constraints.

The allocation degree of freedom can be defined as follows for the mapping A allocating C to S: Let RE be the set of all available servers. Then, the subset of servers $RE_C \subset RE$ to which C could potentially be allocated can be identified as follows:

$$RE_C = \left\{ S^* \in RE \,\middle|\, (\forall t \in RT_C \; \exists t' \in RT_S : t = t') \right\}$$

If $|RE_C| > 1$, there is an allocation degree of freedom at A with the possible values RE_C.

If linking resources are considered, different allocation changes for different components may be in conflict with each other. An interaction constraint must exclude candidate models where communication partners cannot communicate with each other.

Let *Components* be the set of all component allocation instances in the system. Let *Sender* $\subseteq$ *Components* be the set of all components that send messages to C (both locally or remotely) and let *Receiver* $\subseteq$ *Components* be the set of all components that receive messages from C (both sets may overlap). Let LT_p be the set of linking resource types that each communication partner (sender or receiver) $p \in Sender \cup Receiver$ requires. Recall that for a component allocation instance c, $c.server$ denotes the server to which c is allocated.

Let the *linked*$(1, S_1, S_2)$ express that a linking resource l connects the two server S_1 and S_2 so that components allocated to S_1 can send messages to components allocated to S_2.

In the result model after applying all changes, the following interaction constraint must hold for the chosen server S^*: The server must be connected to the servers of all communication partners with the appropriate linking resources.

$$(\forall c \in Sender \; \forall t \in LT_c \; \exists l : linked(l,c.server,S^*) \wedge t_l = t)$$
$$\wedge(\forall c \in Receiver \; \forall t \in LT_c \; \exists l : linked(l,S^*,c.server) \wedge t_l = t)$$

This interaction constraint (or a similar constraint expressing the same concepts) should be defined in the CBA metamodel to describe valid instances of the metamodel.

(Primary) Changeable elements: The model element that maps a component instance to a server, i.e. ComponentAllocationInstance.server.

Quality Effects: Allocation is crucial for performance of distributed systems, as the distribution of components to servers determines how well the system load is distributed among the available resources. However, distribution of components also leads to communication overhead, because local communication of components allocated to a single server is much faster that remote communication of components allocated to different servers.

For performance, the effects of allocation can be well anticipated for simple systems where one type of resource usage determines the result (e.g. CPU-bound applications). If in such cases, the single components contribute similarly to the overall quality (e.g. for performance: that have a similar load in the given usage scenario), the effect of allocation depends on the number of components: the less components are available in the system, the more a single allocation change can affect performance. If more factors contribute to the overall performance of the system (e.g. communication overhead, multiple resource types (CPU, HDD), and software locks), the effects of allocation changes are harder to anticipate and require a full analysis of the system's quality (e.g. by simulation).

In addition, allocation influences reliability, because components deployed on one server fail together if the server itself fails. Depending on the number of used servers, the costs of the system changes. In contrast, different allocation options are cost-neutral for a fixed number of servers. Finally, security threats can arise if sensitive components are allocated to servers that are easier to access.

Allocation also affects costs if the number of servers to allocate the components to is changed. If components are re-allocated to more expensive servers (expensive in terms of procurement costs, of operating costs, or pay-per-use costs), the costs of the system is increased, and vice versa. Finally, allocating a system to many servers can decrease maintainability, because providing updates of components becomes more complex.

Metamodel-specific definitions: PCM and ROBOCOP definitions are provided in Appendix C.5

Example: Consider the PCM example from Figure 2.13, page 61. As described in the overview section 6.2, three instances of the allocation degree of freedom can be identified, because each of the three components can be allocated to a different server. Because all components in this example only use one resource type (CPU) and all three servers are connected with a linking resource (a LAN), we do not have to consider the resource types and linking resources in the following.

Figure 7.3 shows an example where–compared to the initial system configuration–the allocation of PaymentSystem has been changed to server S2. This single allocation change has high impact on performance and cost: The mean response time increases from 7.3 sec to 17.8 sec. While the utilizations of server 1 to 3 were 0.57, 0.5, and 0.58, respectively, in the initial system, the utilization of server 2 has now increased to 0.93, while server 3 is not used. The costs have decreased from 1078.55 units to 923.87, because the costs for server 3 can be saved. Reliability improved from 1.14E-3 to 8.04E-04 due to fewer hardware failure options (the system is only subject to two servers failing) and less remote communication. To conclude, the allocation strongly affects the quality properties in this example.

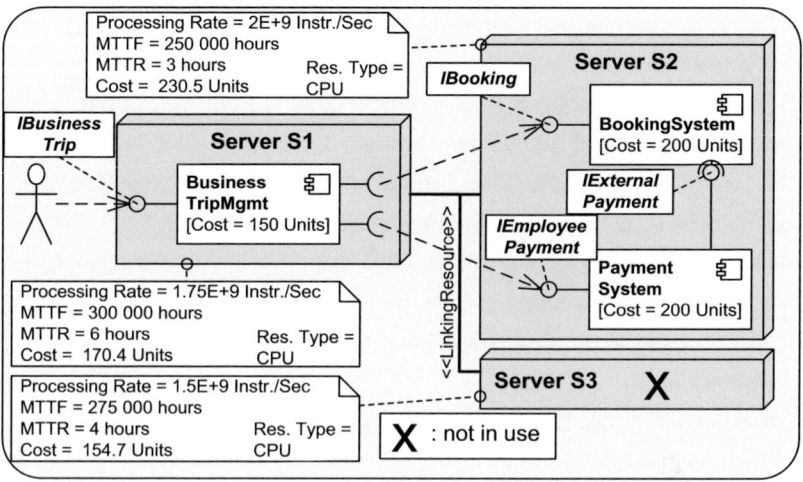

Figure 7.3.: Example for Changed Allocation

7.3.2. Allocation with Replication

Rationale: A component instance can as well be replicated on the deployment layer, i.e. this component instance on the software level is mapped to several servers by defining several component allocation instances for it (cf. Figure 2.1, page 29 in Section 2.1).

There are two purposes for having multiple component allocation instance of one component instance: Replication and Load Balancing. The goal of replication is to prevent failures of a single server to cause a system failure. Either all redundant servers process each request (active replication), or the requests are directed only to a single replica, and the other servers act as fail-over (passive replication). In load balancing, a load manager distributes incoming requests to several server instances to achieve a higher system capacity. A mixture of both types is a setting in which the free capacities of a passive replication are at the same time used for load balancing. For both types, a manager component has to be added that distributes requests to the different servers. Allocation with replication is not available in all components models, and thus is discussed separately from the Allocation degree in the following.

Description: The server multiplicity is defined in the allocation, which specifies the mapping from components to servers. For a metamodel to support allocation with replication, it has to allow an n:m mapping of components in the system (i.e. component instances) to servers. While we allocated each component instance to only a single server in all previous examples, here, a component instance can be allocated to multiple servers, resulting in several component allocation instances for one component instance on the system level.

For the definition, let us assume that the metamodel under study distinguishes component instances assembled in the system from component allocation instances deployed to resource containers, as shown in Figure 2.1, page 29.

Let A be the component allocation instance mapping a component instance C to a set of servers $S = \{S_1, ...S_n\}$. As with the allocation degree, an architecture model is only valid if the servers in S offer all the resources that C needs. The definition of this degree of freedom is analogous to the allocation degree. Let us reuse the variables from the allocation degree of freedom so that RE denotes the set of all available servers and $RE_C \subset RE$ denotes the set of servers that C could be allocated to based on the resource types and linking resources. Then, for the allocation with replication degree, the set of possible values for A is the power set of RE_C excluding the empty set:

$$\mathscr{P}_{\setminus \emptyset}(RE_C) = \{U \,|\, U \subseteq RE_C \wedge U \neq \emptyset\}$$

If $\left|\mathscr{P}_{\setminus \emptyset}(RE_C)\right| > 1$, there is an allocation degree of freedom at A with the possible values $\mathscr{P}_{\setminus \emptyset}(RE_C)$.

As for the simple allocation degree, different allocation with replication degrees may interact. The same interaction constraint as for the simple allocation degree must hold for all chosen servers after all changes have been applied. We reuse the variables from the "Allocation" Degree so that *Components* is the set of all component allocation instances in the system, *Sender* $\subseteq$ *Components* is the set of all components that send messages to *C* (both locally or remotely) and *Receiver* $\subseteq$ *Components* is the set of all components that receive messages from *C* (both sets may overlap). Additionally, LT_p denotes the set of linking resource types that each communication partner (sender or receiver) $p \in Sender \cup Receiver$ requires. Then, the interaction constraint to hold is:

$$(\forall c \in Sender \; \forall t \in LT_c \; \exists l : linked(l, c.server, S^*) \wedge t_l = t)$$
$$\wedge (\forall c \in Receiver \; \forall t \in LT_c \; \exists l : linked(l, S^*, c.server) \wedge t_l = t)$$

In addition to the number of servers that a component is replicated to, the replication strategies such as load balancing strategies (e.g. random or based on utilization of the servers) can be varied if the metamodel supports more than one strategy. This is considered a separate degree here and discussed below as a "Further configuration of the software stack" parameter.

In metamodels where the above distinction of component instances in the assembly and component allocation instances in the allocation is not explicitly modelled, the component instances in the assembly could be copied and thus explicitly replicated as a degree of freedom. However, with this technique, we cannot distinguish between two instances of a component that have been deliberately introduced in the architecture model and play different roles, e.g. due to different configuration, and replicated components. This inaccuracy may lead to invalid models if in the first case, components are replicated and the load is spread to all instances of this component. Thus, this technique is not further discussed here.

Another option how to model a restricted form of allocation with replication is described as the "Server replication degree" in the next Section 7.3.3.

(Primary) Changeable elements: The model element that maps a component instance to a server, i.e. ComponentAllocationInstance.server.

Quality Effects: The quality effects of the "Allocation with replication" degree includes all quality effects of the simple "Allocation" degree. Additional effects stem from the replication of components, i.e. if A defines a mapping to more than one server. Depending on the type of replication, this degree of freedom affects performance or reliability, but always costs. Pure replication can improve reliability while also increasing costs. Pure load-balancing can improve performance while also increasing costs. With the mixture of the types, both performance and reliability can be improved. Additionally, maintainability may be decreased due to higher complexity of the replication mechanisms.

Metamodel-specific definitions: PCM definitions are provided in Appendix C.6.

Example: Let us assume that we have a forth server S_4 available in our running example from figure 2.13, page 61 with the server configuration shown in Figure 7.4. Then, we can allocate the BusinessTrip-Mgmt component to both server S_1 and S_4 as shown in the figure. In the PCM model, there is one assembled component instance of BusinessTrip-Mgmt in the architecture model, but there are now two AllocationContexts that allocate this AssemblyContext to one server each. The arriving requests are randomly distributed to one of both (see description of simplified PCM extension above). Note that the simplified graphical syntax used in the other examples assumed a 1:1 mapping of AssemblyContext and AllocationContext and is thus not applicable here any more. This is why we have split the system view from the allocation view in figure 7.4. The AllocationContexts are represented by the arrows marked with <<allocatedTo>>, while the component symbols represent the AssemblyContexts.

This candidate model has an improved response time of 6.34 sec (vs 7.30 sec), higher costs of 1248.93 (vs 1078.55) and an unchanged reliability. The load that was previously assigned to server S_1 and caused a utilization of

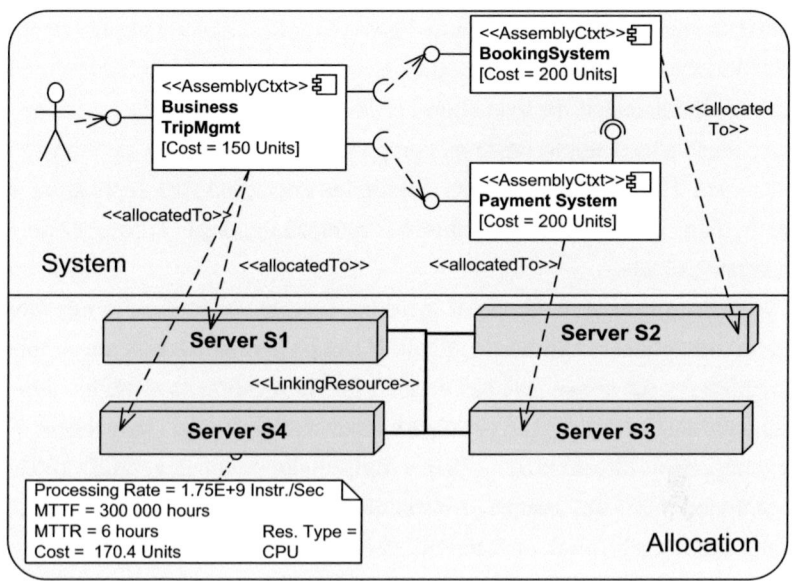

Figure 7.4.: Example for Changed Allocation with Replication

0.57 in the initial candidate model is now spread to two server, resulting in a utilization of 0.285 for both.[1].

7.3.3. Server Replication

Rationale: The above definition of "Allocation with Replication" potentially describes a huge number of possible allocations for a single component, because the number of elements in the power set is $\left|2^{RE_C}\right|$. For systems that have a more restricted allocation of components, the set can be reduced and expressed differently. For example, we could require for a system that servers are replicated homogeneously (i.e., together with all components on it, leading to identical server replicas) to make the system more manageable and the overview easier. For example, if a server is rep-

---

[1]The model does not contain an overhead for the load distribution to both servers. This implementation detail could for example be included by using completions (cf. Section 2.4.4)

licated, system administrators know that one replica server can provide all the functionality of the second replica server, so one server may be turned off for maintenance if the load allows it. In the general allocation described above, each server might host one component that is uniquely deployed to that server. The advantage of such a restricted allocation with replication is that the number of possible allocations is reduced to possibly more sensible candidate models.

Description: In this degree of freedom, servers are replicated together with all components allocated to them. It can be combined with the simple allocation degree above. We can express this replication as a single multiplicity parameter of a server, denoted `Server.multiplicity`, independent of the components allocated to it. Such a multiplicity parameter could already be included in the metamodel. Alternatively, a server can be copied in the model and the allocation of components to it can be adjusted accordingly.

The metamodel has to support multiplicity of servers for this degree of freedom to be applicable. In particular, a semantics of the multiplicity for the analyses needs to be provided. For example, requests could be randomly assigned to one of the servers, the additional servers serve as passive or active replicas, or mixed forms of both. Note that if the metamodel supports several replication schemes here and allows to configure them on the model level, the choice of a replication scheme is an additional degree of freedom discussed below with the "Further configuration of the software stack" degree of freedom.

(Primary) Changeable elements: The model element that describes the multiplicity of a server: `Server.multiplicity`.

Quality Effects: The effects of the server replication degree are the same that are added to the simple "allocation" degree by the "Allocation with replication" degree: Depending on the type of replication, this degree of freedom affects performance or reliability, but always costs. Pure replication can improve reliability while also increasing costs. Pure load-balancing can improve performance while also increasing costs. With the mixture of

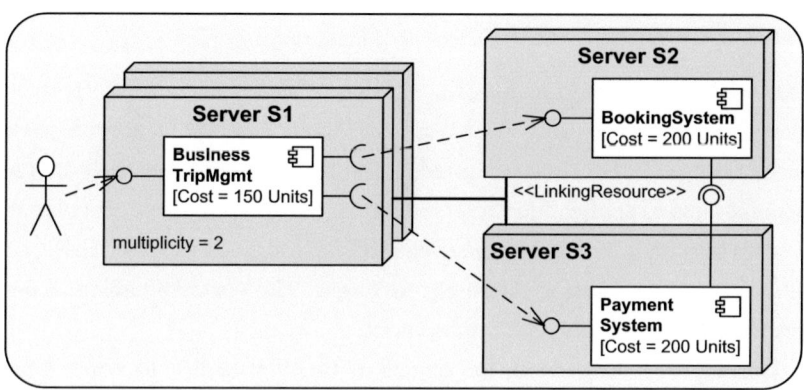

Figure 7.5.: Example for Server Replication

the types, both performance and reliability can be improved. Additionally, maintainability may be decreased due to higher complexity of the replication mechanisms.

Metamodel-specific definitions: PCM and CBML definitions are provided in Appendix C.7.

Example: Consider the PCM example from Figure 2.13, page 61. As an example, we replicate server S_1 with all its components (here only BusinessTripMgmt). The resulting candidate model is shown in figure 7.5. We use the newly introduced ResourceContainer.multiplicity to model that the server is replicated, i.e., that we get two instances of the server.

This candidate model is expressing the same system than modelled in the example for the "Allocation with replication" degree. Thus, the results of this candidate model are the same as for that example. The candidate model has an improved response time of 6.34 sec (vs. 7.30 sec), higher costs of 1248.93 (vs. 1078.55)and an unchanged reliability. The load that was previously assigned to server S_1 and caused a utilization of 0.57 in the initial candidate model is now spread to two servers, resulting in a utilization of 0.285 for both.

7.3.4. Resource Selection

Rationale: The functionality of the system is independent of the properties of the used resources. Resources are mainly hardware resources such as CPU and HDD in most metamodels, but they can represent software resources such as application servers or virtual machines. Components in the system require a certain resource type to function, such as CPU, HDD, or specific resources like special-purpose chips. The concrete choice of the resource to use for this type can be varied.

Description: In general, the degree of freedom here is to select a resource from a predefined repository of available resources with different quality characteristics and costs. For example, CPUs with different processing rates can be used or hard drives with different availability characteristics.

Let RR be a resource repository that contains available resources $r \in RR$ for the system under study, such as an Intel Pentium XY 3GHz CPU. Each resource has a resource type t_r, e.g. CPU. Each server $S \in RE$ of the system offers resources for a set of resource types RT_S.

For each resource type $t \in RT_S$ offered by a server S, the set of resources from the repository that may be used in server S for type t is given as:

$$R_t = \{r \mid r \in RR \wedge t_r = t\}$$

Let $r_{(S,t)}$ be the property that defines which resource is used in server S for resource type t. Then, if there is more than one resource available for type t, i.e. if $|R_t| > 1$, there is a resource degree of freedom at $r_{(S,t)}$ with the possible values R_t.

(Primary) Changeable elements: The model element that describes a resource of a server, i.e. Server.resources.

Quality Effects: The choice of hardware resources may have influence on performance, reliability, security, and costs. Resources with higher processing rate or lower latency may lead to better performance of the overall system. Resources with higher availability may help the system to fail less often. Built-in security mechanisms such as encryption could improve security. Finally, different hardware resource options lead to different costs for procurement and/or operation.

Metamodel-specific definitions: PCM and Robocop definitions are provided in Appendix C.8.

Example: Consider the PCM example from Figure 2.13, page 61. As described in the overview section 6.2, three instances of the resource degree of freedom can be identified, because each of the three servers has one resource of type CPU.

In the example, we assume that 13 different CPU speeds between 1GHz and 4GHz are available. Let us further assume that the MTTF linearly depends on the processing speed: The faster the CPU, the more reliable it is, too. This relation is certainly not generally true, but is assumed for this example. Then, processor type P_1 with speed 1GHz has a MTTF of $200000h$, and the other processor types have a higher MTTF linearly to their increased processor speed. For example, processor type P_{13} with speed 4GHz has a MTTF of $4 \cdot 200000h = 800000h$. The MTTR is the same for all available resources.

We determined the costs in this example based on the Intel CPU price list of February 2010 (Intel Corporation, 2010). From the data for the Xeon Server/Workstation (LGA1366 / LGA771) CPU with 45 nm and 4 Threads, we extracted a power function $cost = 0.7665 \, procRate^{6.2539} + 145$ which describes the relation between processor speed $procRate$ and costs and which fits the data with a high coefficient of determination $R^2 = 0.965$. Thus, to give some examples, the processor configuration P_1 costs $0.7665 \cdot 1^{6.2539} + 145 = 145.7665$ dollars, while the processor configuration P_7 with speed 2GHz costs $0.7665 \cdot 2^{6.2539} + 145 = 203.49566$ dollars.

As an example, we can change the processing rate of all servers to 1GHz (candidate model 1), to 2GHz (candidate model 2), to 3 GHz (candidate model 3), or to 4 GHz (candidate model 4). Additionally, we look at two

Cand. model	P. speed S_1 S_2 S_3	POFOD	Quality Costs	Mean RT	Utilization of S_1	of S_2	of S_3
1	1 1 1	0.001168	987.30	∞			
2	2 2 2	0.001132	1160.49	5.49789	0.4999	0.4998	0.4348
3	3 3 3	0.001120	3200.65	2.84986	0.3327	0.3324	0.2891
4	4 4 4	0.001114	14377.34	1.93253	0.2497	0.2496	0.2172
5	3 3 2	0.001123	2520.60	3.55571	0.3324	0.3320	0.4330
6	2 3 2	0.001129	1840.54	4.5164	0.4997	0.3329	0.4342

Table 7.3.: Evaluation of the PCM Example with Changed Processing Rates (Columns "P. speed") (Costs in units, mean response time (column "Mean RT") in seconds.

candidate models with mixed processing rates (candidate model 5 and candidate model 6). The results of the analyses are shown in table 7.3. The candidate model with the lowest processing rate is overloaded and cannot cope with the workload, thus, an infinite response time was determined. With increasing processing rate, the POFOD and response time decrease; however, the costs increase rapidly due to the power function. The two candidate models with mixed processing speeds (candidate model 5 and candidate model 6) give intermediate results. In these cases, the utilization of the servers varies more, because the load in the example system in the initial allocation is quite evenly spread over the system. If the allocation is changed, too, the effect of the processing rate changes can change significantly.

7.3.5. Resource Property Change

Rationale: For systems that contain many resource selection choices, enumerating all options may become cumbersome. Instead of selecting a resource from the repository *RR* which enumerates all options, the available resource can also be specified as a function of how to change resource properties. However, the effects on all server properties must be well-defined.

Description: A high number of different choices for a resource type, e.g. CPUs with speed varying from 1.5GHz to 4GHz in small steps or CPUs with varying number of cores, can also be modelled as a changeable property of the server. However, the effect of the changeable property (e.g. CPU speed, or both speed and availability) on the remaining properties of the resource (such as costs) need to be modelled because the properties are usually not independently changeable. A mathematical function for example can express the costs in relation to the processor speed. Overall, for each choice of the resource, the resource properties need to be well-defined.

For example, let us assume that for a system under study, the CPU speed can be varied between 1.5GHz and 3GHz ($G = [1.5,3] \subset \mathbb{R}$) and mean time to failure (MTTF) of a CPU can be varied between 200000 hours and 300000 hours ($M = [200000, 300000] \subset \mathbb{R}$). Let us further assume that the costs of CPUs can be defined as a function $C : G \times M \rightarrow \mathbb{R}$ on speed and MTTF. Then, the set of available resources RR is spanned by a function $F : G \times M \rightarrow RR$ creating a resource r with speed $r.speed = x$, MTTF $r.MTTF = y$ and costs $r.costs = C(x,y)$. As we see in this example, the set RR is highly problem specific and depends on the available resources for the specific system at hand as well as on the properties a resource has in the metamodel. Software architects have to decide for a system at hand to model RR in an abbreviated way using functions or to enumerate all options.

In cases where more than one property of the resources can be varied independently of each other and functions to the remaining properties of the resource can be specified, the resource degree of freedom can also be split into independent subordinate resource property degrees which separately modify a resource property. Such a distinction can be beneficial in the later exploitation of the degrees of freedom by optimization techniques, because it brings additional structure to the problem. However, in cases where the available resources cannot be expressed as such as combination of properties, all elements in RR have to be enumerated.

(Primary) Changeable elements: Any set of properties of a resource, for example the processing rate and the costs.

Quality Effects: Depending on which properties are changes, this degree can have influence on performance, reliability, security, and costs like the "Resource Selection Degree" described above.

Metamodel-specific definitions: PCM and Robocop definitions are provided in Appendix C.9.

Example: As an example, consider the PCM example from Figure 2.13, page 61 and the example for the "Resource Selection Degree" in the previous Section.

Let us assume that we are interested in any processing rate in the interval [1GHz, 4GHz]. Then, we can as well model the example with this degree.

7.3.6. Further Configuration of the Software Stack

Rationale: A system may comprise more than the components that realize the business logic. Components are deployed into application servers that provide the required execution environment, which again runs in an operating system. To communicate, components may use message-oriented middleware. Altogether, these software elements make up the software stack of the system. Two examples of software stacks are shown in figure 7.6. The topmost layer of application components is often conceived to be "the system", because it contains the business logic of the system and realizes the system's functional requirements, while the lower layers of the stack provide standard functionality. Nonetheless, the lower layers affect quality attributes, and decisions have to be made on these levels, too.

Configuration of the software stack may be available in the architecture model, so that their effect on quality attributes can be evaluated. Models have been proposed for operating system (OS) scheduler configuration (Happe, 2008), middleware in general (Woodside et al., 2002), or message-oriented-middleware configuration (Happe et al., 2010); and can be envisioned for other configurable properties of operating systems, virtual machines, or middleware. In addition, software stack elements can be ex-

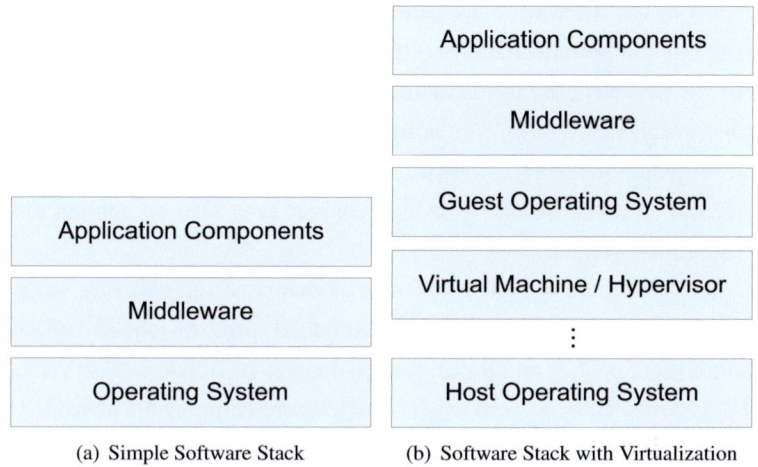

(a) Simple Software Stack (b) Software Stack with Virtualization

Figure 7.6.: Examples for Software Stacks

changed by other products if models for the quality impact are available:
for example, different Java Virtual Machines (JVMs) could be used (Sun's
JVM, Oracle's JRockit JVM, ...), different operating systems could be selected (Windows, Linux, ...), or different application servers can be used
(IBM's Websphere, Apache Geronimo).

Description: Because the software stack is often not central when modelling a component-based software architecture like the components themselves are, the way how the software stack is modelled in a given software
architecture metamodel may vary.

We distinguish two main types of software stack representation: The
software stack can either be explicitly modelled as an infrastructure model
as suggested by Hauck et al. (2009), or its effects can be added to the quality
model as completions, as suggested by Woodside et al. (2002) and realized
in e.g. Happe et al. (2010); Kapova and Reussner (2010) (cf. Section 2.4.4).
In general, all configuration and selection options that are concerned with

elements of the software stack below the application component level are considered configuration of the software stack options in the following.

For the first type, the infrastructure is modelled using specialized model elements (e.g. software layers), or using the same model elements as found on the application level (e.g. software components). In both cases, different degrees of freedom described in this chapter may also be applied to the infrastructure models.

If the metamodel contains different elements of the software stack as separate components, the previously introduced software-related degrees of freedom (Section 7.2) and the allocation degrees of freedom (Section 7.3.1 and 7.3.2) may be applied to these infrastructure components as well.

More complex infrastructure models may open up new types of degree of freedoms that are not inherent to component-based software architectures and thus not covered here (e.g. whether to use virtualization and how many layers of virtual machines to use). They can be added as custom degrees of freedom (see below). They all can be flattened and expressed by component configuration and completions, however, it might be more useful to introduce a new degree of freedom type for easier modelling and understanding.

Thus, the configuration of explicitly modelled infrastructure is covered by the previously described degrees of freedom and potentially additional metamodel-specific degrees.

The second option of software stack representation as model completions is covered by a more general degree of freedom "Completion Configuration" described in Section 7.3.7.

(Primary) Changeable elements: See respective degrees of freedom from Section 7.2, Section 7.3.1 or Section 7.3.2.

Quality Effects: All quality effects described in sections 7.2, 7.3.1 and 7.3.2 may occur. Performance and reliability are influenced by the lower levels of the software stack just as by the application components. Maintainability may also be affected if the operation of the software stack requires effort, in particular if complex manual configuration or even extensions of the implemented functionality are required.

Metamodel-specific definitions: See respective degrees of freedom from Section 7.2, Section 7.3.1 or Section 7.3.2. CBML and ROBOCOP model all relevant components in one model and do not distinguish between application components and further software stack components. Thus, no specific software stack degree of freedom is needed. If software stack elements are modelled as normal components, all previously discussed degrees of freedom can be directly applied to them.

Example: As an example, consider the software stack illustrated in Figure 7.7 by Hauck et al. (2009), which shows a example with a business layer component, an application server component, and a JVM component.

In this example, different JVM implementations may be available and expressed as component selection. Additionally, the allocation of virtual machines to lower layer virtual machines in a virtualized environment with several virtualization layers can be expressed as the allocation degree of freedom.

7.3.7. Quality Completion Configuration

Rationale: Quality completions (cf. Section 2.4.4) have been suggested to include low-level detail required for accurate predictions into a software architecture model in a non-intrusive way. The modelled low-level aspects, such as performance aspects of communication middleware, may offer configuration options, which also have an effect on the quality properties of the system. Thus, when when evaluating an improving the quality attributes of an architecture, it is useful to also consider the configuration options provided by completions.

Description: As described in Section 2.4.4, quality completions can be modelled using feature models (annotated with model transformation fragments which capture the quality effect of each configuration option) and

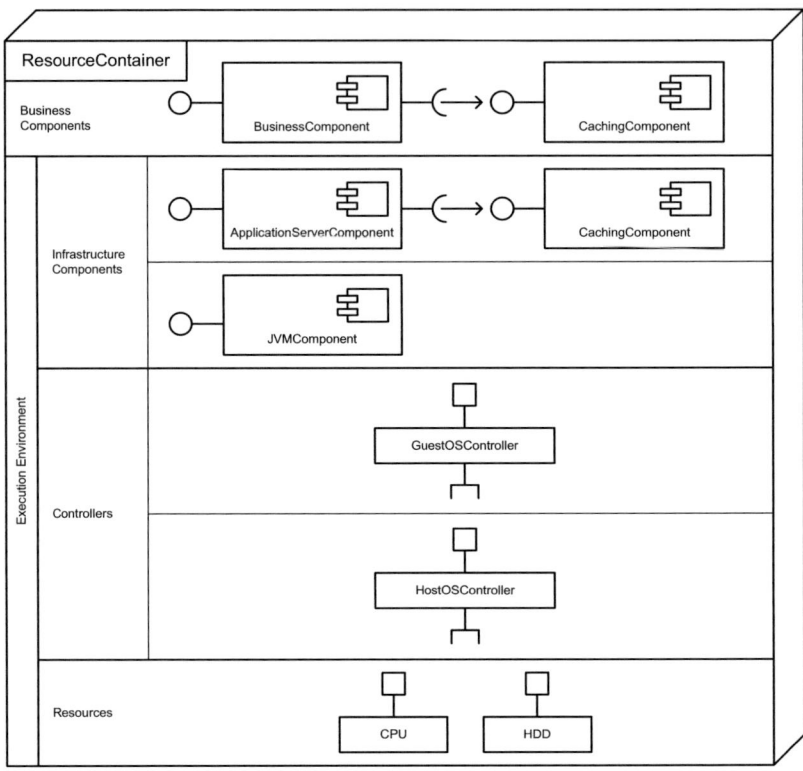

Figure 7.7.: Example of an Explicit Modelling of Infrastructure Components by Hauck et al. (2009)

feature configurations (used to annotate the software architecture and describe the chosen configuration). Each feature model can describe a tree of features, i.e. some features may only be selected if a parent feature is selected. Additional constraints between features may be added as well (cf. (Czarnecki and Eisenecker, 2000)).

Two options exist to consider quality completion configuration as an degree of freedom. First, the configuration of one quality completion (e.g. communication middleware configuration) can be considered one degree of freedom. In this case, the set of all possible configurations form the design option set. For example, consider the "message channel configuration" in the feature model for communication middleware configuration Figure 2.10, Section 2.4.4: Here, a "point-to-point channel" or a "publish subscribe channel" can be selected (exclusive or). If the "publish subscribe channel" is chosen, an additional option is to choose "durable subscribers". Thus, the three overall design options of "message channel configuration" are {point-to-point channel}, {publish subscribe channel }, and {publish subscribe channel, durable subscribers}. If we include the rest of the communication middleware configuration feature model, the design option set grows large, as many features can be combined.

The second option is to consider each feature as one degree of freedom. Thus, to continue our example, we could have two degrees of freedom for the "message channel configuration": The first degree of freedom is whether to use "point-to-point channel" or a "publish subscribe channel", as we have an exclusive or choice here. The second degree of freedom is whether to use "durable subscribers" or not, as this is an optional feature. The choice made for this degree of freedom is only relevant if the "publish subscribe channel" feature has been selected in the parent degree of freedom (similar to degrees of freedoms that are opened up by adding model elements, cf. Section 6.4.1). The advantage of this approach is that the relation of choices described by the feature model are better reflected. However, many degrees of freedom are introduced.

An intermediate approach is to split the feature model into several degrees of freedom, but not necessarily one per feature. For the communication middleware configuration example, three separate degrees of freedom could describe the three features on the upper level of the tree, while each such degree describes all design options of its child features. Heuristics could be devised to automatically derive a set of degrees of freedom for a given feature model, e.g. based on the used constructs (exclusive or, optional features), based on the depth of the tree, or based on the design option set size (e.g. a maximum size of 6). Alternatively, the splitting of each feature model could be defined manually to better reflect the different inner aspects of a quality completion.

Changeable (Primary) Elements: The model elements that describe the completion configuration. If feature models are used, the primary changeable element is the annotated feature configuration.

Quality Effects: Any

Metamodel-specific definitions: PCM and CBML definitions are provided in Appendix C.10.

Example: An example for the PCM is the above-described messaging middleware configuration, described in more detail by Happe et al. (2010), Kapova and Becker (2010), and Kapova (2011).

7.4. Custom Degrees of Freedom

In the two previous subsections, we discussed degrees of freedom that are inherent to component-based software architectures. Depending on the used software architecture metamodel and the concrete software system under study, additional degrees of freedom may be available. If such additional degrees of freedom affect a common quality attribute, these degrees should be considered as well, because an isolated improvement of e.g. first the general CBA degrees and then next the metamodel-specific degrees or the system-specific degrees may lead to suboptimal solutions. In contrast, additional degrees of freedom that do not have effects on quality attributes in common with the degrees of freedom presented in the previous sections can and thus should be considered separately to reduce decision complexity.

The two types of additional degrees of freedom are described in the following:

7.4.1. Metamodel-specific Degrees of Freedom

Rationale: The used software architecture metamodel may offer additional degrees of freedom because the metamodel covers more than the aspects of component-based software architectures described in this work (see Section 2.1).

For example, the metamodel could support to assign developers to components to plan the development schedule, estimate development costs, or the predict reliability based on developer experience. In some development contexts, such decisions may affect the software architecture design[2].

Description: Metamodel-specific value rules need to be defined when instantiating a metamodel-specific degree of freedom. Selection rules, interaction constraints, and added elements are optional.

(Primary) Changeable elements: Custom defined.

Quality Effects: Any

Example in the PCM: Subsystem Selection A set of components together can form an delimited part of the system, called a subsystem, which itself is not a component (e.g. because it is no unit of allocation, or due to other reasons) but which can still be considered a a unit in terms of replacing it. Other subsystems that provide the same functionality, but have different quality properties, can be used to replace the given subsystem in the architecture.

The definition of a subsystem replacement is similar to the component selection degree. The difference is that the contents of a subsystem may be allocated separately. Thus, when replacing a subsystem in a PCM model, the allocation model has to be adjusted, too. Thus, when replacing a subsystem Sub1 with the inner allocated components Sub11, Sub12, and Sub13 with a SubSystem Sub2 with the inner allocated components Sub21, Sub22,

---

[2]Personal communication with Clemens Szyperski, who said that one main driver of how a system is divided into components has been the number of available developer teams in his projects at Microsoft.

and Sub23, we need to delete the AllocationContexts of Sub11, Sub12, and Sub13 and create new AllocationContexts for Sub21, Sub22, and Sub23.

Note that we deliberately do not allow to replace subsystems by components and vice versa. Components and Subsystems are different in their meaning, so that an automated replacement amongst both does not seem appropriate. However, the two degrees of freedom Component Selection and Subsystem Selection could be as well merged into one that also supports the replacement among both types. The quality effects of the Subsystem selection degree are the same as already described for the Component Selection and the Allocation Degree.

See Appendix C.11 for the formal PCM definition.

7.4.2. System-specific Degrees of Freedom

Rationale: The software architect may identify additional design decisions that are still undecided for the concrete system under study, that do not affect functionality or only affect it in an insignificant way, and that affect the quality attributes of interest. In that case, the software architect can manually specify system-specific degrees of freedom.

For example, the software architect may specify that a set of three connected components together with the interfaces connecting them could be replaced by an alternative design of two other components connected by different interfaces. Such a decision does not fall in the component selection degree of freedom, because the interfaces are not matching, but can be specified manually.

Another example are internal decisions inside components. Potentially, the software architect may know about internal design decisions that the developers have to make when implementing a component, and can model these in advance to predict the effects on the overall quality and instruct the developers how to realize the component. For example, a specialized algorithm could be tuned for performance, but the tuning leads to additional costs and worse maintainability. If the software architect can estimate the local quality effects of different tuning levels in advance (e.g. what are the resource demands), he can model the tuning level as a degree of freedom and then let the automated improvement find out how much performance tuning is useful in the overall system context or whether other measures to improve performance are more cost effective.

Description: A system-specific degree of freedom can change a single primary model element in the model or be defined more broadly so that it can be instantiated for several model elements.

Software architects can manually model the system-specific DoF on the metamodel level, have the tool instantiate them automatically, and then select the instantiations of the DoF that are feasible in the design space review step.

A simpler way of specifying a system-specific degree of freedom would be that the software architect only annotates a model element with a range of possible values (or several model elements with a tuples of values) and possibly the related performance, reliability and cost effects. In our tuning example, the software architect would annotate the internal action to be tuned with resource demand and maintainability and development costs, and would define several estimated tuples for the anticipated tuning levels. Alternatively, he could define a function that expresses the relation of resource demand (as the modifiable variable) to maintainability and costs (as outputs of the function), similarly to the continuous definition of resource degrees of freedom (see Section 7.3.4). However, for such simplified specification, a language for specifying custom degrees of freedom on the model level would be required, which is subject to future work.

More complex degrees of freedom can be modelled by manually specifying a model transformation that applies a certain change to the model. For example, one could model the addition of a cache component for parts of the system where the cache hit probability can be estimated. Again, a language for simplified modelling on the model level would be required.

Apart from the possible simplifications, the DoF metamodel already provides the expressiveness to define any degree of freedom that has a primary changeable element on the metamodel level. Software architects can also deliberately decide to model degrees that violate the degree of freedom constraints presented in Section 6.1, and then select the applicable degree of freedom instances in the design space review step.

(Primary) Changeable elements: Any metamodel element.

For the simplified specification on the model level, the changeable elements are determined for a specific system at hand (i.e. for a specific software architecture model at hand).

Quality Effects: Any

Metamodel-specific definitions: As this type of degree of freedom is defined for a specific system, we do not discuss a generic example on the metamodel level here.

Example: For our simple example, a system-specific additional degree of freedom could be to add a QuickConfirm component between BusinessTripMgmt and BookingSystem that checks a requested booking whether it is one of the standard bookings and if yes, it asynchronously calls BookingSystem and then returns the control flow to the BusinessTripMgmt with a confirmation of the booking, without waiting for the response. Figure 7.8 shows the QuickConfirm component.

Figure 7.9 shows the resulting model if this change is applied to the initial model. This degree opens up a new Allocation Degree, here the allocation to S2 has been chosen. Figure 7.9 is just one example of how to apply this change. Like every degree of freedom, this degree can be combined with other degrees instantiated for the example system.

7.5. Limitations

For a system whose design does not follow the component-based paradigm (cf. Section 2.1), our method can only be applied with limitations. First, as a

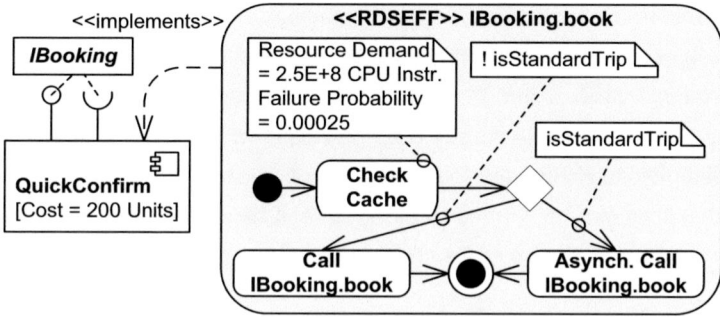

Figure 7.8.: QuickConfirm Cache for the Example of a System-Specific Degree of Freedom

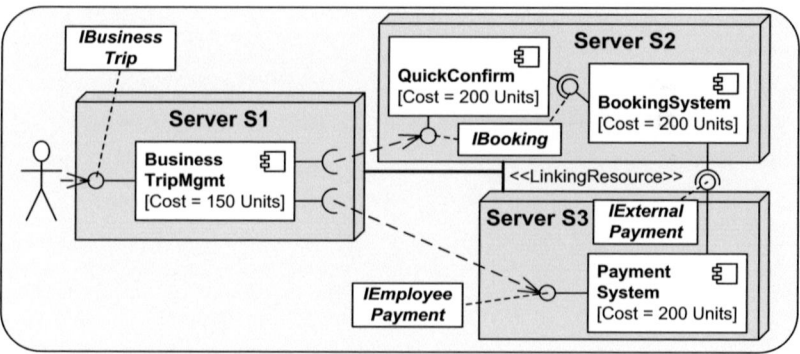

Figure 7.9.: System Using the QuickConfirm Cache for the Example of a System-Specific Degree of Freedom

precondition, a component-based model has to be created for the system. A number of components need to be identified, as no degrees of freedom will be available for a monolithic system. Reengineering tools like presented by Krogmann et al. (2010) may be used to extract component models from the system. Still, if the implementation does not follow the component-based principles such as communication via defined interfaces, the software architect has to review the found degrees of freedom carefully and decide whether they can be applied to the system at hand. Possibly, he needs to define additional design space constraints.

7.6. Summary

This chapter presents the degrees of freedom that are available in CBA in general. Software-related degrees change the application-layer software of the system. Deployment-related change the mapping of the application-layer software to hardware, the configuration of hardware, and further options in the software stack. For most of the presented degrees, the formal definition for the degree in the PCM is given.

8. Optimization

This section describes our optimization method for efficiently finding good architectural models in the design space defined in the previous section. The optimization method is metamodel-agnostic and thus can be applied to any CBA model for which degrees of freedom have been defined. Furthermore, even the realization as a software tool can be implemented without knowledge on the CBA metamodel. To solve the optimization, multi-objective evolutionary optimization is applied.

Section 8.1 describes the optimization problem and discusses the applicable optimization techniques. Section 8.2 presents how we apply evolutionary optimization to the problem. In Section 8.3, we present our extension to evolutionary optimization that allows to include more domain-specific knowledge as tactics operators.

Section 8.4 presents the architecture for a CBA optimization framework that automates the described optimization method while being independent of the used CBA metamodel. Finally, Section 8.5 discusses additional aspects and concludes the chapter.

8.1. Optimization Problem

In this section, we present the optimization problem to find the optimal software architecture models in the design space described in the previous chapter. Having defined the optimization problem, we can apply optimization techniques to automatically solve it and thus automatically improve the given initial software architecture model.

Section 8.1.1 formally describes the optimization problem that results from the degree of freedom definitions of the previous chapter. To select an appropriate optimization technique, Section 8.1.2 discusses the properties of the optimization problem. Finally, Section 8.1.3 explains why we choose metaheuristics to solve the optimization problem.

8.1.1. Formalization of the Optimization Problem

An optimization problem is defined for a specific architectural model M, a set of DoFI D derived for M, and a set of quality criteria (cf. Section 2.2.2) of interest, which we denote as set of objectives O. To define the optimization problem, we discuss the objective function to evaluate candidates and the decision variables to represent candidates in the following. To improve the readability, we drop the indices M and D from the unconstrained design space $\mathcal{D}$, the feasible design space $\mathcal{F}$, and the function T.

The quality evaluation function Φ_q^* (cf. Section 2.4) defines the quality evaluation with respect to quality criterion q of an architecture model. However, Φ_q^* is not defined on the unconstrained design space $\mathcal{D}$, because $\mathcal{D}$ may contain models that do not conform to the metamodel, e.g. because they violate static semantics. Thus the quality prediction may be undefined. To enable reasoning on the unconstrained design space, let us define a more robust evaluation function on top of Φ_q^*. To do so, we add a value *undef* to the domain of the quality criterion q: $\mathcal{V}_q := \mathcal{V}_q^* \cup undef$. Then, we define the robust candidate evaluation function as:

Definition 8.1 Candidate Evaluation Function

The *candidate evaluation function* for a quality criterion q for the unconstrained design space $\mathscr{D}$ is defined as

$$\Phi_q : \mathscr{D} \to \mathscr{V}_q$$

with

$$\Phi_q(a) := \left\{ \begin{array}{ll} \Phi_q^*(a) & \text{if } a \blacktriangleleft MM \\ undef & \text{else} \end{array} \right.$$

To define an optimization problem, we require an order $\leq_i$ on the quality metric's domains which defines preferable values (cf. Section 3.2.2).

Definition 8.2 Order on a Quality Metric Domain

An *order on a quality metric domain* describes which quality values are preferable in this domain and is denoted as $\leq_{qm}$ for a quality metric qm. The order $\leq_{qm}$ is defined as the total order on the quality criterion domain $\mathscr{V}_{qm}$ so that

$$a \leq_{qm} b \Leftrightarrow a \text{ is better than or equal to } b \text{ in terms of } qm$$

with $a, b \in \mathscr{V}_{qm}$. We define *undef* to be the worst value in $\mathscr{V}_{qm}$ under $\leq_{qm}$.

For example, a response time of 2 seconds is better than a response time of 5 seconds. For probability of expected service delivery on demand, 0.9 is better than 0.8. The order $>_{qm}$ is defined as the opposite, but in this case strict order: $a >_{qm} b \Leftrightarrow a$ is worse than b in terms of the quality metric qm ([1]).

We assume in the following that every quality metric's domain has such a total order. Note that there are quality metric domains in which such an

---

[1]Formally, $>_{qm}$ is the complement of $\leq_{qm}$.

275

order does not come naturally, for example the quality metric "response time distributions". These quality metric cannot be used directly but have to be refined to result in a quality metric with an order. To continue the example, we could refine the metric "response time distribution" by applying a function for percentiles, e.g. what response time 90% of the requests fulfil. Quality metrics that cannot be ordered in this way have to be split into multiple metrics, each reflecting an aspect that is not comparable with the others.

In the following, we furthermore assume that a distance metric d_{qm} is defined for each $\mathcal{V}_{qm}$ so that we can quantify the distance of two values in $\mathcal{V}_{qm}$. This assumption is later used to assess candidates within a Pareto front. Many quality domains already have a metric: For example, for mean response time, the time difference of two candidates can be used. Some quality criteria, however, do not have an inherent metric. For example, if we assess the security of a system by different levels low, medium, high, we do not have a metric. In such cases, we define a default metric that assign natural numbers to each value in the quality domain based on their position in the total order $\leq_q$. For security, we might assign the numbers low = 1, medium = 2 and high = 3, so that the distance $d(\text{high,low})$ is $|1 - 3|$.

The optimization problem for a single quality criterion q then is to find the best candidate a with respect to $\Phi_q(c)$. The best candidate is a candidate a^* for that

$$\forall a \in \mathcal{F} : \Phi_q(a) \leq_{m(q)} \Phi_q(a^*) \implies \Phi_q(a) = \Phi_q(a^*)$$

As we use the symbol $\leq_{m(q)}$ here, we also say that a is the minimal candidate.

As described in the previous chapter, the design space of candidates can be expressed with a set of decision variables. The function T maps a decision vector to an architecture candidate. Thus, we can define the optimization problem on the decision vectors instead directly on the candidates.

Applying the function T on a decision vector $x \in \mathscr{O}$ represents a candidate $T(x)$.

Thus, we can write the optimization problem classically as:

$$Opt_q : \min_{x \in \mathscr{O}} \Phi_q(T(x)) \text{ subject to } c \in \mathscr{F}$$

For the multi-criteria optimization problem, we can combine the set $Q = q_1, \ldots, q_n$ of n considered quality criteria in a vector-valued objective function called *multi-objective candidate evaluation function*

$$\Phi_Q : \mathscr{D} \to \mathscr{V}_{m(q_1)} \times \cdots \times \mathscr{V}_{m(q_n)}$$

$$\Phi_Q(a) \mapsto (\Phi_{q_1}(a), \ldots, \Phi_{q_n}(a))$$

Let $\overset{\prec}{\min}$ denote minimization for Pareto optimality with respect to all $\leq_{m(q)}$, $q \in Q$ as described in Section 3.2.2. Then, the multi-criteria optimization problem can be defined as follows

$$Opt_Q : \overset{\prec}{\min_{x \in \mathscr{O}}} \Phi_Q(T(x)) \text{ subject to } c \in \mathscr{F}$$

The solution to this optimization problem is a set of Pareto-optimal candidates, which we denote with $P(D, Q)$.

8.1.2. Properties of the Optimization Problem

For the optimization problem defined in the previous section, we can apply optimization techniques to automate the search for optimal candidates in the design space. A large number of optimization techniques for different types of problems have been proposed. The choice of an applicable optimization technique depends on the properties of the optimization problem. Thus, in this section, we discuss the properties of the optimization problem defined in the previous section, before selecting an appropriate optimization technique in the next section.

The problem is *multi-objective*, i.e. the objective function maps one candidate to a set of quality criteria. The different quality criteria can be in conflict with each other, but not necessarily. For example, if in a model where more expensive processors are also more reliable, and where no other degrees of freedom that affect reliability are given, performance and reliability are not in conflict. Often, however, performance, cost, and reliability are mutually in conflict. For example, distributing the system to several servers can improve performance, but can worsen reliability as more points of failures are introduces. Additionally, costs are increased. At the same time, more reliable resources may be more expensive. Formally, the objective function Φ_Q does not introduce a total order on $\mathscr{F}$, but only a partial order (Pareto, 1896; Zitzler, 1999).

For complex quality attributes such as performance and reliability, the quality effect of design option depends on other chosen design options. For example, selecting a component that has fewer CPU demand but higher HDD load may be beneficial for performance in a candidate where the component's server has high CPU utilization already but low HDD utilization. However, for a candidate where this component is deployed to a server with low CPU utilization and high HDD utilization, it worsens performance. Even if we know for some degrees of freedom that a design option will always have a positive effect on the quality criterion, we cannot quantify it in advance without solving the model. For example, although we can predict that increasing the server speed in an open workload[2] will improve response time, we do not know how much, as this depends on the utilization of all servers. Thus, we have *no isolated quality effect* of a design option in general.

The problem usually has *discrete decision variables*. While some DoFI might be modelled with a continuous variable (e.g. "Non-functional Component Configuration Parameters" or "Resource Selection" modelled by a continuously changing variable), most DoFI have a discrete set of design

---

[2]In a system with a closed workload, this example is not even right in general

options (all other DoFI from Chapter 7). Some design option sets are unordered (for example the available servers in the Allocation Degree).

The range of values is constrained by practical reasons (for example, no arbitrarily fast CPU or arbitrarily large thread pool is possible in practice). Thus the discrete design option sets are finite and every discrete decision variable can only take a limited number of values. There is no infinite number of threads possible, for example, but there is a current maximum over all possible operating systems and environments. For continuous decision variables, an approximation with floating point values, which is a finite set, is used in computing anyway. Thus, continuous decision variables can only take a limited, but potentially large, number of values.

The size of the decision space depends on the instantiated DoFI in D. For a set of DoFI D with discrete design option sets only, the size is $|\mathcal{O}| = \Pi_{d \in D} |designOptions(d)|$. Thus, already with a few DoFI, each having a number of design options, the decision space becomes large. For example, the decision space of the example in Section 6.2 with its 7 DoFI (three with design option set size three, three with size 13, and one with size 2) is $3^3 \cdot 13^3 \cdot 2 = 118638$. If DoFI with infinite design option sets are present, the decision space is infinite in theory. However, considering approximations with float values again, the *design space is finite*, but very large, too.

We want to support expressive quality prediction techniques such as LQN solution using mean value analysis (cf. Section 2.4). Additionally, the improvement method should be extendable to other any quantitative quality prediction techniques for any quality criteria. Thus, we cannot assume any properties of the quality criterion evaluation functions Φ_q and thus cannot assume any properties such as linearity, continuity, or differentiability for the combined objective function Φ_Q. We say that Φ_Q is a *black-box function*.

Additionally, the evaluation of the quality properties is *computationally expensive*. Even if the approximate analytic LQNS analysis for PCM models is used, the evaluation of a candidate can take several seconds or minutes, depending on the requested accuracy. Similarly, the reliability prediction for the PCM may take long for complex models and high prediction accuracy. While the accuracy of the predictions is not required to be very high for candidate evaluation, the quality evaluation is still orders of magnitude longer than the logic of e.g. an evolutionary algorithm (selection, mutation, and reproduction steps as described in Section 8.2). Thus, an exhaustive enumeration of all possible solutions is not feasible for a large decision space.

To summarize, our optimization problem has the following properties

- Multi-objective: The objective-function Φ_Q objective function maps one candidate to a set of quality criteria.

- No isolated quality effect: The effect of single design option cannot be predicted in isolation in general, but only together with chosen values for the other degrees of freedom.

- Discrete decision variables: A subset of the decision variables is discrete.

- Finite design space: The set of design options is finite (or can be simplified to be finite) and the set of DoFI is finite.

- Black-box function: No assumptions possible for properties of the objective function Φ_Q.

- Computationally expensive: As we use expressive quality models, determining Φ_Q for a candidate is computationally expensive.

Simple instantiations of the optimization problem do not have all these properties. For example, if only costs in the PCM are considered, the quality effect of design decisions can be determined in isolation, because our cost model only sums up the costs of components and servers. Additionally, the problem is then not multi-objective. However, we will not consider such simple versions of the problem further, because they are of limited practical use.

8.1.3. Applicable Optimization Techniques

For the optimization problem characterized in the previous section, we cannot apply classic techniques such as Branch-And-Bound (Dakin, 1965) (see Section 3.3), because we cannot make any assumptions about the objective function. A common class of optimization techniques that does not make any assumptions about the problem, but allows any black-box function as objective function are metaheuristics (cf. Section 3.4). Metaheuristics have been successfully applied to similar problems in software engineering (Harman, 2007).

We chose not to use a rule-based approach (which employ local search techniques). Rule-based methods (Xu, 2008; Cortellessa and Frittella, 2007; Parsons and Murphy, 2008; McGregor et al., 2007) target to find designs that satisfy a set of predefined quality requirements. As discussed in Section 5.1, we expect that software architects cannot specify meaningful quality requirements in advance, but need an approximation of the Pareto-front in order to understand the design problem and trade-off the available quality criteria.

Additionally, rules target to improve a single quality criterion. Applying only rules for one criterion may thus result in a candidate that is optimal with respect to this criterion, but exhibits bad values for other quality criteria. Mixing rules for all criteria could result in an undirected exploring of the search, e.g. if a rule for one criterion reverts a rule of another criterion. Thus, to use such rules for multi-objective problems with multiple quality criteria, an additional high-level search algorithm is required that decides what rules to apply, possibly based on Pareto-dominance. Thus, single-objective rules alone cannot solve the multi-objective problem efficiently.

Finally, the rule-based methods are restricted to limited degrees of freedom each. No a-priori knowledge about the effects of many of the degrees of freedom is available. For example, in the PCM, rules for the exchange of components would require a numerical solution for optimal component composition, which is not possible in general because of the parametrization of the component SEFFs. For other degrees of freedom, such as allocation, rules can give guidance, but cannot foresee the complexity of performance metrics introduced by software resources and contention effects. For example, if passive resources such as thread pools are involved, allocation of components to servers cannot be solved based on the resource demand of components only. Additionally, network utilization had to be taken into account.

Metaheuristics can search regions of the search space for which no prior knowledge about the relation between choices and resulting quality properties exists. They only require a quantitative evaluation function for each quality criterion based on an architecture model and make no more assumptions on the function's properties or the model's properties (black-box function).

Still, the existing knowledge about the design space is not ignored by our method, but integrated as tactic operators described in Section 8.3.

Methods that do not require any a-priori preference articulation, but target to provide a well-spread Pareto-front are beneficial to provide the software architect with a set of solutions to assess the trade-offs and decide for one candidate (cf. Section 3.2.1). Here, methods that explore the Pareto-front using Pareto dominance seem promising because they are independent of weighting the objective functions and can find a well-spread Pareto-front (cf. (Deb, 2001, p.172 et seq.) and (van Veldhuizen and Lamont, 1998)). Methods that use objective function weighting during the exploration may result in a not uniformly-spread Pareto front (cf. example in (Deb, 2001, p.173)).

As described in Section 3.4, population-based metaheuristics are useful for multi-objective problems because they generate multiple solutions in one run (Deb, 2001, p.7). In our problem, the evaluation of a candidate (especially for performance) is computationally expensive (e.g. simulation or LQN solution), which makes the possible parallel evaluation of population-based methods desirable.

To summarize, we identify three properties for an optimization technique to be promising for our optimization problem:

Metaheuristic to allow for any black-box objective function and multiple objective functions

Pareto-based because no weighting of objectives is required

Population-based because the fitness evaluation can be parallelized

In this work, we use evolutionary algorithms (as for example described by Deb (2001)), which are a popular type of population-based metaheuristics. Evolutionary algorithms have been found useful for multi-objective problems (Coello Coello, 1999). Several evolutionary methods that target to find a well-spread front have been suggested (Deb, 2001, p.172–176). The optimization problem presented in Section 8.1.1 can be directly handled by an evolutionary algorithm with a fixed genome length, with each gene representing one DoFI.

We do not use Ant Colony Optimization (cf. (Blum and Roli, 2003, p.289 et seqq.)) because partial solutions cannot be evaluated with the quality prediction techniques. One would require a heuristic that evaluates the attractiveness of partial solutions, i.e. solutions where only some choices have been made while for others no values have been chosen. Thus, the constructive approach of Ant Colony Optimization does not seem well applicable in this problem.

Most multi-objective simulated annealing (MOSA) (Suman and Kumar, 2006) are not population-based or use weights to combine the objective functions and thus are not used. Hybrid methods that combine MOSA with evolutionary methods have been suggested and could be used here as well.

Simple Estimation of Distribution Algorithms (EDAs, cf. (Blum and Roli, 2003, p.288 et seq.)) that assume no interactions of decision variables are not promising because such independence of the decision variables is not given in our problems. For quality optimization, especially performance, the decision variables may highly depend on each other. For example, the effect of the processor speed of a server on the mean response time highly depends on what components are allocated to it. Thus, the effect of single genes to the objective function cannot readily be estimated by a distribution function. Other types of optimization approaches that build probabilistic models during the search and consider interaction of decision variables could be promising (survey by Pelikan et al. (2002)), however, and could be studied in future work.

More multi-objective population-based metaheuristics that use Pareto-dominance have been suggested and could be evaluated further to be used in this work as well. An example is particle swarm optimization (Parsopoulos and Vrahatis, 2002; Coello Coello and Salazar Lechuga, 2002).

Evolutionary methods are the most commonly used multi-objective population-based metaheuristics. Here, it has been shown for several case studies that elitist algorithms are superior (Deb, 2001, p.375 et seqq.,p.379) (Coello Coello et al., 2007, p.304). In this work, we adopted the elitist evolutionary optimization technique NSGA-II (Deb et al., 2000). We chose NSGA-II because it has been very commonly used in optimization literature (Coello Coello et al., 2010). It has performed better than another popular algorithm SPEA-2 (Zitzler et al., 2002a) on a number of test problems when two objectives are optimized while at the same time having a lower computational complexity than SPEA-2 (Deb et al., 2003).

Note, however, that SPEA-2 is expected to produce better distribution in three and more dimensions, while having higher computational costs (Deb et al., 2003). A clustering-based crowding measure has been suggested for

NSGA-II (Deb et al., 2003) that could be used in our method for optimization problem instances where the number of objectives is 3 or higher.

Another interesting algorithm that particularly focusses on problems with expensive evaluation functions is ParEGO (Knowles, 2006). ParEGO builds an approximated model of the search landscape while optimizing with the goal to converge to promising solutions quickly, without too many function evaluations. However, ParEGO targets problems where the candidate evaluation takes minutes or hours so that only up to 250 candidate evaluations can be performed. Evaluations in our work are faster, so that more evaluations can be performed. The current ParEGO implementation is reported to deteriorate in speed for more than 200 evaluations [3], so it could not be used as-is.

In future work, it could be beneficial to adopt more recent results in the field of evolutionary algorithms with respect to dominance relations, other preference relation, or archiving strategies, as sketched in Section 3.5.3. However, it is difficult to assess which technique is best in general because the optimization techniques' performance depends on search problem at hand. Comparisons of evolutionary optimization techniques in the literature depend on the evaluated case study. Furthermore, Wolpert and Macready (1997) have stated that all optimization techniques perform the same on average when being applied to all possible optimization problems. Thus, from reports that an algorithm has performed better than NSGA-II on a test problem, we cannot conclude that it will perform better for our software architecture optimization problem. An experimental evaluation of numerous optimization techniques for our type of optimization problem is a large effort and outside the focus of this work.

As a consequence, in this work, we focussed more on how to adapt the NSGA-II algorithm to our problem at hand using domain-specific knowledge (Section 8.3) and considering potentially available quality bounds (Section 8.2.5.2) instead of experimentally evaluating which existing evol-

---

[3] Documentation in main class in http://dbkgroup.org/knowles/parego/ParEGO.tar.gz

utionary optimization techniques to use as a basis. Our extensions can as well be applied to any other evolutionary optimization technique used as a basis.

In the following, we describe our an evolutionary optimization technique based on the NSGA-II evolutionary algorithm.

8.2. Evolutionary Optimization

This section describes how we apply evolutionary optimization to the described optimization problem. Our technique is based on the NSGA-II evolutionary algorithm (Deb et al., 2000). The following subsections describe how the steps of an evolutionary optimization are realized in this work, and discuss the decisions made.

Section 8.2.1 gives an outline on our evolutionary optimization technique. The following sections discuss details of the optimization technique, namely the representation of candidates (Section 8.2.2), the evaluation of candidates (Section 8.2.3), the reproduction of candidates, considering constraints (Section 8.2.4), and the strategies for candidate selection (Section 8.2.5). Finally, Section 8.2.6 briefly discusses stopping criteria for the algorithm.

Section 8.3 then describes our extension to evolutionary optimization that allows to include more domain-specific knowledge as tactics to guide the search.

8.2.1. Outline

Figure 8.1 shows the process model of our method and puts the evolutionary optimization step into context. The optimization is described here exemplary for our current realization with the PCM and the NSGA-II evolutionary algorithm (Deb et al., 2000) (cf. Section 3.5.3) as implemented in the Opt4J framework (Lukasiewycz et al., 2010). It can as well be used

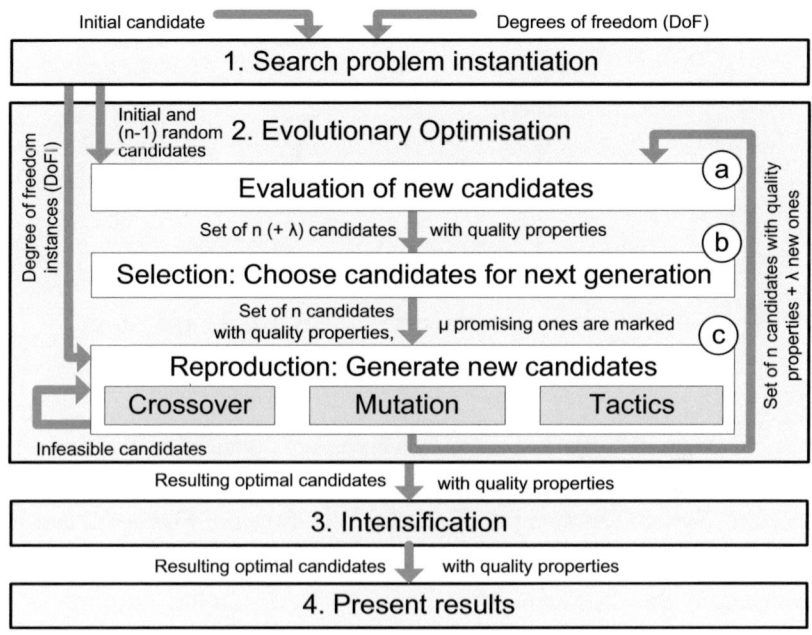

Figure 8.1.: Evolutionary Optimization Process

for other software architecture modelling languages and other population-based metaheuristic search techniques, because the process is generic.

The process starts with an initial model of a component-based software architecture (initial candidate) and modifies it along the degree of freedom instances. As the software model contains all required annotations, all steps of the search can be completely automated.

In step 1 *Search Problem Formulation*, the DoFI are instantiated automatically based on the DoF description and the initial model (cf. Section 6.4.1). After this step, the software architect may review the found DoFI and adjust them, e.g. by removing unwanted options or adding additional system-specific degrees.

Step 2 is the *Evolutionary Optimization*. To better convey the optimization step, the first two iterations of an exemplary run for the Business Trip

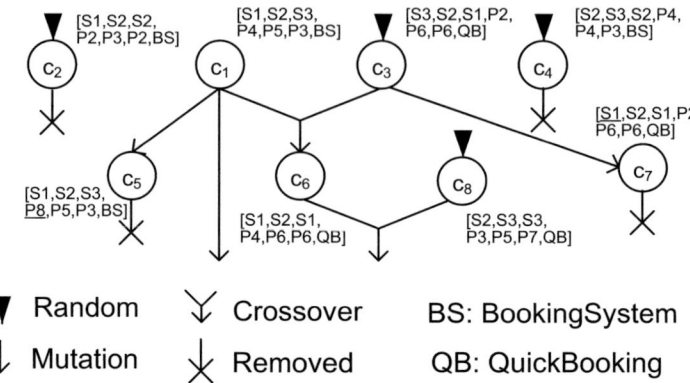

Figure 8.2.: The Beginning of an Exemplary Optimization Run

Booking System example (cf. Figure 2.13) is shown in Figure 8.2 and is used to explain the steps in the following. To better convey the concepts, we simplify the steps here. More detail is provided in the following sections. The run starts with the initial given candidate c_1.

The evolutionary algorithm is configured with population size n and additional parameters, explained in the next sections. After the search problem formulation, $n - 1$ random decision vectors are generated to form the initial population. Then, the following optimization steps a–c are repeated until a stop condition (see below) is fulfilled:

(a) **Evaluation:** In the first step, each newly derived candidate is evaluated for each quality criterion of interest. To do so, every decision vector is translated to a software architecture model and this model is evaluated using standard techniques (e.g. LQN) as described in Section 2.4. As a result, each candidate is annotated with the determined quality properties. In our example, candidates c_1 to c_4 are evaluated in the first iteration, and candidates c_5 to c_8 are evaluated in the second iteration. The results for each candidate are depicted in Figure 8.3.

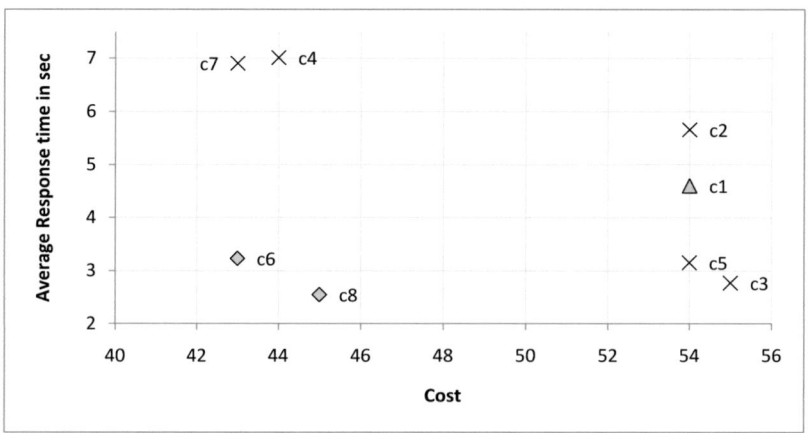

Figure 8.3.: Resulting Candidates after 2 Iterations (Pareto-optimal Candidates: $\Diamond$, Initial Candidate: $\triangle$, Others $\times$)

(b) **Selection:** The selection step removes unfit candidates and selects candidates for reproductions.

After the first iteration, the population grows after each reproduction step. In the selection phase, the population is again reduced by removing less promising candidates. The selection strategy must balance between exploitation and diversity: It must prefer better candidates so that the quality of the population increases over times. On the other hand, it should keep a variety of different candidates, even if some are inferior, so that the search does not prematurely converge to a local optimum. For our example, let us assume that we simply filter Pareto-dominated candidates and only keep Pareto-optimal ones. Then, candidates c_2 and c_4 are removed in the selection phase of iteration 1, and candidates c_5 and c_7 are removed in the selection phase of iteration 2.

Furthermore, μ candidates are selected for reproduction. In this example, all candidates except the removed ones are selected. Details on the selection can be found in Section 8.2.5.

(c) **Reproduction:** Based on the μ selected candidates, λ new candidate solutions are derived by "mutation" or "cross-over" or they are randomly created. With mutation, one or several design options are varied. In our exemplary run, based on the initial candidate c_1, a new candidate c_5 with changed processor speed for server 1 is derived in the first iteration. Candidate c_7 derives from c_3 in the first iteration by reallocating QuickBooking to S1. With cross-over, the genotypes of two good candidate solutions are merged into one, by taking some of each candidates design option values for the cross-over. For example, candidate c_1 and candidate c_3 are combined by cross-over in the second iteration to produce c_6.

If a candidate is created that is infeasible due to model constraints (cf. Section 6.4.3), or that is already in the population, it is discarded and a random candidate is generated instead. More details on the reproduction step can be found in Section 8.2.4. In Section 8.3, we discuss how performance domain specific tactics are integrated here to guide the search. For example, a tactic moves a component from an over-utilized server to a lightly utilized server.

Over several iterations, the combination of reproduction and selection lets the population converge towards the front of *globally* Pareto-optimal solutions. If the search also keeps a good diversity of candidates, we can find solutions near to the global optima. In our example, a resulting solution with a good trade-off is c_6, shown in Figure 8.4. It is superior to the initial candidate in average response time (3.23 sec) and cost (43), and has just as slightly higher probability of failure on demand (74E-04).

The most common stop criterion is a predefined maximum number of iterations, after which the algorithm stops and outputs the front of Pareto-optimal candidates obtained so far. More sophisticated stop criteria use convergence detection to estimate whether a continuation of the search

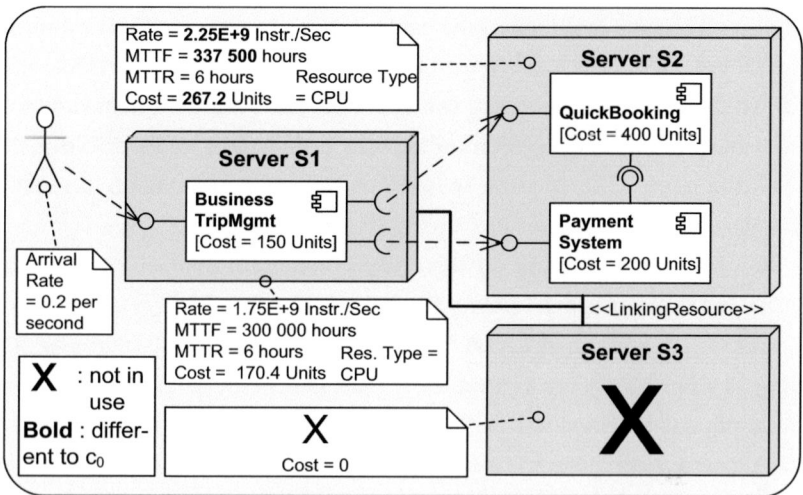

Figure 8.4.: Example PCM Model for Pareto-optimal Candidate c_6

would improve the current results, and stop the search if this is not expected. Such criteria are discussed in Section 8.2.6.

In a final *Intensification* step (step 3), the neighbourhood of the found Pareto-optimal candidates is searched for even better candidates. For each candidates found by the previous step, it is checked whether any tactic can be applied to further improve it. This step is described in more detail in Section 8.3.3.

Finally, in the forth step *Present Results*, the resulting Pareto-optimal candidates are presented to the software architect who can make well-informed trade-off decisions.

8.2.2. Candidate Representation

The candidate representation is straightforward with our formulation of the design space (cf. Section 6.4) and evolutionary algorithms. A candidate model is represented by a candidate vector in the decision space. This representation can directly be used as the genome of the evolutionary algorithm. For each DoFI, one gene captures the chosen value for the design option set. The genes are typed based on which DoF the DoFI belongs to. Then, the genetic operators can determine the possible values directly from the DoFI's design option set and can even handle genes of different DoF differently. The decision space in our problem formulation has fixed dimensions, so the genome has a fixed length.

A DoFI d' may depend on the chosen values for another DoFI d, as discussed in Section 6.4.1. Only if a subset of values for d is chosen, the choices for d' have an effect on the quality properties. Thus, varying d' as long as other values are chosen for d does not progress the search. This knowledge is reflected in this work by introducing non-coding regions in the genome. Each gene has a flag whether it is currently active or not in a candidate. This flag expresses that the gene will certainly have no effect if it is inactive and thus should be ignored by genetic operators. Thus, genetic drift (i.e. the filling of the population with quasi-equal candidates that bring to benefit to the search) due to inactive regions (Aguirre and Tanaka, 2005, Sec.6.2) is prevented. Note that the flag does not ensure that a gene will certainly have effect on a quality attribute if it is active.

Inactive genes are determined in two ways: First, if a DoFI d opens up new DoFI d' in the automated DoFI instantiation by adding new model elements (cf. 6.4.1), we know that d' is active only for values of d's primary changeable element that lead to the addition of this model element. We can keep track of the opened DoFI in the automated DoFI instantiation algorithm (page 216 in Section 6.4.1) in lines 57–68.

Second, the DoF description is enriched by additional constraints if applicable. For example, the speed of a processor is only relevant for performance if at least one component is deployed to the server containing the processor. This condition can be expressed by an OCL constraint that describes the conditions under which instances of this DoF are inactive. To continue the example, the OCL constraint for the Allocation DoF in the

PCM is given below, with the variable allocation denoting the unique alloc-ation model.

```
context ResourceContainer
  def : isActive : Boolean =
    allocation . allocationContext
      ->exists(ac | ac.resourceContainer = self)
```

Third, software architects might manually specify conditions when genes are active for their system-specific degrees of freedom.

The resulting metamodel for candidate vectors in EMOF is shown in Figure 8.5. Corresponding to the metamodel for DoFIs (Figure 6.9), which has specialized classes for design option sets with different value types, candidate vectors are modelled depending on the data type of their values. For each DoFI, a Choice defined the chosen values and thus represents a gene. For integer and real values, the classes ContinuousRangeChoice and DiscreteRangeChoice are used to select one value from the design option set of the corresponding range degree of freedom. For design option sets where metamodel elements are referenced, the ClassChoice refers to the chosen Entity.

OCL constraints (not shown here) ensure that a choice matches the type of referenced degree of freedom, so that a ClassChoice can only be used if the referenced DoFI is a ClassDegree.

With our candidates representation, not every candidate encoded by a genome is a feasible candidate, because the decision vectors only describe the unconstrained design space, not the feasible design space. However, we assume that few candidates in the design space are infeasible compared to the total number of candidates, because degrees of freedom usually describe independent choices. One of the core ideas of component-based software design is the encapsulation of concepts, so this assumptions seems valid. In the CBSE degree of freedom we have discussed so far, only the allocation degrees require interaction constraints. Here we may assume, at least for business information systems, that servers are pairwise connected (e.g. if they all reside in a computing centre), and that they offer similar resources.

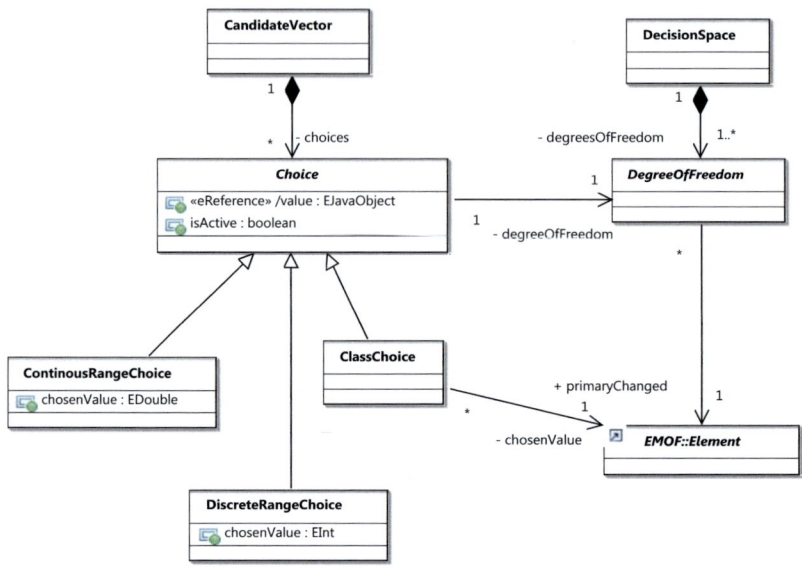

Figure 8.5.: Metamodel for Candidate Vectors in EMOF

The optimization of arbitrary configurations (cf. Section 7.3.6), however, may lead to more constraints if the feature model is highly constrained.

For systems and CBA metamodels this assumption does not apply to, more sophisticated constraint handling strategies or even a different candidate representation may be required. If the infeasible candidates are limited to interactions of few DoFI, these degrees could also be joined to form one composed DoFI that enumerates all feasible combinations of the inner DoFIs design option sets. However, such a composite degree cannot be exploited by crossover operators any more, and thus might lead to worse optimization performance.

8.2.3. Candidate Evaluation

This section presents the candidate evaluation. First, Section 8.2.3.1 discusses how the quality function formally presented in Section 8.1.1 is modelled and realized in the evolutionary optimization technique. Then, Section 8.2.3.2 describes the candidate vector evaluation during the optimization.

8.2.3.1. Quality Function Definition

The evaluation function Φ_Q is conceptually described in Section 8.1.1. However, concrete quality prediction techniques, such as LQNS and SimuCom, are metamodel-specific: they require an input model in a certain format (e.g. LQN or Palladio). In this section, we discuss how to bridge the gap between the metamodel-specific prediction technique and a metamodel-agnostic optimization method.

The main tool to close the gap is a common CBA-metamodel-agnostic quality metamodel for describing quality criteria and quality properties. This metamodel serves as an interface between the prediction technique and the optimization. An adaptor for each prediction technique declares which quality criteria the technique supports. Additionally, it offers to evaluate a passed candidate model for a set of quality criteria. The results are stored in the common quality property model. In the optimization technique, the optimization problem is defined using terms of the common quality metamodel.

For the quality model in EMOF, we adopted the Quality of service Modelling Language (QML) (Frølund and Koistinen, 1998), which has been originally proposed to model quality requirements for a system. The relevant concepts in QML are the following: In a Contract Type in QML, a quality Dimension describes the domain and order of a quality criterion. For example, a Dimension can be response time with real-numbered values and a decreasing order (i.e. a smaller value is beneficial). A Contract in QML defines Constraints for these dimensions. A Constraint defines an Evaluation Aspect for a Dimension and a worst acceptable value. An Evaluation Aspect defines how the Dimension is interpreted, e.g. what point estimator such as mean or percentiles should be considered. Here, as we are interested in Pareto-fronts to study trade-offs, we added the possibility to specify Objectives. Objectives only define the Evaluation Aspect, without defining a worst acceptable value. The new common superclass of Constraint and Objective is Criterion, as it corresponds to the definition of a quality criterion (cf. Section 2.2.1).

We metamodelled QML in EMOF and extended it so that it can be annotated to CBA models specified in EMOF. Appendix D presents QML, shows the resulting EMOF metamodel, and discusses the adoptions in more detail.

To express the results of a quality prediction, we model quality properties as shown in Figure 8.6. The quality property specification refers to the QML criterion definition used to defined the optimization problem (cf. Appendix D). Values of quality properties can be integer values (Integer-QualityProperty), double values (DoubleQualityProperty), or other values defined in the QML definition of their respective dimension. OCL constraints (not shown here) ensure that the QualityProperties match the domain of the referenced QML Criterion. In some cases, a quality property for a quality criterion cannot be determined for a candidate vector, because the candidate model is invalid or because the quality prediction could not provide a meaningful value. In that case, no QualityProperty is defined for this criterion and this candidate vector, which corresponds to an undefined value.

An adaptor for a quality prediction technique then has to provide the following interface.

Declare Dimensions: The quality prediction adaptor declares a set of quality Dimensions it supports (for example, response time or PO-FOD), referring to a repository of QML dimensions.

Name supported Evaluation Aspects: For a given dimension, a quality prediction adaptor lists the supported Evaluation Aspects, such as mean, variance, percentiles, etc.

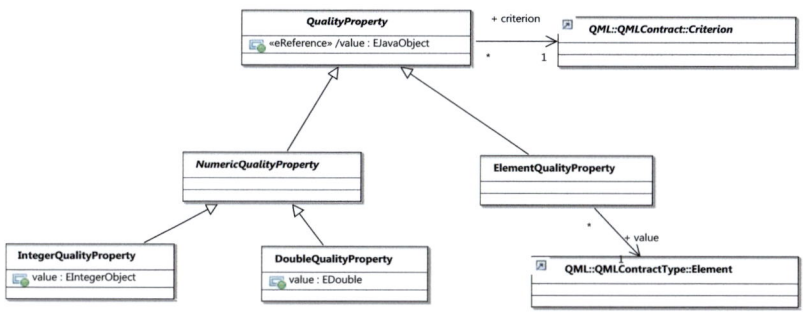

Figure 8.6.: Quality Property Model in EMOF

Evaluate model and return Quality Properties: Finally, when a candidate model is passed to the quality prediction adaptor, it evaluates the model using the underlying quality prediction technique, determines the result values for the requested dimension and evaluation aspect, and returns the resulting QualityProperty element.

8.2.3.2. Candidate Evaluation during the Search

Candidate evaluation consists of three steps, informally shown in Figure 8.7. First, the genome, i.e. in our case the candidate vector, is translated to the so-called phenotype, which in our case is a candidate model. Second, the quality prediction for the quality attributes of interest is executed for the candidate model, e.g. with SimuCom or LQNS for Palladio. Third, the quality property of interest, e.g. the mean response time of one service of the system, is extracted from the results.

In the candidate translation step, a candidate vector (i.e. a genome) uniquely identifies a candidate model. The candidate transformation function T, which creates a candidate model from a candidate vector based on the initial candidate model, is discussed in Section 6.4.2. The function can be defined generically for a metametamodel.

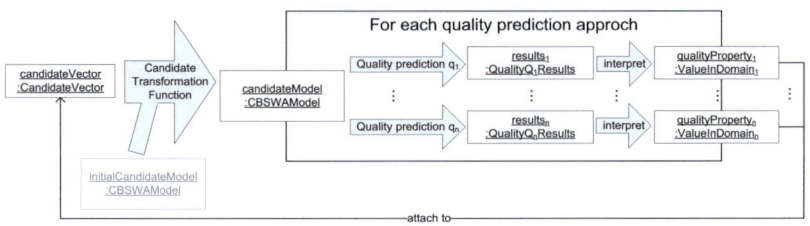

Figure 8.7.: Candidate Evaluation Steps

If the metametamodel supports reflection, such as EMOF and Ecore in EMF do, these capabilities can be used and a single generic transformation can represent T, as shown in Appendix B.3 for EMF.

Otherwise, a higher-order transformation T needs to be created for the metamodel, that automatically creates a transformation T_i for each DoF g_i. A straightforward option would be to write a generic model-to-text transformation (e.g. with the XPand language (Efftinge et al., 2008, chapter II.5)) that creates the DoF-specific transformations T_i, which can then be used during optimization.

In the candidate model evaluation step, the created candidate model, conforming to the CBA metamodel at hand, is fed into the quality prediction (cf. Section 2.4). For example, for performance quality criteria, the candidate model can be transformed into a queueing network model and solved with e.g. Layered Queueing Network Solver (LQNS) (Franks et al., 2009). The result of this step is a prediction-model-specific output. For example, LQNS annotates the predictions results, i.e. response times of all LQN entries and utilization of all LQN processors, to the input LQN model.

If the accuracy of quality evaluations can be configured, it could be increased in this phase. For example, the LQNS tool allows to configure a convergence value that defines what accuracy is required in the analysis of a candidate. The larger the convergence value, the faster the candidate can be evaluated, but the more inaccurate are the results. While it it useful to have quick candidate evaluation at the beginning of the evolutionary al-

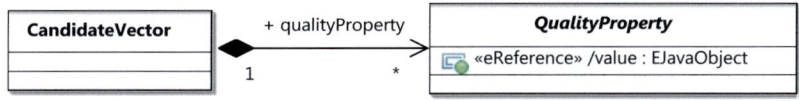

Figure 8.8.: Metamodel for Evaluated Candidate Vectors in EMOF

gorithm, it is more important to have accurate results in later phases and in the intensification phase. Furthermore, different candidate evaluation techniques could be used depending on the phase of the optimization, as for example suggested by Buchholz and Kemper (2006).

In the last step of result interpretation, the quality properties of interest must be retrieved from the quality prediction results and stored with the candidate vectors. For our EMOF model, we attach the quality property of interest presented in the previous subsection to the candidate vector as shown in Figure 8.8. For performance, additional quality properties such as utilization of servers are stored in a result decorator model (Krogmann et al., 2009) so that tactics can interpret them (cf. Section 8.3). Similarly, more detailed result models can be added for other quality properties to make use of domain-specific knowledge.

8.2.4. Candidate Reproduction

We use the two standard operators crossover and mutation (cf. Section 3.5.2) and our tactics operators. The use of tactics operators is described in Section 8.3.2.

The following briefly describes how the two standard genetic operator types *mutation* and *crossover* are used in this work (Section 8.2.4.1). Then, we discuss how produced candidates that are infeasible due to design space constraints are handled in Section 8.2.4.2.

8.2.4.1. Reproduction Operators

If no tactics are used, we randomly choose whether to apply the crossover operator based on the configurable crossover probability. Additionally, each candidate (resulting from the crossover or unchanged) is mutated.

To increases the diversity of the population, we check the outcome of the reproduction step for duplicates (i.e. whether a generated candidate has been considered before), and if yes, we replace them with random candidates.

In the context of quality optimization of CBA, there are some degrees of freedoms that do not have an order (e.g. component reallocation). Thus, a hybrid mutation operator that applies different mutation strategies to different types of degrees of freedom has been chosen, as suggested by Deb and Goyal (1996). When the hybrid mutation operator is applied, it changes each gene in the genome as follows: For the part of the genome representing degrees of freedom with an order and a meaningful distance (i.e. ContinuousRangeDegrees), the gene is varied by a small random amount using a polynomial distribution (cf. (Deb and Goyal, 1996)). For genes representing choices of DiscreteRangeDegreess or EnumerationDegrees, a new value is randomly chosen from all allowed values following a uniform distribution.

We use probabilistic mutation with a mutation rate in this work (cf. Section 3.5.2.1). To be able to steer the intensity of mutation, we added an additional mutation intensity factor that can be used to increase or decrease the mutation probability. Our mutation rate is

$$\text{mutation rate} = \min\left(\frac{\text{mutation intensity}}{\text{number of genes}}, 1\right)$$

An mutation intensity of 1 leads to the often used mutation rate of $\frac{\text{mutation intensity}}{\text{number of genes}}$, while a higher mutation intensity increases the rate up to one, and a lower intensity decreases the rate.

An extension to the optimization presented in this work could be the use of adaptive mutations that vary the mutation rate, mutation intensity, and/or mutation strategy over time. A recent review on different mutation strategies can be found by Deep and Thakur (2007).

Concerning the crossover operator, the genome in this work has with fixed length, so we use same crossover point in both genomes. Because the location of a gene in the genome is arbitrary in this quality optimization of CBA problem (see 8.2.2), we expect crossover operators that do not respect the gene location to result in better solutions. Thus, we use the uniform crossover operator (cf. Section 3.5.2.2).

8.2.4.2. Design Space Constraints

In our problem formulation, different types of constraints in the design space need to be considered (cf. Section 6.4.3). First, the unconstrained design space spanned by our candidate representation contains infeasible candidates (cf. Section 8.2.2). Second, the software architect may decide to add additional system-specific constraints to the problem that are not covered by the degrees of freedom but rather caused by aspects of the CBS not captured in the CBS model.

As mentioned in Section 8.2.2, we assume infeasible candidates are rare in the unconstrained design space. Thus, we can apply a simple constraint handling technique and discard new candidates that are infeasible (also called death-penalty method) (Coello Coello, 2002) in the reproduction step. Instead, a new random candidate is generated. To exclude the case that the new random candidate is infeasible, too, we repeat the random creation until a feasible candidate is found or a maximum number of tries has been reached.

More sophisticated constraint handling approaches have been suggested (see (Deb, 2001, p.126 et seqq.)), but we expect that a more efficient approach does not lead to significantly better optimization performance due to our assumption that infeasible candidates are rare. If this assumption is found to be wrong for specific systems or in general in the future, other constraint handling methods could be integrated. However, because infeasible candidates possibly cannot be evaluated for their quality attributes, fitness penalty-based methods are not suitable. Constructive methods could be used to repair a infeasible candidate by analysing the violated OCL constraints and varying the candidate until all constraints are satisfied. This approach can become computationally complex.

8.2.5. Candidate Selection

In this section, we discuss the strategy used for candidate selection. Section 8.2.5.1 briefly discusses why we chose the NSGA-II selection as the baseline for our approach. Section 8.2.5.2 presents an addition to the selection strategy that can be used if upper bounds for acceptable quality are known, e.g. budgets for costs or maximum response times accepted by users.

8.2.5.1. Basic Selection Strategy

As described in Section 3.5.3, multiple selection strategies have been proposed. Tournament operators have been shown to perform well (Deb, 2001, p.89), as has elitism in the search (Deb, 2001, p.240). Additionally, Pareto-based fitness assignments are useful if no weights for the objectives are known, because they enable a well spread of candidates approximating the true Pareto front (Deb, 2001, p.173). Thus, we decided to use a selection strategies with these properties in this work.

To assess the fitness of candidates in the selection process, we use the NSGA-II fitness scheme based on Pareto rank and crowding distance as described in Section 3.5.3, as this strategy has lead to good results in many problems. The tournament selection operator selects the candidate with the higher fitness in a tournament. The number of tournament rounds can be configured.

Newer and promising fitness schemes exist, such as by Zitzler and Künzli (2004), but their performance has not been studied on as many problems as NSGA-II's performance yet. Recently, Zitzler et al. (2010) suggested to make the fitness assignment and thus the specification what type of Pareto front approximation is sought more configurable. It would be interesting to integrate such configurable algorithms in our work and study the effects of different selection strategies in more detail.

8.2.5.2. Considering Quality Requirements in Selection

As discussed in Section 5.1, the goal of an quality improvement process is to find the Pareto front of candidates optimal under a number of quality properties of interest. As we usually cannot model the user preference in advance, the optimization problem cannot be reduced to a single-criteria problem.

Still, as discussed in Section 5.1, there may be information on the worst acceptable value of a quality criterion. For example, a cost budget could be given. Such a quality requirement can both be defined for a quality criterion to be optimized (e.g. we are interested in low cost but at the same time there is an upper cost limit) or for a quality criterion that is not considered in the optimization (e.g. there is a cost budget, but there is no reason to spend less than the budget).

We consider quality requirements in the selection step of the optimization. A candidate that does not fulfil one or more quality requirements is *quality-infeasible* and a candidate that fulfils all quality requirements is *quality-feasible*. We use QML (cf. Appendix D) to model the worst acceptable values for quality criteria independently of the objectives defined for the optimization problem. Basically, a quality requirement defines a worst acceptable value r_q for a quality criterion q.

Definition 8.3 Quality-infeasible Candidate

A candidate c is *quality-infeasible* with respect to a set of quality require-ments R defined for a set of quality criteria Q, if at least one of its quality properties $\Phi_q(c)$ is larger than the worst acceptable value for q:

$$quality\text{-}infeasible(c,R) \Leftrightarrow \exists q \in Q : r_q \leq_q \Phi_q(c)$$

A candidate that is not quality-infeasible is called *quality-feasible*.

With this definition, note that the quality properties of the system in differ-ent situations can be considered. For example, we may want to optimize the mean response time of a system for the most common usage scenario A, while also fulfilling that 90% of requests in a rare peak load usage scen-ario P should have a response time of 10 second or less. In this case, we define the quality criterion "mean response time of A" to be an objective and we define a quality requirement on the quality criterion "90% quantile response time of P" with the upper limit 10 second.

The quality requirements are constraints in the objective space for the optimization problem. We consider this type of constraints during the se-lection step instead of discarding them right after evaluation, because (1) at least one quality function evaluation is required to detect a violation, so computational effort has already been spent, and, more importantly, be-cause (2) we cannot assume that the constraints only exclude some candid-ates from the set of feasible candidates as we can assume for the design space constraints (cf. Section 8.2.4.2) so we may need to consider quality-infeasible candidates, too, when optimizing in highly quality-constrained problems (cf. discussion of ignoring infeasible solutions by Deb (2001, p.291)).

We modified the fitness in the selection step to prefer any feasible candid-ates over quality-infeasible candidates and to discriminate between quality-feasible candidates. Two main approaches how to consider constraint violations have been suggested. In the penalty function approach, a penalty is added to the fitness candidates with violated constraints. The disadvantage is that this approach is sensitive to the parameter of how much penalty is assigned (Coello Coello, 2002). Several methods have been proposed that modify the fitness without requiring parameters. Two of them are the constraint domination method of Deb (2001, p.301 et seqq.) and the goal attainment method of Fonseca and Fleming (1993). We included both methods in our optimization approach so that the user can choose one.

In both methods, feasible candidates are preferred over quality-infeasible candidates in the selection. The difference lies in the comparison of quality-infeasible candidates.

The *constraint-domination* approach d discriminates between quality-infeasible candidates based on the amount of quality criterion violation. How the constraint violation is calculated is not defined by Deb (2001) but only illustrated with an example. To be independent of the absolute values of the objectives, we normalize the difference between the quality requirement and the quality property of c with the current range of values for this quality criterion in the population. Let q be the quality criterion to consider, let r_q be the required value, let $\min_q$ be the minimum value of q in the current population and let $\max_q$ be the maximum value of q in the population. Then, the constraint violation for q is

$$
v_q(c) := \begin{cases} \frac{|\Phi_q(c) - r_q|}{\max_q - \min_q} & \text{if } r_q <_q \Phi_q(c) \wedge \max_q > \min_q \\ |\Phi_q(c) - r_q| & \text{if } r_q <_q \Phi_q(c) \wedge \max_q = \min_q \\ 0 & \text{if } r_q \geq_q \Phi_q(c) \end{cases}
$$

The overall constraint violation $v(c)$ of a candidate is $v(c) = \sum_{q \in Q} v_q(c)$.

For example, if a candidate violates a mean response time requirement of 5 seconds because it has a mean response time of 6 seconds, we first determine the minimum and maximum mean response times in the current population (let use assume these are 3 seconds and 7 seconds). Then, we normalize the violation of $6 - 5 = 1$ with this range of $7 - 3 = 4$. Thus, the constraint violation is $\frac{1}{4}$ in this example.

The consideration of quality-infeasibility and constraint violation is added to the fitness assignment scheme with higher priority than the Pareto rank and the crowding distance. The resulting fitness scheme f_d in the presence of quality requirements is determined so that $f_d(c) > f_d(c')$ iff:

- c is quality-feasible and c' is quality-infeasible, or

- c and c' are quality-infeasible and $v(c) < v(c')$, or

- c and c' are quality-feasible and $f(c) > f(c')$

The *goal attainment* approach g discriminates between quality-infeasible candidates based on the Pareto dominance of unsatisfied quality criteria. If a candidate c is quality-feasible and c' is not, c is preferred. Otherwise, Pareto dominance only considering the quality criteria of the violated quality criteria of c, denoted $V_c \subseteq Q$, is determined. We denote this Pareto dominance as $\prec_{V_c}$. If c dominates c' under $\prec_{V_c}$, c is preferred. Otherwise, if the quality properties of the violated requirements of c of both candidates are equal, c is preferred to c' if c fulfils more quality requirements or if c dominates c' in its fulfilled requirements $F_c = Q/V_c$, denoted as $\prec_{F_c}$. Thus, the resulting fitness scheme $f_g(c)$ is determined so that $f_g(c) > f_g(c')$ iff:

- c is quality-feasible and c' is quality-infeasible, or

- c and c' are quality-infeasible and $c \prec_{V_c} c'$, or

- c and c' are quality-infeasible and $\forall q \in V_c : \Phi_q(c) = \Phi_q(c')$ and $\exists q \in F_c : q \in V_{c'}$, or

- c and c' are quality-infeasible and $\forall q \in V_c : \Phi_q(c) = \Phi_q(c')$ and $c \prec_{F_c} c''$, or

- c and c' are quality-feasible and $f(c) > f(c')$

This method is only defined for quality requirements on quality criteria that are objectives, too. The detailed definitions of the methods are found by Noorshams (2010).

The evaluation of the optimization performance gain due to quality requirements consideration with both methods is presented in Section 9.5.4.

We also studied the option to provide a quality criterion value at which the quality criterion is satisfied, so that we are not willing to trade other quality criterion for further improvement of this quality criterion. For example, a mean response time of 1 second may be considered to be enough, and we do not want to sacrifice other quality criteria (such as POFOD or costs) for further improvement of response time beyond 1 second. However, by Noorshams (2010), we found that this information does not help to focus the search and to improve the optimization performance in the studied examples. Although these observations are not necessarily transferable to the general case, we do not discuss this possibility further in this work.

8.2.6. Stop Criteria

Stop criteria for multi-objective evolutionary optimization are an open problem (Harman, 2007, Sec.6.1). In the context of this work, Dimitrov (2010) has devised and implemented a set of stop criteria. Simple stop criteria stop after a number of iterations or after a certain time is elapsed. Pareto-front based criteria compare the current Pareto front with the Pareto front found n iterations earlier (where n is configurable) and stop the search of no new candidates or few new candidates (relative to the size of the front) are found. Finally, indicator-based criteria stop the search if a quality indicator value (cf. Section 3.5.5) does not change significantly (e.g. more than a configurable threshold) over a number of iterations n. Here, a stop criterion based on the coverage indicator has been implemented.

More sophisticated stop criteria taking into account the stochastic nature of evolutionary algorithms such as described by Trautmann et al. (2009) and later works could be used to stop the optimization as early as possible.

8.3. Informed Quality Improvement

As discussed in Section 4.2, problem-specific knowledge can be integrated into a metaheuristic in several ways (Cheng et al., 1999). First, the problem representation itself contains knowledge about the domain. In this work, the genetic encoding only expresses valid architectures, i.e. feasible solutions are constructed. Second, the initial population may be constructed instead of being randomly generated by considering domain-specific knowledge (Grefenstette, 1987).

Third, the performance of the search can be enhanced by problem-specific knowledge. In evolutionary methods, heuristic operators can be defined that contain problem-specific knowledge. In this work, we suggest use detailed domain-specific rules (as used in the rule-based methods) in a new type of heuristic operator.

This section is organized as follows. First, several domain-specific tactics for performance, reliability and costs are described in Section 8.3.1. In particular, we focus on performance tactics. Then, Section 8.3.2 describes how the tactics are integrated in the optimization approach as tactics operators in detail. Finally, we discuss two approaches to create a starting population in Section 8.3.4.

8.3.1. Improvement Tactics

Architectural tactics for quality attribute improvement of software architectures encode design knowledge and rules of thumb (Bass et al., 2003). They are intuitively applied by experienced architects when designing an architecture. In this section, we present how to encode these informal rules of thumb into processable modification rules for a CBA metamodel (e.g.

for on the PCM). These encoded rules can then speed up the optimization, as they can be used to modify CBA models in an effective way in the reproduction step, instead of simply applying random operators such as crossover and mutation, which can yield many suboptimal solutions.

This section describes the incorporation of tactics into our optimization approach. We briefly explain the considered scope of tactics (Section 8.3.1.1). Then, the following sections provide a list of generic tactics for performance (Section 8.3.1.2), reliability (Section 8.3.1.3), and costs (Section 8.3.1.4). The codification of these tactics as rules is CBA-metamodel specific. Thus, to illustrate the tactics, we sketch in each of these sections how the tactics can be mapped to the PCM.

8.3.1.1. Scope

This work consider tactics on the level of the *software architecture* at design time, particularly in the domain of component-based distributed systems. Some of these tactics may also be applicable on embedded or mobile systems. As this work targets improving an architecture model instead of an implementation, code-level tactics are excluded here. Rules are only applied on a CBA model instance, which describes a system as an assembly of component and connectors, component behaviour, and component deployment to hardware nodes.

We assume a component-based development process, where possibly black-box components from third party vendors are assembled. In such a process, it might be complicated to change the implementation of individual components as the code may not be accessible. Therefore, we have marked tactics that require to alter component implementations as "*Change component*" in the following tables. These tactics may therefore not always be automatically applicable. Depending on the expressiveness of the CBA metamodel, user interaction may be required to determine how the component can be changed to realize the tactic.

The following tables 8.1, 8.2 and 8.3 provide an overview of well-established tactics. The listings try to be comprehensive, but we do not claim completeness. The tactics are grouped into software, hardware, and network heuristics. The third column in each table describes how the rules can be applied to PCM instances as one example of a CBA metamodel.

The tactics may not be applicable for every CBA metamodel, as the metamodels have a varying level of abstraction. Additionally, the tactics require a different level of quality prediction results. Thus, they can also only be used with quality prediction techniques with sufficiently expressive results. At the same time, specific CBA metamodels and specific quality prediction techniques and methods may offer additional tactics that are not covered here. Bachmann et al. (2003) discuss how architectural tactics can be derived for a given architecture model and quality prediction technique.

8.3.1.2. Performance Tactics

The list of performance tactics in Tables 8.1 and 8.2 have been aggregated from multiple sources about performance improvement on the architectural level. The SPE book (Smith and Williams, 2002b) highlights technology-independent performance principles, patterns and anti-patterns. Further rules have been integrated from Microsoft's performance improvement guide (Microsoft Cooperation, 2004) and literature on architectural tactics (Bass et al., 2003; Bachmann et al., 2005; Rozanski and Woods, 2005; Taylor et al., 2009).

Classical performance analysis guides (Jain, 1991; Menascé et al., 2004) focus on queueing models and simulation, but provide only limited hints on how to improve performance on an architectural level. Contrary to other methods (e.g., (Xu, 2010; Parsons and Murphy, 2008)) our list of performance heuristics is not tied to a specific performance model, such as LQN, or technology, such as EJB, but more generically applicable.

	Name	Rule [Principle]	Modelling in Palladio CM
Software	Asynchronous Communication	Let components exchange data asynchronously to avoid synchronization delays. ["Parallel Processing Principle"]	*Change components:* change interfaces and RDSEFFs of blocked components to support asynch. comm., add cost.
	Caching	Keep the most frequently used data in a cache in main memory to allow quick access. ["Centering Principle"]	Create a cache component either immediately serving a request with a cache hit probability or delegating the request, add costs.
	Concurrency / Parallelisation	Introduce parallelism using multithreading or multiple processes. ["Parallel Processing Principle"]	*Change components:* use fork actions in RDSEFFs and reduce resource demand per thread, add costs.
	Coupling and Cohesion	Ensure a loosely coupled design that exhibits an appropriate degree of cohesion. ["Locality Principle"]	*Change components:* Merge components with a high interaction rate. Build subsystems, add costs.
	Internal Data Structures and Algorithms	Use appropriate data structures and algorithms within the components. ["Centering Principle"]	Identify component with highest resource demand and exchange them with different component implementations.
	Fast Pathing	Find long processing paths and reduce the number of processing steps. ["Centering Principle"]	Introduce additional components to serve the most frequently used functionality in a dedicated way, add costs.
	Locking Granularity	Acquire passive resources late and release early, minimize locking. ["Shared Resources Principle"]	*Change components:* change RDSEFFs and minimize the time between Acquire and Release Actions, add costs.
	Priorisation	Partition the workload and prioritize the partitions so that they can be efficiently queued. ["Centering Principle"]	Not yet supported.
	Resource Pooling	Ensure effective use of pooling mechanisms (Objects, Threads, Database connections, etc.). ["Fixing-Point Principle"]	Identify passive resources with the highest waiting delay and adjust their capacity.
	State Management	Use stateless components where possible to keep them decoupled and allow scalability. ["Shared Resources Principle"]	Not yet supported.

Table 8.1.: Performance Improvement Tactics (Koziolek et al., 2011a)

Hardware	Component Reallocation	Allocate software components from saturated resources to underutilized resources. ["Centering Principle"]	Identify resources with U>=maxThreshold & reallocate components to resources with U<=minThreshold
	Component Replication	Start multiple instances of the same component and spread the load on multiple servers. ["Spread-the-load Principle"]	Identify components accessed by many users, create multiple component instances and introduce load balancer component.
	Faster Hardware	Buy faster hardware to decrease the node utilization and response times. ["Centering Principle"]	Increase processing rate of bottleneck processing resources, increase hardware costs
	More Hardware	Buy additional servers and spread the load among them. ["Spread-the-load Principle"]	Increase the number of processing resources, introduce load balancer (incl. costs), increase hardware costs
Network	Batching	Avoid network accesses by bundling remote requests. ["Processing vs. Frequency Principle"]	Insert messaging components that bundle remote requests to batches and unpack them at the receiver side, add costs.
	Localization	Allocate frequently interacting components on the same hardware devices. ["Locality Principle"]	Identify components with a high interaction rate and reallocate them to the same resources.
	Remote Data Exchange Streamlining	Decrease the amount of data to be send across networks (e.g., using compression). ["Centering Principle"]	Create a compression component that shrinks the size of the data transferred, but adds a resource demand to the CPU.

Table 8.2.: Performance Improvement Tactics (continued) (Koziolek et al., 2011a)

The PCM-specific short rule descriptions in column three of Tables 8.1 and 8.2 can be implemented to manipulate PCM models. Notice that despite of their brevity some of the rules encapsulate complex relationships. For example, different kind of database performance improvements, such as query optimizations or different schema layouts are summed up in the heuristic "Data structure and Algorithms", because in an architecture model such as the PCM these changes are reflected only in changes to the resource demands of services of the database component. The large number of known concurrency patterns (Schmidt et al., 2000) is summed up in the heuristic "Concurrency". The rules marked with "change component" require additional annotation or user interaction, because the PCM models are not expressive enough to automatically apply these rules.

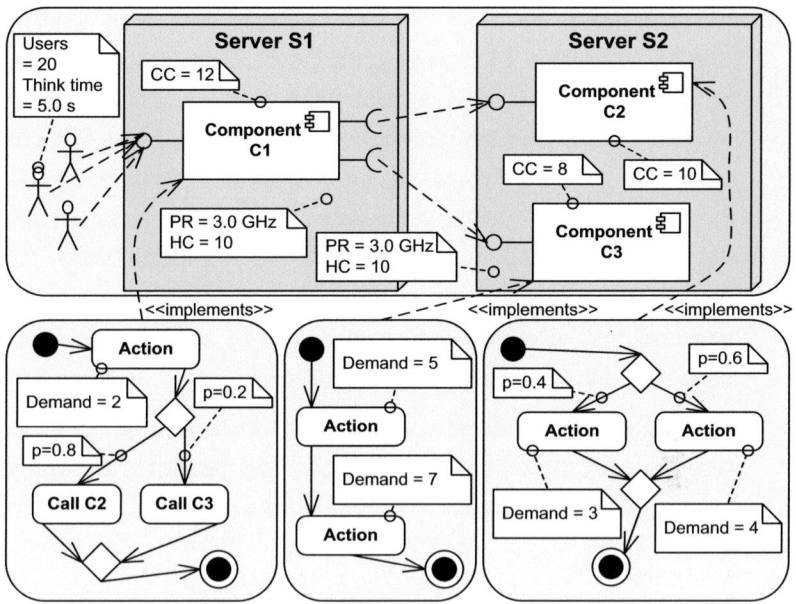

Figure 8.9.: Example System for Tactics

In the following, we discuss several tactics and their realization for the PCM in more detail. For each tactic, we detail rationale, precondition, action, additional effects and extensions below, if available. Note that we assume in the tactics that all servers are connected by linking resources. If this is not the case, rules to exclude invalid tactic applications have to be added analogously to the "Allocation degree" presented in Section 7.3.1.

Figure 8.9 shows an example system that we use to convey the tactics in the following. The performance of this example system is analysed using LQNS. The tools calculate an expected mean user response time of 8.8 seconds, a CPU utilization $U(S1)$ of 17% for server S1, a CPU utilization $U(S2)$ of 88% for server S2, a POFOD of 0.016, and costs of 407 monetary units.

Spread the Load In distributed systems, components can be allocated to different servers. To improve performance, the overall load should be spread evenly across the system. Thus, some components should be reallocated from highly utilized servers to servers with low utilization. If the right components are reallocated, this tactic can improve performance, while being cost-neutral. This tactic realizes the "spread the load" principle (Smith and Williams, 2002b) and thus solves the performance antipattern "unbalanced processing in concurrent processing system" as described by Smith and Williams (2002a) and in (Trubiani and A. Koziolek, 2011).

Precondition: The utilization difference between the highest utilized resource r_h of resource type t (e.g. CPU) and the lowest utilized resource r_l of the same type t is above a threshold U_{spread}:

$$U(r_h) - U(r_l) \geq U_{\text{spread}}$$

Additionally, the server S_h that contains r_h hosts several components.

Action: One of the components allocated to server S_h is randomly chosen and reallocated to server S_l. In the PCM, component reallocation is realized by changing the allocation model. For the chosen component, the allocation mapping is updated to point to the newly chosen server S_l.

Additional effects: The reallocation is cost-neutral. However, it may introduce additional network processing overheads if components are separated that communicate intensely. Reallocation can impact reliability both positively or negatively depending on the involved servers and components (cf. reallocation tactics in table 8.3).

Example: In the running example, component C3 could be reallocated from server S2 (CPU utilization 88%) to server S1 (CPU utilization 17%).

Extensions: Communication frequencies could be taken into account when choosing a component to reallocate (i.e. this tactic could be combined with the "reduce remote communication tactic" below). Similarly, the demand of a component could be taken into account, both for the chosen resource type as well as fr other resource types (such as HDD), to achieve a balanced load more quickly. An elaborate version of this tactic could use the Multifit-COM algorithm suggested by Woodside and Monforton (1993) that uses the bin-packing algorithm Multifit (Coffman et al., 1978) to allocated components to servers considering resource demand and communication demand in a simplified performance model. The accuracy of the found solution will depend on the appropriateness of the used performance model, and cannot consider additional degrees of freedom.

Scale-up Bottleneck Resources: Highly utilized bottleneck resources (CPU, HDD, network) that slow down the system should be made faster by buying faster resources (scaling up). This tactic improves performance most likely, however, it is limited by the maximally available resource speed.

Precondition: The highest utilized resource r_h is utilized above a threshold ($U(r_h) \geq U_{\text{scale-up}}$).

Action: Increase the processing rate of resource r_h by an increase factor f which can be configured by the user and is set to 1.25 as a default. If the result is higher than the maximum processing rate, choose that maximum. If the resources are chosen from a discrete set, choose the cheapest resource r' with a processing rate $PR(r') > PR(r_h) \cdot f$. In the PCM, the resource environment model is modified.

Additional effects: Hardware costs are increased. If hardware reliability changes due to faster hardware, this tactic also affects reliability.

Example: The processing rate of the bottleneck CPU in server S2 could be increased by 25%.

Scale-out Bottleneck Server: As processing rates of resources cannot be increased unlimitedly, at some point, additional servers and hardware need to be added (scale out) to relieve highly utilized servers and cope with high load. However, scaling out is limited by the software design. Currently, we consider the maximum number of servers to be the number of components (i.e. the maximum scale-out is that each component is deployed to one dedicated server). This tactic is not effective if a single component causes most of the load in the system.

Precondition: The highest utilized resource r_h is utilized above a threshold $(U(r_h) \geq U_{\text{scale-out}})$ and the maximum number of servers has not yet been reached.

Action: Reallocate one component from the server S_h with the bottleneck resource r_h to a new server. In the PCM, the allocation model is changed (cf. "spread the load" tactic).

Additional effects: Hardware costs are increased. Possible, a performance overhead for the additional network communication is introduced.

Example: A third server S3 could be added and component C3 could be reallocated to it.

Extension: The extensions of the "spread the load' tactic also apply here. Additionally, a single component could also be deployed to multiple servers using load balancing techniques and possibly synchronization strategies (both not yet supported by the PCM).

Reduce Remote Communication If components that frequently communicate with each other are deployed on different servers, the remote communication can be an extensive overhead to the overall response time of the system and the linking resource can become a bottleneck resource.

Precondition: The highest utilized linking resource l_h is utilized above a threshold ($U(l_h) \geq U_{remote}$). Then, we determine whether the reallocation of one of the components using l_h could be beneficial by checking the ratio of local calls versus remote calls over this linking resource for all components deployed to servers connected by this linking resource as follows:

Let $S = \{S_1, ..., S_n\}$ denote the set of servers connected by the linking resource l_h. Let C_s denote the set of components allocated to $s \in S$. Let $local(c)$ denote the number of local calls sent or received by a component c and let $remote(c,s)$ denote the number of remote calls that c sends to or receives from server s. These values are determined in relation to a usage scenario using an extended version of the PCM dependency solver (H. Koziolek et al., 2007).

Then, we can check whether there is a component c^* on any of the servers connected by l_h (i.e. $c^* \in \bigcup_{s \in S} C_s$) which has more remote calls to one of the other connected servers than local calls (i.e. $\exists s \in S : remote(c^*,s) > local(c^*)$). If there are several such components, we choose the component with the highest ratio $\frac{remote(c^*,s)}{remote(c^*,s)+local(c^*)}$. Then, it may be beneficial to reallocate component c^* to server s.

Action: If such a component c^* can be found, reallocate c^* to server s.

Additional effects: The reallocation is cost-neutral. However, it may introduce more unbalanced load on the adjacent servers. Reallocation can impact reliability both positively or negatively depending on the involved servers and components (cf. reallocation tactics in table 8.3).

Example: Let us consider a variation of the example system. Assume that components C1 and C2 communicate frequently in our example (e.g. C1 calls C2 seven times per request on average) while C1 and C3 communicate less often (only 0.2 times on average per request).

Additionally, let us assume that the linking resource connecting the two servers is utilized above a threshold, e.g. 85%. Then, we can reallocate C2 to server S1 to reduce the usage of the linking resource.

Extension: Another approach to reduce remote communication could be to compare the time each request spends on the network. If the time spend on the network exceeds a certain ration of the overall response time of the request (e.g. 25%), we can try whether a better allocation of components leading to less remote communication is possible. Note that in this case, the linking resource is not necessarily highly utilized, but rather leads to a too high latency.

Remove One-lane bridge "One-lane bridge" is a performance antipattern (Smith and Williams, 2000) which describes a situation where requests compete for too few shared passive resources (e.g. database connections, file handles, or thread pools). To solve the antipattern, the number of available passive resources should be increased. Note that for passive resource with an initial capacity of one, increasing the capacity is usually not possible because the passive resource models a region of mutual exclusion. We have described this tactic in (Trubiani and A. Koziolek, 2011).

Precondition: There is a passive resource p that has a long queue length q (i.e. longer than a threshold q_{olb}) and that has a capacity c larger than one. Additionally, requests for this passive resource p are delayed, i.e. the time h they hold p is significantly shorter than the time w they wait for p (again, significantly shorter is determined by a threshold value w_{olb}, i.e. $\frac{h}{h+w} < w_{olb}$).

Action: Increase the capacity of passive resource p by an increase factor, but at least by one. The default values for the increase factor is 0.5.

Additional effects: In the PCM, this tactic has no additional effects. However, one may want to consider increased costs for more passive resources, or decreased reliability due to more internal parallelism in the respective quality models.

Example: Let us consider a variant of the example model. Assume that requests to component C2 and C3 access a passive resource, e.g. a thread pool of fixed size on server S2. Additionally, assume that server S2 has four processing cores available and that C2 and C3 also access the hard drive of S3. Then, in a scenario with high load and a thread pool size of $2(^4)$, it could happen that the hold time of the passive resource is only 3 seconds on average, while the waiting time is 4 seconds. Then, the thread pool size of server S2 could be increased.

Extension: This tactic could additionally take the resource demand of the underlying active resources into account and only be applied if the underlying active resource are partially idle while requests are blocked by the passive resources, as sketched in the example above. This can especially happen in layered systems tasks of a given layer have to wait for requests to a lower layer while at the same time blocking new requests of the given layer. This observation has been one reason to introduce layered queueing networks (Franks et al., 2009).

Concerning the optimal size of thread pools, Chen et al. (2002) have suggested a benchmarking approach to determine the performance properties of J2EE middleware with varying number of threads. Such models could be considered here as well to improve the performance prediction for varying number of threads and the application of tactics.

We have presented more tactics derived from known performance antipatterns (Smith and Williams, 2000, 2002b,a, 2003) in (Trubiani and A. Kozi-

---

[4]In this simple example, we have to use such an unrealistic value for the thread pool size to be able to explain the problem.

olek, 2011): "Blob" (or God class (Smith and Williams, 2000)), "Unbalanced Processing in Pipe-and-Filter Architectures" (Smith and Williams, 2002a), "Circuitous Treasure Hunt" (Smith and Williams, 2000) (requires an annotation that identifies the components acting as databases (Trubiani and A. Koziolek, 2011)), "Empty Semi Trucks" (Smith and Williams, 2003), and "Traffic Jam" (Smith and Williams, 2002b). Their preconditions are described in (Trubiani and A. Koziolek, 2011, Sec.4.1) for the PCM. However, the action of these tactics cannot be automated in the PCM without additional annotations, thus, we do not discuss them here in more detail. The antipattern "Extensive processing" (Smith and Williams, 2002a) is not discussed here, too, because only a small aspect of it can be automatically solved in the PCM. Possibly, the application of some of these antipatterns could be completely automated for other CBA metamodels or with additional annotations to the PCM as future work.

PCM instances can be improved for performance with these tactics, as demonstrated in Section 9.5.2 and by Trubiani and A. Koziolek, 2011.

8.3.1.3. Reliability Tactics

Numerous publications focus on reliability analysis (Musa et al., 1987) and software fault tolerance techniques (Pullum, 2001; Kienzle, 2003). Additionally, several authors have described architectural tactics for reliability (Bass et al., 2003; Rozanski and Woods, 2005; Taylor et al., 2009). From these sources, Table 8.3 aggregates several reliability tactics, as compiled by Brosch et al. (2011b). The terms Mean time to failure (MTTF) and Mean time to Repair (MTTR) are properties of hardware resources, which are often specified by hardware vendors and which can be used to calculate the overall system's reliability (Brosch et al., 2011b).

In practice, a common tactic for reliability-critical systems is to introduce redundant hardware (e.g., stand-by nodes, RAID discs, etc.). Some safety-

	Name	Rule	Modelling in Palladio CM
Software	Design Diversity	Realize one algorithm in n different ways. Apply a voting algorithm that chooses a result (e.g., majority voting).	*Change components:* Decrease internal action failure probability, increase costs, increase resource demands.
	Heartbeat / Ping	Periodically test the availability of components, initiate immediate repair upon failures.	Decrease MTTR of resources, add monitoring costs, resource demands.
	High reliable software components	Apply a high-quality development process to software components for high reliability.	*Change components:* Decrease internal action failure probability, increase costs
	Rejuvenation	Automatically restart components, after failures or periodically.	*Change components:* Decrease internal action failure prob., increase resource demands & cost for restarts / monitoring
Hardware	Dependency-Aware Reallocation	Allocate components together that depend on each other, so that hardware failures impact a smaller set of components	Reallocate components based on the execution paths, allocate components together that fail together anyway.
	High available hardware	Operate the system on hardware with low failure rates and low service times in case of failure.	Increase resource MTTF, decrease MTTR. Increase hardware costs, servicing costs.
	Redundant hardware	Buy additional servers and replicate components to them.	Increase resource MTTF, decrease MTTR. Increase hardw. costs, resource demands. Add overhead for fail-over.
	Sensitive Component Reallocation	Allocate reliability-sensitive software components to high availability resources.	Identify processing resources with A>=maxThreshold & reallocate critical components to them.
Network	High reliable network	Use network links with high capacity and reliability (e.g. TCP).	Decrease communication link failure probabilities, increase network costs.

Table 8.3.: Reliability Improvement Tactics (Brosch et al., 2011b)

critical systems use design diversity to increase reliability, which however introduces high development costs.

While the table shows in the PCM-specific column three how the the reliability tactics can be applied on PCM instances, most of them require the identification of reliability-critical components. This identification can be done by a sensitivity analysis, where component failure probabilities are varied in the model to find out there influence on the system reliability. This step is not yet automated for the reliability analysis of the PCM. Thus, we do not discuss reliability tactics in more detail here.

8.3.1.4. Cost Tactics

Although costs are usually not considered a quality property of software architectures, their minimization is of high business interest. Here, we only consider costs that can be predicted based on the software architecture model as presented in Section 2.5.5. First of all, costs can be minimized by choosing a less expensive option for a degree of freedom. For example, the cheaper components can be selected or cheaper hardware can be chosen. Additionally, all tactics that improve one of the other quality properties and increase costs can be inverted. In this work, we consider two costs tactics of this type:

Scale-Down Idle Resource: Inversely to the "scale-up bottleneck resource" tactic, this tactic decreases resource speeds of infrequently used resources, because we expect that performance is only slightly degraded, while costs are saved. This tactic is only applicable if faster resources are also more expensive.

Precondition: The resource with the lowest utilization (r_l) is utilized less that a threshold ($U(r_l) \geq U_{\text{scale-down}}$).

Action: Decrease the processing rate PR of r_l by an decrease factor d which can be configured by the user and is set to 0.75 as a default. If the result is lower than the minimum processing rate of the resource, choose that minimum. If the resources are chosen from a discrete set, choose the fastest resource r' with $PR(r') < PR(r_l) \cdot d$. In the PCM, the resource environment model is modified.

Additional effects: Performance is degraded. If hardware reliability changes due to slower hardware, this tactic also affects reliability.

Example: The processing rate of the CPU of S1 ($U(CPU_{S1}) = 17\%$) could be decreased by 25% in the example.

Consolidate Servers: Inversely to the "scale-out bottleneck server" tactic, lowly utilized servers can also be consolidated and their components can be joined one server to save cost. For simplicity, we only consider one resource type at a time for this tactic.

Precondition: The utilization of a resource r_l in a server S_l is lower than a threshold: $U(r) \leq U_{\text{cons}}$. Additionally, the other servers are estimated to have enough space capacity for the resource type t of r_l to host the components from server S_l. This is estimated by assigning each component on S_l an equal share of the utilization: Let n be the number of components allocated to S_l, then each component is assumed to cause a load of $U(r_l)/n$.

Then, we try to find an assignment of the n components to other servers so that the resource $r_{S,t}$ of these servers are expected to not have a higher utilization than a threshold U_{maxcons}. We execute a greedy assignment that (1) orders the servers based on their spared capacity for the resource type t (i.e. based on the utilization values for the resources $r_{S,t}$, in ascending order) and (2) iterates through the servers and assigns the largest possible number x of components to each server S so that the utilization is expected to be lower than the threshold U_{maxcons}, i.e. the largest x that satisfies

$$\frac{x \cdot U(r_l)}{n} + U(r_(S,t)) \leq U_{\text{maxcons}}$$

The search stops as soon as all components have been assigned or if all servers have been considered and space components could not be allocated. In the first case, a tactic candidate is created.

Action: Reallocate all components from S_{12} to the other servers as determined by the greedy assignment, so that S_{12} is no longer used.

Additional effects: Performance is degraded. Also see "spread the load" tactic in Section 8.3.1.2.

Example: Assume that the load of the running example was lower and the CPUs of both servers had a utilization of lower that 25%. Then, all three components could be allocated to server S1, and the cost of S2 could be saved. *Extension:* First of all, the real demands of the components for the resource type in question could be used to determine whether other servers could host them, and a more sophisticated algorithm than the greedy approach described above could be used. Furthermore, the tactic could be extended to account for all resource types used in the system at once and determine a server to remove where all resources have low utilization. Additionally, the processing rates of the servers could be taken into account when estimating the capacity. Finally, even communication could be taken into account. Overall, the extensions of the "spread the load" tactic are applicable here as well.

8.3.2. Tactics Operators

The architectural tactics are integrated in the optimization approach in the reproduction step for three reasons. First, applying a tactic means to generate a new candidate from an existing one, so the reproduction step is a natural choice. Second, the quality properties must be already predicted for the candidates, so tactics can only be applied on evaluated candidates. Third, we want to focus on promising candidates and improve these even further. Thus, the tactics are applied after the selection step.

The tactics are integrated as new operators in the reproduction step (step 2c) of PerOpteryx. In the reproduction step, the precedence of crossover, mutation, and tactics needs to be defined. Figure 8.10 shows the control flow of the reproduction step as an UML activity diagram. In addition to conditions for decision nodes, we added probabilistic choices by defining the probability of taking each decision (see key).

The input of the step are two candidates c_1 and c_2 selected for reproduction. First, it is randomly decided whether to apply tactics or not based on a configurable *tactics probability*. If no tactics are applied, it is randomly decided whether to perform a crossover based on the crossover rate. Afterwards, the two (resulting) candidates are mutated.

If tactics are applied, both candidates are handled separately. For each candidate c_i and tactic, the preconditions are evaluated. If the precondition of a tactic is fulfilled, a new candidate is generated based on the tactic, and added to the set of result candidates C_i. If no tactic precondition matches, the result candidate set C_i remains empty and a mutation is performed for c_i. If tactics have been applied, one candidate is selected from the result candidate set for each parent candidate c_i based on weights described below. The result of the reproduction step are two new candidates.

If the preconditions of multiple tactics match, multiple candidates are generated in the tactics step. To decide for one candidate, we assign weights between 0 and 1 to both the tactic (weights W) and the candidate (weights V). Tactic weights W_t are configured for each tactic t and define how promising this tactic is in general. Candidate weights $V_t(c_t)$ are functions that assign weights to a generated candidate c_t based on the input candidate's applicability for tactic t. Then, one candidate is chosen from candidate set C. Each candidate c_{t*} is chosen with probability

$$Prob(c_{t*}) = \frac{W_t \cdot V_t(c_{t*})}{\sum_{c_t \in C} W_t \cdot V_t(c_t)}$$

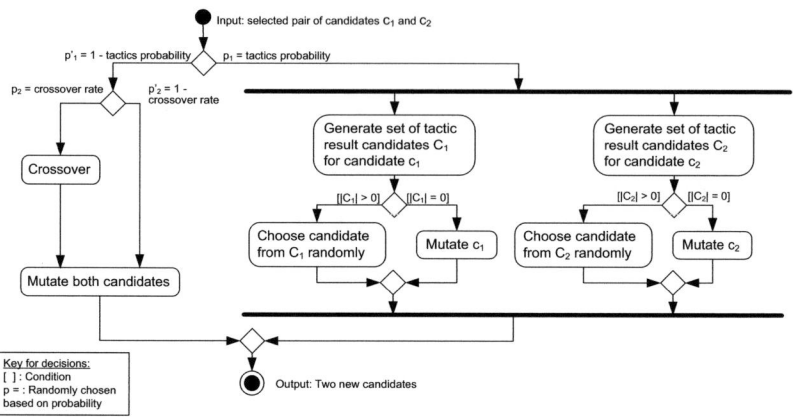

Figure 8.10.: Integration of Tactics in the Reproduction Step. Cf. Fig 8.1 for an
Overview of the Complete Process.

We chose the following candidate weight function V_t for our current tactics. Let c be the input candidate, r_h be the resource with the highest utilization, r_{l1} be the resource with the lowest utilization, and r_{l2} be the server with the second lowest utilization. $U(r)$ denotes a resources r's utilization. The weights are only calculated if the preconditions of the tactics match, so the values always range between 0 and 1.

Spread the Load: $V_{\text{spread}}(c) = U(r_h) - U(r_l)$. In our running example, we get a weight of $0.88 - 0.17 = 0.69$ for reallocating C3 to S1.

Scale-Up Bottleneck Resource: $V_{\text{scale-up}}(c) = \frac{U(r_h) - U_{\text{scale-up}}}{1 - U_{\text{scale-up}}}$. In our running example, if $U_{\text{scale-up}}$ is 80% we get a weight of $\frac{0.88 - 0.8}{1 - 0.8} = 0.4$ for the tactic candidate with a higher processing rate of the CPU in server S2.

Scale-Out Bottleneck Server: $V_{\text{scale-out}}(c) = \frac{U(r_h) - U_{\text{scale-out}}}{1 - U_{\text{scale-out}}}$. In our example, if $U_{\text{scale-out}}$ is 80% we get a weight of $\frac{0.88 - 0.8}{1 - 0.8} = 0.4$ for adding a third server.

Reduce Remote Communication:
$V_{\text{remote}}(c) = \frac{remote(c^*,s)}{remote(c^*,s)+local(c^*)} \cdot \frac{U(l_h)-U_{\text{remote}}}{1-U_{\text{remote}}}$. In our varied example
for this tactic, if U_{remote} is 80%, we get $\frac{7}{7+0} \cdot \frac{0.85-0.8}{1-0.8} = 0.25$.

Remove One-Lane Bridge: $V_{\text{olb}}(c) = \frac{w_{\text{olb}} - \frac{h}{h+w}}{w_{\text{olb}}}$. In our example, we
get $\frac{0.5\frac{3}{3+4}}{1-0.5} = 0.14$.

Scale-Down Idle Resource: $V_{\text{scale-down}}(c) = \frac{U_{\text{scale-down}}-U(r_{l1})}{U_{\text{scale-down}}}$. In our
example, if $U_{\text{scale-down}}$ was 25%, we get a weight of $\frac{0.25-0.17}{0.25} = 0.32$
for decreasing S1's CPU processing rate.

Consolidate Servers: $V_{\text{cons}}(c) = \frac{U_{\text{cons}}-U(r_l)}{U_{\text{cons}}}$. Assume a variant of the
example where all three components are deployed to dedicated serv-
ers, and the CPUs r_2 and r_3 of server S2 and the new server S3, respectively, have utilization values of $U(r_2) = 65\%$ and $U(r_3) = 13\%$.
Then, servers S1 and S3 can be consolidated by moving component
C3 to server S1.

This approach allows us to take both the expected impact of a tactic and its
applicability to a concrete input candidate into account.

In (Cortellessa et al., 2010b), we have furthermore presented an approach
how to dynamically determine the tactics weights for the antipattern-based
tactics based on the violation of quality requirements or quality bounds.
However, this approach is only applicable if preferences for quality requirements or bounds are available.

Several extensions of these tactic operators approach are possible: An
interesting extension would be to monitor their performance over the course
of an optimization run and adjust the probability of their execution based
on how successful they have been. Their performance could be assessed
by determining how many candidates are produced that (1) dominate their
parent, or (2) become a new Pareto-optimal candidate, or (3) improve the
current population by other metrics, such as coverage or hypervolume (cf.
Section 3.5.5 for these metrics) compared to the previous population.

Furthermore, some degrees of freedom could be restricted to only be changed by tactics. For example, the software architect may decide that the replication of servers (cf. Section 7.3.3) is unwanted and only should be considered if servers are overloaded. Thus, we could add the configuration option that the software architect may choose for every degree of freedom whether it should be varied by all operators or only by tactic operators. Possibly, after a tactic operator has changed a candidate vector, the other operators could be allowed to revert this decision on all degrees of freedom, too.

Finally, we could add an option that the software architects themselves can specify knowledge about the search for the given system at hand. Software architects may already have knowledge about the interactions of several degrees of freedom. For example, they may expect that a system can either be hosted on a single powerful machine, or be distributed on several smaller machines. They may want to exclude other combinations of server configuration and component allocation explicitly to reduce the size of the design space, so that search can become more efficient. However, if such knowledge is only heuristic (i.e., it is not necessarily true for all possible candidates), it could be integrate it in the optimization approach as tactics instead of formulating it as constraints the design space. In this case, software architects can implement a new tactic operator and add it to the optimization approach.

8.3.3. Intensification using Tactics

It has been recognized that evolutionary algorithms have good diversification properties (cf. Section 3.5), but that they may miss better solutions that are close to the evaluated solutions (Grefenstette, 1987)(Blum and Roli, 2003, p.300). Thus, they do not necessarily terminate with local optima at the end of a search. Better solutions may be reachable by a local search around the final candidates determined by the evolutionary algorithm (Miettinen et al., 2008a, p.441),(Deb, 2001, p.466 et seqq.) in an additional *intensification step* (cf. Figure 8.1 on page 287).

In this work, we apply our tactics in the intensification step, i.e. the application of tactics defines the neighbourhood to explore in this step. Alternatively, a local search based on the degrees of freedom could be used here as well; however, as many degrees do not have an order, each candidate has a large number of neighbours in the design space. Thus, evaluating all neighbours could be too computationally expensive, so that we focus on neighbours created by tactics.

Possibly, the thresholds in the preconditions of the tactics can be reduced in this phase to get a larger neighbourhood to be explored. Section 9.5.3 shows how the final results of evolutionary search can be further improved by this approach.

Similarly, other methods such as path relinking (described by Ehrgott and Gandibleux (2004)) which creates a candidate in between two parent candidates in the decision space, could be used to refine the Pareto-front after the evolutionary optimization.

8.3.4. Starting Population Heuristics

Generating starting populations based on domain-specific knowledge has potential to improve optimization performance (Grefenstette, 1987). If a good starting population is provided, the optimization can save initial iterations. However, the starting population must be diverse to enable exploration.

In the context of this work, we have developed two alternatives to generate starting populations. First, an analytic analysis of those parts of the optimization problem that are analytically tractable with simplified quality evaluation functions (*hybrid optimization*) is presented in Section 8.3.4.1. Second, as component allocation is crucial for performance, we devised a starting population heuristic that creates a diverse set of *allocation schemes*

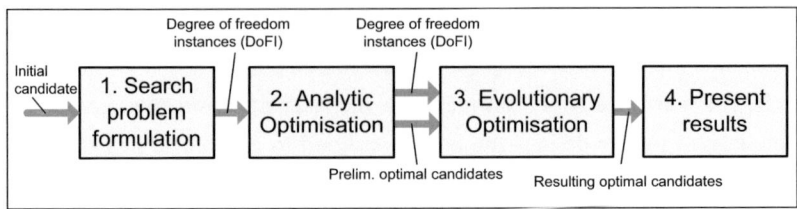

Figure 8.11.: Hybrid Optimization Analytically Providing a Starting Population (Martens et al., 2010)

in Section 8.3.4.2. Which of the two approaches is applicable for a concrete problem at hand depends on the considered degrees of freedom.

8.3.4.1. Hybrid Optimization

Figure 8.11 shows the combination of analytic and evolutionary optimization as presented in (Martens et al., 2010). To generate a starting population, an analytically tractable simplified version of the optimization problem is explored. Two simplifications are made (1) the considered DoFI are reduced and (2) a simplified quality prediction is used.

The set of degrees of freedom is reduced and mapped to a set of binary decision variables and constraints. Two degrees of freedom that overlap in their effect, i.e. their combination does not result in a linear combination of effects (e.g. a component can be exchanged and at the same time reallocated) are problematic: Additional decision variables have to be introduced to represent the combination of the two degrees. Thus, the approach suffers from combinatorial explosion already in the problem formulation. As a result, usually a subset of the degrees of freedom of interest can be explored by the analytical approach.

So far, we considered selection of components, server processing rates, and the allocation of some of the components. An extension for more degrees of freedoms is planned.

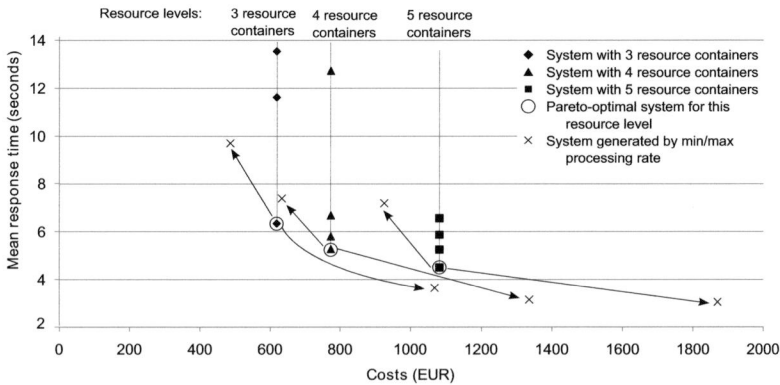

Figure 8.12.: Allocation Scheme Starting Population (by Beyer (2010))

Furthermore, this approach uses a simplified quality evaluation function for each quality criterion. For performance, we used product form solutions for queueing networks (Jain, 1991), which assumes exponential distribution of all parameters and do not support aspects such as e.g. passive resources. Additionally, reliability and costs can be considered.

The resulting linear optimization problem is solved using the ε constraint method (cf. Section 3.3) and linear programming for the sub-problems. More details can be found in (Martens et al., 2010).

8.3.4.2. Allocation Schemes Starting Population

Component allocation is a crucial influence factor on performance. Thus, we expect a diverse population with respect to allocation to be beneficial for the optimization of systems with allocation degrees of freedom.

The allocation scheme starting population (Beyer, 2010) systematically generates a number of allocation for the system, varies the processing rates of the used servers, and then selects the best ones as the starting population. Figure 8.12 schematically shows the algorithm and its motivation.

As an input, a minimum number of servers and a maximum number of servers. The number of servers is called resource level in the following. An additional input is the number of allocations to consider per resource level. Then, per resource level, the algorithm generates a number of random allocations. Because all candidates of one level use the same servers, they all have the same costs. Each candidate is evaluated for performance. Then, the best candidate per resource level is chosen (circled in Figure 8.12), and the processing rate of its resources is systematically varied (in the figure, two additional processing rate configurations are generated per candidate, using the maximum and minimum processing rate, respectively).

As a result, the optimization starts already with the number of servers that seems appropriate for the overall workload. However, such a starting population can also be deceptive, because it only considers the initial choices for other degrees of freedom. If, for example a system is strongly influenced by a component selection choice, the allocation scheme starting population only explores the best options for the initially used component.

Initial experiments are reported by Beyer (2010) and had promising results. However, to fully understand the impact of this starting population generation, more experiments with varying degrees of freedom should be conducted in future work.

8.4. CBA Optimization Framework

Figure 8.13 shows the architecture of the generic CBA optimization framework. The CBA optimization framework defines the DoF metamodel (cf. Section 6.3) including the candidate representation (cf. Section 8.2.2). It wraps the candidate representation so that the general-purpose optimization framework can handle it. Additionally, the CBA optimization framework defines the quality metamodel (cf. Section 8.2.3.1). The DoF metamodel, the quality metamodel, and the CBA metamodel have to defined in the same meta-meta-modelling language such as EMOF.

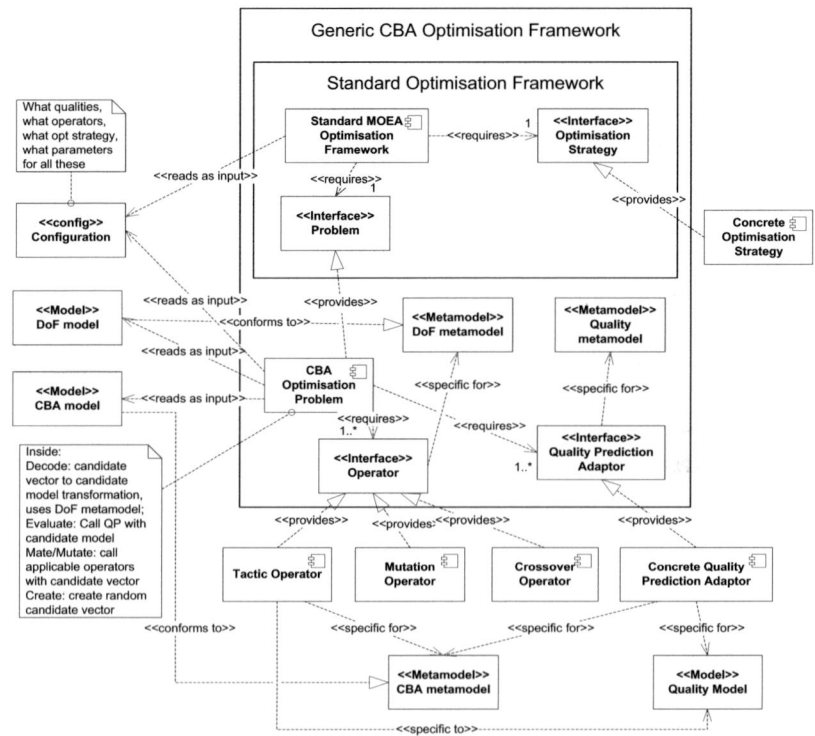

Figure 8.13.: Architecture of Generic CBA Optimization Framework

Operators and quality prediction techniques can be added dynamically as plugins (e.g. using Eclipse's extension point mechanism). Operators provide the Operators interface that is specific to the DoF metamodel. They declare which genetic operator they support (i.e. mating of two or more candidates or mutation). Tactics operators (see Chapter 8.3) are additionally specific to a CBA metamodel and one or several quality properties. If applicable, a software architect can provide additional custom tactics for the given system at hand.

Quality prediction techniques (e.g. SimuCom, PCM2LQN) are connected to the framework using the Quality Prediction Adaptor interface that

333

is specific to the quality metamodel. Quality Prediction Adaptors declare which quality property their quality prediction techniques can determine, what evaluation aspects (such as mean, median, etc.) they support and for which CBA metamodel they are specific.

The input CBA models and the derived DoFI define the design space. DoFI are defined using the DoF metamodel, so that all framework parts can handle them. The CBA model conforms to the CBA metamodel which again conforms to the chosen metametamodelling language such as EMOF. The generic framework handles the model only based on the chosen meta-metamodel, so it supports any CBA metamodel. However, the quality prediction adaptors and tactics operators are limited to one CBA metamodel.

The framework can use a general-purpose multi-objective optimization framework such as Opt4J (Lukasiewycz et al., 2010) or PISA (Bleuler et al., 2003) for the generic optimization tasks. This general-purpose framework defines the interfaces Problem and Optimization Strategy. The exact design of Problem interface is different in different general purpose frameworks. For example, an Opt4J problem is defined by implementing several interfaces. These interfaces are the genotype and phenotype of the problem as well as a creator, a decoder and an evaluator that handle candidates (Lukasiewycz et al., 2010). Additionally, problem-specific operators can be defined. In PISA, the problem is defined by implementing a Variator module (Bleuler et al., 2003, p.5), which has the same responsibilities. Thus, the CBA optimization framework is specific for the chosen general-purpose framework when implementing its Problem interface. At the same time, the CBA optimization framework could implement the Problem interface of several general-purpose frameworks.

The interplay of the different framework parts can be configured. The user can configure which of the available quality prediction adaptors and operators should be used to evaluate and vary, respectively, candidates. Only quality prediction adaptors and tactics operators that match the meta-

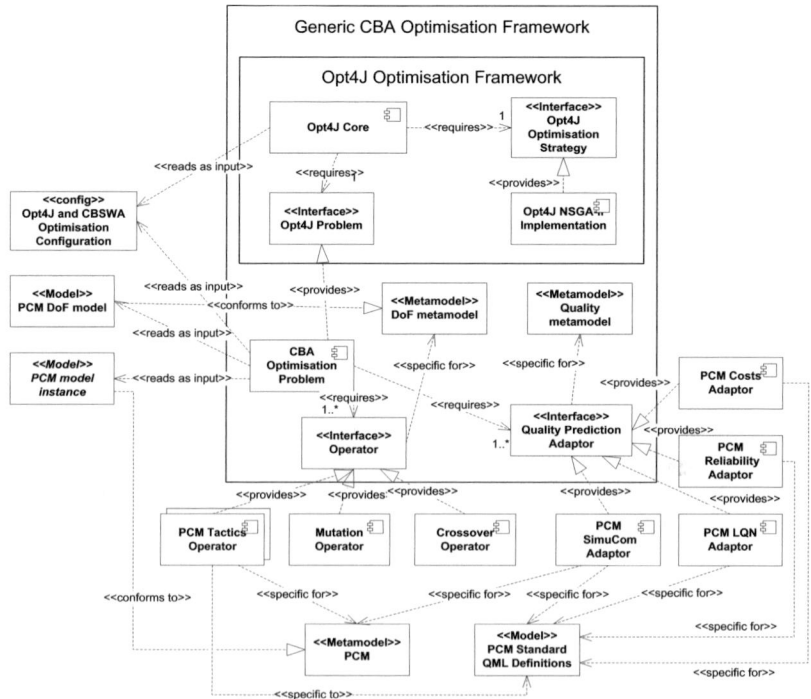

Figure 8.14.: CBA Optimization Framework using PCM and Opt4J

model of the input CBA model can be selected. Together, this defines the optimization problem.

Additionally, general optimization parameters, such as which available optimization strategy (which can also be dynamically added via plugins) is used, the population size, and further parameters of the optimization strategy, can be configured.

Figure 8.14 shows an example configuration of the CBA Optimization Framework for the PCM and using Opt4J. The models outside the generic framework core are PCM specific, and the Problem interface is defined by Opt4J.

Our currently implemented tool PerOpteryx partially realizes this framework and is described in Section 9.2. Additionally, we have studied the feasibility of the framework by implementing a CBA-metamodel-agnostic transformation that reads in a DoF model for component selection in the PCM, a candidate vector, and an initial PCM model, and applies the chosen values to produce a changed CBA model. This transformation is independent of the used CBA metamodel (in our case PCM), as the transformation handles the model only using EMF (the Eclipse version of EMOF) reflection capabilities.

8.5. Discussion

In this section, we discuss the influences of optimization problem properties on the expected performance of the optimization approach. Additionally, the optimization approach presented in this chapter relies on a number of assumptions (Section 8.5.2) and has several limitations (Section 8.5.3).

8.5.1. Influences on Optimization Performance

For different software architectures under study and the respective degrees of freedom and quality properties of interest, an optimization problem is formulated and solved as described in this chapter. In this section, we discuss the influence of the parameters of such problems on the optimization approach's performance. Optimization performance combines the search duration and the quality of the found results.

In our optimization problems, the evaluation of the candidate evaluation function is time-consuming for performance and reliability (cf. Section 8.1.2 and Section 9.4.3.1) and is high compared to the overhead of the evolutionary algorithm for candidate selection and candidate reproduction. Thus, the search duration in work can be considered to be the product of the time needed to evaluate all quality properties of a candidate and the number of candidate evaluations:

Search duration = average candidate evaluation duration *
number of candidate evaluations

The time needed to evaluate a candidate depends on the used quality prediction technique. Results for scalability of these techniques can be directly
applied here. For example, the duration until an LQNS analysis converges
depends on the level of contention in the modelled system: If only few users
use the modelled system, the performance results can be quickly obtained
in few iterations of the LQNS algorithms, while the analysis of highly utilized systems requires more iterations. Franks (1999) discusses more run
time influences for LQNS and LQSim. The time needed for analysis can
be influenced by requiring a certain accuracy (e.g. for LQNS, a convergence value to achieve can be set, while performance simulations with e.g.
SimuCom can be configured with a number of measurements or confidence
levels). Thus, we do not empirically study this aspect further in this work
and focus on the number of candidate evaluations in the following.

The number of candidate evaluation required before the algorithm converges reflects the hardness of the optimization problem excluding the quality evaluation function. For evolutionary optimization, several influence
factors on the optimization algorithm's performance have been observed.
Before discussing these in the context of software architecture quality optimization in Section 8.5.1.2, we fist summarize some general insights from
the literature in Section 8.5.1.1.

8.5.1.1. Complexity of Optimization Problems

First of all, the number of objectives is a major influence factor. The more
objectives are considered, the larger usually the number of optimal solutions is (as the Pareto front becomes larger, from a curve in two-objective
problems to a surface in three-objective problems to any hypersurface in
n-objective problems. It has been recognized that high dimensional problems are problematic for most multi-objective evolutionary optimization

techniques (Deb, 2008). Extensions to e.g. NSGA-II have been proposed (Saxena et al., 2009) that improve the convergence of NSGA-II and thus are a research direction towards solving high-dimensional problems (Saxena et al., 2009, p.551), although they do not provide an final and mature solution.

Apart from that, additional optimization properties have been discussed and studied in the context of finding appropriate test problems for multi-objective evolutionary algorithms (Coello Coello et al., 2007, Chapter 4). We can use these results here to reason on possible properties of the software architecture optimization problem for different studied software systems and how the expected performance of our approach depends on the problem properties. Because the following discussion is not specific for software architecture optimization problems, we use use the general terms of gene, genome, and objective instead of our specific terms of design options, candidate vector, and quality property, respectively.

Many aspects of problem complexity can be described with the notion of a *search landscape* or fitness landscape. The search landscape describes the relation between genes, their neighbourhood relation, and objective function in evolutionary optimization. In single-objective optimization with few genes, the search landscape can be visualized easily: Figure 8.15 shows a search landscape for an optimization problem with two genes g1 and g2 with values ranging from -3 to 3 each, and a resulting objective o with values ranging from -5 to 5. Assuming that the problem is an maximization problem, the global optimum lies at value 1.5 for g1 and value 0 for g2, resulting in an objective function value of 5.

Based on this notion of a search landscape, we can reason on properties of an optimization problem. Although little work has been done on the landscape analysis for multi-objective problems so far (Coello Coello et al., 2007), observations have been made, some of which we present in the following. In the simple example in Figure 8.15, two additional local maxima are present, thus, the landscape is *multi-modal*. Multi-modality makes an

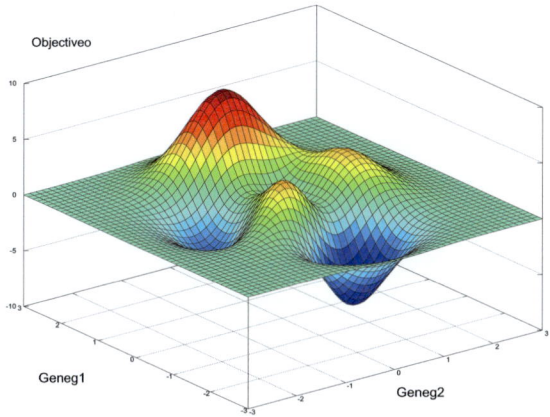

Figure 8.15.: Example Search Landscape

optimization problem more complex because the search will spend time or get stuck in the local optima (Deb, 2001, p.347).

In this example, the landscape is *smooth*: Each small change of a chosen value of a gene results in a small change in the quality property. The opposite of a smooth landscape is a rugged landscape where a small change in the genes may result in a large change of objective, possible even non-continuous jumps. Rugged search landscapes are more difficult for optimization techniques (Deb, 2001, p.347), although this can be somewhat mitigated by larger population sizes (Deb, 2001, p.101).

For evolutionary optimization techniques, the reproduction operators have to be taken into account when reasoning in the search space, because they impose the actual neighbourhood structure of the problem. The problem becomes simpler if "points in the objective space are also nearby in the permutation space" (Knowles and Corne, 2002, Sec.5), i.e. nearby in the decision space with respect to the used reproduction operators. This property is also called locality (Coello Coello, 2002).

More genes that deactivate others are likely to increase the complexity of the problem. This phenomenon is called *epistasis* in the context of evolutionary algorithms (Coello Coello et al., 2007, p.301): Epistasis means that genes in the genome interact, i.e. that the contribution of a gene to the fitness function depends on the values of other genes[5]. A high epistasis makes a problem difficult (Aguirre and Tanaka, 2005, p.355). In contrast, low or no epistasis makes the problem trivial as simple hill climbing can solve it. Still, epistasis is said to have a lower influence on the problem complexity than the number of objectives.

Finally, the *size of the search space*, i.e. the number of genes and the number of possible value per gene is another influence factor: More options result in a larger search space. If the optimization problem is complex due to the reasons mentioned above, the size of the space makes it even more difficult. In contrast, a simple optimization problem is less sensitive to the size of the search space: For example, if only a single optimum is present in the search landscape (i.e. no multi-modality), then the problem can be solved easily with hill climbing and the size of the search space has little influence.

8.5.1.2. Complexity of Software Architecture Optimization Problems

Based on the general observations recounted above, we can reason on the complexity of software architecture optimization problems. First of all, the number quality properties influences the optimization problem complexity as each quality property is an objective.

The search landscape depends on the considered degrees of freedom. In the following, we will discuss the influence of the degrees of freedom presented in Chapter 7.

---

[5]Some researchers (e.g. (Weise et al., 2008)) have a more strict definition: In their view, epistasis means that one gene has effect on several properties of the phenotype. We follow the more general definition here that epistasis denotes any interaction of genes that lead to different contribution to the fitness.

Usually, the problem will be multi-modal. For example, when considering the allocation of components to servers in our simple example in Figure 2.13 (page 61, Section 2.5), moving the BusinessTripMgmt component to server 2 will deteriorate the performance if the system is under high load. If we additionally move component BookingSystem back to server 1, the performance will be similar to the initial value again (assuming similar configuration of the two servers). Other degrees of freedom can also result in multiple modes, especially if performance is considered, because the performance of the overall system depends on many aspects.

The search space can also be rugged, again depending on the degrees of freedom. Allocation can lead to high ruggedness, but this depends on the number and load of the components under study: If the demand of components is unevenly distributed in the system, i.e. there are some components that pose a high load to their servers, a single change can have major impact on performance (i.e. solutions that are close in design space are not close in the objective space). Furthermore, the neighbourhood of each candidate when considering allocation is large, as every single component reallocation to a different server is a neighbouring solution. Thus, problems with many allocation degrees probably take more time to find a good approximated Pareto front.

The selection of components and the change component parameters can have a similar rugged effect, because the alternative components can have an arbitrary effect on the quality properties in general, and the change of component parameters can lead to a completely different behaviour of the component. Usually, however, we can expect that component alternatives will not be too different from the replaced component as they have to provide the same functionality; we can also expect that component parameters will only change certain aspects of a component's behaviour and thus their change leads to small changes in the quality properties, too.

Other degrees of freedom are less problematic with respect to ruggedness, because their change has usually a local effect. Still, in special cases changes of their values can also lead to huge change in the quality properties.

Finally, the allocation degrees are additionally problematic because of epistasis. If no component is deployed to a server, the server configuration is irrelevant. Still, the optimal server configuration of the unused server is not evolved while it is not in use, so that if a component is allocated to it later during the search, the configuration can only then be evolved which requires additional search iterations. Component selection degrees also have epistasis if composite components are introduced or removed that open up new component selection degrees.

To summarize, the optimization problem complexity depends on the number of considered quality properties and the considered degrees of freedom, with allocation degrees and component selection degrees expected to lead to more complexity than the other degrees of freedom.

8.5.2. Assumptions

The assumptions of the approach are summarized in the following. Some have been mentioned in more detail in other parts of this chapter, too.

Accurate quality models: We assume that the used quality models accurately reflect the quality properties of the system under study. As a principle of quality prediction for CBA, component quality models should be valid for different contexts the component is used in (Szyperski et al., 2002, p.55–57). However, such models are not always available for components. If, for example, the performance of a component has been measured to create the performance annotations of the CBA model, the observed properties may be specific to the used resource environment or middleware. More effort is needed to create reusable quality specification of components. We assume that such reusable specifications are used and that their portability to other platforms and contexts is assured. For specifications with limited portability (i.e. that are specific for certain properties of the environment such as a specific processor or middleware), the degrees of freedom that changes these properties of the environment cannot be explored.

In Section 9.4.1.1, we present a number of previous studies that show the portability of PCM models for a number of degrees of freedom. Additionally, we have studied the portability of quality models concerning allocation for an example system ans present the results in Section 9.4.1.2.

Few infeasible candidates: We assume that only few interactions between degrees of freedom exist so that only few candidates in the design space are infeasible. The main principle of CBSE is to build reusable building blocks (Szyperski et al., 2002) that encapsulate complexity and can be reused in different contexts, which at the same time means that they can be reused in different combinations (cf. Section 8.2.2). As a result, we use a simple constraint handling strategy that discards candidates that violate design space constraints in the reproduction step (cf. Section 8.2.4.2). If this assumption is violated in certain settings, more elaborate constraints handling techniques (Coello Coello, 2002) could be integrated in our approach.

Combined optimization of all degrees is required: We assume that the optimization problem cannot be split into several independent simpler optimization problem that could be subsequently solved. First, especially performance is a cross-cutting properties that emerges from all factors of a performance model (Woodside et al., 2007). The performance properties of a system thus can only be vaguely approximated with simpler sub-optimization problems. Although some systems may allow splitting different concerns into separate optimization problems, this is difficult to decide for a software architect. Additionally, if such separation comes with simplified performance model, a software architect who is not an expert on performance analysis may not know whether the assumptions of an underlying performance model are fulfilled. Here, an expressive performance model is beneficial.

Order and metric for each quality criterion: We assume an order and a distance metric for each quality metric, as described in Section 8.1.1.

8.5.3. Limitations

In the following, we distinguish between limitations of the optimization approach in general (Section 8.5.3.1) and additional current limitations of the tactics incorporation (Section 8.5.3.2).

8.5.3.1. General Limitations

The first limitation listed here is a principle limitations of the approach. The other two limitations could be overcome in future work.

No guaranteed optimality: The optimization approach itself is a best-effort approach and does not guarantee to find the real Pareto-front, i.e. the globally optimal solutions, because metaheuristics are used.

Considerable time consumption: As the evaluation of each candidate solution, mainly due to the performance evaluation, takes several seconds, the overall approach is considerably time consuming, even if tactics operators are used. A distribution of the analyses on a cluster of workstations could lead to significant improvements. For certain systems, it could also be possible to split the optimization problem into several independent parts that are solved separately and thus quicker. However, an automated approach that can detect this possibility for a system at hand would be required. As a result, software architects should run the architecture exploration in parallel to other activities or over night. The application of our approach for runtime (semi-)autonomous adaptation that is supposed to react quickly to changes (e.g. in the workload) is thus limited (but at the same time, this is not the goal of our approach, cf. Section 5.1).

No regard for uncertainties: For the results, uncertainty of estimations, uncertainty of the workload, and the resulting risks are not taken into account. Here, sensitivity metrics could be an additional quality criterion and we could integrate robust optimization techniques such as discussed by Miettinen et al. (2008a, p.450 et seqq.) into our approach.

8.5.3.2. Current Limitations of Tactics

The tactics proposed in Section 8.3 currently have a number of limitations that could be addressed by future work.

Restricted number of tactics: No reliability tactics are formalized yet. More performance and costs tactics could be formalized.

No sequencing of tactics: The current tactics approach applies one tactic at a time and then evaluates the quality properties again. In future work, it could be studied whether a good sequence of tactics can already be found when evaluating a candidate, so that the search converges even faster. For example, spreading the load could be combined with scaling up or scaling down resources to balance the load more effectively.

Limited rationale for tactic parameters: More systematic methods to determine the thresholds and weights used by the tactics need to be developed.

One resource per server: Currently, the tactics can handle only one processing resource per server, so that we can easily define a server's utilization. This can easily be extended to consider multiple resources in one server, e.g. CPU and HDD.

8.6. Summary

This chapter presents an optimization approach based on the formulation of the design space from the previous chapter 6. Based on the discussion of the resulting optimization problem and its characteristics, we chose evolutionary optimization to improve the initial CBA candidate and find the Pareto-front of optimal candidates. The candidate representation is derived from the design space formulation.

Our realized optimization approach is based on the NSGA-II algorithm. We discuss in this chapter how the steps of candidate evaluation, candidate selection, and candidate reproduction are realized for the optimization problem.

To improve the performance of the optimization, we incorporate domain-specific knowledge from architectural tactics in form of tactics operators. Finally, we present the resulting CBA framework, which can optimize CBA models independent of the used metamodel and the used quality prediction technique, and which allows to plug in additional quality predictions and tactics operators.

In the next chapter, we present the evaluation of our approach.

Part III.

Validation and Conclusion

9. Validation

This chapter describes the validation of the automated improvement approach as a step in the CBSE development process as presented in Chapter 5 based on two case study systems. We claim that our approach supports the software architect in improving a CBA based on model-based quality predictions, assuming that a software architecture model with quality annotations is available. The validation is structured into two main goals: (1) To assess the validity of the automated improvement method in terms of the accuracy of the results and the applicability of the method and (2) to evaluate the performance of the optimization step quantitatively.

Regarding the first goal, our claim has to be evaluated based on different levels of validation of prediction models suggested by Böhme and Reussner (2008b). In this work, we address several aspects: First, we validate the *accuracy* of model predictions for the example quality attribute performance, and we validate the accuracy of the improvement method in terms of capability to find an approximation of the true Pareto-optimal candidates. Second, we validate the *applicability* of our method by evaluating the appropriateness of the design space formed by the combination of degrees of freedom, and we discuss further applicability aspects of our approach. Additionally, we sketch future further validation studies, e.g. for cost/benefit evaluation.

Regarding the second goal, we evaluate the *performance* our optimization step quantitatively. In particular, we study the effects of our enhancements (tactics, quality requirements, starting population) of the standard evolutionary optimization as described in Section 8.3 in several experiments, comparing the quality of the found solutions and the time to find equivalent solutions.

This chapter is structured as follows. First, Section 9.1 describes the evaluation goals in more detail and derives questions for both goals. In Section 9.2, we present the implementation of the optimization framework used in this chapter. Section 9.3 presents the two case study systems. Then, Section 9.4 described the results for the validity of our automated improvement approach and Section 9.5 describes the quantitative evaluation of the optimization step's performance.

9.1. Validation Goals and Derived Evaluation Questions

The validation goals for the two validation aspects are presented below in Section 9.1.1 and Section 9.1.2, respectively. For both goals, we derive validation questions and also describe questions that are out of scope of this work.

9.1.1. Validity of the Automated Improvement Method

The goal of this work is to provide an automated approach that supports software architects in improving a CBA based on model-based quality predictions. The validity of model-based prediction approaches in general can be studied on several levels (Böhme and Reussner, 2008b), ranging from the accuracy of the predictions to the benefits of the approaches in software development projects. Similarly, the validation of our approach, which extends and supports model-based predictions, needs to be validated on these levels.

In the following, we first present the three levels of validation for model-based prediction approaches and extend them to consider the improvement support in Section 9.1.1.1. We derive validation questions addressed in this work in Sections 9.1.1.2 and 9.1.1.3. Finally, we discuss what validation aspects are out of scope of this work in Section 9.1.1.4, and sketch how to validate these aspects in future work.

9.1.1.1. Validation Levels for Model-based Quality Improvement Approaches

Böhme and Reussner (2008b) have introduced validation levels for model-based prediction approaches. Alternative terms for these levels have been described by (H. Koziolek, 2008). We combine both views below.

The validation levels have been suggested to assess prediction approaches. We extend the validation level description below to explicitly cover the improvement step, either manual or automated, as well.

Level I: Accuracy Validation The first level of validation studies the accuracy of the prediction approach by comparing prediction results to the observed properties of the studied subject. For example, predicted response times can be compared to measured response time of an implementation. On this level, the assumption is that an accurate input model is given as required by the prediction approach. Böhme and Reussner call this level of validation "metric validation". For (automated) improvement support, two additional aspects are of importance.

Accurate Predictions: The prediction model must deliver accurate predictions also when it is varied: Every candidate model that is automatically derived from the given accurate input model need to result in accurate predictions. For manual improvement support, this aspect is less relevant if the candidate models are manually created based on suggestions of the improvement support.

Optimal Results: Additionally, it should be validated whether the approach can indeed find model candidates with improved quality properties, or even optimal quality properties. For an automated search-based improvement approach, this aspect implies that the automated search finds the optimal candidates or an approximation thereof. For manual improvement support (e.g. (Cortellessa and Frittella, 2007)), it has to be validated whether better candidates are reachable assuming perfect user behaviour.

If both these aspects are fulfilled, the result models are accurate, i.e. they reflect systems with approximately optimal quality properties with respect to the explored design space, cf. Figure 5.5, page 155 from Chapter 5.

Level II: Applicability Validation The second level of validating model-based prediction approaches is concerned with applicability: The question is whether users of the approach can obtain the necessary information, create the prediction models, execute the prediction, and interpret the prediction results. For an automated improvement approach, some of these properties are inherited, others become irrelevant, and more are added, as described in the following.

First, an automated improvement approach inherits the applicability regarding required information and model creation from the used model prediction methods. If the automated improvement requires further input models, the ability to create these needs to be studied.

Furthermore, an automated improvement approach targets to conduct the design space exploration of a subset of the true design space for the software architect. Thus, with respect to applicability, it needs to be studied whether the subset is a relevant subset of the true design space, i.e. whether the exploration provides useful information to the software architect.

Then, in an automated improvement approach, the predictions are executed automatically and the prediction results are automatically analysed to find the best candidates. Then, the only remaining applicability aspect to validate is whether the user can understand the results and make decisions based on them.

To summarize, the applicability aspects to validate for an automate improvement method is whether a user can provide the input models, whether the method explores a relevant subset of the design space, and whether the user can understand the approaches' results and make decisions based on them.

Level III: Cost/Benefit Validation   Finally, the third level is concerned with the cost/benefit evaluation of a prediction approach. The use of an approach usually comes at a certain cost, e.g. the cost and effort to create the input models and the time to make predictions and interpret the results. These costs need to be compared to the expected benefit of prediction approaches. An example benefit is the improvement of the modelled subject based on insights from the predictions. For performance predictions of CBA, an expected benefit is, for example, reduced late life-cycle effort to fix performance problems.

The validation of costs and benefits is the most expensive level of validation. For a controlled study, the same software project has to be executed twice, once using the prediction approach, once without using it or using competing approaches. Thus, this form of validation is rarely executed by researchers. Böhme and Reussner call this level of validation "benefit validation".

Due to its comprehensiveness, the third level is unchanged for improvement support approaches. However, due to the high effort, we cannot conduct a level III validation in this work. We discuss future work validation studies for level III in Section 9.1.1.4.

9.1.1.2. Derived Validation Questions for Accuracy

In the following, we derive the accuracy validation questions from the discussion above.

Model Accuracy: Level I   Because our approach supports any quality evaluation function, the validation of any such function is out of scope of this work and accuracy of predictions must be separately shown for different quality prediction approaches in general.

Accuracy of other performance prediction approaches have been studies in several case studies, cf. (H. Koziolek, 2010). Accuracy of reliability predictions is difficult to validate, because system failures in real systems are rare events and difficult to measure. Thus, only some reliability prediction approaches have been validated empirically (Gokhale, 2007; Immonen and Niemelä, 2008). Accuracy of costs estimation have been validated in other works. Costs for hardware and for bought third-party components can be collected from vendors. Costs for in-house development can be estimated, e.g. using the COCOMO tool suite (Boehm et al., 2000), although only with limited accuracy.

However, our approach assumes in particular that quality predictions for models are accurate for changes along the degrees of freedom. To achieve this, the quality annotations of a component must result in accurate predictions in different contexts (Becker et al., 2006),(Reussner et al., 2011, Sec.2.4). Thus, the goal in CBA quality prediction approaches is to specify *parametrized* component quality annotations independently of the later context. Due to complex interactions of the component and its environment, this is difficult to achieve. At the same time, this accuracy of models along changes in the CBA model is crucial for the optimization.

We thus pose the first evaluation question:

Q1.1 Can models that were automatically modified according to the specified degrees of freedom still result in accurate performance predictions?

Because this work focusses on performance as a quality attribute, we focus on performance predictions with the PCM here. To answer this question, we first review and evaluate the existing studies of PCM model accuracy with respect to model parametrization and model accuracy in the presence of changes. We observe that although many parametrization aspects have been covered elsewhere, the accuracy of models when the allocation is changed has not been studied before. Thus, we add an additional validation for this aspect to the body of work. To validate the accuracy in this study, we compare the results of an optimization run with performance measurements of the realized candidates.

The detailed review of existing studies, the set-up of the allocation experimental evaluation, and the results are presented in Section 9.4.1.

Approximating the True Pareto Front: Level I In addition to finding any improved architecture candidates based on accurate predictions—which is, nonetheless, already a viable support for the software architect itself—another aspect of an automated improvement support is whether it can find an approximation of the optimal candidates in the considered design space. The resulting question is:

Q1.2 Can the search find an approximation of the true Pareto front?

The true Pareto front of the design spaces and optimization problems considered in this work could only be determined by exhaustive search. However, the search space in our case studies is too large and prohibits enumerating and evaluating all possible candidates. We can, however, get an insight into the properties of the design space by considering the results of many searches. Here, only considering the results of evolutionary optimization runs may be misleading, because all runs may mistakenly converge to the same local optimum if the considered search space happens to be deceptive (Deb, 2001, p.347). Thus, we additionally consider the results of random search, which is not prone to premature convergence to local optima. From the results of all these searches, we calculate the overall Pareto-optimal front, and assess the quality of approximation manually. To do so, we can analyse the found optimal candidates and try to manually find additional candidates dominating the found front.

9.1.1.3. Derived Validation Questions for Applicability

The applicability aspects to validate for an automate improvement method are whether a user can provide the input models, whether the method explores a relevant subset of the design space, and whether the user can understand the approaches' results and make decisions based on them.

On top of the input CBA model, our approach does not require further information from the user. The approach automatically instantiates the degrees of freedom based on the DoF, i.e. based on a description on the metamodel level. These DoF are created once per metamodel by experts (for example, we have presented the DoF for the PCM in this work).

Software architects may review the found degrees of freedom and possibly delete some. This is less effort than the manual task of first coming up with possible design alternatives and then assessing their usefulness. Then, the optimization step of our approach is automated and thus requires no manual effort.

Thus, the remaining aspects are the relevant design space and the decision making, discussed in the following.

Relevant Design Space: Level II In an automated improvement approach, we are by definition limited to the information contained in the CBA model and CBA metamodel, so that the complete design space that the software architect considers when designing an architecture cannot be covered. Thus, the design space that can be searched by our tool to support the software architect is a strict subset of the true design space.

The question to validate here is whether the design space considered in this work is a relevant subset so that the found optimal solutions provide relevant information to the software architect:

Q1.3 Does our design space represent a relevant subset of the complete design space software architects are faced with?

To answer this question, we first study whether the discussed degrees of freedom actually occur in example systems. Additionally, we analyse the impact of the degrees of freedom on the quality of the example system. We do not study all proposed DoF because the existence of some meaningful DoF already justifies our approach.

Furthermore, as discussed in Chapter 5, quality criteria often conflict, especially when considering costs as one quality criterion. Whether an optimization of CBA is multi-objective depends on the considered quality criteria. We assume that two or more conflicting quality criteria are considered. Then, the question to validate is whether our formulation of the design space, which is an incomplete subset of the true design space, actually reflects the conflict in the quality criteria.

Note that we do not claim that every instance of the optimization problem is multi-objective, because some combinations of degrees of freedom, especially when combining few of them, may lead to correlating quality properties, even though the quality attributes are known to usually conflict. We show that the optimization of performance, reliability, and costs as an example of quality optimization is indeed a multi-objective problem and that the Pareto-front contains meaningful trade-offs from which the software architect can choose.

We present the detailed validation plan and the results for this question in Section 9.4.3.

In all cases, we can only show that it is possible to create meaningful models and meaningful degrees of freedom. At the same time, there are certainly software systems that are hard to model because of complicated performance effects or other quality property effects and there are software systems where the described degrees of freedom have only little effect and other design decisions (that possibly cannot be automatically studied) are relevant. Thus, we do not claim that our observations for the case study systems in the following are transferable to all other software system.

357

Understanding and Decision Making: Level II As we exclude the applicability of the separate model-based quality prediction approaches, the remaining aspect concerning the applicability of our automated improvement approach is the whether a user can understand the approaches' results and make decisions based on them.

A validation of this aspect can be derived from the preliminary study in Rohrberg (2010). An empirical study with 8 participants was conducted, who were trained in making quality predictions with the PCM and had a background software engineering knowledge. The participants were asked to analyse the results of our automated improvement approach and choose one candidate based on their own preferences. They were asked to state any insight they got into the trade-off problem at hand during the analysis. Most participants were confident in the decision they made, indicating that they were able to understand the results. Additionally, they were mostly able to answer a questionnaire on the quality properties of the available candidates and the conflicts among them. Thus, this initial study indicates that the results of the automated improvement can be understood by a trained user.

We do not include the details of this study into this work because of its preliminary nature and space restrictions, thus, we do not pose any questions here. More details on the study, including the posed questions, a detailed discussion of the results, and the threats to validity, can be found in Rohrberg (2010). Still, the study is preliminary and a more thorough evaluation is subject to future work.

9.1.1.4. Out of Scope Validation Activities

We do not conduct additional applicability validations of model-based prediction approaches, because any prediction approach for CBA can be used in our approach. For the PCM, the applicability of creating such models has been evaluated with a series of empirical studies (Martens et al., 2011), leading to the conclusion that parametrized, reusable models can indeed be created by users.

A cost/benefit evaluation (level III) of our approach is subject to future work because of its high effort. The most expressive form of study, as described above, would be to execute the same software project twice, once using our improvement approach, once by a control group not using our approach.

We could compare the quality of their final software system, their insight into the problem, and the time they needed for their evaluations and decisions. For valid results regarding analysis and decision making, the studied system would have to be realistic and the software architect would have to have much insight into the context and stakeholder desires of the system. Thus, an evaluation in a lab setting with students, which would have a moderate effort, would lead to high threats to validity. However, such an experimental evaluation in a practical setting is too expensive and time consuming to be realized in this work, and remains subject to future work.

Different levels of control groups could be used: An evaluation of our approach compared to the manual result interpretation of model-based prediction results would require the control group to work with model-based quality prediction approaches, too, so that all effects can be attributed to the automated improvement approaches.

However, because there have been no published cost-benefit studies for any model-based quality prediction approach (a single preliminary study in Williams and Smith (2003) investigates the required refactorings and performance fixes, comparing two releases of a software where the second had used performance prediction), a study that compares using our improvement approach to using no model-based predictions at all could result in even more interesting results. Such a study would combine the effects of model-based quality prediction and our approach.

Ultimately, alternative improvement support should be compared to our approach. However, this type of study is beneficial only after the above sketched studies have been evaluated.

9.1.2. Validation of the Optimization Step

As a second aspect, we validate our suggested extensions to evolutionary optimization quantitatively. We first discuss how the optimization method can be validated in Section 9.1.2.1 before presenting the posed questions in Section 9.1.2.2. Finally, we describe validation activities that are out of scope in Section 9.1.2.3.

9.1.2.1. Performance Assessment for Multi-objective Optimization

Metaheuristic optimization approaches such as evolutionary optimization do not guarantee to find the true global Pareto optimum (Blum and Roli, 2003, p.271). The result of an optimization run is usually an approximation of the true Pareto front with unknown quality (Zitzler et al., 2002b, p.117). As discussed in Section 3.5.4, convergence properties have been shown for elitist multi-objective evolutionary algorithms that do not discard any optimal solutions. However, this property does not apply to evolutionary algorithms that limit the size of the population for practical reasons. For example, in NSGA-II and SPEA-2, optimal candidates may be discarded by the crowding selection operator (NSGA-II) (Deb, 2001, p.252) or the clustering algorithm (SPEA-2) (Deb, 2001, p.268). Furthermore, this theoretical property does not allow to make conclusions about the quality of the achieved front after a number of iterations.

Thus, we compare our proposed extensions of the evolutionary optimization (tactics, quality bounds, and starting population heuristic) to the baseline methods of (1) unchanged evolutionary algorithm and (2) random search.

To compare any two approaches (e.g. random search and evolutionary search), we compare the outcome of optimization runs after a number of iterations using metrics to assess the quality of the Pareto-fronts. This is the standard technique when assessing multi-objective optimization approaches (Deb, 2001). Additionally, we study the development of the metrics over the course of the optimization to assess how quickly the search finds good solutions. Together, we can assess the achieved quality of the solutions after a number of iterations as well as the time needed for the optimization and the time to find equivalent results. We call both aspects together the *performance* of an approach in the following [1].

An analytic comparison of multi-objective metaheuristics (in particular evolutionary algorithms) is difficult in general (Deb, 2001, p.375). Especially together with the stochastic and complex nature of performance and reliability evaluation, an analysis of the performance in general is infeasible. Thus, multi-objective evolutionary algorithms (and other metaheuristics) are commonly compared based on test problems (Deb, 2001, p.375). Here, the performance of metaheuristic optimization approaches depend on the chosen test problem (Coello Coello et al., 2007, Chapter 4), so that to assess the suitability of an optimization approach for a certain domain, a test problem from that domain should be chosen. Naturally, we select test problems from the domain of CBA to compare different optimization approaches. Still, even within this domain, the performance of optimization

---

[1] The terms quality and performance are thus overloaded in this work due to the connection to different research communities: When referring to software systems and software architectures, the term "quality" denotes the quality attributes of software system (as predicted based on a model of the architecture), and the term "performance" denotes the time behaviour and resource efficiency properties of the modelled system as described in Section 2.2.1. When referring to the optimization approach validation, we use the common wording in metaheuristic optimization research (Deb, 2001; Zitzler et al., 2002b): The term "quality" denotes the quality of the found Pareto-front (as assessed with quality indicators and using the Pareto dominance relation, cf. Section 3.5.5) and the term "performance" denotes the combined examination of quality and needed time. The terms are related: the former is concerned with the assessment of software systems and architectures in general, while the latter is concerned with the assessment of our optimization approach, which is also a software system.

approaches may depend on the concrete CBA at hand. Thus, we can only study the performance of our approach for test problems, without being able to show the validity of the results for all possible CBA optimization problems as defined in this work.

9.1.2.2. Derived Validation Questions

In this work, we suggest three extensions of the baseline evolutionary optimization.

1. The use of tactics operators to include domain-specific knowledge as presented in Section 8.3.2

2. The use of tactics in a final intensification phase, as presented in Section 8.3.3

3. The use of quality bounds to focus the search on interesting regions as presented in Section 8.2.5.2

4. The use of domain-specific knowledge to generate starting populations, as presented in Section 8.3.4

The benefit of the starting population generation has been evaluated elsewhere, as described below. Thus, based on the discussion in the previous section, we pose the following three questions:

Q2.1 How much is the optimization's performance improved by using tactics in a case study?

Q2.2 How much is the optimization's performance improved by an intensification phase at the end of the search in a case study?

Q2.3 How much is the optimization's performance improved by using quality bounds in a case study?

The benefits of analytically generating an initial starting population based on simplified quality prediction and limited degrees of freedom (hybrid optimization, cf. Section 8.3.4.1) has been investigated by us in (Martens et al., 2010). We observed that the analytic starting population provided valuable input to the evolutionary optimization in the considered case study, while the evolutionary algorithm was able to refine the results. The benefits of generating a diverse starting population based on different allocation schemes (cf. Section 8.3.4.2) has been investigated by Beyer (2010) for one case study, resulting in the observation that the optimization performs better in all phases of the optimization. In both cases, however, the results as-is are limited to case studies actually considering the selection of degrees of freedom. The allocation scheme only considers the allocation degree of freedom. The hybrid optimization only considers component selection and limited allocation degrees of freedom, and may suffer from combinatorial explosion if more degrees of freedom are selected.

We first discuss the metrics to assess the performance of optimization approaches in Section 3.5.5. Then, in Sections 9.5.2 to 9.5.4, we study the effect of our extensions to consider tactics, quality requirements, and starting population heuristics.

9.1.2.3. Out of Scope Validation Activities

The following aspects are not validated empirically in this work.

- We do not evaluate the choice of metaheuristic with experiments because the choice is not fixed in our approach. As described in Section 8.4, other metaheuristic search approaches could be plugged into the optimization framework as well. In Section 8.1.3, we discuss why evolutionary optimization and in particular the chosen NSGA-II based method seem beneficial.

- We do not compare our approach to rule-based approaches because the assumptions of both are different. Rule-based approaches such as

Performance Booster (Xu, 2010) assume one quality criterion to be optimized with potentially others (here: costs) as constraints. In this assumed setting and for systems where all optimal solutions to this model (like the case studies by Xu (2010)) are reachable by the rules, a rule-based approach is superior to our approach, as it is tailored to the problem. However, for our problem formulation that multiple conflicting quality criteria should be optimized, the rule-based approaches cannot be applied as is. Thus, no meaningful setting for a comparison is available.

- We do not experimentally validate the influence of problem parameters (e.g. number of degrees of freedom, number of design options per degree, and used types of degrees of freedom) on the optimization performance, because software architecture optimization problems have a large number of properties influencing the performance. In general, evolutionary optimization has been recognized as a flexible optimization technique (Deb, 2001, p.164), and thus should result in useful (even though always approximate) results for most types of problems except isolated special cases. At the same time, a limited number of experimental evaluations can only give a limited insight into the interactions of properties in general. See Section 8.5.1 for the discussion of influences on the optimization performance.

9.2. Tool Implementation

This section presents the current implementation of the optimization tool, called PerOpteryx. It is used in the following experiments to validate our approach. The tool does not yet support the generic optimization framework described in Section 8.4 because it is yet specific to the PCM metamodel. The validation questions posed above and the experimental evaluation in the next sections, however, do not require this generality, so we can use the PerOpteryx tool for evaluation here.

Section 9.2.1 describes the architecture of the current implementation, and Section 9.2.2 provides more detail on the used PCM-specific DoFI metamodel used in PerOpteryx.

9.2.1. PerOpteryx Architecture

The current architecture of the PerOpteryx tool is shown in Figure 9.1. The tool uses Opt4J (Lukasiewycz et al., 2010) as an general-purpose optimization framework. Five quality prediction adaptors (two for performance (LQNS or SimuCom), one for reliability (PCM2Markov) and one for costs (PCM2Costs)) have been implemented. Currently, the evaluation of candidates is sequential, but it could as well be parallelized to λ parallel evaluations, i.e. every newly generated candidate is evaluated in parallel.

Two standard operators (cf. Section 8.2.4) and a number of tactics operators (cf. Chapter 8.3) have been implemented. See Section 8.4 for a description of the framework parts.

The PerOpteryx implementation is yet specific to the PCM metamodel, i.e. it does not conform to the CBA optimization framework presented in Section 8.4 with that respect. The DoF metamodel is partially used and is discussed in the next section.

The following degrees of freedom in the PCM are supported by the tool at this time

- Component Selection (Section 7.2.1)

- Passive Resource Multiplicity (Section 7.2.3)

- Allocation (Section 7.3.1)

- Resource Property Change for changing the processing rate (Section 7.3.5)

Like the PCM, PerOpteryx uses Ecore instead of EMOF. As described in Section 2.5.2, Ecore and EMOF are effectively equivalent, so we do not distinguish them further.

365

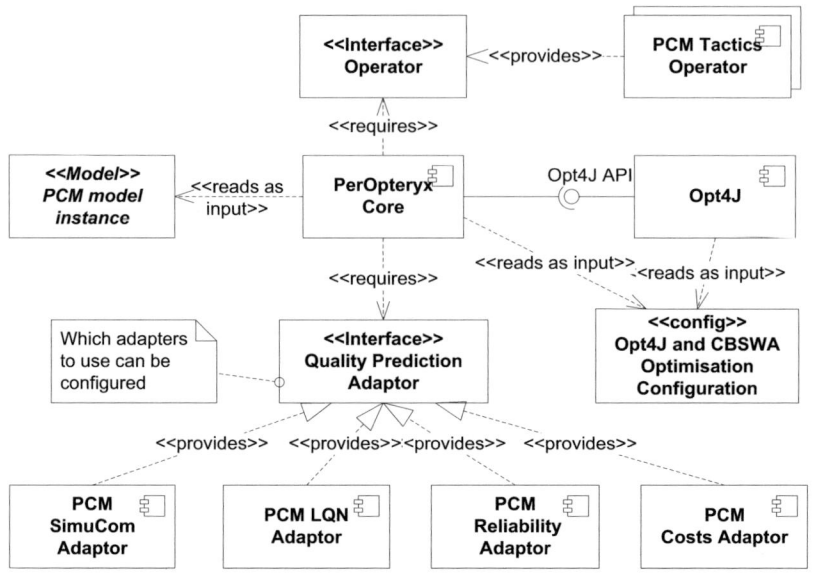

Figure 9.1.: PerOpteryx Tool

Constraint checking is not yet implemented, as the currently supported DoF in Palladio have not required this so far.

If not mentioned explicitly in the following sections, the following default configuration for PerOpteryx was used. The maximum number of iterations is the default stop criterion with the maximum number of iterations set to 200. The default population size is 20 and the default crossover rate is 0.9. Tactics and starting population heuristic are disabled by default. If tactics are enabled, the default probability to apply tactics is 0.6. The order and probability of the applied operators is described in Section 8.3.2.

The tournament level for the NSGA-II selector is set to 3 (cf. (Deb, 2001). For crowding distance assignment, the objective values are scaled by the current minimum value and maximum value in the population (like presented in Deb (2001), this was not present in the initial presentation of NSGA-II in Deb et al. (2000)).

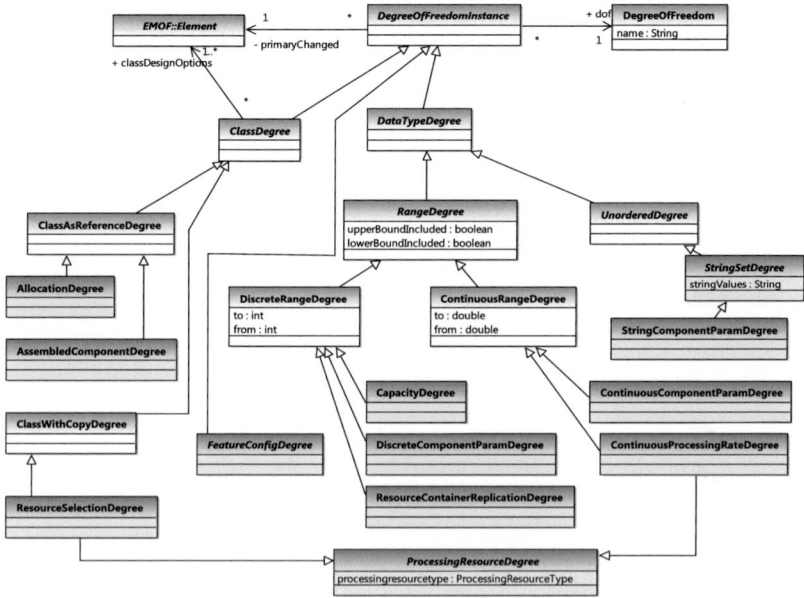

Figure 9.2.: Degrees of Freedom in PerOpteryx

Additionally, we have studied the feasibility of our approach by implementing a prototype CBS-metamodel-agnostic transformation that reads in a DoF model for component selection in Palladio, a candidate vector, and an initial Palladio model, and applies the chosen values to produce a changed CBS model. This transformation is independent of the used CBS metamodel (in our case PCM), as the transformation handles the model only using EMF (the Eclipse version of EMOF) reflection capabilities.

9.2.2. Degree of Freedom Instances in PerOpteryx

The PerOpteryx degree of freedom model adds one (or several) meta-classes per conceptual degree of freedom (as described in Section 6.3.3) to the generic model of Figure 6.9. These meta-classes are annotated by OCL constraints to constrain the primary changed elements and the design option set. The constraints for the annotated model elements have been omitted in this figure to save space. As described in Section 6.3.3, because Properties cannot be referenced in EMOF, the primary changed element is usually restricted to the model element that contains the primary changeable element property. For example, the Component Selection Degree has the primary changeable element AssemblyContext.encapsulatedComponent, so the referenced primary changed element is restricted to be an AssemblyContext.

An exception are degrees where a single element from a property with multiplicity larger than one is changed, such as the Resource Selection Degree. To identify the changed element here, there are several option. Because the property ResourceContainer.activeResourceSpecifications is a composite property (see discussion in Section 6.3.3), we can refer to ProcessingResourceSpecification here because one instance of ProcessingResourceSpecification uniquely defines the place in the system to change. When applying a change produced by the degree of freedom, we then have copy the attributes values from the template ProcessingResourceSpecification, which is in the resource repository, to the changed ProcessingResourceSpecification to keep the correct reference.

Alternatively, we can add additional information to the degree to identify the ProcessingResourceSpecification from the ResourceContainer.activeResourceSpecifications list. For the Resource Selection Degree, we chose the latter option and add the ResourceType of the ProcessingResourceSpecification to the degree, so that the Resource Selection Degree references the ResourceContainer and the ResourceType to uniquely identify a ProcessingResourceSpecification. This option is suitable because a ResourceContainer may only contain one ProcessingResourceSpecification per ResourceType, and it makes the exchange of ProcessingResourceSpecifications technically easier, because we can copy a ProcessingResourceSpecification from the repository and do not have to copy the values of all attributes separately.

For the configuration parameter degree, several meta-classes are added to the PerOpteryx degree of freedom model. A configuration parameter degree can be modelled by either a continuous range or a discrete range or a set of strings, thus, there are three different classes in the degree of freedom model: DiscreteComponentParamDegree, ContinuousComponentParamDegree, and StringComponentEnumDegree.

9.3. Case Study Systems

This section presents the two case study systems our method was applied to: These are a business reporting system (BRS) (Section 9.3.1) and an industrial control system (ICS) from ABB (Section 9.3.2), which shows the industrial applicability of our approach.

9.3.1. Business Reporting System

In this section, we first introduce the architecture and the Palladio model of our first system under study, the so-called business reporting system. Then, we describe the degrees of freedom in this system and formulate the search problem.

The system under study is the so-called business reporting system (BRS), which lets users retrieve reports and statistical data about running business processes from a data base. It is loosely based on a real system (Wu and Woodside, 2004b). Fig. 9.3 shows some parts of the PCM instance of the BRS visualized using annotated UML diagrams. It is a 4-tier system consisting of several software components.

The WebServer component handles user requests for generating reports or viewing the plain data logged by the system. It delegates the requests to a Scheduler component, which in turn distributes the requests to the GraphicalReporting component or the OnlineReporting component, depending on the type of request. These components generate the reports using data retrieved from the respective core reporting engine

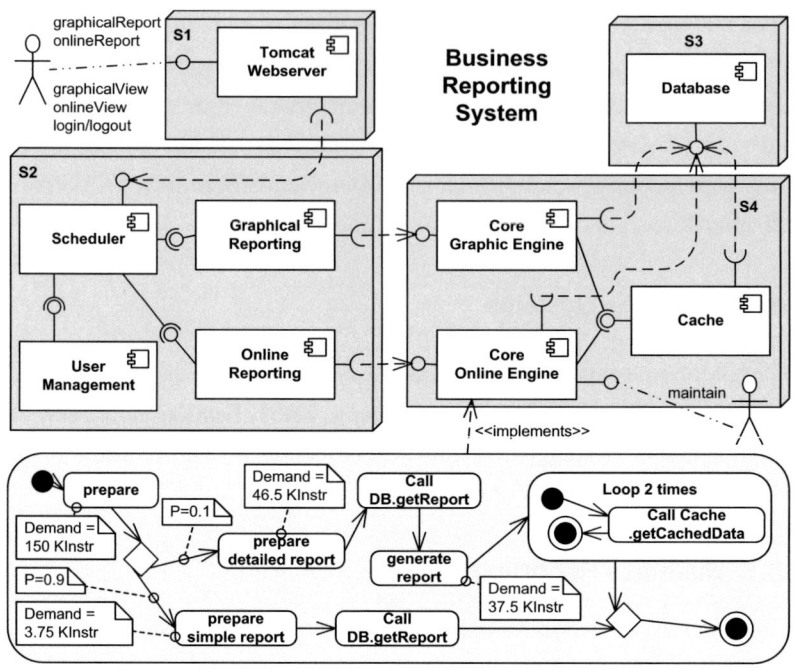

Figure 9.3.: Business Reporting System: PCM Instance of the Case Study System

(CoreGraphicEngine or CoreOnlineEngine). The core reporting engines query the Database, for some requests directly, for others using a Cache component. The Scheduler also communicates with the User-Management for user login and logout requests as well as to log the user requests over time.

Besides the static view of the system, Fig. 9.3 also contains a behavioural view of the CoreOnlineEngine.getReport service in form of an RD-SEFF in the lower half of the figure. The RD-SEFF contain the resource demands, failure probabilities, and call propagations later predictions will be based on. The components are allocated on four different servers connected by a network. Each server has a CPU with a processing

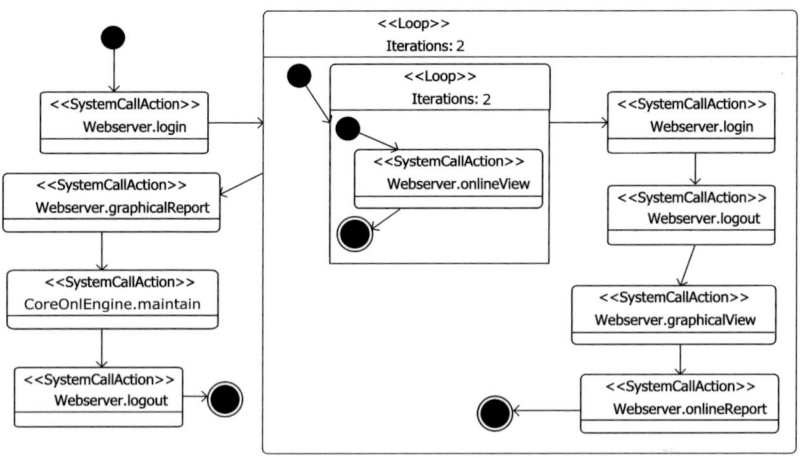

Figure 9.4.: Usage Scenario for the BRS System

rate of 1.5 GHz. Our case study analyses a usage scenario in which all six services of the system are used, shown in Figure 9.4. The inter-arrival time of the open workload is exponentially distributed with a mean value of 1.

For the performance prediction, we transform the model into a LQN using PCM2LQN (H. Koziolek and Reussner, 2008) and solve it with the LQNS tool. The performance prediction with the LQNS tool shows that the system is overloaded, i.e. its queue lengths grow over time and operational equilibrium is not reached (Jain, 1991). Even though the model does not converge because of the overload situation, the LQNS tool still outputs a predicted mean response time that can be used by the optimization as a measure of the quality of the candidate. In this case, the predicted value is 25.3 seconds. The utilization of server 2 is reported to be 100.9%, thus, server 2 is the bottleneck in this system.

The reliability prediction includes software, network and server hardware failures. Some internal actions of components were annotated with failure probabilities. We assumed that the servers have a mean time to failure (MTTF) of 43800 hours and a mean time to repair (MTTR) of 3 hours.

Component	Action accept request graphical		Action accept request online		Action accept view graphical		Action accept view online		
	dem.	failure prob.	dem.	failure prob.	dem.	failure prob.	dem.	failure prob.	costs
WebServer	0.5	2.8E-6	0.5	5.4E-6	0.05	3.5E-6	0.05	3.0E-6	100
WebServer2	0.3	2.8E-6	0.3	5.4E-6	0.05	3.5E-6	0.05	2.0E-6	150
WebServer3	0.5	6.0E-6	0.5	7.0E-6	0.04	3.5E-6	0.04	3.2E-6	80

Table 9.1.: Component Selection in BRS: Changes to Initially Used Component (dem. = demand, failure prob. = failure probability)

The network has a failure probability of 10^{-6}. For the reliability prediction, we use the PCM Markov translator (Brosch et al., 2010), which predicts a probability of failure on demand for the system of $8.07 \cdot 10^{-4}$. This means that each user request will be successful with a probability of 99.92 percent.

The BRS server costs depend on the chosen CPU processing rate pr in GHz. For the costs model, we analysed Intel's CPU price list (Intel Corporation, 2010). We fitted a power function to this data, so that the resulting costs of one server s is $cost_s = 0.7665 \ pr_s^{6.2539} + 145$ with coefficient of determination $R^2 = 0.965$. The overall server costs of one candidate is the sum of the costs of all used servers plus the costs of the components. The costs of the initial system are 718.7 units.

To formulate the search problem for the business reporting system, first the system specific degrees of freedom have to be determined. For our case study, we consider the following degrees of freedom: component selection, server processing rates, and component allocation.

Component selection is possible in this system as it contains several replaceable standard components. The WebServer can be realized using third party components. The software architect can choose among multiple functional equivalent components with different non-functional properties and cost. For the BRS, we have modelled two additional web servers which have different performance and reliability properties, but also higher or lower cost than the components in the initial system. The demands and probability of failure of the internal actions are shown in table 9.1.

Server processing rates can be adjusted at multiple locations in the model as it contains up to nine servers. It is expected that the overall performance of the system increases most significantly when using faster processing rates for highly utilized components. We assume here that the bounds for the processing rate are 1/2 of the initial rate (lower bound) and 2 times the initial rate (upper bound). The processing rate is modelled as a continuous variable.

Component allocation can be crucial for the non-functional properties and cost of the system. It could be possible to allocate multiple components on the same server without affecting the performance or reliability significantly. This could allow to remove some servers to save cost. In this problem, we allowed the components to be allocated to up to four servers.

The genome of the initial candidate is [1.5, 1.5, 1.5, 1.5, WebServer, server1, server2, server2, server2, server4, server4, server4, server3, server2]. It reflects the processing rates in GHz, the selected web server component as well as the component allocation to different servers (in the order they are described above, e.g., WebServer is deployed on server 1, Scheduler is deployed on server 2, and the UserManagement (last entry) is deployed to server 2).

If we only consider 4 steps to vary the processing rate of servers, which is actually a continuous variable, the resulting optimization problem has the following size (we denote the number of components, servers, etc., using the cardinality symbol):

$$\text{number of candidates} = |\text{servers}|^{|\text{components}|} \cdot |\text{web server components}|$$
$$\cdot\,|\text{rate steps}|^{|\text{servers}|}$$
$$= 4^9 \cdot 3 \cdot 4^4$$
$$= 201326592$$

As the evaluation of each candidate takes about 50 seconds (for the business reporting case study using the fast LQN solver, cf. Section 9.5.2), the time needed for the full exploration of the design space would be 319.2 years. Some of the candidates in the design space are equivalent, though: If we exchange S1 and S3 in the example, i.e. if we deploy the WebServer component to S3 and the Database component to S1, the resulting candidate has the same quality properties than the initial candidate, and does not have to be evaluated anew. If we exclude all permutations of servers that lead to equivalent candidates, the number of allocation option to evaluate is 11051 (cf. (Beyer, 2010)) and the number of required evaluations is $11051 \cdot 3 \cdot 4^4 = 8487168$. Still, the time needed for the evaluations would be 13.5 years.

9.3.2. ABB Process Control System

The second case study shows the applicability of the method in an industrial context on a large scale system. In this case, we analysed an industrial process control system (PCS) from ABB, which is used in many domains, such as power generation, pulp and paper handling, and oil and gas processing. The PCS manages industrial processes by periodically collecting sensor data like temperature, flow, or pressure, processing the data and visualizing the data for human operators. Operators may use the system to control actuators in the process such as pumps, valves, and heaters. Additionally, the system may execute predefined action on its own.

Our case study focusses on the server-side part of an ABB PCS. We do not consider the embedded field devices in this work. The server-side application comprises of several million lines of C++ code. Due to the proprietary nature of this system, the author of this work could not access and study the system herself, but worked together with ABB researchers who created the models and run the optimization. Thus, no in-depth detail of the system can be provided.

Fig. 9.5 shows a part of the PCM model of the system. Researchers at ABB have modelled 28 components of the system, each one having at least

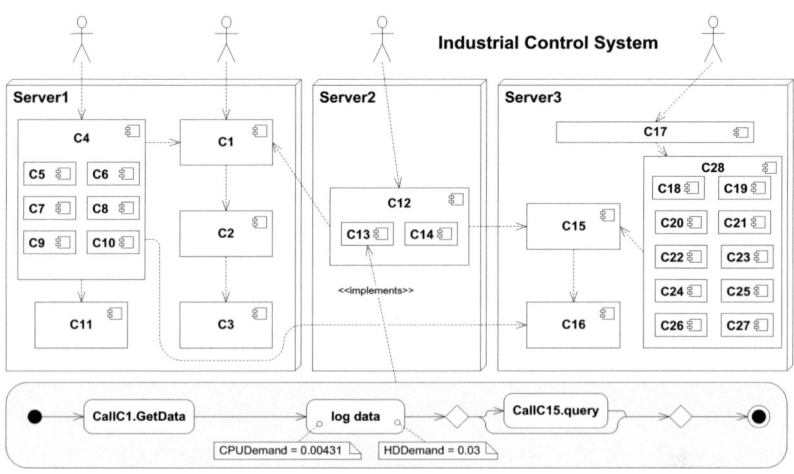

Figure 9.5.: PCM Model of the Industrial Control System (by H. Koziolek et al., 2011c

one resource demand, which were determined from performance measurements on a running instance of the system. The resource environment is adaptable to customer requirements and consists of three servers in the initial configuration. For the hardware resources, we used a costs model similar to the former case study. One behaviour model for component C13 is shown in Fig. 9.5 at the lower part. Additionally, four of the most important usage scenarios of the system were modelled.

More details on the model creation for the ABB PCS have been published in H. Koziolek et al., 2011c. Reliability annotations are not available for this system; thus, only performance and costs are considered here.

The quality properties of interest for our optimization are performance (in terms of mean response time of the described usage scenario) and costs as modelled with the PCM costs model.

As degrees of freedoms, it is possible to replace component C1 and C13 by alternative implementations with different performance and costs. Table 9.2 shows the different options. For C1, there is one alternative com-

Component	HDD demand	CPU demand	costs	Probability to call C2
C1-2	N/A	-7.3%	+200%	N/A
C13-2	+ 33%	- 50%	+20%	lower
C13-3	- 17%	- 19%	+200%	lower

Table 9.2.: Component Selection in ABB PCS: Relative Changes to Initially Used Component

ponent C1-2 that has less CPU demand (in relation to C1) but higher costs. For C13, there are two different alternatives. Component C13-2 has less CPU demand, but more HDD demand and higher costs. Component C13-3 has lower CPU and HDD demand, but much higher costs.

Furthermore, the allocation of the components to hardware resources can be adjusted. Up to five servers are available. The composed structures C4 and C28 are subsystems, thus their content may be allocated independently. Component C12 is a composite component and can only be allocated as one. Thus, we get 24 allocation degrees of freedom for C12 and all basic components except C13 and C14.

Additionally, the processing rates of the servers can be lowered to save costs or increased. For each CPU, we assume a possible range from -50% to +100%.

9.4. Improving CBA based on Model-based Quality Prediction

In this section we present the validation settings and results for Goal 1, the validation of the architecture improvement support in the context of the CBSE development process. Section 9.4.1 is concerned with question Q1.1, i.e. the accuracy of the models. Section 9.4.2 discusses question Q1.2 of whether an approximation of the true optimum can be found. Finally, Section 9.4.3 presents the set-ups and results for question Q1.3 of whether the considered design space is relevant.

9.4.1. Model Accuracy

In this section, we address the first question regarding the optimization problem:

Q1.1 Can models that were automatically modified according to the specified degrees of freedom indeed be used for valid performance predictions?

The question of model accuracy is independent of the optimization approach of this thesis, but applies to any model-based quality prediction approach. Additionally, it depends on the used meta-modelling language. Thus, to study the validity of the software architecture models in general is out of scope of this thesis, but is of importance for any proposed quality prediction approach.

However, the optimization relies in particular on the accuracy of the models even if the model is changed. This means that a model must be accurate not only for the system configuration it has been created and calibrated for, but also for changed system configuration (i.e., for different candidates). Thus, the single component models must be parametrized to account for a varying environment. Our optimization approach assumes that the models are parametrized and that they are accurate for all candidates without calibrating the model for each possible candidate.

In the following, we discuss the existing work on accuracy of parametrized models achievable with the PCM in Section 9.4.1.1 and identify a gap concerning component allocation. Our additional study closes this gap and is presented in Section 9.4.1.2.

9.4.1.1. Existing Model Accuracy Studies for the PCM

For the PCM, numerous case studies validated that accurate models can be created (H. Koziolek and Firus, 2006; H. Koziolek et al., 2006; H. Koziolek, 2008, Happe et al. (2006); Becker (2008a); Becker et al. (2009); Happe et al. (2010); Hauck et al. (2009); Kuperberg et al. (2008); Huber et al. (2010); Krogmann (2010)). Thus, in this work, we do not further study that accurate models can be created.

In some of the previously mentioned studies (H. Koziolek and Firus, 2006, Happe et al. (2006); Hauck et al. (2009); Huber et al. (2010)), PCM models for a system under study have been created and calibrated using measurements of the system. Then, the predicted performance properties are compared to measurements of the system. While these studies validated the accuracy of the given model at hand, they do not allow conclusions on the model accuracy in the presence of model changes without new calibration of the models.

In most of the above studies ((H. Koziolek et al., 2006; H. Koziolek, 2008), Becker (2008a); Becker et al. (2009); Kuperberg et al. (2008); Krogmann (2010)), the accuracy of models in a changed system has been studied already, though:

Design alternatives: Two studies (H. Koziolek et al., 2006, Becker (2008a)) validated the accuracy of the models across design alternatives. The model is calibrated for an initial system design. Then, a design alternative (in this case the addition of a compression component) is modelled. The performance properties of the new component are measured in isolation. Then, the predictions for the design alternative are successfully compared to measurements of an analogously changed system. These studies show that PCM performance predictions can be accurate across component selection if the components are properly parametrized. In these studies, the important parameter to model was the size of the processed data.

Usage: Two studies (H. Koziolek, 2008, Krogmann (2010)) are concerned with the accuracy of models for changing usage profiles. Although this is not directly a degree of freedom in this work, usage changes are also relevant if component selection and component allocation changes, because such changes may lead to different internal usage profiles at internal interfaces.

Configuration: Two studies (Becker et al., 2009; Happe et al., 2010) evaluated the accuracy of messaging completions across different configuration. In both cases, the effects of messaging configuration such as message size, messaging protocol, and use of security measures (encryption or authentication) were measured in isolation. Then, the performance effects are weaved into to PCM model and compared with overall system measurements. These studies show that the configuration of middleware can be parametrized.

Resource Environment: One study (Kuperberg et al., 2008) evaluated the accuracy of models across different platforms, and even created the component models independently of the target platform. The component's resource demands were characterized in terms of executed Java byte-code instructions, and the processing speed of the target platform was characterized using micro benchmarks of single Java byte-code instructions on the target platforms. Measurements of the component on a test platform were required to estimate the impact of just-in-time compilation. Component models, just-in-time estimation and resource environment model were combined and provided accurate predictions of the systems on the target platform with a prediction error of less than 10% in most cases.

These studies show that indeed parametrized models can be created which are reusable for different execution contexts. However, these studies focus on changed components, additional components or other changes of the component topology. Changes of the execution environment are so far limited to changes to middleware configuration. As the accuracy of models across different component allocation is a crucial degree of freedom in this work, we add a further study to the above body of work. The study and its results are presented in the next section.

In other CBA metamodels, the parametrization is less pronounced, but also available. In CBML, a component can be configured with parameters (Wu and Woodside, 2004a) (similar to component parameters in the PCM). Using these parameters, different environments in which a component is used can be reflected. as well as varying input parameters can be reflected. ROBOCOP (Bondarev et al., 2005) also supports such component configuration parameters, and additionally allows to specify resource demands, control flow constructs, and input parameters to other called services that depend on input parameter values (similar to the usage profile modelling and propagation in the PCM). Thus, the usage profile can be propagated through a system.

Both CBML and ROBOCOP also distinguish between the resource requirements of a component (tasks using replaceable processors in CBML, component resource model in ROBOCOP) and the provided resource environment (processor bindings to actual processors in CBML, performance models for hardware blocks in ROBOCOP), see Section 2.6 for more details on the models. Thus, they support the separated specification of components and used resources and thus account for the allocation degree of freedom.

9.4.1.2. Allocation Validation Study

While numerous studies have validated that accurate PCM models can be built (cf. Section 9.4.1.1), the validity of the models when the allocation of components is changed has not been published yet. Therefore, in this section, we present a case study validating the accuracy of models when changing allocation. To better connect to our optimization approach, we used the optimization to determine optimal candidates for the case study set-up.

Then, we measure two optimal candidates and one suboptimal candidate. To assess the accuracy, we determine the relative prediction error e based on the predicted mean response time mrt_{pred} and the measured mean response time mrt_{meas} as $e = \frac{mrt_{meas} - mrt_{pred}}{mrt_{meas}}$. Additionally, we compare whether the optimal candidates are indeed better than the suboptimal candidates.

In the following, we first describe the measurement set-up. Based on this measurement set-up, we ran an optimization to determine optimal and suboptimal candidates. The optimization set-up is described below. Then, we compare the measurement results for the three selected candidates to the predicted values.

Measurement Set-up   We use the Business Reporting System described in Section 9.3.1 in this study. The assumed workload for this study was an open workload with an constant inter-arrival rate of 1.5 seconds, i.e. every 1.5 seconds a user arrives at the system and executed the usage scenario shown in Figure 9.4. Both loop iterations within the usage scenario were set to 5 repetitions.

The available hardware environment are a PC with an Intel Core2 Quad CPU Q6600, with 2.4 GHz per core, and a IBM Think Pad T60 with an Intel Core2 T7200 processor with two 2 GHz cores, connected by PowerLAN[2], a router and wireless to reflect a more complex network environment. We installed three application servers on the two physical machines, two on the quad core and one on the Think Pad. To exclude influences of the multiple cores on the measurements, we restricted each application server to use only one core of the machine. Thus, we have a resulting three virtual machines with one core each.

For the implementation of the Business Reporting System, we use the PCM to ProtoCom transformation (Becker, 2008b). This transformation generates an executable prototype system which is a set of EJB components. While this prototype does not provide any functionality, it can be deployed in an application server, uses processing resources, and thus can be

---

[2]technology to set up a local area network over power line, also called dLAN (direct LAN) or Powerline Communication (PLC)

used to measure the system. In particular, when measuring the prototype, the effects of the application server and the remaining software stack can be captured, as well as the network influence. The amount of processing can be parametrized so that varying processing rates can be emulated. Thus, this prototype allows to study allocation degrees of freedom and resource property change degree of freedom.

Using this prototype of the BRS system, the resource environment model was created and calibrated. We measured the delay of the network communication and the inter-application server communication in a single-user and a multi-user scenario, using different configuration of the system than used later in the validation measurements. Then, we modelled the resulting distribution as network latency distribution in the PCM.

For measurements, we used the built-in instrumentation capability of ProtoCom, which has only negligible overhead. As load driver, a Proto-Com usage scenario can be started from a web browser.

Optimization Set-up and Selected Candidates   The goal of the optimization step is to find candidates with optimal cost and response time trade-offs. The initial system model was an arbitrary allocation of the components to the three servers (shown in table 9.4 below), where each server was configured with a low processing rate. This initial candidate has low costs, but is overloaded by the workload described above, so that no meaningful response time values can be predicted or measured (the LQN solver predicted a mean response time of 2390 seconds, while the measurement fails due to to many started threads). Because an overloaded system is unacceptable, any found candidate that is not overloaded is better than this initial candidate.

The degrees of freedom of our prototype system are the following. Each of the nine components can be allocated to any of the three servers, leading different network communication. Thus, we get nine allocation degrees of freedom. Additionally, the effective processing rates of the servers can be varied by varying the amount of processing of the prototype components, which is reflected by three resource property degrees of freedom. Finally, the three alternative web server components described in Section 9.3.1 have been considered, resulting in one component selection degree of freedom.

We configured the PerOpteryx tool with a population size of 20 and 310 iterations. All tactics described in Section 8.3.1 except the "Remove One-lane Bridge" tactic were enabled with the configuration shown in table 9.3. The "Remove One-lane Bridge" has been disabled because the model does not contain any passive resources, so the tactic's condition is never fulfilled. The probability to apply tactics in the reproduction step was 0.6 (cf. Section 8.3.1). After the optimization, tactics with lower thresholds were again applied to the Pareto-optimal candidates, if applicable, in the intensification phase.

For quality analyses, we use the LQNS tool and the costs analysis. The LQNS tool was configured to continue analysis even if the system seems to be overloaded ("Stop on message loss pragma" has been set to false, cf. (Franks et al., 2008, p.45)). If the "stop on message loss pragma" is enabled (which is the default configuration), the LQNS tool aborts analysis if the system is overloaded and reports and the quality analysis reports infinite response time. If the pragma is set to false, the LQNS tool predicts a mean response time value for each candidate, even though it is know to be inaccurate. This allows the algorithm to distinguish better between candidates: For example, two overloaded candidates have predicted response times of 250 and 1000 seconds. Then, even though both systems are overloaded, the first candidate is more promising. With the enabled pragma, both candidates would be assigned an infinite value for response time, so that no distinction is possible. Additionally, we configured an upper quality bound for response time of 15 seconds, so that the algorithm does not focus on searching such uninteresting overloaded candidates.

From the resulting set of Pareto-optimal candidates, we choose two optimal candidates (no. 1 and 2) and a suboptimal candidate (no. 3) shown in

Tactic	threshold	additional configuration	tactic weight
Spread the load Scale-up bottleneck resources Scale-out bottleneck server Reduce remote communication	$U_{\text{spread}} = 0.5$ $U_{\text{scale-up}} = 0.8$ $U_{\text{scale-out}} = 0.9$ $U_{\text{remote}} = 0.8$	$f = 0.25$	$W_{\text{spread}} = 1$ $W_{\text{scale-up}} = 0.1$ $W_{\text{scale-out}} = 0.5$ $W_{\text{remote}} = 1$
Scale-down idle resource Consolidate servers	$U_{\text{scale-down}} = 0.2$ $U_{\text{cons}} = 0.3$	$f = 0.25$	$W_{\text{scale-down}} = 0.1$ $W_{\text{cons}} = 1$

Table 9.3.: Configuration of Tactics in Allocation Study

Candidate no.	Predicted Costs	Predicted MRT	CPU rate of s1	CPU rate of s2	CPU rate of s2	Chosen web server	Alloc. of web server	Alloc. of OnlineReporting	Alloc. of CoreOnlineEngine	Alloc. of CacheInfo	Alloc. of UserManagement	Alloc. of Scheduler	Alloc. of CoreGraphicEngine	Alloc. of Database	Alloc. of GraphicalReporting
0	564.0	2389.68	10	10	10	W	s1	s1	s1	s1	s1	s2	s2	s2	s3
1	734.3	9.15	12.3	12.1	15.5	W3	s3	s3	s3	s2	s3	s3	s2	s2	s1
2	1147.7	6.24	16.4	15.3	16.9	W	s3	s2	s2	s2	s3	s3	s2	s2	s1
3	1005.5	10.6	18.8	15	15	W	s1	s1	s1	s1	s1	s1	s1	s1	s3

Table 9.4.: Allocation Validation Study: Initial Candidate no. 0 and Chosen Candidates no. 1–3

table 9.4. MRT stands for mean response time, W stands for `WebServer`, W3 for `WebServer3`, and s1 to s3 stand for servers 1 to 3.

When comparing these candidates with other candidates and investigating the models, we observe that the optimization algorithm has deployed components together that communicate much, and thus splits the system into several physical tiers. The amount of remote communication has been reduced as much as possible by the algorithm. Other candidates that allocate the candidates so that the communicate more remotely lead to an overloaded network resource.

Cand. No	Predicted MRT mrt_{pred}	Measured MRT mrt_{meas}	Relative error e
1	9.15	9.84	-0.070
2	6.24	5.81	0.074
3	10.56	9.97	0.060

Table 9.5.: Measurement vs Predictions for Selected Candidates

Measurement Results   We measure the system for the selected three candidates and compare the measurement results to the predictions. Table 9.5 shows the results. We observe that the prediction is close to the measurement results and that the relative prediction error e is low.

The predictions report moderate utilization values for the servers (between 25% and 70%), thus, the candidates are not overloaded. The measurement results also show a steady behaviour and indicate that the candidates are not overloaded.

As a result, we observe that the response time for candidates with changed allocation can be accurately predicted, even if the models are created and calibrated without knowledge of the final allocation. Thus, the PCM models can be parametrized for allocation. The candidate that is predicted to be suboptimal is indeed suboptimal, assuming a realistic costs model.

Still, it should be noted that the creation of such parametrized models is difficult. Thus, several works have been suggested to support the component developer or software architect in the task of creating parametrized models for their components or black-box subsystems (Wu and Woodside, 2008; Krogmann et al., 2010; Westermann and Happe, 2010; Hauck et al., 2011).

At the same time, we observe that the optimization did not find the possibility to allocate all components on servers 2 and 3, which can communicate faster than with server 1. The server consolidation tactic fails here (e.g. when applied to candidate 1 or candidate 2), because the CPUs of the two remaining servers 2 and 3 are too slow to host the GraphicalReporting in these configurations. The optimization did not generate a candidate with allocation to two servers and at the same time increased CPU processing rate of servers 2 and 3. As a result, we have created a new tactic that increases the processing rate of the servers to which components of the removed server are reallocated. This is an example of how insight in the problem domain can lead to new performance tactics.

9.4.1.3. Results for Question Q1.1

We conclude that accurate models for performance predictions can be built. Having surveyed existing studies on parametrization conducted for the PCM, we conclude that accurate parametrized models for varying component environment such as design alternatives (i.e. component selection), usage profile changes, middleware configuration changes, and resource environment changes can be created. The remaining gap of allocation changes has been successfully closed by a new study.

However, even though we have validated that accurate models can be build, the remaining question is whether software architects in practice can actually do so. Here, (more) level II validations are required for all model prediction techniques are required. Our method has an additional problem in that software architects may use degrees of freedom for which their models are not accurately parametrized, e.g. because a third party has provided the model. However, this mistake could as well be made in a manual improvement approach and is a general problem of model-based prediction approaches.

9.4.2. Approximating the True Pareto Front

In this section, we study the question :

Q1.2 Can the search find an approximation of the true Pareto front?

for the business reporting system. As discussed above, we assess the approximation found by a combination of search runs. Section 9.4.2.1 refers to the set-ups for this evaluation, and Section 9.4.2.2 describes the results and answers the validation question.

9.4.2.1. Experiment Set-up

We use the results of 33 optimization runs conducted for the validation of the optimization step in Section 9.5 with different search strategies (evolutionary search with different population size and crossover configuration, tactics-enhanced search, and random search). The optimization runs together evaluated 83921 candidates which we denote by *allC* (possibly including duplicates).

9.4.2.2. Results for Question Q1.2

Figure 9.6 shows the combined Pareto front calculated over all candidates, i.e. $P(allC)$. Two dimensions are pairwise compared to each other. The diagonal define the axes of the plots. Each field in the figure shows the quality property defined in its column on the x axis and the quality property defined in its row on the y axis. For example, the plot in row 2 column 1 compares POFOD and costs, with POFOD on the x axis and costs on the y axis. While Figure 9.6(a) shows the unfiltered results, we have omitted the three candidates with mean response time larger than 15 seconds in the second Figure 9.6(b) to better show the interesting knee region.

We observe that the main trade-off exists between costs and response time. The Pareto front for these two criteria is smooth, suggesting that the searches have indeed converged to a (local) optimum an this point, possibly the global optimum. Interestingly, the searches have found two bands of candidates: An outer band with many candidates that have optimal cost and performance trade off, and an inner band with better reliability values at the cost of both cost and response time.

Analysing the choices of the optimal candidates, we observe that the bands reflect different number of used servers. Figure 9.7 shows the costs

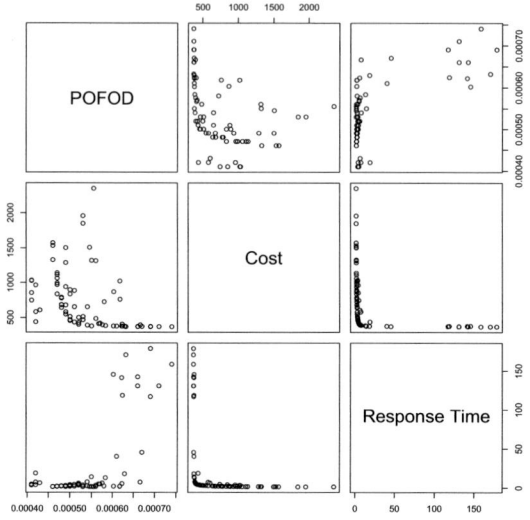

(a) All Candidates in the Overall Pareto Front

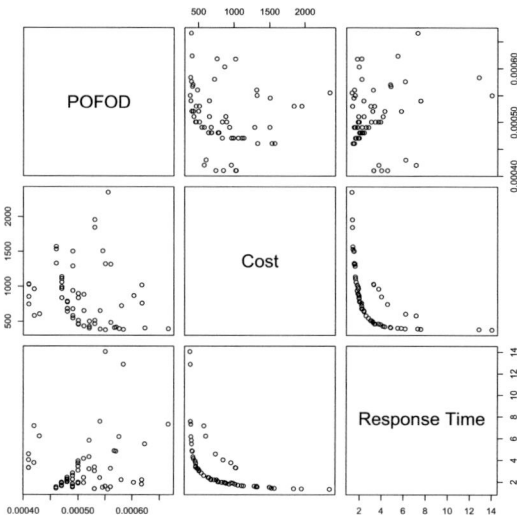

(b) Candidates with Response Time Smaller than 15

Figure 9.6.: Scatter-plots for the Overall Pareto Front

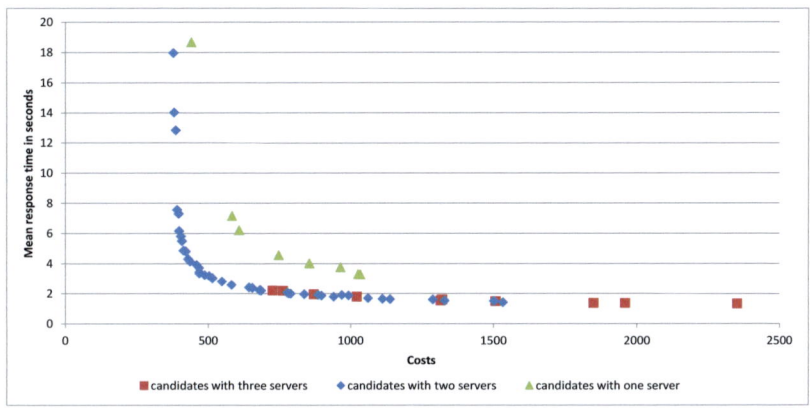

Figure 9.7.: Costs-performance-trade-off in the Overall Pareto Front for Varying Number of Servers

performance trade-off of $P(allC)$ with the number of servers used by each candidates. We observe that all candidates of the inner band are deployed to a single server with high processing rates. The shape of the band reflects different processing rate configuration of the single chosen server. No network communication is needed, so no network-indices failures can happen, which leads to the improved reliability.

In the outer band, candidates are deployed to two or three servers. The three most expensive candidates are deployed to three servers, as the processing rate of two servers cannot be increased beyond 3 GHz in our problem. In the costs range of 750–1600, there is both: While the candidates with two servers achieve a higher utilization of each server and thus use the available processing capacity efficiently, the candidates with three servers have more total processing power due to our exponential processor cost model, and thus achieve the same response time for the same price.

No candidates with four servers was found to be Pareto-optimal. We manually analysed whether a candidate with four servers could be optimal as well, and present the results in the following. Due to our exponential

Component	Relative CPU load
WebServer	0.13
Scheduler	0.13
Database	0.21
CoreOnlineEngine	0.03
Cache	0.04
GraphicalReporting	0.32
OnlineReporting	0.08
UserManagement	0.06
CoreGraphicEngine	0.00

Table 9.6.: CPU Resource Demand in BRS System

costs model, one might expect that a candidate with low processing rate configuration and four servers is more cost-efficient than a solution with three servers while providing the same response time. However, the components of the business reporting system have different resource demands. Table 9.6 shows the relative resource demand of each component, analysed using the usage scenario presented in Section 9.3.1 with a single user only. We observe that a the GraphicalReporting component alone causes 32% of the CPU resource demand in this scenario, and the Database component 21%. If these component are deployed to a dedicated server each with minimal processing rate, the servers are overloaded in the studied multi-user scenario as described in Section 9.3.1. Thus, the deployment of four servers with minimal processing rates is not possible. Manually gradually increasing the resource speeds until the system is feasible leads to suboptimal candidate. Thus, the optimization result that no candidate with four servers is optimal is correct.

All three web server components are used in the candidates of the found front. Most candidates in the high-reliability band use WebServer2. While WebServer2 has the same probability of failure than the WebServer component, it has less resource demand and higher costs. This combination is beneficial in the one-server setting: The server already has a high load and needs fast processing resources, and due to the exponential costs model, the increase of processing speed to host the WebServer component is more expensive than using WebServer2. Note that while we can understand these effects when analysing the found Pareto-front, they are not be intuitively clear and thus are difficult to find in a manual approach.

In the costs-performance trade-off band, the two-server candidates in the costs range up to 435 use the cheaper WebServer3 component, while the more expensive candidates in the costs range starting from 890 all use Web-Server2. This is sensible because in the more expensive candidates, the use of WebServer2 saves more resource costs due to the exponential costs model. Candidates in the intermediate range and candidates with three servers use all three web server components. Overall, the use of the WebServer component is rare.

The processing rate choices result in the shape of the two bands. The continuous processing rate has comparably straightforward impact on the response time. Note that the true Pareto front, in theory, has infinitely many candidates, because we consider a continuous processing rate range. A search based approach can only find an approximation, and we deduce that intermediate solutions are also available in both bands. A higher number of candidates in the front, however, does not necessarily provide additional benefit to the software architect, because more candidates have to be considered after the search.

Having analysed the different types of choices in detail, we deduce that the found Pareto front probably is very close to true Pareto front, The true Pareto front probably has a similar shape with the two bands, although the number of candidates on each band is likely to be much higher due to the continuous processing rate.

Thus, we conclude that the $P(allC)$ is a good approximation of the true Pareto front.

9.4.3. Design Space

In this section, we study the question:

Q1.3 Does our design space represent a relevant subset of the complete design space software architects are faced with?

To evaluate this question, we apply the optimization approach to both case study systems presented in Sections 9.3.1 and 9.3.2. From one optimization run per case study system, we can answer the question.

The available degrees of freedom of the example systems have already been described in Section 9.3. Thus, here we check whether the candidates found by the optimization using these degrees differ in their quality properties. We report the distribution of values for each objective for (1) all candidates evaluated during the optimization run and (2) for the finally determined optimal candidates.

Second, we report the found Pareto-optimal candidates. A set of multiple candidates shows that a trade-off is present between the optimal candidates. If the problem was no multi-objective one, only a single optimal candidate would be reported.

Section 9.4.3.1 presents the results for the Business Reporting System and Section 9.4.3.2 for the ABB system. The question is first answered separately for each case study system and then Section 9.4.3.3 summarizes the findings.

9.4.3.1. Business Reporting System

Before reporting the results, we describe details on an optimization run performed on the Business Reporting System model below. Then, the results for question 3 are presented.

Experiment Set-up For the evolutionary optimization of the model, we configured Opt4J to run for 200 iterations and to produce 20 candidates per iteration. The LQN solver was configured with a convergence value of 0.001 and an iteration limit of 20 (see (Franks et al., 2008) for details). The PCM Markov model solver was configured to determine the reliability with an accuracy of 5 decimal places, the remaining configuration was the standard configuration so that both software and hardware failures were taken into account.

The automatic improvement process took 21 hours, produced 2110 valid architectural candidates and made performance, reliability, and cost predictions for them. Thus, the average creation, transformation, and prediction time per candidate was 36 seconds. The overhead of the evolutionary algorithm (Pareto front calculation, crowding distance calculations, etc.) is negligible. Most of the time is spent for the LQN analysis, while the reliability analysis only requires less than half a second and the costs analysis only a few milliseconds. 43 of the candidates were deemed Pareto-optimal by the evolutionary algorithm. Note that the optimization run might not be finished yet after this time. In this section, we do not study whether the found solutions are close to the true Pareto optimum.

The arrival rate for the BRS usage scenario was configured to be exponentially distributed with a mean value of 1 second. The servers were assumed to be connected by a fast network connection with 1.5 milliseconds latency.

The current implementation evaluated candidates sequentially, so the optimization effectively used only one core in this set-up. The evolution process run time could be shortened significantly by executing the candidate analyses per candidate concurrently (e.g., on multi-core processors or in a distributed environment). We consider this enhancement—which is straightforward, as candidates of one iteration can be analysed independently of each other—to our tool as future work.

Results Figures 9.8 to 9.10 compare the quality properties of all evaluated candidates (light grey histogram) with the optimal candidates' values (dark blue histogram). Table 9.7 shows the minimum and maximum values of all evaluated candidates, showing that there is a considerable effect on

Quality criterion	minimum in all evaluated candidates	maximum in all evaluated candidates	mean of all evaluated candidates	mean of optimal candidates
POFOD	0.00052	0.00099	0.00077	0.00065
Costs	410	2844	1136	1041
Mean response time	1.4	313.51	38.83	10.99

Table 9.7.: Descriptive Statistics for Quality Properties in BRS Run

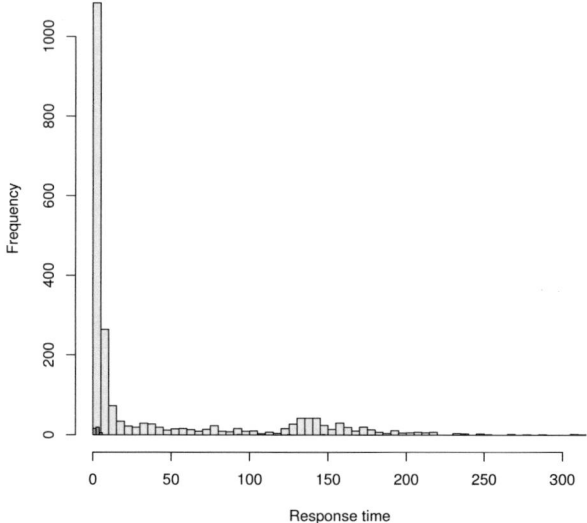

Figure 9.8.: Response Time Histogram for BRS Run (light grey histogram: all evaluated candidates, dark blue histogram: optimal candidates)

each quality property. Additionally, we observe that the optimal candidates have better mean values for all three objectives, as shown in table 9.7.

Figures 9.11 and 9.12 show two of the optimal candidates with their quality properties. The candidate in Figure 9.11 is a comparably fast candidate with higher costs, but also good POFOD. The candidate in Figure 9.12 is slower, but only half as expensive while having even better POFOD (due to the allocation to two servers, the hardware reliability is better). Both candidates use WebServer2, but there are candidates in the Pareto front that use WebServer and WebServer3, too.

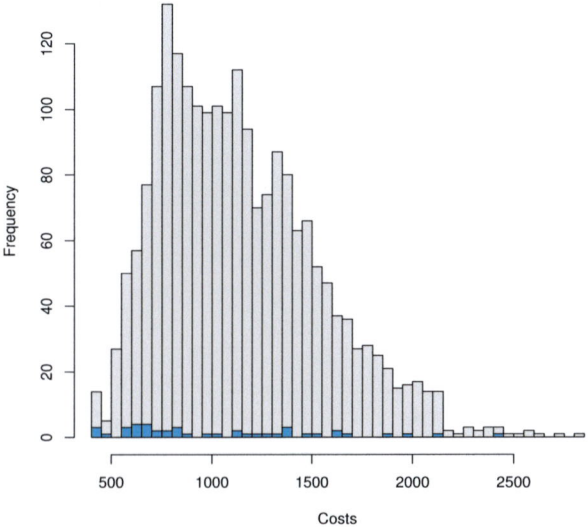

Figure 9.9.: Costs Histogram for BRS Run (light grey histogram: all evaluated candidates, dark blue histogram: optimal candidates)

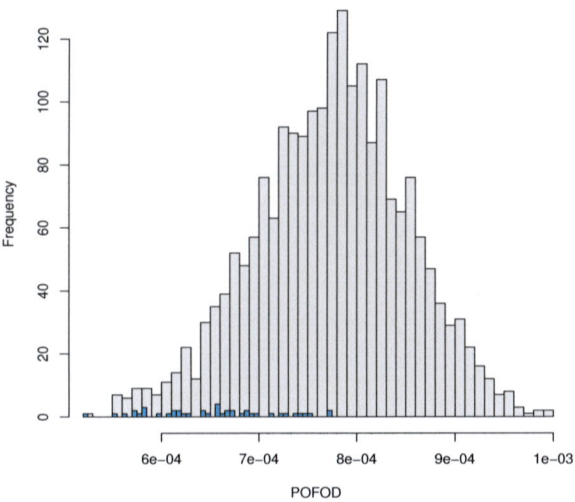

Figure 9.10.: POFOD Histogram for BRS Run (light grey histogram: all evaluated candidates, dark blue histogram: optimal candidates)

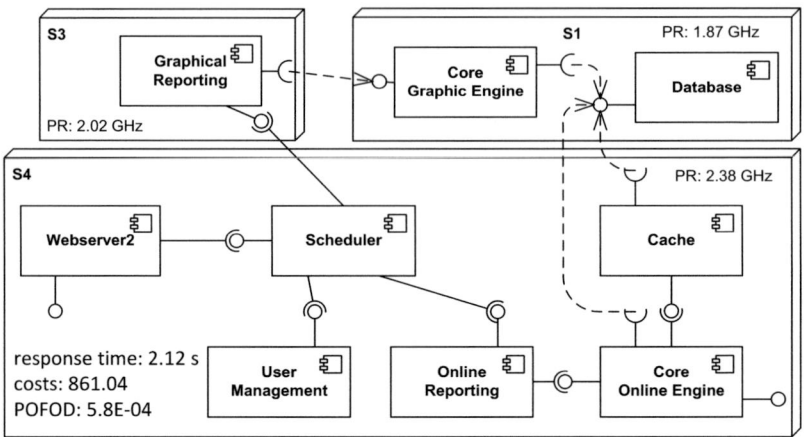

Figure 9.11.: Example: A Pareto-optimal BRS Candidate

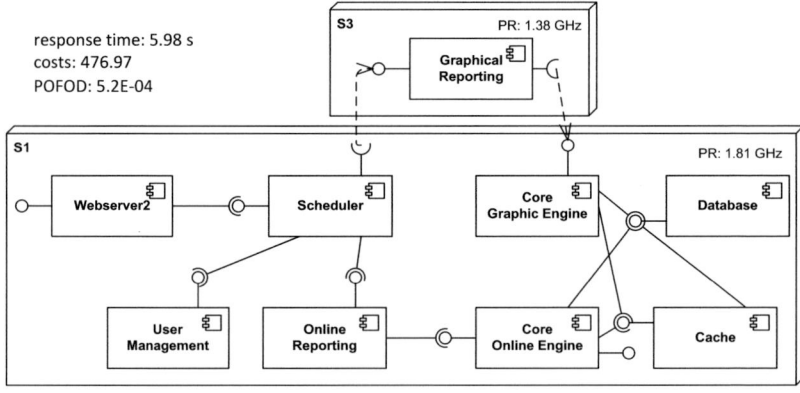

Figure 9.12.: Example: Another Pareto-optimal BRS candidate with Longer Response Time and Lower Costs

We see that the degrees of freedom are indeed meaningful in the BRS and lead to candidates with varying response time, costs, and reliability properties as shown in Figures 9.8 to 9.10. Additionally, we showed that the Pareto-optimal BRS candidates indeed represent different options of how to configure the system, as demonstrated by the two example candidates in Figures 9.11 and 9.12.

Regarding the conflict of quality criteria, Figure 9.13 shows the resulting Pareto front in a scatter-plot, pairwise comparing two dimensions to each other. The diagonal define the axes of the plots. Each field in the figure shows the quality property defined in its column on the x axis and the quality property defined in its row on the y axis. For example, the plot in row 2 column 1 compares POFOD and costs, with POFOD on the x axis and costs on the y axis. While Figure 9.13(a) shows the unfiltered results, we have omitted the three candidates with mean response time larger than 50 seconds in the second Figure 9.13(b) to better show the interesting knee region.

We observe that the qualities costs and response time have a string conflict as shown by the curve in these two dimensions. For the other combination of quality, no strong conflict is observed: the candidates are distributed over the scatter-plots. Still, we observe that an improved POFOD may come with worse costs and response time, because the candidates in the inward side of the costs-response time curve are optimal due to their better POFOD values.

Figure 9.14 shows connects the points of the resulting Pareto front with a surface to better visualize the front. The two sub-figures show the front from different angles, see the figure captions for an an explanation of the axes. Again, the values are filtered so that candidates with mean response time larger than 50 are not shown.

As a result, we observe that the studies problem for the BRS is indeed a multi-objective problem.

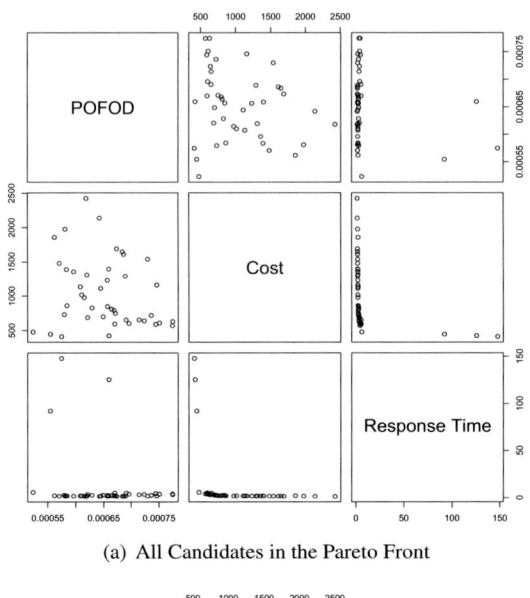

(a) All Candidates in the Pareto Front

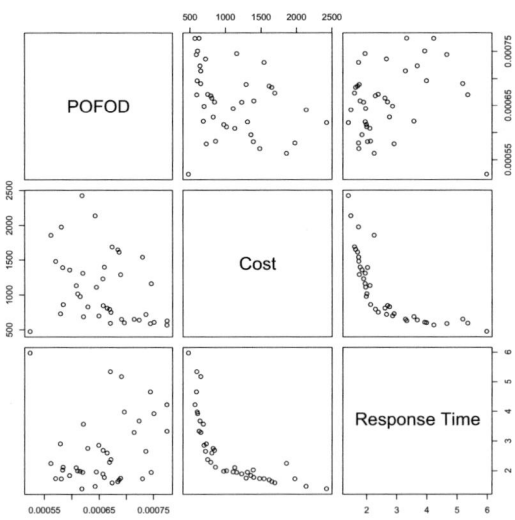

(b) Candidates with Response Time Smaller than 50

Figure 9.13.: Scatter-plots for the Resulting Pareto Front

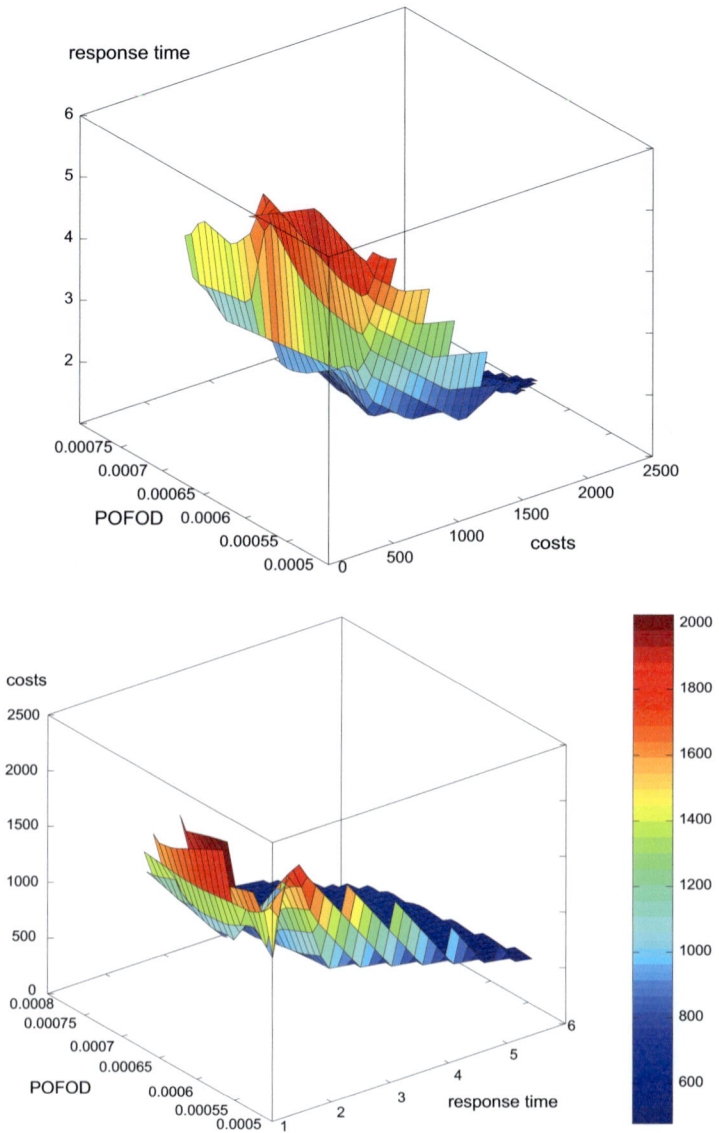

Figure 9.14.: Surface Visualization of the resulting Pareto front

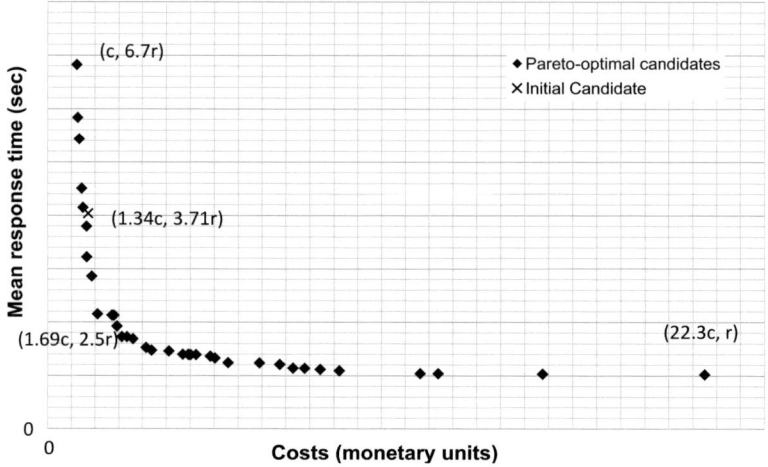

Figure 9.15.: Sample Pareto Front of an Optimization Run for the ABB PCS (Units Obfuscated)

9.4.3.2. ABB System

Experiment Set-up For the ABB PCS, we configured the optimization to run for 200 iterations with a population size of 20. The use of tactics was enabled (the influence of tactics is discussed in Section 9.5.2 in more detail). For the performance prediction, we configured the LQNSolver with convergence value 0.001, iteration limit 50 and under-relaxation coefficient 0.5 (cf. (Franks et al., 2008)).

Figure 9.15 shows the resulting Pareto front generated by the optimization run at iteration 200. PerOpteryx found 36 Pareto-optimal candidates. We also observe that the initial candidate is dominated by the found front, even though it is close to the front of optimal candidates.

Results Concerning the design space, we observe that the DoFIs have an influence on both response time and costs. Even though we cannot provide the predicted costs and performance values in Figure 9.15 because they must not be disclosed, we observe that there is a trade-off. Additionally, as the point of origin in the figure marks the value 0 for both quality properties, we can observe that the response time ranges from some non-disclosed value r for the most expensive candidate in the lower right corner to $6.7r$ for the slowest candidate in the upper right corner. Costs range from a non-disclosed value c to $22.3c$. We observe that the quality effect of the DoF is substantial.

The initial candidate is already a near-optimal configuration in this setting, which is to be expected because it is a recommended configuration of the system. The results of our optimization identify other possible configurations with different cost and performance trade-offs: One example candidate had its costs reduced by 23.1%, while the response time increased by 19.4% which is tolerable within customer requirements. For this candidate PerOpteryx suggested to use the standard variants of components C1 and C13, to purchase a slightly more powerful CPU for server 1, and then to deploy all components on this server, so that the others servers can be removed to save costs. Indeed this candidate reflects a realistic configuration of the system that is sold to smaller customers (A. Koziolek et al., 2011a).

Concerning conflicting quality criteria, we see that the resulting Pareto-optimal set consist of multiple candidates that reflect a trade-off situation with many intermediate solutions between the two extremes $(c, 6.7r)$ and $(22.3c, r)$. For example, two intermediate solutions are $(1.34c, 3.71r)$ and $(1.69c, 2.5r)$ shown in the Figure.

9.4.3.3. Results for Question Q1.3

For both case study systems, we observe that the design space is relevant and lead to different candidate systems with varying quality properties. Furthermore, we observe that the optimization problem is indeed a multi-objective problem. Finally, we see that the design space in our case studies

401

contains many candidates, so that a manual exploration would be time-consuming. Altogether, we conclude that the information provided by the automated approach is useful for the software architect. Because achieving the results has almost no manual effort, we thus expect a positive costs/benefit for the automated improvement given accurate prediction models. Still, the evaluation of costs/benefit for model-based quality prediction is subject to future work, as discussed in Section 9.1.1.4.

9.5. Validation of the Optimization Step

In this section we present the validation settings and results for Goal 2. We evaluate our extensions to evolutionary algorithms for improving software architectures by comparing them to the baseline approaches of standard evolutionary algorithms and random search. First, in Section 9.5.1, we discuss how two optimization techniques can be compared and define the metrics used in this section. In sections 9.5.2 to 9.5.3, we study the effect of our extensions to consider tactics, quality requirements, and starting population heuristics by comparing the optimization performance to the baseline techniques of a standard evolutionary algorithm and random search. Section 9.6 concludes.

9.5.1. Comparing Optimization Techniques

The performance of an optimization approach is typically measured by assessing the quality of the solutions and the time needed to generate the solutions (Zitzler et al., 2008). Section 3.5.5 described comparison techniques for multi-objective evolutionary algorithms. In this section, we describe how the comparison methods have been adopted and used in this work.

First, to account for the stochastic nature of evolutionary algorithms, all experiments are replicated several times. For each experiment setting S (e.g. running the evolutionary optimization with tactics in a certain configuration), a set of runs $\{S_r | r = 0, \ldots, n\}$ is performed. At each iteration i, a run S_r has produced a Pareto front, i.e. a sample, which we denote with $P(S_r^i)$. To compare optimization approaches, we do not require a complete characterization of the random variable $P(S^i)$, but we are only interested in the distribution of the quality metrics (see below). Statistical tests are performed for a chosen iteration to assess the results.

To assess the quality of the results, Pareto dominance ranking (cf. Section 3.5.5.1) provides an objective comparison of optimization results. In cases where fronts are incomparable, we additionally chose to use two quality indicators, namely a modified coverage indicator (Section 9.5.1.1) and the hyper-volume indicator (Section 9.5.1.2) as described below in this work.

Section 9.5.1.3 describes how all three methods are used together in this work to assess an optimization approach's quality.

9.5.1.1. Coverage Indicator

The standard coverage indicator (cf. Section 3.5.5.2) may be misleading if the Pareto fronts overlap each other with varying distances to the true optimal Pareto front, and if the fronts contain a different number of solutions. Additionally, both directions $\mathscr{C}(P_1, P_2)$ and $\mathscr{C}(P_1, P_2)$ have to be considered to assess the difference of the fronts.

To overcome both problems, we (1) additionally measure the size of the dominated space using the hyper-volume indicator $\mathscr{S}(P)$ (Zitzler and Thiele, 1999) to assess the quality of each Pareto front P separately and (2) modify the coverage metric $\mathscr{C}(P_1, P_2)$ to make it symmetric.

For the consideration of quality requirements (cf. Section 8.2.5.2), we additionally include the quality requirements and the concept of quality-feasible candidates in the coverage metric, resulting in the following definition: Let P_1 and P_2 be *quality-feasible, non-dominated sets*[3] and $Q \subseteq P_1 \cup P_2$

---

[3]In a non-dominated set, the elements are pairwise non-dominated (cf. (Deb, 2001)). In a quality-feasible set all candidates are quality-feasible.

be the quality-feasible, non-dominated set of $P_1 \cup P_2$. Our coverage metric $\mathscr{C}^*$ is defined as

$$\mathscr{C}^*(P_1, P_2) := \frac{|P_1 \cap Q|}{|Q|} \in [0, 1]$$

If $\mathscr{C}^*(P_1, P_2) > 0.5$ then P_1 is considered better than P_2 because P_1 has a higher contribution to Q than P_2. Note that if no quality requirements have been defined, all elements in a non-dominated set are quality-feasible by definition.

We use our own implementation to calculate the coverage indicator and perform statistical tests with the R tool (R Development Core Team, 2007).

9.5.1.2. Hyper-volume Indicator

To measure the size of the dominated space, we use the hyper-volume measure (cf. Section 3.5.5.3). We define the reference point and an indicator based on the hyper-volume as follows.

If no quality requirement is given for an objective, we use the maximum values in all Pareto-optimal candidates of all runs as the reference point. If quality requirements are defined for an objective, the quality requirement value is the coordinate of the reference point for this objective, so that the indicator measures the size of the *feasible* space covered by a Pareto front.

We define the reference point $z_{F,Q,R}$ for a set of Pareto fronts F to be compared (e.g. all fronts generated by 10 runs of two optimization approach each), a set of quality criteria Q and a set of quality requirements R (possibly empty) as

$$z_{F,Q,R} = (z_0, \ldots, z_{|Q|}) \text{ with, for } i \in 0, \ldots, |Q|,$$

$$z_i = \begin{cases} r_{q_i} & \text{if there is a requirement } r_{q_i} \in R \\ & \text{for criterion } q_i \in Q \\ \max(\{\Phi_{q_i}(c) \mid c \in \bigcup_{P \in F} P\}) & \text{else} \end{cases}$$

Based on the hyper-volume measure $hvolume(P, z)$, we define the hyper-volume indicator for two Pareto fronts P_1 and P_2 to be compared, a set of quality criteria Q, a set of quality requirements R (possibly empty) and a reference point z as

$$\mathscr{S}_z^*(P_1, P_2) = hvolume(P_1, z) - hvolume(P_2, z)$$

If the hyper-volume indicator $\mathscr{S}_z^*(P_1, P_2)$ is positive, P_1 covers more of the (feasible) design space and is better with respect to this indicator. If $\mathscr{S}_z^*(P_1, P_2)$ is negative, P_2 is better with respect to this indicator. Note that one cannot deduce that P_1 or P_2 is objectively better.

We use a Java implementation of the hyper-volume indicator provided with the jMetal framework (Durillo et al., 2010). The implementation is based on the original indicator definition of (Zitzler and Thiele, 1999) and is called with the normalized objective values. Statistical tests are performed with the R tool (R Development Core Team, 2007).

9.5.1.3. Combination of Quality Metrics

The three metrics described above result in a differentiated comparison of Pareto fronts. The Pareto dominance ranking is consistent with the principle of Pareto dominance, so it is tested first and if one optimization approach has significantly better results with respect to this metric than another one, it can be deemed at better for the studied problem and setting. If the Pareto Dominance Ranking does not provide significant results, the two chosen quality indicators complement each other well.

The coverage indicator compares two fronts based on Pareto dominance, so it does not require additional preferences. However, the indicator does not take the distance of the Pareto fronts to the origin into account. An example is shown in Figure 9.16 for a maximization problem: The coverage indicator is 0.5. However, the area between the fronts (grey areas) is

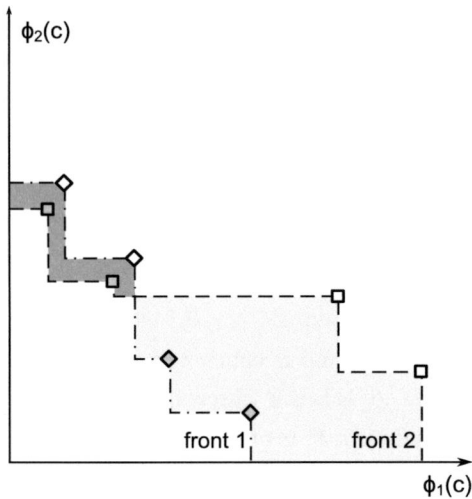

Figure 9.16.: Potential Problem of the Coverage Indicator (by Noorshams (2010), Original Source (Zitzler, 1999)) in a Maximization Problem

different in size, so one might want to prefer front 2. Additionally, if one front P_1 contains an area of solutions that are very close to each other and not dominated by front P_2, the coverage of P_2 is positively influenced even though such a cluster of similar solutions is not useful for the user.

The hyper-volume indicator can detect this discrepancy between coverage indicator value and preferences and is considered a useful indicator (Fonseca et al., 2006). Another advantage of the hyper-volume is its compatibility with the Pareto Dominance Ranking (i.e. if a front is better w.r.t. dominance ranking it is also better w.r.t. the hyper-volume indicator). This property is known as monotonicity (Zitzler et al., 2008, p.382). The main weakness of the hyper-volume indicator is the required reference point, as the indicator is susceptible to the choice of reference point (Zitzler et al., 2008, p.382), but all monotonic unary indicators have this limitation.

9.5.1.4. Time Metrics

Based on the metrics to compare the quality two Pareto fronts described in the previous section, we define a speed-up metric to compare the time efficiency of two optimization techniques.

The time savings metric $\mathcal{T}$ determines how many iteration steps earlier one optimization run has found a solution with equivalent quality. Because each iteration has a similar duration, this measures the computational effort of a run while is is independent of execution time measurement errors such as additional load on the executing machine. To compare a run A with another run B, we determine the smallest iteration step x in which run A has a Pareto front $P(A^x)$ that is superior or equivalent to the results of run B at the final iteration i_{max} (front $P(B^{i_{max}})$). For the coverage, we determine the smallest x so that: $C^*(P(A^x), P(B^{i_{max}})) > 0.5$. For a fair comparison, we also determine the smallest iteration y in which run B has already found a front $P(B^y)$ that is equivalent to the front $P(B^{i_{max}})$: $C(P(B^y), P(B^{i_{max}})) \geq 0.5$. Then, run A has found an equivalent solution $y - x$ iterations earlier. $\mathcal{T}$ is defined as the relative runtime improvement of run A over run B with respect to quality metric $q \in \{\mathcal{C}^*, \mathcal{S}^*\}$:

$$\mathcal{T}_q(A, B) = \frac{(y - x)}{y}$$

For the hyper-volume, the definition is analogous with the smallest x so that $S^*(P(A^x), P(B^{i_{max}})) > 0.0$ and y so that $S^*(P(B^y), P(B^{i_{max}})) \geq 0.0$. We denote the metric using the coverage as $\mathcal{T}_{\mathcal{C}^*}$, and the metric using the hyper-volume as $\mathcal{T}_{\mathcal{S}^*}$.

9.5.1.5. Summary

To summarize, we use the following quality and time metrics to compare optimization runs of two settings S and T.

M.1 Pareto dominance ranking $rank(P(S_r^i))$ and $rank(P(T_r^i))$ over all considered iterations i

M.2 Coverage indicator $\mathscr{C}^*(P(S_r^i), P(T_r^i))$ over all considered iterations i

M.3 Hyper-volume indicator $\mathscr{S}_z^*(P(S_r^i), P(T_r^i))$ over all considered iterations i

M.4 Time savings with respect to coverage $\mathscr{T}_{\mathscr{C}^*}$

M.5 Time savings with respect to hyper-volume $\mathscr{T}_{\mathscr{S}^*}$

9.5.2. Tactics

In this section, we study the effects of our tactics operators on the optimization performance.

Q2.1 How much is the optimization's performance improved by using tactics in a case study?

To answer the question, we study optimization runs for the two case studies describe in Section 9.3. We use the metric defined in the previous section to compare the performance of the tactics operator extension as described in Section 8.3.2 to a standard evolutionary algorithm (i.e. the evolutionary optimization as described in Chapter 8 without the extensions described in Section 8.3 and without quality requirements as described in Section 8.2.5.2). The intensification phase is not used (to evaluate its effect separately). For the Business Reporting Case study, we also compare the results to random search. Additionally, the effect of the antipattern-inspired tactics have been evaluated in isolation in Trubiani and A. Koziolek, 2011.

Section 9.5.2.1 presents the set-up and results for the Business Reporting System case study, and Section 9.5.2.2 for the ABB case study. Finally, Section 9.5.2.3 concludes and answers question Q2.1.

9.5.2.1. Business Reporting System

For the Business Reporting System, we compare our tactics extension to the baseline evolutionary algorithm and to random search.

Experiment Set-up We analysed 10 tactics-guided optimization runs T_r, $0 \leq r \leq 9$, each starting with the initial candidate and 19 random candidates (different for each run) as population p_r. PerOpteryx was configured with $i_{max} = 200$ iterations, population size 20, number of offspring $\lambda = 10$, mutation rate 1, crossover rate 0.95, and tactics probability 0.6.

Then, each optimization run evaluated around 2000 candidates and ran for about 20 hours on one 2.4 GHz core of Intel Core2 Quad CPU Q6600 of a PC (which hosted up to three optimization runs in parallel).

To compare the quality and duration of tactic-guided optimization (T) with unguided optimization (B), we ran another 10 unguided optimization runs B_r and 10 random searches R_r, $0 < r < 9$, each starting with the same population p_r as its guided counterpart T_r. The random search is a simple procedure that generates a configurable number of random candidates in each iteration as defined by the number of offspring parameter λ. Thus, the random search evaluates as many candidates as the evolutionary searches.

Then, we can compare $P(T_r^i)$, and $P(B_r^i)$ pairwise for each r and thus exclude influence of the starting population p_r on the results. We also compare $P(R_r^i)$ pairwise with the respective runs. Although the random search is not influenced by the starting population, the found Pareto front may contain the initial population still after a number of iterations. A pairwise comparison ensures that all searches use the same starting point.

For this case study, we considered the five tactics presented in Section 8.3.2 with the following weights and thresholds:

- **Spread the Load:** The threshold for high utilization is $U_{spread} = 0.4$. The weight W_{spread} is 0.8.

- **Scale-up Bottleneck Server:** The threshold for high utilization is $U_{\text{scale-up}} = 0.8$. The increase factor f is 20%. The weight $W_{\text{scale-up}}$ is 0.1.

- **Scale-out Bottleneck Server:** The threshold for high utilization is $U_{\text{scale-out}} = 0.8$. The weight $W_{\text{scale-out}}$ is 0.5.

- **Reduce Remote Communication:** The threshold for high utilization is $U_{\text{remote}} = 0.8$. The weight W_{remote} is 0.1.

- **Scale-down Idle Server:** The threshold for low utilization is $U_{\text{scale-down}} = 0.2$. The decrease factor is 20%. The weight $W_{\text{scale-down}}$ is 1.

- **Consolidate Server:** The threshold for low utilization is $U_{\text{cons}} = 0.3$. The weight W_{cons} is 1.

The "Remove One-lane Bridge" tactic has not been used because the model does not contain any passive resources.

For the performance prediction, we configured the LQN-Solver with convergence value 0.001, iteration limit 50 and underrelaxation coefficient 0.5 (cf. (Franks et al., 2009)).

In additional exploratory experiments, we also varied the crossover rate (other values 0.9 and 0.8), the mutation rate(values 1, 2/n, 1/n), and the population size (values 40, 60, and 100). However, no discernible effect on the results was achieved.

Results With respect to Pareto Dominance ranking, the resulting fronts $P(T_r^i)$, $P(B_r^i)$, $P(R_r^i)$ are incomparable. Thus, we refer to the quality indicator for assessing the benefits of the tactics extension.

Figures 9.17 to 9.20 show the evolution of the coverage metric $\mathscr{C}^*$ and the hyper-volume metric $\mathscr{S}^*$ over time. We observe that the tactics runs quickly gains an advantage over the comparison runs.

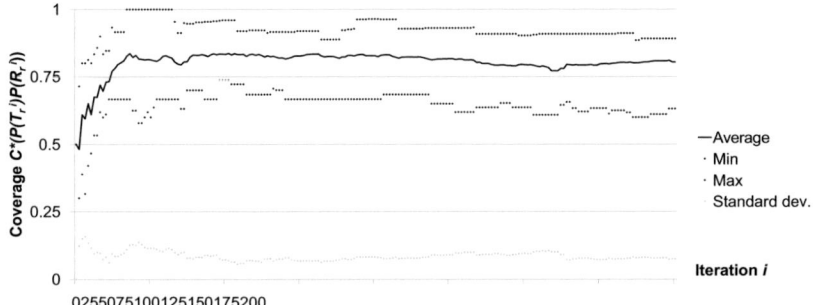

Figure 9.17.: Results for M.1: Pareto Front Coverage $C^*(P(T_r^i), P(R_r^i))$ of Runs Using Tactics T over Random Search Runs R for $r \in 0, ..., 9$ (Business Reporting System)

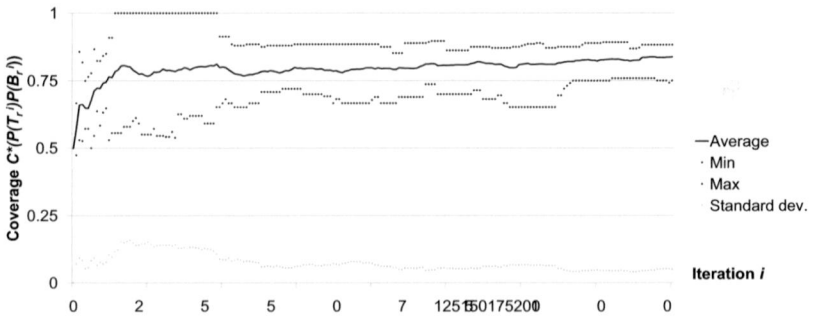

Figure 9.18.: Results for M.1: Pareto Front Coverage $C^*(P(T_r^i), P(B_r^i))$ of Runs Using Tactics T over Standard Evolutionary Optimization B for $r \in 0, ..., 9$ (Business Reporting System)

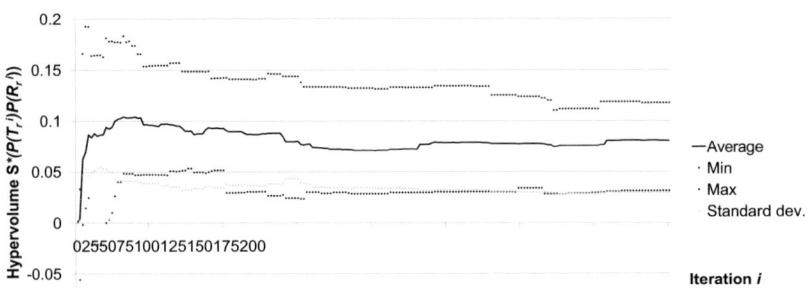

Figure 9.19.: Results for M.1: Hyper-volume Indicator $S^*(P(T_r^i), P(R_r^i))$ of Runs Using Tactics T over Random Search Runs R for $r \in 0, ..., 9$ (Business Reporting System)

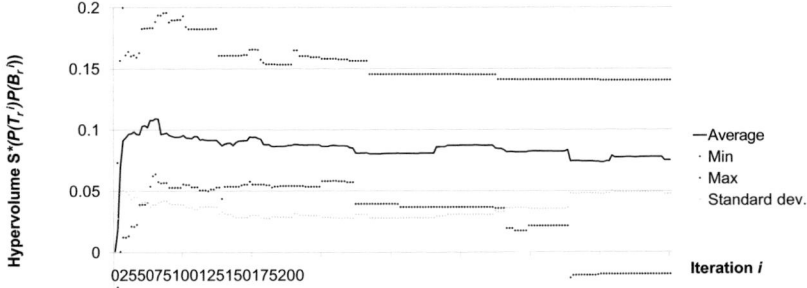

Figure 9.20.: Results for M.1: Hyper-volume Indicator $S^*(P(T_r^i), P(B_r^i))$ of Runs Using Tactics T over Standard Evolutionary Optimization B for $r \in 0, ..., 9$ (Business Reporting System)

Statistical tests using Wilcoxon signed-rank test (Siegel and Castellan, 1988, p.87) (as implemented in the R tool (R Development Core Team, 2007)) confirm that the difference between the tactics runs and the base runs are significant. We tested the null hypothesis that the mean is ≤ 0.5 (for the coverage metric $\mathscr{C}^*$) or ≤ 0 (for the hyper-volume metric $\mathscr{S}^*$) in a one-sided test over runs $0 \leq r \leq 9$. For all iterations later than iteration 7, the null hypotheses can be rejected with 99% confidence. We can conclude that the true mean of the coverage metric $C^*(P(T_r^i), P(R_r^i))$ or $C^*(P(T_r^i), P(B_r^i))$ over runs $0 \leq r \leq 9$ is larger than 0.5 and the true mean of the hyper-volume

Comparison	Statistically significant $(p = 0.01)$ at iteration i	p value at iteration i	Average time saving $\mathscr{T}_q$, $q \in \{C^*, S^*\}$
$\mathscr{C}^*(P(T_r^i), P(R_r^i))$	$i = 7$	0.00098	0.59
$\mathscr{C}^*(P(T_r^i), P(B_r^i))$	$i = 3$	0.0029	0.90
$\mathscr{S}^*(P(T_r^i), P(R_r^i))$	$i = 3$	0.0029	0.80
$\mathscr{S}^*(P(T_r^i), P(B_r^i))$	$i = 3$	0.00098	0.87

Table 9.8.: Statistical Significance and Time Savings Average

metric $S^*(P(T_r^i), P(R_r^i))$ or $S^*(P(T_r^i), P(B_r^i))$ over runs $0 \leq r \leq 9$ is larger than 0 for iteration $i \geq 7$. Table 9.8 shows the test statistics and lists the smallest iteration i for each test and quality metric at which the difference becomes significant.

To assess the duration of the runs, we consider the time savings with metric $\mathscr{T}_q$, again for the pairs of runs with the same starting population. The considered final iteration is iteration 200. As described above, for each run r, we determine the smallest x so that the tactics run T_r is better than the compared run B_r or R_r at the final iteration with respect to a quality metric. Then, we compare the smallest y at which the compared run B_r or R_r already has equivalent results to its final iteration with respect to the considered quality metric.

Figure 9.21 shows the resulting relative time savings $\mathscr{T}_q$. We observe that in most cases, the time saving is larger than 0.5, which means that the tactics run only need half the time to achieve solutions of the same quality than runs with standard evolutionary algorithms or random search. None of the tactics runs was slower than a comparison run. The average time savings metric $\mathscr{T}_q$ results are shown in the last column of table 9.8.

Here, statistical tests with the Wilcoxon signed rank test again confirm that the increase of speed is significant. We tested the null hypothesis that the relative time saving $\mathscr{T}$ is equal or smaller than 0, which is rejected with

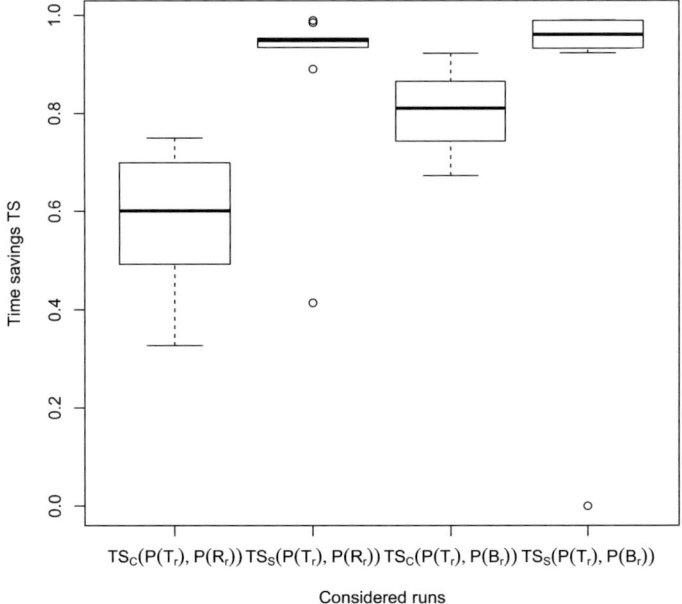

Figure 9.21.: Time Savings for BRS. The Label TS_C Denotes the Time Savings Metric $\mathcal{T}_c$.

a confidence level of 99% for all combinations of comparison and quality metric (as shown in Figure 9.21).

Interestingly, the standard evolutionary algorithm has not performed better than random search in our Business Reporting System experiments. This indicates that the optimization problem is indeed difficult. Arns et al. (2009) have also found that the optimization of complex qualities such as performance is difficult using standard evolutionary algorithms. Deb (2001, p.353 et seq.) has described that parameter interactions make a problem difficult. In our case, the effect of a single allocation gene change may dramatically influence the results, at least on the performance dimension. Furthermore, the allocation choices and processing rate choices have strong interactions: Processing rate choices for highly utilized servers can have a large effect, while processing rate choices for lowly utilized servers have almost no effect. In such cases, it may be difficult for the evolutionary algorithm to identify good building blocks, because the recombination of many building blocks leads to suboptimal candidates. Possibly, the standard evolutionary algorithm could perform better for other configuration parameters. We have, however, not noticed an effect when changing the configuration parameters as described for the Business Reporting System.

9.5.2.2. ABB System

For the ABB system, we compare our tactics extension to the baseline evolutionary algorithm only.

Experiment Set-up   Again, we analysed 10 tactics-guided optimization runs T_r, $0 \leq r \leq 9$, each starting with the initial candidate and 19 random candidates (different for each run) as population p_r. PerOpteryx was configured with $i_{max} = 200$ iterations, as initial experiments showed that the Pareto fronts do not change much afterwards, population size 20, number of offspring $\lambda = 10$, mutation rate 1, and crossover rate 0.75. In these experiments, tactics were only applied if the algorithm did not choose to perform a crossover (as described in more detail in (A. Koziolek et al., 2011a)). Each optimization run evaluated around 2000 candidates and ran for 5 to 6 hours on one 2.4 GHz core of a standard PC.

For comparison, we ran another 10 standard optimization runs B_r, $0 < r < 9$, each starting with the same population p_r as its guided counterpart T_r. Then, we can compare $P(T_r^i)$ and $P(B_r^i)$ pairwise for each r and thus exclude influence of the starting population p_r on the results.

For this case study, we considered the five tactics presented in Section 8.3.2 with the following weights and thresholds:

- **Spread the Load:** The threshold for high utilization is $U_\text{spread} = 0.4$. The weight W_spread is 1.0.

- **Scale-up Bottleneck Server:** The threshold for high utilization is $U_\text{scale-up} = 0.75$. The increase factor f is 25%. The weight $W_\text{scale-up}$ is 0.1.

- **Scale-out Bottleneck Server:** The threshold for high utilization is $U_\text{scale-out} = 0.8$. The weight $W_\text{scale-out}$ is 0.5.

- **Scale-down Idle Server:** The threshold for low utilization is $U_\text{scale-down} = 0.25$. The decrease factor is 25%. The weight $W_\text{scale-down}$ is 0.1.

- **Consolidate Server:** The threshold for low utilization is $U_\text{cons} = 0.3$. The weight W_cons is 1.

The "Reduce Remote Communication" tactic and the "Remove One-lane Bridge" tactic have not been used because the network influence was not considered in this case study and the model does not contain any passive resources.

For the performance prediction, we configured the LQN-Solver with convergence value 0.001, iteration limit 50 and underrelaxation coefficient 0.5 (cf. (Franks et al., 2009)).

Results The optimization runs found on average 33 Pareto-optimal candidates per run. Again, we study the development of coverage metric C^* as the search advances in Fig. 9.22. We observe that the average coverage is again larger than 0.5 starting from few iterations and increases to a value of around 0.67 at iteration 142, and then stays at that level until iteration 200. This time, the worst-performing run using tactics, i.e. the minimum coverage, is inferior to its unguided counterpart until iteration 117, but then also improves to values larger than 0.5. The Wilcoxon signed-rank test confirms

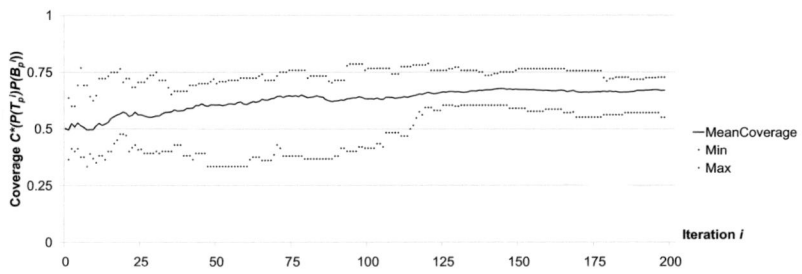

Figure 9.22.: Results for M.1: Pareto Front Coverage $C^*(P(T_r^i), P(B_r^i))$ of Runs Using Tactics T over Unguided Runs B for $r \in 0, ..., 9$ (ABB system)

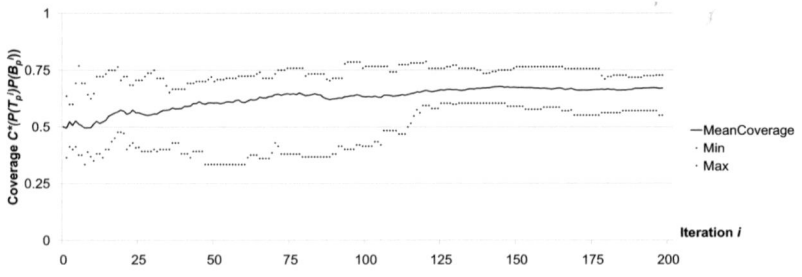

Figure 9.23.: Results for M.1: Hyper-volume Indicator $S^*(P(T_r^i), P(B_r^i))$ of Runs Using Tactics T over Unguided Runs B for $r \in 0, ..., 9$ (ABB system)

that the average coverage $C^*(P(T_r^i), P(B_r^i))$ is significantly larger than 0.5 for all $i > 62$ ($\alpha = 0.99$).

The largest coverage advantage is reached around iteration step $i = 160$. Where $175 \leq i \leq 200$, saturation effects yield a smaller advantage. At this stage, the heuristic search cannot improve its Pareto-set by a large extend, possibly because the found candidates are located near the global optimum. Thus, the unguided search, finding more Pareto-optimal candidates by chance now, can reduce the gap.

The hyper-volume indicator evolution is shown in Figure 9.23. Here, the tactics-guided run has a disadvantage in the first 12 iterations, but then quickly catches up to a difference of almost 0.01. In the remainder of the runs, the hyper-volume indicator remains almost stable with a slight decrease. Statistical tests using the Wilcoxon signed-rank test show that the hyper-volume indicator is significantly larger than 0 for all $i > 62$ ($\alpha = 0.99$).

With respect to the coverage metric, the optimization runs with tactics were able to find an equivalent front 107 iterations earlier than their counterpart without tactics on average. Thus, for our formerly defined metric $\mathcal{T}_{\mathcal{C}^*}$, we get an average 56% savings of runtime. The time saving is statistically significant in a Wilcoxon signed-rank test ($\alpha = 0.99$). We also noted that all optimization runs with tactics found more Pareto-optimal candidates than their counterpart without tactics. With respect to the hyper-volume metric, the time savings metric is $\mathcal{T}_{\mathcal{S}^*} = 0.85$, i.e. 162.3 iterations earlier on average. The speed up is statistically significant ($\alpha = 0.99$), too.

The implemented tactics inserted 457.4 candidates into the population on average during each 200-iteration run. The "Spread the Load" tactic (229.0) generated most candidates, followed by "Consolidate Server" (186.6), "Scale-out Bottleneck Server" (40.5), and "Scale-up/Scale-down Bottleneck Server" [4] (1.3).

9.5.2.3. Results for Question Q2.1

As a result, we observe that the tactics operators are able to improve the search and lead to a speed up of between 56% in average for the ABB system with respect to coverage $\mathcal{C}^*$ and 90% in average for the BRS system with respect to the size metric $\mathcal{S}^*$ for our test problems.

Due to the observed limitations of the standard evolutionary algorithm for the Business Reporting System (cf. Section 9.5.2.1), the use of tactics to guide the search is important.

---

[4] Both tactics have been implemented by one tactics operator, so that it could not be distinguished from the optimization logs which direction was applied.

9.5.3. Intensification Phase

In this section, we study the effects of the intensification phase (as described in Section 8.3.3) using the Business Reporting case study.

Q2.2 How much is the optimization's performance improved by an intensification phase at the end of the search in a case study?

Section 9.5.3.1 describes the set-up for this evaluation, and Section 9.5.3.2 describes the results and answers the validation question.

9.5.3.1. Experiment Set-up

We study the effect of an intensification phase after the tactics runs T_r from Section 9.5.2. The intensification phase was configured to apply tactics to each candidate of T_r's final result $P(T_r^{200})$ after 200 iterations. The thresholds for the tactics used as defined in Section 9.5.2. The weights are irrelevant, because all tactics are applied if their precondition matches (as described in Section 8.3.3). We refer to these intensification runs as I_r in the following. The intensification runs stop as soon as no more preconditions match. Let $P(I_t^*)$ denote the resulting Pareto front after the intensification phase.

For comparison, we continued the tactics runs T_r for at least an equal number of evaluations, as defined in the following. Let $eval(S_r^i)$ denote the number of candidate evaluations performed by a optimization run S_r until iteration i. We continued each T_r for the minimum number of iterations j so that $eval(T_r^{i+j}) \geq eval(I_r^*)$. Then, we compare $P(T_r^{i+j})$ and I_r^* using the hyper-volume indicator and the coverage indicator.

The comparison is rather biased towards the continued tactics run T_r^{i+j}: First, it potentially considers more candidates from that run. Second, we study the intensification of a tactics-enabled run T_r^{200}, not a pure evolutionary run. Thus, the runs have previously benefited from the same domain-specific knowledge (see Section 9.5.2).

Indicator	mean	std	min	max	sig.?	p-value
Coverage indicator $\mathscr{C}^*$	0.676	0.043	0.625	0.767	yes	0.00098
Hyper-volume indicator $\mathscr{S}^*$	0.0139	0.024	-0.012	0.0642	no	0.01855

Table 9.9.: Intensification Phase Results (sig. = significant)

9.5.3.2. Results for Question Q2.2

The intensification phase explored between 36 and 133 additional candidates, with 71.2 evaluations on average. This corresponds to 4 to 14 iterations of the continued tactics run.

The Pareto dominance ranking method does not result in any statistically significant results, thus we proceed to the quality indicators.

Table 9.9 shows descriptive statistics (std denoting standard deviation) and the results of a Wilcoxon signed-rank test with significance level $\alpha = 0.05$. Regarding the coverage, the intensification run produced significantly better results. All runs were superior. Regarding the hyper-volume indicator, one intensification run I_5 was inferior to its tactics counterpart T_5. While the mean hyper-volume indicator is still positive, the results are not significant.

Thus, in run 5, the randomness of the continued tactics run was able to find a better candidate with respect to hyper-volume that the intensification phase, applying tactics rules only. In all other runs, and also in all runs with respect to coverage, the intensification phase was more efficient.

Based on this single case study, a generalization is difficult. However, as the setting was rather biased towards the continued tactics run, our claim is rather supported than rejected. As a result, we conclude that the intensification phase seems to be beneficial.

The results also indicate that the amount of tactics knowledge used during the evolutionary optimization could be increased, e.g. by increasing the tactics probability, possibly even setting it to the value 1. However, as parameter settings is an open issue in evolutionary algorithms in general

(Nannen et al., 2008), we do not further pursue this questions in this work, leaving it as an issue for future work.

9.5.4. Quality Requirements Effect

In this section, we study the effects of the quality bounds extension presented in Section 8.2.5.2 on the optimization performance.

Q2.3 How much is the optimization's performance improved by using quality bounds in a case study?

Section 9.5.4.1 describes the set-up for this evaluation, Section 9.5.4.2 describes the results and Section 9.5.4.3 answers the validation question.

9.5.4.1. Experiment Set-up

The validation of the quality requirements effects has been conducted earlier than the other validation aspects and thus uses a different version of the BRS model. The validation is also described at (A. Koziolek et al., 2011b).

To study the effects of different quality requirement values on the results, we ran the optimization for four different levels of requirements (weak, i.e., only few candidates are excluded from the Pareto front, to strict, i.e., many candidates are excluded). Table 9.10 shows the four different scenarios. The requirements are modelled with our metamodel of QML (Noorshams et al., 2010). For each scenario $scen \in \{W, M, S, O\}$, we optimized the system once for each constraint handling technique $c \in \{C, G\}$, resulting in 8 optimization settings $WC, WG, ..., OC, OG$, i.e. the set of optimization settings $\{W, M, S, O\} \times \{C, G\} = OptSettings$. As a baseline, we optimized the system without constraint handling (setting B). For each optimization setting $s \in OptSettings$, 10 runs $s_r, 0 \leq r \leq 9$ have been conducted.

Scenario	costs	POFOD	mean response time
(W) Weak requirements	3000	0.00175	5.0 sec
(M) Medium requirements	2000	0.0015	3.0 sec
(S) Strict requirements	1500	0.0015	2.5 sec
(O) Only costs requirements	1000	∞	∞

Table 9.10.: Quality Bound Scenarios

9.5.4.2. Results

The Pareto dominance ranking method does not result in any statistically significant results, thus we proceed to the quality indicators.

Figure 9.24 illustrates the result of the optimization run MC_0 with medium constraints using the constrained tournament method C. 7 Pareto-optimal candidates that satisfy all three bounds were found and are marked with triangles.

In the following, we present the results by scenario. As the differences of the studied scenarios are small, no statistically significant results were obtained. More runs of each setting could be conducted to achieve more conclusive results.

Figures 9.25 and 9.26 show the coverage measure and the size measure for scenario W. The coverage measure is around 0.5 in average over most of the iterations for both constraint handling methods C and G. With both measures, thus, no improvement towards the basic approach is visible. The size of the dominated feasible space grows similarly for all approaches, too.

Figures 9.27 and 9.28 show the coverage measure and the size measure for scenario M. For both the coverage measure and the size measure, the runs with constraint handling start well (coverage > 0.5 and size larger than size of basic approach). However, the basic approach catches up: At iteration 200, all approaches perform equally well (G has a slightly better coverage, C a slightly larger dominated space, so none performs better than the other).

Figures 9.29 and 9.30 show the coverage measure and the size measure for scenario S with strict quality requirements. Here, we see an improve-

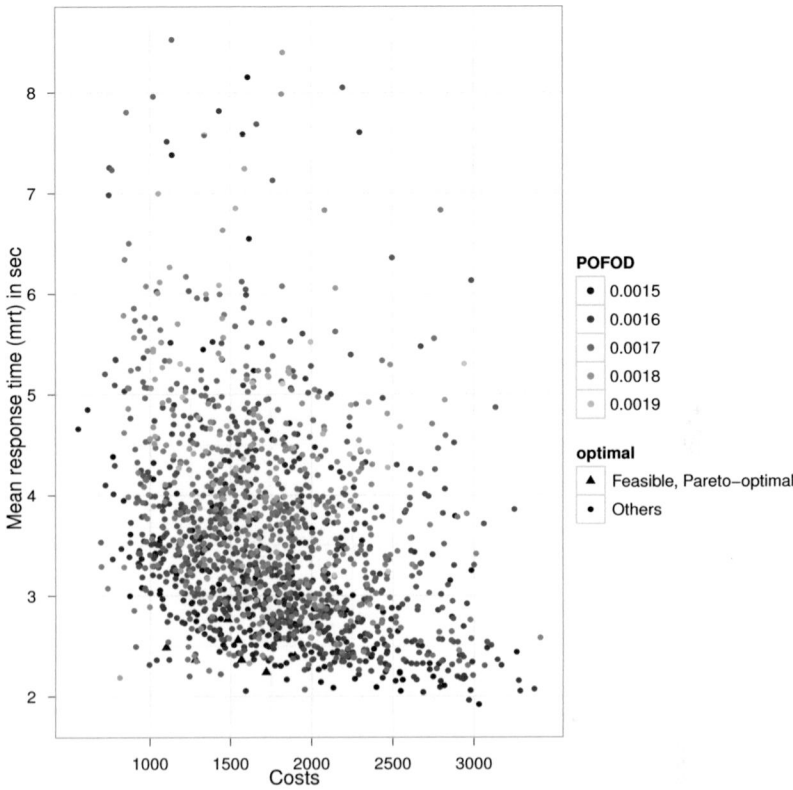

Figure 9.24.: Result of an Optimization Run MC_0 with medium requirements $scen = M$ and the Constrained Tournament Method $c = C$.

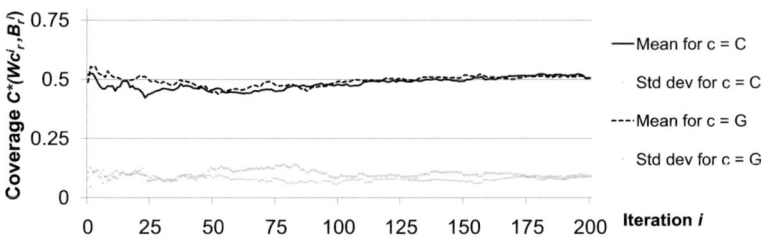

Figure 9.25.: Coverage Measure $\mathscr{C}^*(Wc_r^i, B_r^i)$ in Scenario W, Aggregated over Runs r, for Both Methods $c \in \{C, G\}$

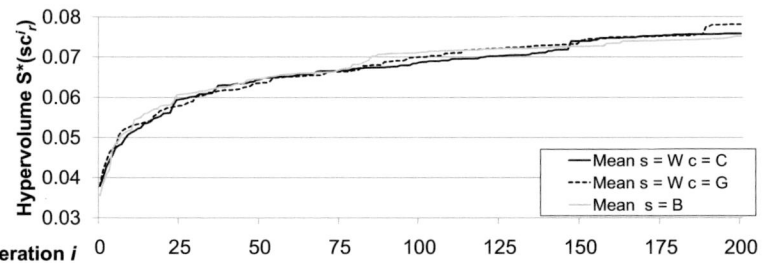

Figure 9.26.: Size of the Dominated Space $\mathscr{S}^*(Wc_r^i)$ in Scenario M, Compared to the Basic Scenario $\mathscr{S}(B_r^i)$, Aggregated over Runs r, for Both Methods $c \in \{C, G\}$

ment of the search: The coverage measure of method C is higher that 0.5 during all iterations, and the size measure is significantly larger than for the basic approach, too. Method G does not perform as well, even has a coverage < 0.5 at the beginning while still having a better size measure than the basic approach.

Finally, figures 9.31 and 9.32 show the results for the common case of a budget-only limitation. While both constraint handling method do not perform well in the first 75 iterations, they catch up and provide better results in the last iterations, both regarding coverage and size measure.

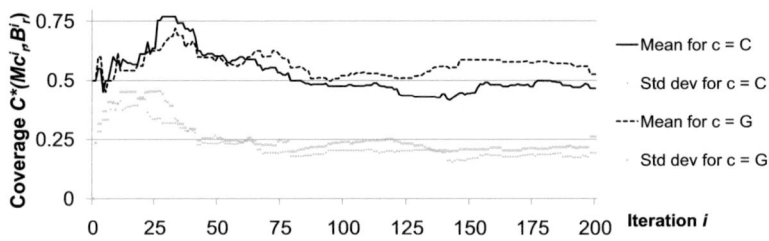

Figure 9.27.: Coverage Measure $\mathscr{C}^*(Mc_r^i, B_r^i)$ in Scenario M, Aggregated over Runs r, for Both Methods $c \in \{C, G\}$

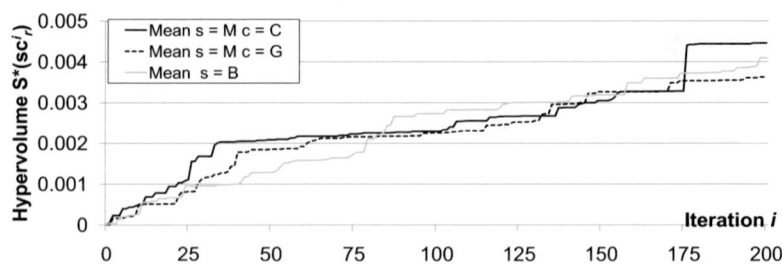

Figure 9.28.: Size of the Dominated Space $\mathscr{S}^*(Mc_r^i)$ in Scenario M, Compared to the Basic Scenario $\mathscr{S}(B_r^i)$, Aggregated over Runs r, for Both Methods $c \in \{C, G\}$

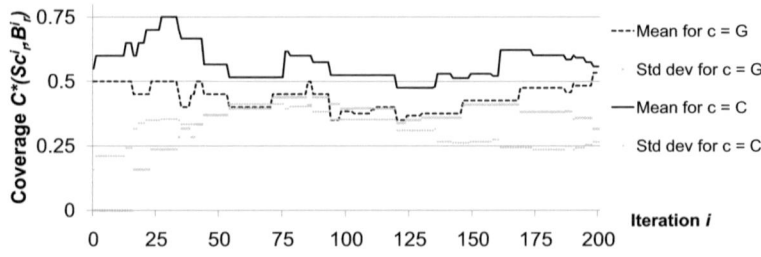

Figure 9.29.: Coverage Measure $\mathscr{C}^*(Sc_r^i, B_r^i)$ in Scenario S, Aggregated over Runs r, for Both Methods $c \in \{C, G\}$

425

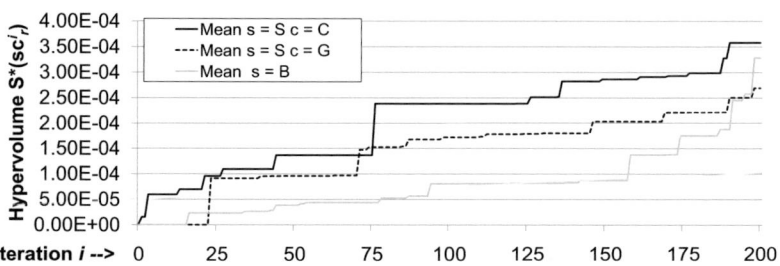

Figure 9.30.: Size of the Dominated Space $\mathscr{S}^*(Sc_r^i)$ in Scenario S, Compared to the Basic Scenario $\mathscr{S}(B_r^i)$, Aggregated over Runs r, for Both Methods $c \in \{C, G\}$

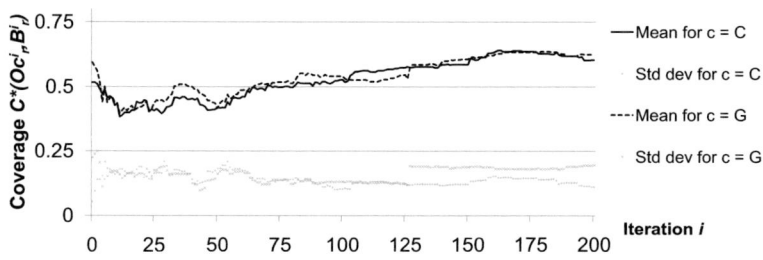

Figure 9.31.: Coverage Measure $\mathscr{C}^*(Oc_r^i, B_r^i)$ in Scenario O, Aggregated over Runs r, for Both Methods $c \in \{C, G\}$

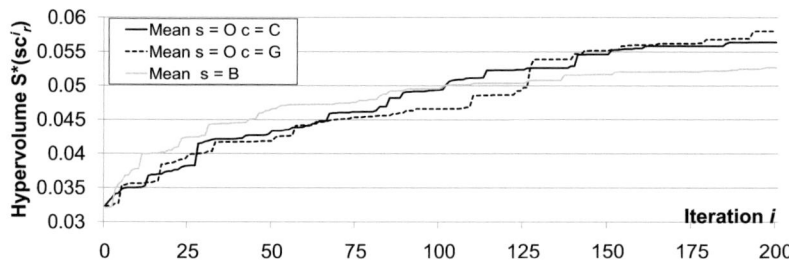

Figure 9.32.: Size of the Dominated Space $\mathscr{S}^*(Oc_r^i)$ in Scenario O, Compared to the Basic Scenario $\mathscr{S}(B_r^i)$, Aggregated over Runs r, for Both Methods $c \in \{C, G\}$

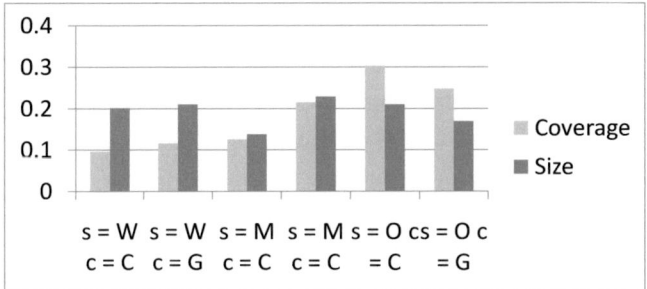

Figure 9.33.: Time Savings

To assess the duration of the runs, we consider the time savings with metric $\mathscr{T}$. Figure 9.33 shows the relative time savings for scenarios W, M, and O. In scenario S, too few solutions were feasible and Pareto-optimal at the end, so that a sensible assessment of the time saving is not possible.

We observe that for all scenarios, the constraint handling methods was able to find an equivalent front faster than the basic approach. The average time saving is 11.1% with respect to $\mathscr{C}^*$ and 11.8% with respect to $\mathscr{S}^*$, and with the most time saving in scenario O with the constrained tournament method (30.3% for $\mathscr{C}^*$ and 21.0% for $\mathscr{S}^*$, average 25.6%).

In further experiments (Noorshams, 2010), we have also studied to add lower bounds indicating that a quality values is good enough so that further improvement does not bring additional benefit, i.e. that other quality properties should not be traded off for more improvement of this value. However, we found that including such lower bounds does not significantly improve the optimization performance, neither in isolation nor in combination with upper bounds as presented in this work.

9.5.4.3. Results for Question Q2.3

As a result, we observe that the quality bounds slightly improve the search performance in our case study scenarios. However, the results are not statistically significant. The effect of the quality bounds seems to depend on the size of the feasible and infeasible design space: The quality bounds have almost no effect in lowly constrained scenarios W and M. In scenario S, the constrained tournament method C performs well in both coverage and even more so regarding the size of the dominated feasible space. The goal attainment method is less successful. In scenario O, both constraint handling methods perform well.

From these observations, we suppose that using quality bounds to focus the search is only effective if a large portion of the search space are excluded by the quality bounds, such as given in scenarios S and O. In the two first scenarios, fewer solutions on the Pareto-front are infeasible, so that the constraint handling is seldom used and thus cannot steer the search well. Because it is not necessarily known in advance whether given requirements are strict or lax, the constraint handling methods should always be used, as they do not worsen the performance of the search. More runs of each setting could be conducted to achieve more conclusive results.

As future work, a combination of quality bounds with tactics operators is promising: If a quality bound is violated, tactics operator that strive to improve the violated quality criterion can be favoured or even deterministically chosen to "repair" the current candidate.

9.6. Summary

This chapter presents the validation of our automated improvement method according to two main goals: First, we study the validity of our automated improvement approach in context of the CBSE development process. Second, our extensions to standard evolutionary optimization, namely tactics operators, quality bounds in selection step, and starting populations, are experimentally evaluated.

With respect to the first goal, we found that

- Candidate models can deliver accurate performance prediction based on a manually created initial model: The optimization relies in particular on the accuracy of the models even if the model is changed. We have reviewed the existing validation for changes along different degrees of freedom. A gap concerning the validity of allocation change has been closed by our new allocation validation case study.

- An approximation of the true Pareto front can be found, and provides meaningful insights into the design space.

- The spanned design space contains considerable potential for improving quality attributes, and thus represents a relevant subset of the complete design space software architects have to consider.

With respect to the second goal of validating our extensions to standard evolutionary optimization, we found that

- Tactics operators are able to find better solutions or are able to find equivalent solutions in less time. Thus, they improve the optimization step.

- An intensification phase seems to further improve the optimization, even after optimization runs with tactics.

- Quality bounds seem to improve the optimization for highly constrained problems. However, no statistically significant results could be achieved yet. Because the quality bounds do not seem to worsen the search performance, they can be used also in cases where the level of constrainedness is unknown. More experimental evaluation is needed to better assess the quality bounds effect.

In addition to the possible topics for future work mentioned throughout this chapter, a possible further research direction is the learning of parameter relations during the search. For example, in the Business Reporting System case study, we observe after a number of iterations that most Pareto-optimal candidates use 3 or less servers. Thus, the number of servers can be reduced in the problem, so that the search can focus more effectively on the promising parts. Such learning could also be achieved by interaction of users and optimization during the search: If intermediate search results are reviewed by the users, they can identify such relations and modify the optimization problem during the search.

10. Conclusion

This chapter concludes the thesis, summarizing the main contributions and validation results in Section 10.1. Section 10.2 describes the benefits of this work for the software architect and software development in general. Section 10.3 provides a brief summary of the assumptions and limitations discussed throughout the thesis, and discusses the main assumption of having quality-annotated architecture models available as input. Finally, Section 10.4 describes issues and questions for short-term and long-term future work.

10.1. Summary

This thesis provides an automated method to improve component-based software architectures based on model-based quality prediction, thus providing support for trade-off decisions in the requirements analysis phase.

The main contributions of this work are summarized in the following (they are discussed in more detail in Section 1.4).

Process: We have identified the information needs of software architects and stakeholders that can be filled with an automated method based on model-based quality prediction. Based on this, we extend a process model for the development of new component-based systems with our method and include a more solid process for determining appropriate quality requirements. The method provides quantitative feedback from model-based quality predictions for software architects, requirements engineers, and stakeholders to be used in archi-

431

tecture design and requirements analysis. Furthermore, we embed the method in other scenarios such as software evolution scenarios or capacity planning.

Framework: We have provided a framework for multi-objective optimization of software architectures based on quality predictions. This framework is independent of the used CBA metamodel and quality analysed due to its flexible and extendible *degree of freedom model*. Additionally, it allows to include domain-specific knowledge in form of architectural tactics operators known from literature and operationalized in this work.

Framework Instantiation: To instantiate this framework, we have provided concrete degrees of freedom for CBA affecting performance, reliability, and costs as well as performance and costs tactics for the Palladio Component Model.

To validate the proposed method, we have (1) validated the accuracy and applicability of our method and (2) evaluated the performance of our extensions to the optimization step. Two case study system have been considered, the first being a business reporting system (BRS), which is loosely based on a real system (Wu and Woodside, 2004b); the second being an industrial control system (ICS) from ABB, which shows the industrial applicability of our approach.

To validate the accuracy of the predictions when the models are changed, we surveyed existing accuracy validation for the PCM and provide an additional study showing the models can deliver accurate performance prediction even if the original allocation is changed. Furthermore, to assess the accuracy of the optimization in terms of finding an approximation of the true Pareto front, we discuss the optimality of results for a case study, and conclude that a close approximation of the true optimum has been provided by our method.

To validate the applicability of our method, we study whether the design space considered by our method in two case studies is a relevant subset of the complete design space. Here, we have studies whether the degrees of freedom actually occur in the case study system, how large their influence on the quality criteria is, and whether they indeed conflict in these scenarios. We found that the design space indeed contains a large number of candidates with varying quality properties, and that in both case study systems, a trade-off situation among the quality criteria was given. Altogether, we conclude that the information provided by the automated approach is useful for the software architect.

With respect to the second goal of validating our extensions to standard evolutionary optimization, we found that tactics operators were able to find better solutions or are able to find equivalent solutions in less time in both case studies. Thus, they improve the optimization step.

Furthermore, the intensification phase seems to further improve the optimization, even after an optimization runs with tactics has been conducted before. Quality bounds seem to improve the optimization for highly constrained problems. For less constrained problems, no improvement was observed. More experimental evaluation is needed to better assess the quality bounds effect.

10.2. Benefits

The results of this thesis support the software architect in improving component-based software architectures based on model-based quality prediction. They thus provide quantitative support for trade-off decisions in the requirements analysis phase. As a distinctive feature of our method compared to existing solutions, we elaborate on the connection to requirements engineering, provide a flexible and extendible formulation of the design space, and include domain-specific knowledge in the form of architectural tactics. The benefits of our work are the following.

Automated Design Space Exploration: Our method automates feedback and interpretation of results of model-based quality analysis that the software architect had to carry out manually with high effort before. As the considered design space is potentially large, the effort for manual exploration is unreasonably high, or even prohibitive so that good solutions would remain undetected in many typical scenarios in current software development.

The benefit of such assistance is *reduced effort* due to the partial automation of the design space exploration task. As our proposed approach does not require additional input information, the human user saves time. Thus, costs are saved in the development process. Additionally, it has been recognized that automated, search-based approaches can help to produce unexpected, but *valuable solutions* that humans would have overlooked because of bias (Harman, 2007, Sec.7.3), time constraints, or limited insight into the problem.

Input for Trade-Off Decisions in Requirements Analysis and Architecture Design: As our method uses multi-objective optimization, it provides a set of Pareto-optimal candidates to the software architect and stakeholders, thus providing a quantitative basis for *well-informed trade-off decisions*.

The information can be used in the requirements analysis phase to clarify, negotiate, and agree on quality requirements and the expected costs. Thus, our methods enables a stronger interaction of architecture design and analysis, potentially leading to a better fulfilment of stakeholder needs.

The method does not require the stakeholders to specify fixed quality requirements at the beginning of a development process, which are later endangered to be dismissed if they prove to be infeasible. Instead, defining only quality criteria and then negotiating based on quantitative data allows stakeholders to focus on the most relevant quality criteria, to consider the feasibility and incurred costs, and to realize them at low costs.

Flexible and Extendible Design Space Formulation: Our degree of freedom metamodel allows to specify quality-relevant degrees of freedom for a given CBA metamodel. A tool then explores the spanned design space automatically. Our method is *generic* as it can be applied for any CBA metamodel: thus, it does not force the software architect to use a specific CBA modelling language, and can be applied for any project with model-based quality prediction based on an architecture model.

Furthermore, the design space formulation is flexible and extendible because software architects can select generic CBA degrees of freedom to consider and model additional degrees of freedom, if required. Additional degrees can be modelled either for the given CBA in general, or specifically for the system at hand. For modelling system-specific degrees of freedom, any design decision that can be expressed in the architectural model by changing a primary model element can be considered. Thus, the method is not restricted to certain degree of freedom types.

This benefit is not provided by existing approaches, as they do not support the modelling of the optimization problem (cf. Section 4.1.5).

Automated Design Space Instantiation: Our tool PerOpteryx automatically instantiates the design space (by detecting and instantiating degrees of freedom in an input CBA model) and, together with the available and selected quality analyses, instantiates the optimization problem for the user. Thus, the software architect does not have the manual effort of defining the optimization problem. Existing other approaches do not support this task (cf. Section 4.1.5). For example, ArcheOpterix (Aleti et al., 2009a) requires the implementation of Java classes for any new optimization problem.

Flexible Combination of Quality Criteria: Furthermore, our method allows to add additional quality analyses by providing quality prediction adaptors. Here, software architects may also define project-specific quality criteria, for example related to the organization of the project in terms of developer assignment.

435

Efficient Optimization: Existing solutions are divided into rule-based approaches, which apply domain-specific knowledge to improve a single quality attribute, and metaheuristic approaches, which can (in principle) handle any quality criteria, but do not make use of domain-specific knowledge. Our method is the first to combine both approaches by using tactics operators, which benefits the design space exploration as it reduces the time to find solutions (by 50% to 90% on average in our case studies).

Summary: To summarize, the method proposed in this thesis helps software architects (1) by saving significant costs for manually exploring the design space, (2) by providing a more solid process for determining appropriate quality requirements, and (3) by supporting an extensible analysis framework applicable in a large class of practical scenarios.

Furthermore it advances state-of-the-art and benefits researchers in architecture optimization (1) by clarifying the role of model-based quality predictions in the process of quality requirements engineering, (2) by being the first method to offer a flexible and extendible design space formulation, and (3) by being the first method to demonstrate how domain-specific knowledge can be combined with metaheuristic, multi-objective software architecture optimization.

10.3. Assumptions and Limitations

This section (1) points to assumptions and limitations discussed throughout this thesis, and additionally (2) discusses and justifies the main underlying assumption of having quality-annotated software architecture models available as an input.

Pointers to Assumptions and Limitations Discussion: Assumption and limitations of our approach are discussed in the separate chapters in detail. Here, we only point to the relevant sections for different aspects. Section 5.5 describes the assumptions and limitations of the *component-based development process* with quality exploration and the application of our method in other scenarios. Section 6.5 discusses assumptions and limitations of our *design space formulation*, covering the assumed properties of CBA metamodels and the limitations of the resulting design space. Section 7.5 discusses the limitation of our method to *software architecture models that have component-based properties*. Finally, Section 8.5 describes the assumptions and limitations of the *evolutionary optimization step* and the *tactics operators*.

Available Quality-annotated Software Architecture Models: The main underlying assumption of our method is that it requires the use of software architecture models annotated with quality information. The models require quality attribute annotations that reflect the quality properties of the system under study well, as discussed and validated in Section 9.1.1.1. Because creating such models requires considerable effort (e.g., 1-3 persons months in recent large-scale studies Huber et al. (2010); Koziolek et al. (2011c)), we discuss the expected conditions under which the creation of such models is beneficial and under which the application of our proposed method is most useful.

Model-based prediction is especially beneficial for large software projects, where the influence of design decisions on the quality attributes is not yet well understood. For example, for simple development projects in well-understood domains or for small projects, model-based quality prediction might not be required. Performance prediction may be less important for simple desktop applications where the application only has to serve a single user while running on more powerful hardware.

However, as soon as scalability of the system to a large number of concurrent users is required and high workloads are expected, model-based performance predictions are an important means to avoid overloaded servers and dissatisfied users during system runtime. The performance effects of decisions are often unknown based on experience and intuition, as shown by an empirical study by H. Koziolek and Firus, 2005, where even for a rather small system (ca 1 KLOC) the benefits of a structured performance evaluation method has been shown beneficial compared to an ad-hoc approach. Even for existing systems that should be used in new environments (i.e. new usage contexts or new deployment), the quality effects of decisions or changes are hard to predict intuitively, and should be supported by quantitative analyses.

Empirical investigation for the costs and benefits of architecture analysis in general, comparing several projects over eight years at AT&T, report costs savings for large projects (Bass et al., 2003, p.263). More example are discussed by Bass et al. (2003, p.263). Concerning model-based quality prediction, initial empirical studies indicate a benefit for early design time performance prediction, i.e. that the costs for creating the models pays off (Williams and Smith, 2003). Furthermore, we discussed three examples of losses due to a lack of quality consideration in Section 1.1; many more examples have been reported by Glass (1998); Schmietendorf and Scholz (2001) and others.

Nonetheless, more studies in industrial contexts need to be conducted to better understand the costs and benefits of model-based prediction approaches. Additionally, we a deeper understanding and more empirical research on the conditions under which the use of model-based prediction is beneficial.

Here, risk analysis should be a foundation for deciding to adopt prediction techniques. For example, Fairbanks (2010, p.8) suggests a risk-driven approach to software architecture in general, arguing to put just enough effort into modelling and documenting software architecture to reduce risks (i.e. the perceived probability of problems occurring multiplied by the expected losses in case of problems) to an acceptable level. The spent effort of any architecting activity should be smaller than the expected risk reduction. Similarly, effort for quality prediction model creation should be lower than the expected risk reduction regarding quality problems. We expect this risk analysis to be positive for large projects with high business value. Furthermore, the method presented in this thesis is expected to decrease the effort of applying model-based prediction, as it automates the feedback tasks. Thus, our method supports the applicability of model-based quality prediction.

10.4. Future Work

This section discusses ideas and open issues for short term future work (Section 10.4.1) and long term future work (Section 10.4.2). Short term future work requires smaller conceptual contributions and implementation work, while long-term future work requires in-depths new concepts and may for example be tackled in future PhD theses or industry projects.

10.4.1. Short Term Future Work

Modelling Language for System-specific Degrees of Freedom: As described in Sections 6.3.2.5 and 7.4.2, the definition of system-specific degrees of freedom could be simplified by providing a modelling language to describe design options on the model level. Here, model elements need to be annotated with the possible design options. Additionally, the quality effects of the design options must be well-defined.

For system-specific degrees of freedom that require to change several model elements at once, the consistency of all model elements must be retained. In the context of model evolution (e.g. the approach by Gray et al. (2006)), several approaches have been suggested to capture changes of models and make them repeatable and analysable as model transformations. Such descriptions of model changes could be used for defining complex design alternatives.

A sketch of such a language is provided in Section 7.4.2. The benefit of such a language would be the simplified inclusion of any design alternative the software architect wants to consider in the design space exploration process, without the need to define the change on the metamodel level (as required in our current model).

Add Project-Specific Quality Metrics: In addition to existing quality prediction techniques, project-specific quality metrics could be defined by the software architect, especially for quality attributes for which no or only few quantitative prediction approaches are available. Such quality metrics could be defined as any aggregation function on model properties, similar to OPEDo (Arns et al., 2009) or GDSE (Saxena and Karsai, 2010a). For example, software architects may define security of components on a scale from low to high, and define the security of each service provided by the system as the minimum security of all involved components. Then, a coarse security measure can be included in the optimization and trade-off decisions. Rohrberg (2010) has described an example of such a simplified security analysis, which nonetheless can have the ability to highlight and quantify trade-offs and thus be a basis for decisions.

In addition to simplified, project-specific quality metrics, the connection of other quantitative quality prediction techniques (e.g. (Grunske and Joyce, 2008) for security) is desirable.

Learning DoF Effects and Interactions: Optimization approaches that learn properties of a given optimization problem during the search have been proposed (Blum and Roli, 2003, p.288). In the context of this work, algorithms that learn the interactions of degrees of freedom could be beneficial. For example, if one component in the system has a high resource demand, the server it is deployed to should have a high processing rate, and it possibly should be deployed to a dedicated server. However, not all types of learning algorithms seem appropriate: Some approaches, such as simple Estimation of Distribution Algorithms (cf. e.g. (Blum and Roli, 2003, p.288 et seq.), assume no or only limited dependencies between variables, while for our problem, the most promising learning is to detect these interactions. Algorithms that consider multivariate interactions (survey by Pelikan et al. (2002)) are more promising. Additionally, domain-specific learning could be devised. Such learning would use the available information at its best and possible further reduce the number of needed and expensive candidate evaluations.

More Tactics and Hybridization: More tactics can be devised to encode more domain-specific knowledge. The reliability tactics informally described in Section 8.3.1.3 could be formalized.

Furthermore, specialized efficient optimization approaches could be used within tactics. For example, a linear integer programming formulation of the deployment problem, using simplified quality models, could be solved as part of the reallocation tactic to estimate an optimal deployment of components within one reproduction step. While we have already combined the metaheuristic optimization with a simplified analytic optimization that generates a starting population (cf. Section 8.3.4.1), one could employ similar simplified calculations as part of tactics operators. However, it must be ensured that such a combination does not bias the search too strongly towards possibly only locally optimal solutions due to the inaccuracy of the simplified predictions. Here, learning capabilities should be employed (see below)

Degrees of Freedom for other CBA Metamodels: As described in Chapter 6, the degree of freedom metamodel is CBA metamodel independent. In Chapter 7 we have described degrees of freedom for ROBOCOP and CBML. In future work, the described degrees of freedom could be modelled for these CBA metamodels, and the quality analyses available for these metamodels could be connected to our optimization framework, so that design space exploration for these models becomes possible.

Moreover, the definition of degrees of freedom for UML models could be studied. Because the semantics of UML is not as well-defined for e.g. performance prediction as other component-based architecture models (Becker et al., 2009), additional interpretations may have to be assumed. Furthermore, the definition of behaviour as sequence diagrams is a challenge for defining the exchange of components and the possibly resulting change of the system behaviour. Still, defining degrees of freedom for UML models could increase the applicability for the method presented in this thesis.

Compare Performance of Metaheuristics: Although we expect evolutionary algorithms to be a good choice for our optimization problem (cf. Section 8.1.3), other metaheuristics and in particular other, more recent types of evolutionary algorithms could be employed and their performance could be compared for case studies.

As a further extension in context of long-term future work, the performance of optimization techniques could be compared for different types of problems: For example, architectures where the component allocation has a large influence on the quality properties of candidates, a different algorithm could exhibit the best performance than in architectures where allocation choices are limited, but server configuration is more relevant. On top of this, the choice of metaheuristic or evolutionary algorithm for a problem at hand could be adapted during the search based on insights of the problem (e.g. whether the unordered selection degrees such as component allocation or component selection are the main influencing factor for a problem, or whether possibly continuous, ordered degrees are more relevant). For parameter settings of a single algorithm, similar control during the search has been implemented in several works. A survey is provided by Eiben et al. (1999).

Quality bounds and tactics: In our validation, we observed that quality bounds are helpful in highly constrained optimization problems (i.e. the scenario with tight costs constraints), cf. Section 9.5.4. Here, the efficiency of quality bounds could be potentially increased by combining them with tactics operators: For candidates which lie outside the quality bounds, tactics operators can be executed that improve the violated quality, if the candidate fulfils the conditions of the tactics.

10.4.2. Long Term Future Work

Large Scale Validation and Empirical Studies: More validation evaluating the support of decision making and the applicability of our method in industry contexts is desirable. Furthermore, exploratory studies to better understand decision situations could be conducted to drive result presentation and decision support techniques based on the available Pareto-optimal candidates. More validation aspects subject to future work are discussed in Sections 9.1.1.4 and 9.1.2.3.

Costs / Benefit of Model-based Prediction: Instead of validating the costs and benefits of our method in isolation (i.e. comparing it to model-based prediction without feedback mechanisms), it seems more promising and to result in more insight to conduct a combined costs/ benefits study of model-based prediction including automated exploration, preferably in an industrial context.

Smaller studies could be useful to accompany use of prediction techniques in practice and measure the actual effort to create such models in practice. While several studies already have considered this question (e.g. (Williams and Smith, 2003), (H. Koziolek et al., 2011c)), more independent studies are required to achieve a generalizable result. Such costs studies could be accompanied by qualitative analysis of what problems could be avoided, and an estimation of the mitigated late costs, as done by Williams and Smith (2003). Possibly, the results could be compared to historical data where no prediction has been used, to quantify the costs of late quality fixes. A fully controlled study where the same project is conducted twice, once using model-based prediction and exploration, one without such support, may be too costly to be feasible.

Consider Uncertainty of Model Parameters: The quality annotations of software architecture, i.e. the input information to quality predictions, are usually uncertain, especially if their are based on estimations instead of measurements. Here, the uncertainty could be explicitly considered by the optimization, so that solutions that are likely to be optimal even if the estimations vary (i.e. more robust solutions) are preferred to solutions that are sensitive to estimation errors. Jin and Branke (2005) provides a survey on methods that could be applied to consider uncertainty. Recently, Meedeniya et al. (2011b) proposed such an approach for software architecture optimization in the context of ArcheOpterix.

Furthermore, Schmidt (2007) specifically targets problems in which uncertainty arises due to the stochastic nature of the problem (as encountered e.g. for performance simulations), and the proposed methods could be adopted for our work as well. For example, adaptive allocation adapts the number of samples for candidates depending on the uncertainty of their quality properties. Similarly, for candidates that are obviously suboptimal after a short simulation, the simulation can be aborted as the candidate is useless anyway.

Systematic Use of Pareto-optimal Candidates in Requirements Engineering: Our method results in a set of Pareto-optimal candidates which can be used for trade-off decisions in the requirements analysis phase. Here, a method how to systematically use this trade-off in existing requirements engineering processes should be devised to ensure the optimal use of the information. Visualization of the results and decision support (as initially developed by Rohrberg (2010) in the context of this thesis should be developed and studied further.

Furthermore, as observed by Berntsson Svensson et al. (2011), the management of quality criteria is insufficient in many development projects, thus, systematic methods are required. Studies need to accompany new methods to validate their assumptions, and exploratory studies could precede to better understand the decision situation and method needs.

Support Several Metamodels: Our method is currently limited to one input CBA model which is modelled using any, but only one CBA metamodel. If several models are used to describe a system (e.g. a UML model for the static structure and coarse grained behaviour, an SPE model (in

444

form of a software execution graph Smith and Williams (2002b)) for performance analysis, and a Markov Chain-based model for reliability), our method cannot be applied as is.

Here, a general precondition for applying any model-based automated improvement is that changes performed by the design space exploration tool in one of the models can be propagated to the other models, so that the models are consistent. To do so, the used models must be connected to each other by some formalism, ranging form the use of common identifiers to a trace model that captures the relations of model elements in all used models.

An example technique to achieve connection of different metamodels is Dually Malavolta et al. (2010). To use Dually, links between concepts in different metamodels are modelled manually. Then, Dually provides model transformations to transform any instance of one metamodel into the other.

Based on such links, the open question is how to synchronize the models when the models are changed along degrees of freedom. If one of the models contains all relevant information, this model can be manipulated along the specified degrees of freedom and other models can be synchronized using e.g. Dually. However, if the information is distributed among several models (e.g. one model defines the allocation of components to servers, while another one contains fault tolerance mechanisms), degrees of freedom have to operate on several models at once. Thus, more research is required to put this approach into practice.

Combined Consideration of Functional requirements and Quality Criteria: Quality criteria (or quality requirements) are not only subject to trade-off against each other, but may also be traded off against functional requirements. For example, Berntsson Svensson et al. (2011) reports that quality requirements are often dismissed in practice to allocate limited development resources to achieving functional requirements. Here, as both the realization of functional requirements and the improvement of quality criteria may lead to increased costs, both aspects compete with each other.

This approach fits the ISO/IEC 9126-1:2001(E) (2001) standard, where functionality is considered a quality attribute, too, capturing the "capability of the software product to provide functions which meet stated and implied needs" (ISO/IEC 9126-1:2001(E), 2001, p.7).

Thus, the choice to implement certain functionality should also be expressed as a degree of freedom, which incurs costs but provides some functionality value to the stakeholders. The functionality value can be traded-off against costs and other quality criteria. A similar problem has been considered in search-based software engineering as the Next Release Problem (cf. (Harman, 2007, Sec.4.3)), where the goal is to select an optimal set of (functional) requirements to implement in the next release, with respect to customer requests, development resource constraints, and requirements interdependencies. The treatment of functionality value and costs could be adopted from such approaches.

Combine Optimization on Different Levels of Design: Opportunities for optimization can be found on different levels of software design and development. For example, on the highest level, business strategies and business processes are subject to improvement and optimization. A roadmap to combining business process management and software architecture has been suggested by Paech et al. (2009). Another high-level perspective is to consider systems-of-systems or architectural landscapes and their quality attributes.

Furthermore, low level optimization of design and implementation could be combined with this work. For example, Schaefer et al. (2010) suggest a method to optimize the use of parallel programming patters such as pipelining, producer-consumer or fork-join. Here, the optimal selection of parallel programming patterns within a software component depends on which other components are allocated on the same server (i.e. the component allocation degree of freedom), because all resulting threads will compete for the server's resources. Thus, the optimization of parallel programming patterns is not independent of the software architecture optimization presented in this work.

To cope with optimization problems on different levels, one approach could be to encode all of them into one large optimization problem. However, due to the high number of degrees of freedom, such a problem might become too difficult to efficiently find approximations of the optimal solutions. Instead, a meaningful hierarchization of optimization problems at different levels could be reasonable. Here, a challenge is to devise a mechanism to feed back and feed forward the results from one optimization problem into the other.

Support of Runtime Adaptation: As described in Section 5.4, our method as is does not target fast runtime adaptation, i.e. the optimization of systems at runtime to adapt to changed environment. The current, detailed optimization is too expensive in terms of needed computation to provide results quickly and adapt within minutes or even hours. Additionally, the output of our method are Pareto-optimal candidates to provide input for human trade-off decisions. If software systems are to judge autonomously based on optimization, however, the preferences must be defined beforehand.

Still, the concept of degrees of freedom and the spanned design space could be used for runtime adaptation as well. Here, different optimization techniques need to be applied: More approximate, but faster quality predictions than used in this work need to be used. Furthermore, a focus in the neighbourhood of the current candidate could be useful to decrease the costs of reconfiguration at runtime (in terms of incurred resource demand).

Final Remark: To conclude, this thesis is a step towards adopting engineering principles in software engineering. It builds upon component-based software engineering principles, upon parametric contracts, and upon quantitative quality prediction techniques. Based on this, our method supports the software architect to explore the design space of a given software architect by automatically finding the optimal trade-off candidate architectures. Thus, in the requirements analysis phase, stakeholders can negotiate and agree upon relevant quality criteria and preferences based on quantitative information about the system, allowing them to make well-informed decisions whose effects are known.

Appendix

A. Palladio Component Model

All diagrams in Sections A.3 to A.4 are taken from the PCM metamodel definition (revision 8988 of `https://svnserver.informatik.kit.edu/i43/svn/code/Palladio.RSA-Models/trunk/pcm.emx`) as presented by Reussner et al. (2011, chapter 4).

A.1. Key for PCM Diagrams

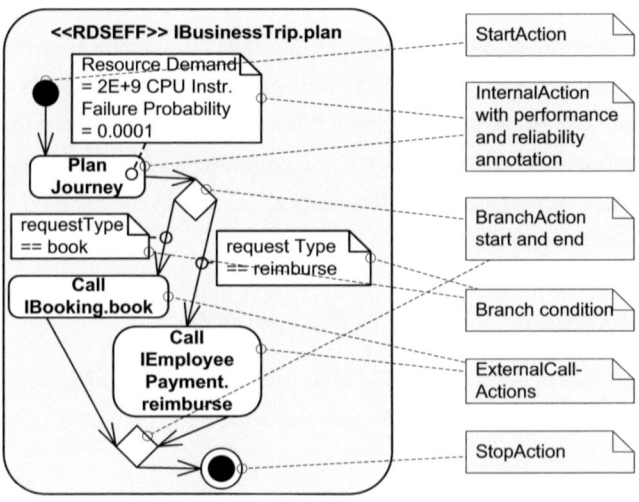

Figure A.1.: Key for RDSEFF Diagram

Figure A.1 shows the key for RDSEFF diagrams used throughout the thesis. Figure A.2 shows the key for the diagram parts showing system and allocation.

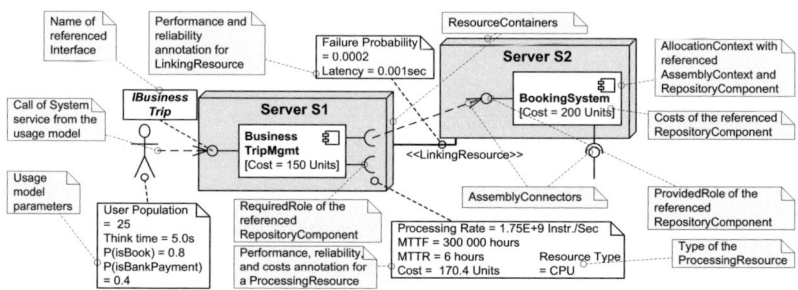

Figure A.2.: Key for Combined System and Allocation Diagram

A.2. Mapping of PCM Concepts to General Concepts

Table A.1 shows the mapping of PCM elements to general CBA concepts. To distinguish PCM from general concepts, only PCM elements are used with upper-case in the table. General CBA concepts are referred to by their name without upper-case letters, such as component or component instance. See the PCM technical report (Reussner et al., 2011) for detailed rationale of the PCM metamodel.

A.3. Inheritance Hierarchy of Components

Figure A.3 shows the composition hierarchy in the PCM. Figure A.4 shows the so-called core entities, and Figure A.5 shows the delegation concepts.

PCM Concept	General CBA Concept(s) and Explanation
AllocationContext	component allocation instance
AssemblyConnector	a connector to connect a required interface with a provided interface within one component assembly.
AssemblyContext	component instance
BasicComponent	primitive components, i.e. components that are not composed.
Composite-Component	composed structures that are components
ComposedPREntity	Full name "ComposedProvidingRequiringEntity", an abstract superclass of composed structures
InterfacePREntity	Full name "InterfaceProvidingRequiringEntity", an abstract superclass of components.
LinkingResource	Link
ProcessingResource-Specification	Resource
ProvidedDelegation-Connector	a connector to connect the outer provided interface of a composed structure to an inner provided interface of an inner component.
ProvidedRole	association class for referencing interfaces, needed because the PCM has no interface instances.
Repository-Component	a component
RequiredDelegation-Connector	a connector to connect the outer required interface of a composed structure to an inner required interface of an inner component.
RequiredRole	association class for referencing interfaces, needed because the PCM has no interface instances.
ResourceContainer	Server
System	the component assembly that forms the system model in the CBA model, i.e. the component assembly that is directly referenced by the root node.

Table A.1.: Mapping of PCM Concepts to General CBA Concepts

451

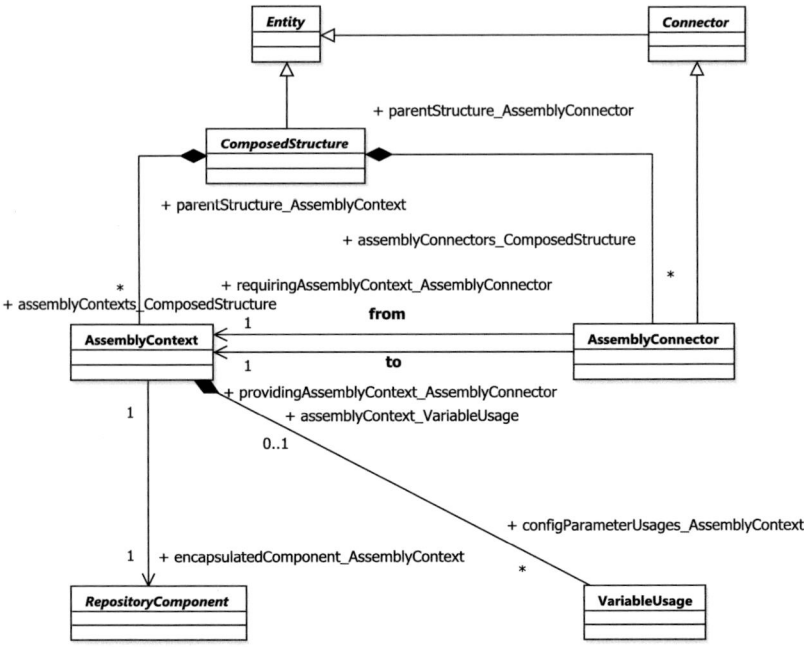

Figure A.3.: PCM Composition

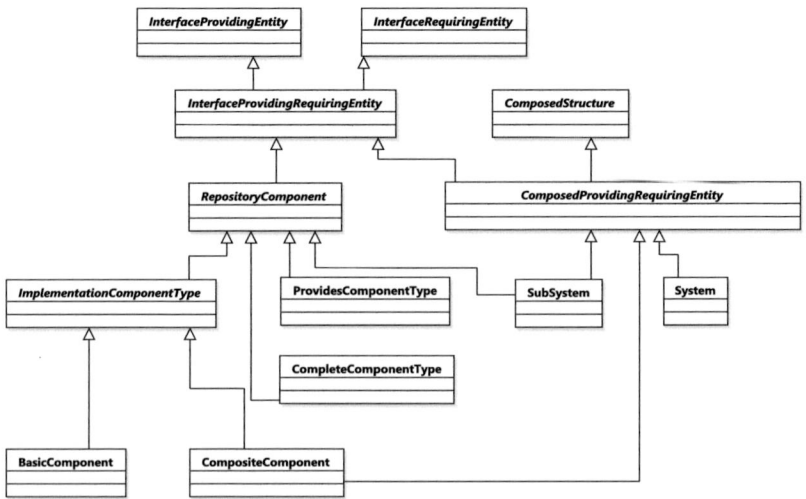

Figure A.4.: PCM Core Entity Overview

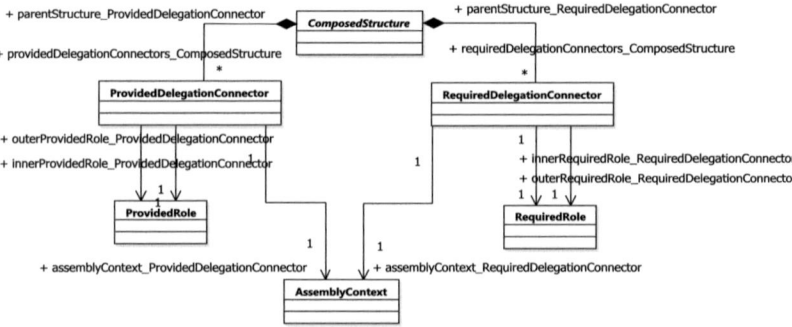

Figure A.5.: PCM Delegation

A.4. RDSEFF Metamodel Elements

Figures A.6 and A.7 show the RDSEFF metamodell, namely the integration of the available behaviour models into the components (Figure A.6), and the actions to model behaviour (Figure A.7).

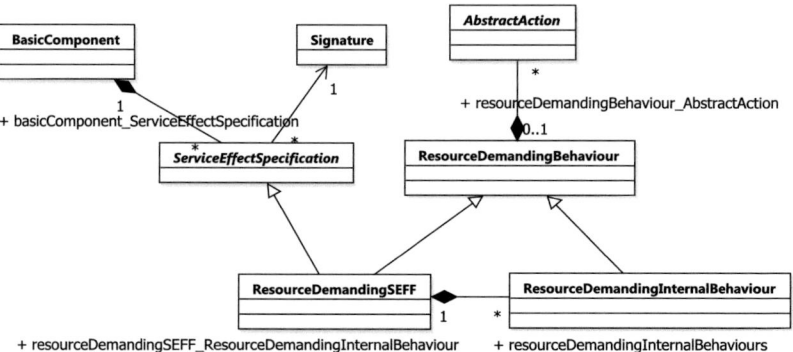

Figure A.6.: PCM Behaviour Overview

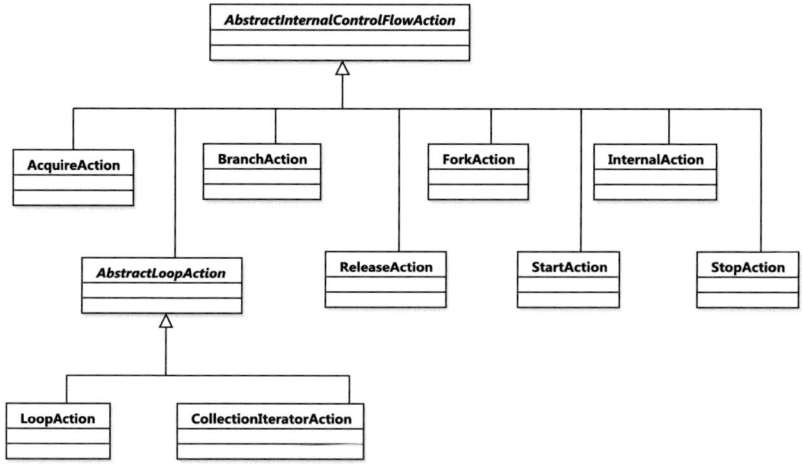

Figure A.7.: PCM Action Hierarchy

A.5. Resource Repository

To specify the possible resources that a server can have, a repository of resources has been created as an extension to the PCM metamodel. Figure A.8 shows the metamodel of the resource repository. The Resource-DescriptionRepository is the model root and specifies possible resources. A possible resource is described by a ResourceDescription, which combines the ProcessingRateSpecification information and the costs of the resource as FixedProcessingResourceCost.

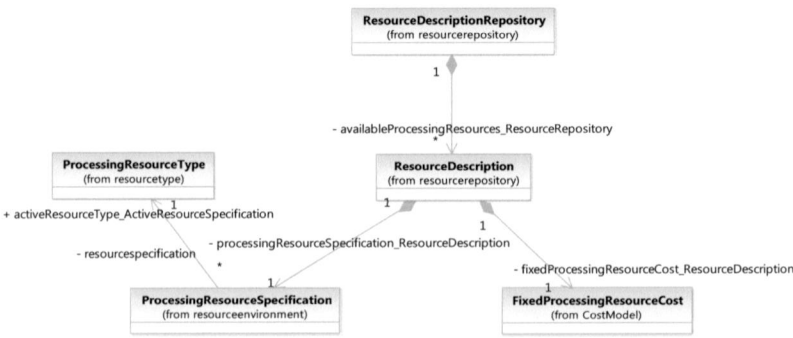

Figure A.8.: Resource Repository

A.6. OCL Constraint for Valid AllocationContexts

The constraint below exclude servers that are not linked to the communication partners. Components cannot define the linking resource they use for communication in the PCM; it is assumed here that the components use higher level communication mechanisms such as remote procedure calls that are unaware of the used communication link, e.g. Ethernet. Additionally, linking resources are always bidirectional in the PCM. Thus, if two components C_1 and C_2 are allocated to two different servers and communicate with each other, it is sufficient that a linking resource connects two servers. The direction of the communication can be neglected.

It is complex to determine the AllocationContexts of all communication partners, because the components in the PCM can be hierarchically composed and several types of composition exist (ComposedComponents and SubSystems, see Figures A.3 and A.4). A number of helper methods are required to navigate through the system.

The interaction constraint below checks whether the chosen server self.-resourceContainer is connected to the servers of all communication partners (retrieved by getSenders and getReceivers) server with a linking resource. The rule is applied to the changed resource container after applying the change. Candidates this rule evaluates to false for are invalid.

```
context AllocationContext
def : isConnectedToAllSendersAndReceivers : Boolean =
— is connected to all servers this component communicates with

self.assemblyContext.getSenders(
  self.assemblyContext.encapsulatedComponent.providedRoles,
  allocation)
  ->union(self.assemblyContext.getReceivers(
  self.assemblyContext.encapsulatedComponent.requiredRoles,
  allocation))
       .resourceContainer
       ->forAll(src | self.allocation.targetResourceEnvironment
        .linkingResources->exists(l |
              l.connectedResourceContainers->includes(src)
          and l.connectedResourceContainers
              ->includes(self.resourceContainer)))
```

To determine the AllocationContexts of the communication partners, the following methods getSenders and getReceivers are used. Three possible cases need to be considered when querying the communication partners and are visualised in figure A.9. The simplest case (case 1 in figure 11.9(a)) is that the current component is connected to the communication partner with an AssemblyConnector. Then, the AssemblyContext at the other end of the connector is the communication partner.

The other two cases concern SubSystems, which are composed structures whose contents can be allocated separately. If the current component is encapsulated in a SubSystem and is connected to ProvidedRoles or

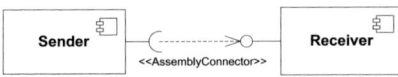

(a) Case 1: Simple case to Determine Communication Partners

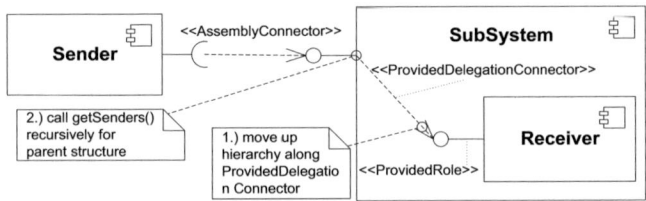

(b) Case 2: Current Component is Contained in SubSystem and Connected to SubSystem Roles

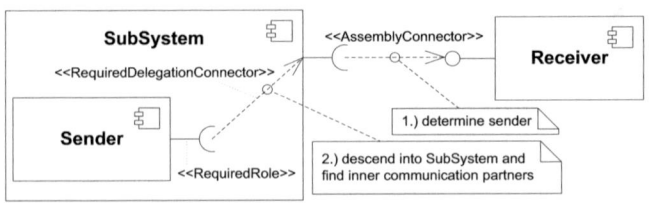

(c) Case 3: The Communication Partner is Contained in a SubSystem which is not Allocated as a Whole

Figure A.9.: Three Cases of Navigation when Determining Communication Partners. Here: Current Component is the Receiver (Situation in get-Senders() method)

RequiredRoles of that SubSystem (case 2), it is required to first move up the hierarchy and then determine the communication partner of the parent structure that match the roles to which the current component is connected.

If a SubSystem is found to be the communication partner and if that SubSystem is not deployed as one (case 3), the query needs to descend into the SubSystem to find the AllocationContexts of the inner components that communicate with the current component from inside the SubSystem. The helper methods to descend into a SubSystem are explained below, starting with getSenders. The three cases an also be mixed and occur more than once: for example, a component can be encapsulated in a SubSystem which is again encapsulated in a SubSystem, and the communication partners of this component can at the same time be encapsulated in a different third SubSystem.

```
context AssemblyContext
— component instances that require this component
def : getSenders ( prs : Set(ProvidedRole), allocation : Allocation )
  : Set(AllocationContext) =

self . parentStructure . assemblyConnectors –>select ( conn |
conn . providingAssemblyContext = self and
prs –>select ( pr | pr =conn . providedRole ))
  –>iterate ( conn : AssemblyConnector , result : Set(AssemblyContext)
       = Set { } ,
     if ( not conn . requiringAssemblyContext . encapsulatedComponent
       . oclIsKindOf ( SubSystem ))
     then
        — Simple case 1: navigate across AssemblyConnector
        result –>including ( allocation . getAllocationContext (
             conn . requiringAssemblyContext ))
     else
       if ( allocation . isAllocated ( conn . requiringAssemblyContext ))
       then
           — SubSystem is directly allocated
           — Also simple case 1: navigate across AssemblyConnector
           result –>including ( allocation . getAllocationContext (
             conn . requiringAssemblyContext ))
       else
           — SubSystem is not directly allocated , descend into it
           — Case 2: Communication partner is a SubSystem
           result –>including ( conn . requiringAssemblyContext
             . encapsulatedComponent . oclAsType ( SubSystem )
                . getAllocationContextsForRR (
                     conn . requiredRole , allocation ))
       endif
     endif
  )
  — also navigate across composed structures ,
  — if this method is called on an allocated component ,
  — composed structures can only be SubSystems and
  — thus are only assembled once in the system .
  — Case 3: The current component is contained in a SubSystem
  –>union ( system . getAssemblyContextsFor ( self . parentStructure )
       . getSenders (
```

```
self.assemblyContext.parentStructure
    .providedDelegationConnectors
    ->select(conn | conn.providingAssemblyContext = self
        and prs->select(pr | pr =conn.providedRole))
        .outerProvidedRole, allocation))
```

Analogously, the method getReceivers handles receivers.

```
context AssemblyContext
— component instances required by this component, find the
— assemblyContexts that are allocated
def : getReceivers(rrs : Set(RequiredRole), allocation : Allocation)
    : Set(AllocationContext) =

self.parentStructure.assemblyConnectors->select(conn |
    conn.requiringAssemblyContext = self
    and rrs->select(rr | rr =conn.requiredRole))
    ->iterate(conn: AssemblyConnector, result: Set(AssemblyContext)
        = Set{},
        —— if the providing AssemblyContext is a SubSystem, then we
        —— may have to look for the inner components if it is
        —— not allocated as one
        if (conn.providingAssemblyContext.encapsulatedComponent
            .oclIsKindOf(SubSystem))
        then
            if (allocation.isAllocated(conn.providingAssemblyContext))
            then
                —— SubSystem is directly allocated
                result ->including(allocation.getAllocationContext(
                    conn.providingAssemblyContext))
            else
                —— SubSystem is not directly allocated, descend into it
                result ->including(conn.providingAssemblyContext
                    .encapsulatedComponent.oclAsType(SubSystem)
                        .getAllocationContextsForPR(conn.providedRole,
                            allocation))
            endif
        else
            result ->including(allocation.getAllocationContext(
                conn.providingAssemblyContext))
        endif
    )
    — also navigate across composed structures
    — if this method is called on an allocated component,
    — composed structures can only be SubSystems and
    — thus are only assembled once in the system.
    ->union(system.getAssemblyContextsFor(self.parentStructure)
```

```
. getReceivers ( self . parentStructure . requiredDelegationConnectors
  ->select ( conn | conn . requiringAssemblyContext = self
    and rrs ->select ( rr | rr =conn . requiredRole ))
      . outerRequiredRole , allocation ))
```

To find the communication partners inside a SubSystem that is not allocated as a whole, the query follows the delegation connectors inside the SubSystem. The roles the current component is connected to are passed as an argument to the helper methods, so that the matching delegation connectors connecting these roles with the internals can be retrieved. Then, the communication partners are the components on the inner side of the delegation connector. If an inner component found like this is again a SubSystem and not allocated as one, the query descends further into it. The method getAllocationContextsForPR below handles receivers.

```
context SubSystem
— handle receivers (SubSystems that provide functionality to the
— current component)
def : getAllocationContextsForPR ( prs : Set ( ProvidedRole ) ,
  allocation : Allocation ) : Set ( AllocationContext ) =

— the delegation connectors that are connected to the roles prs
let providedDelegationConnectors : Set ( ProvidedDelegationConnector ) =
self . providedDelegationConnectors ->select ( conn | prs ->exists ( pr |
  pr = conn . outerProvidedRole )) in

— find inner allocated component for each delegation connector
providedDelegationConnectors ->iterate (
conn : ProvidedDelegationConnector , result : Set () = Set { } ,
let allocationContexts : Set ( AllocationContext ) =
  allocation . getAllocationContext ( conn . assemblyContext ) in
— if the inner component is allocated directly , return it .
if ( not allocationContexts ->isEmpty )
then
  result ->including ( allocationContexts )
else
  — otherwise , if inner is SubSystem , descend into it recursively
  if ( conn . assemblyContext . encapsulatedComponent . oclIsKindOf ( SubSystem ))
  then
    result ->including (
      conn . assemblyContext . encapsulatedComponent . oclAsType ( SubSystem )
      . getAllocationContextsForPR ( conn . innerProvidedRole ) , allocation )
    )
```

```
else
   — If inner is not a SubSystem, return null. This can only
   — happen if this SubSystem is not used at all in the system, so
   — that no allocation exist, because otherwise, non−SubSystems
   — have to be allocated by constraint.
   OclVoid
 endif
endif
)
```

Analogously, the method getAllocationContextsForRR handles senders.

```
context SubSystem
— handle senders (SubSystems that require functionality of the
— current component)
def : getAllocationContextsForRR( rrs : Set(RequiredRole),
  allocation : Allocation) : Set(AllocationContext) =

— the delegation connectors that are connected to the roles rrs
let requiredDelegationConnectors : Set (RequiredDelegationConnector) =
self.requiredDelegationConnectors −>select(conn | rrs −>exists(rr |
  rr = conn.outerRequiredRole)) in

— find inner allocated component for each delegation connector
requiredDelegationConnectors −>iterate(
conn : RequiredDelegationConnector, result : Set() = Set{},
let allocationContexts : Set (AllocationContext) =
  allocation.getAllocationContext(conn.assemblyContext) in
— if the inner component is allocated directly, return it.
if (allocationContexts −>isEmpty)
then
   result −>including(allocationContexts)
else
   — otherwise, if inner is SubSystem, descend into it recursively
   if (conn.assemblyContext.encapsulatedComponent.oclIsKindOf(SubSystem))
   then
      result −>including(
         conn.assemblyContext.encapsulatedComponent.oclAsType(SubSystem)
         .getAllocationContextsForRR(conn.innerRequiredRole, allocation)
      )
   else
      — If inner is not a SubSystem, return null. This can only happen
      — if the SubSystem self is not used at all in the system, so that
      — no allocation exsist, because otherwise, non−SubSystems have
      — to be allocated by constraint.
      OclVoid
   endif
endif
)
```

The method below is responsible for backward navigation from a repository component *rc* to the AssemblyContexts that instantiate *rc*. This is needed to navigate across composed structures: If the contents of composed structures are allocated separately, as it may be the case in SubSystems, one may have to navigate up the composition hierarchy to the SubSystem to determine the communication partner of the inner component. The method below can be used to determine the AssemblyContext(s) of the SubSystem itself, so that the communication partners can be determined.

```
context ComposedProvidingRequiringEntity
— get all AssemblyContexts in this composed entity that refer to the
— passed RepositoryComponent
def : getAssemblyContextsFor( rc : RepositoryComponent )
  : Set(AssemblyContext) =

self.assemblyContexts ->select(ac | ac.encapsulatedComponent = rc)
  ->union(self.assemblyContexts ->select(ac |
    ac.oclIsKindOf(ComposedProvidingRequiringEntity))
      .getAssemblyContextsFor(rc))
```

Finally, the helper method getAllocationContext retrieves the AllocationContext for a given AssemblyContext. An OCL constraint in the metamodel ensures that at most one exists in a conformant model. If the passed AssemblyContext is not allocated, null (i.e. OclVoid) is returned.

```
— get allocation for an assembly context
context Allocation
def : getAllocationContext(a : AssemblyContext) : AllocationContext =

let matchingAllocationContext : Set(AllocationContext) =
  self ->select(allc | allc.assemblyContext = a) in
if (matchingAllocationContext.size > 0)
  matchingAllocationContext.first
else
  if (not a.parentStructure.oclIsUndefined)
  then
    self.getAllocationContext(
      system.getAssemblyContextsFor(a.parentStructure))
  else
    OclVoid
  endif
endif
```

B. Degrees of Freedom and Design Space Appendix

B.1. Notes on Changes

B.1.1. Why all Model Changes can be Considered Updates

In general, there are three types of primitive model changes which can be combined to form more complex changes:

1. Update: An existing element e of a model is assigned a new value. For example, the processing rate of a server (modelled as a parameter of the server) is changed to a higher value. Update changes can also refer to associations of the model. For example, moving component BookingSystem to server S3 in a PCM model means to change the AllocationContext of the BookingSystem instance. In particular, the attribute AllocationContext.resourceContainer is changed to point to server S3, which already exists in the model.

2. Add: New model elements can be created and added to the model. For example, a cache component could be added between Business-TripMgmt and BookingSystem to quickly reply to common trips.

3. Delete: Existing model elements can be deleted and thus be removed from the model. In the initial example model, nothing can be deleted without violating one of the constraints. After adding a cache component, however, this cache can be deleted again.

In this work, we assume that all model elements are connected to each other (at least by a common root model element). Then, both additions and deletions imply an update of other model elements that have an association to the added or deleted model elements.

Consider the examples for addition and deletion above: Adding a cache component between BusinessTripMgmt and BookingSystem in our example PCM model means to (1) update the Repository's property Repository.components to contain an additional BasicComponent that provides the IBooking interface, (2) update the System's property System.assemblyContexts to contain an additional AssemblyContext referencing the new BasicComponent, (3) updating the Allocation model's property Allocation.allocationContexts to contain an additional AllocationContext referencing the new AssemblyContext, (4) updating the System's property System.assemblyConnectors to contain an additional AssemblyConnector to connect the cache and BookingSystem, and (5) updating the AssemblyConnector that previously connected BusinessTripMgmt and BookingSystem to now connect BusinessTripMgmt and the cache.

We can unambiguously express the additions of a BasicComponent, an AssemblyContext, an AllocationContext and an AssemblyConnector by describing these 5 model element updates. To do so, we name the *updated model element* (e.g. Repository.components), its *old value* (e.g. Repository.components = {BusinessTripMgmt, BookingSystem, PaymentSystem }), and its *new value* (e.g. Repository.components = {BusinessTripMgmt, BookingSystem, PaymentSystem, Cache })[1].

As a result, we can simplify the notion of a change and treat all three types of primitive model changes the same. To describe a change, we only need to describe how elements are updated.

B.2. Proof for Design Space Definition

Recall:

$$T_{M,D} : \mathcal{O}_{M,D} \to \mathcal{D}_{M,D}$$

---

[1]While we only listed the components' names here, the actual value of Repository.components is the set of model objects describing the components. The complete serialization of the objects is too long to be represented here.

with

$$(v_1, ..., v_{|D|}) \mapsto M(designOptions(d_1) \leftarrow v_1, ..., designOptions(d_{|D|}) \leftarrow v_{|D|})$$

Theorem 6.3: *The function $T_{M,D}$ is surjective, i.e. every architectural candidate model can be produced by a vector from $\mathscr{O}_{M,D}$:*

$$\forall a \in \mathscr{D}_{M,D} : \exists v \in \mathscr{O}_{M,D} :$$
$$a = M(designOptions(d_1) \leftarrow v_1, ..., designOptions(d_{|D|}) \leftarrow v_{|D|})$$

Proof. Let a be a architectural candidate model with respect to a set of DoFI D and an initial architecture model M. Then by definition

$$candidateModel(a, M, D) \Rightarrow$$
$$\exists c_1, ..., c_n \in \{c \, | \, c \in changes(d), d \in D\} : M \xrightarrow{c_1 \circ ... \circ c_n} a$$

Each $c_i \in \{c_1, ..., c_n\}$ is produced by a DoFI $d \in D$. Let us denote the DoFI that produces c_i by d_i. Let p_i denote the primary changed element of d_i.

Then, we can construct the vector in $\mathscr{O}_{M,D}$ as follows:

We start with the vector describing the initial candidate model $ia_0 = (v_{p_1}(M), ..., v_{p_{|P|}(M)})$. Each d_i has a position j_i in the index set $J = \{1, ..., |D|\}$ that spans $\mathscr{O}_{M,D}$. For a vector of values z, let $z(j \leftarrow v)$ denote that the value at position j is replaces by value v. For a change c, let M_c denote the result model of c.

We exchange the value of d_1's primary changed element in c_1 in ia and produce a new vector of values ia_1. Then, we exchange the value of c_2 in ia_1 and so forth. Formally, for each d_i, we exchange the value in ia_{i-1} to produce the $ia_i := ia_{i-1}(j \leftarrow v_{p_1}(M_{c_1}))$.

Then, ia_n is the vector that represents a.

Note that a DoFI $d \in D$ can be used several times in the set of changes that produce a. For the vector, only the last application of d defines the values of a, as every previous value assignment to the primary changed elements of d is overwritten. □

B.3. Candidate Transformation Function T

This section presents the generic transformation T to derive a candidate model from a candidate vector and an initial model for the DoFI metamodel described in Section 6.3.3. This Java transformation uses model elements as provided by the Eclipse Modelling Framework (EMF) (Steinberg et al., 2008), which can be used to read in and manipulate a serialised EMOF model. The inputs are a model root element model from which all model elements can be reached, and a candidate vector candidate as described in Section 8.2.2. Then, the transformation T for Ecore is:

```
/**
 * The generic transformation method
 * @param rootElements The initial architecture model or the
     architecture model of any other candidate.
 * @param candidate The candidate vector to apply.
 */
public void transform(List<EObject> rootElements, Candidate candidate){

List<Choice> choices = candidate.getChoice();

for (Choice choice : choices) {
  // is choice active?
  if (choice.isActive()){

    DegreeOfFreedom dofi = choice.getDegreeOfFreedom();
    DegreeOfFreedom dof = dofi.getDof();

    // Store for each CED which instances have been selected
    Map<ChangeableElementDescription, Collection<EObject>>
        selectedModelElements = new HashMap<
        ChangeableElementDescription, Collection<EObject>>();

    // set primary element
    Entity modelElement = dofi.getPrimaryChanged();
```

```
EStructuralFeature property = dof.getPrimaryChangeable().
    getChangeable();

setProperty(modelElement, property, choice.getValue());

List<EObject> modelElementList = new ArrayList<EObject>(1);
modelElementList.add(modelElement);
selectedModelElements.put(dof.getPrimaryChangeable(),
    modelElementList);

for (ChangeableElementDescription ced : dof.
        getChangeableElementDescription()){
    if (ced == dof.getPrimaryChangeable())
        continue;

    Collection<EObject> changeableElements = selectionRule(ced,
        rootElements, selectedModelElements);
    selectedModelElements.put(ced, changeableElements);

    EStructuralFeature changeableProperty = ced.getChangeable();

    for (EObject changeableElement : changeableElements) {

        Object newValue = valueRule(ced, changeableElement,
            rootElements);
        setProperty(changeableElement, changeableProperty, newValue);

    }

  }
 }
}}
```

This transformation varies the input model and may result in an invalid model, i.e. a model that only structurally conform to the metamodel, but does not conform to the metamodel with respect to the static semantics. Thus, the input model has to be copied before if it is to be preserved.

Currently, for manually determined DoFI, a custom DoF has to be defined as well for this transformation to handle them. Alternatively, a new type of DoFI could be added to the DoF metamodel that does not refer to a DoF, but lets the user define and model the transformation-relevant information directly for the concrete metamodel or system at hand.

C. Degree of Freedom Definitions for PCM

This section provides the formal definitions of the degrees of freedom identified in Chapter 7 for the PCM and either Robocop or CBML. We use OCL 2.0 (Object Management Group (OMG), 2006b) for the definitions because the latest version of EMOF (2.0, (Object Management Group (OMG), 2009)) refers to UML 2.0 (Object Management Group (OMG), 2005) and OCL 2.0.

C.1. Component Selection

C.1.1. PCM Definition:

In the PCM, the composition of components to form a system is modelled in the System model. Components are instantiated in the system using AssemblyContexts. AssemblyConnectors connect the RequiredRoles and ProvidedRoles of the instantiated components. DelegationConnectors connect the outer roles of a composed structure to roles of the contained components.

To replace a component is used in a System, the AssemblyContext needs to be updated: The Property AssemblyContext.encapsulatedComponent references the component to instantiate from the Repository. Additionally, to keep the model consistent, the AssemblyConnectors need to be updated to refer to the RequiredRoles and ProvidedRoles of the new component. For all AssemblyConnectors that connect a ProvidedRole of the replaced component to other components that require this functionality, the property AssemblyConnector.providedRole needs to be updated. For all AssemblyConnectors that connect a RequiredRole of the replaced component to other components that provide the requested functionality, the property AssemblyConnector.requiredRole needs to be updated. If the component instance resides at the border of a composed structure, i.e. if its roles are directly connected to the outer roles of the composed structure, also the delegation connectors (ProvidedDelegationConnector, RequiredDelegationConnector) need to be updated analogously to the AssemblyConnectors.

If the new component requires less functionality than the previous component, some AssemblyConnectors or DelegationConnectors become superfluous and need to be removed by deleting them from the list of connectors of their parent ComposedStructure.

Thus, the set of properties whose instances can be changed is $changeable(g) = \{$AssemblyContext.encapsulatedComponent, AssemblyConnector.providedRole, AssemblyConnector.requiredRole, ComposedStructure.assemblyConnectors, ProvidedDelegationConnector.innerProvidedRole, RequiredDelegationConnector.innerRequiredRole, ComposedStructure.requiredDelegationConnectors $\}$, while AssemblyContext.encapsulatedComponent is the primary changeable element.

To describe the replacement of one component, all changeable model elements have to refer to the same place in the architecture, which is expressed by the following selection rules. First, only components can be exchanged. SubSystems, which may also be referenced by AssemblyContext.encapsulatedComponent, cannot be replaced because the allocation of the inner components requires additional adjustment. For SubSystems in the PCM, a separate degree of freedom is defined in Section 7.4.2. Additionally, rules describe how to get the matching instances that contain the changeable elements AssemblyConnector.providedRole, AssemblyConnector.requiredRole, ComposedStructure.assemblyConnectors for the selected AssemblyContext.

Rule *selectionRule*(AssemblyContext.encapsulatedComponent) to select the components that might be replaced, which are all components that are reachable from the architecture model and that are not SubSystems:

```
context System
def: getReplaceableComponents : Set ( AssemblyContext ) =
  self . getAllInnerComponents

context ComposedStructure
def: getAllInnerComponents : Set ( AssemblyContext ) =
  self . assemblyContexts
    −>select(c | not c. encapsulatedComponents . oclIsKindOf ( SubSystem ))
  −>union ( self . assemblyContexts . encapsulatedComponents
    −>select(c | c. oclIsKindOf ( ComposedStructure ))
      . oclAsType ( Set ( ComposedStructure )). getAllInnerComponents )
```

Rule *selectionRule*(AssemblyConnector.providedRole) to select the AssemblyConnectors where AssemblyConnector.providedRole needs to be updated, given the AssemblyContext *self* that contains the chosen instance of AssemblyContext.encapsulatedComponent:

```
context AssemblyContext
def: getConnectorsToUpdateProvidedSide : Set ( AssemblyConnector ) =
  self . parentStructure . assemblyConnectors
    −>select(conn | conn . providingAssemblyContext = self )
```

Rule *selectionRule*(AssemblyConnector.requiredRole) to select the AssemblyConnectors where AssemblyConnector.requiredRole needs to be updated, given the AssemblyContext *self* that contains the chosen instance of AssemblyContext.encapsulatedComponent:

```
context AssemblyContext
def: getConnectorsToUpdateRequiredSide : Set ( AssemblyConnector ) =
  self . parentStructure . assemblyConnectors
    −>select(conn | conn . requiringAssemblyContext = self )
```

Rule *selectionRule*(ComposedStructure.assemblyConnectors) to select the ComposedStructure where ComposedStructure.assembly-Connectors may have to be updated, given the AssemblyContext *self* that contains the chosen instance of AssemblyContext.encapsulated-Component:

```
context AssemblyContext
def: getComposedStructureToUpdateConnectors : ComposedStructure =
  self . parentStructure
```

The value rules are the following: The *valueRule*(AssemblyContext.encapsulatedComponent) is:

context AssemblyContext
def : getCompatibleComponents : **Set** (RepositoryComponent) =
  repositories.components—>select(c|
    c.offersAllInterfaces(self.allNeededProvidedInterfaces())
    && c.requiresAtMostInterfaces(self.allAllowedRequiredInterfaces()))

  — *get all Interfaces that this AssemblyContext needs to provide*
  — *(because the connected components require them)*
  def: allNeededProvidedInterfaces: **Set**(Interface) =
    self.parentStructure.assemblyConnectors—>select(a|
      a.providingAssemblyContext = self).requiredRole.requiredInterface

  — *get all Interfaces that this AssemblyContext can require*
  — *(because the connected components provide them)*
  def: allAllowedRequiredInterfaces: **Set**(Interface) =
    self.parentStructure.assemblyConnectors—>select(a|
      a.requiringAssemblyContext = self).providedRole.providedInterface

context RepositoryComponent
  — *check whether the component provides all the passed Interfaces*
  def: offersAllInterfaces(i : **Set**(Interface)): **Boolean** =
    i—>forAll(i : Interface | self.providedRoles.providedInterface
    —>exists(pi | pi.isEqualOrDescendantOf(i)))

  — *check whether the component requires at most the passed Interfaces*
  def: requiresAtMostInterfaces(i : **Set**(Interface)): **Boolean** =
    self.requiredRoles.requiredInterfaces—>forall(ri |
      i—>exists(i | i.isEqualOrDescendantOf(ri)))

context Interface
  — *check whether this interface can replace the parameter interface*
  — *because they are the same or this interface is a descendant of*
  — *the parameter interface.*
  def: isEqualOrDescendantOf(i: Interface) : **Boolean** =
    (self = i **or** self.parentInterfaces.isEqualOrDescendantOf(i))

valueRule(AssemblyConnector.providedRole) is:

context AssemblyConnector
def: getProvidedRoleForNewComponent : ProvidedRole =
  — *any provided role of the new encapsulated component that offers*
  — *the interface required by the AssemblyContext on the other side*
  self.providingAssemblyContext.encapsulatedComponent.providedRoles

```
->select(pr | pr.providedInterface
  .isEqualOrDescendantOf(self.requiredRole.requiredInterface))
  ->asOrderedSet()->select(r | r = first())
```

Remark: The statement ->select(r | r = first()) is used here and in the following to get a result set with one element, if available, or an empty result set. The value rule for ProvidedDelegationConnector.innerProvidedRole is almost identical, only that the new encapsulated component is reached by "self.assemblyContext".

valueRule(AssemblyConnector.requiredRole) is:

```
context AssemblyConnector
    — a required role of the new encapsulated component that offers
    — the interface required by the AssemblyContext on the other side
    — so that each required Roles is only bound once.
  def: getMatchingRequiredRole : Set(RequiredRole)
  self.requiringAssemblyContext.encapsulatedComponent.requiredRoles
    ->select(rr | self.providedRole.providedInterface
      .isEqualOrDescendantOf(rr.requiredInterface)
    and
      — there is not already another AssemblyConnector that
      — connects this role in this AssemblyContext
    not self.parentStructure.assemblyConnector->exists(c |
        c.requiringAssemblyContext = self.requiringAssemblyContext
      and c.requiredRole = rr)
    )->asSequence()->select(r | r = first())
```

Here, it is assumed that the value rules are executed sequentially, and not at the same time. For example, if there are three AssemblyConnectors that connect three RequiredRoles of a component to be replaced and the three roles refer to the same Interface, the first execution of the above rule for the first AssemblyConnector selects any of these roles, the second execution for the second AssemblyConnector selects one of the two remaining roles, and the third execution for the third AssemblyConnector selects the last RequiredRole. Thus, all three roles are bound: Because the roles refer to the same interface, it does not matter which one is bound in which AssemblyConnector. The value rule for RequiredDelegationConnector.innerRequiredRole is almost identical, only that the new encapsulated component is reached by "self.assemblyContext".

The AssemblyConnectors and RequiredDelegationConnectors that cannot be bound by the above rule, i.e. where the value rule results in an empty set (because either the respective Interface is not required any more, or because the Interface is required fewer times) have to be deleted. The ComposedStructure may only contain AssemblyConnectors with complete provided role links and required role links, as selected by the following *valueRule*(ComposedStructure.assemblyConnectors):

```
context ComposedStructure
  self.assemblyConnectors ->select(conn |
    conn.getMatchingRequiredRole()->notEmpty()  )
```

The value rule to delete superfluous RequiredDelegationConnectors is almost identical, only that the list of conectors to delete from is reached by "self.requiredDelegationConnectors".

Component selection in the PCM may open up new component selection degree of freedom instances, if the new component is a composite component that has inner components that can be replaced, i.e. that introduces new AssemblyContexts to consider. Thus, the added element is Assembly-Context. No additional interaction constraints are required.

Note that we assume in this example that components that provide the same functionality also require the same resources. For example, a storage component requires hard drive, while most business-logic components only need a CPU. If resource requirements were to be considered in more detail and if component allocation (cf. Section 7.3) is considered as a degree of freedom, an interaction constraint would have to be added which checks whether the server teh component instance is currently deployed to also offers the required resources.

C.1.2. ROBOCOP Definition:

The component selection in ROBOCOP is realised with the Binding in the ScenarioModel. To exchange a component, all Bindings that bind the ServiceInstances of the component needs to be updated. Thus, the changeable metamodel elements are $changeable(g) = \{$Binding.from, Binding.to, Binding.fromPort, Binding.toPort$\}$. The primary changeable elements is Binding.from. When a new ServiceInstance is selected there, all other properties have to be updated accordingly to refer to the Ports of the new ServiceInstance, thus the selection rules are similar to the PCM case.

For a component in the initial system, alternative components are Components that offer the same Interfaces via their Services and Ports. Thus, the value rules are similar to the PCM.

No interaction constraints are required. In contrast to the PCM, no new DoF are opened up because ROBOCOP does not support composite components (H. Koziolek, 2010).

C.2. Non-functional Component Configuration Parameters

C.2.1. PCM Definition:

Component configuration parameters are modelled on the type level by the ImplementationComponentType.componentParameterUsage property, which references a VariableUsage containing the specification of a parameter as a PCMRandomVariable, and possibly a default value. On the instance level, component configuration parameter values can be redefined by attaching a VariableUsage to an AssemblyContext as AssemblyContext.configParameterUsages. Thus, the metamodel element to be updated in a degree of freedom is the AssemblyContext.configParameterUsages property:

$$changeable(g) = \{AssemblyContext.configParameterUsages\}$$

The valid values depend on the concrete component that is parametrised, thus they can only be determined on the instance level and need to be annotated to the component instance. No interaction constraints are required.

The PCM does not distinguish yet between non-functional component configuration parameters and other component configuration parameters that affect functionality. Thus, the information whether a component configuration parameter has no functional effect has to be annotated manually. Alternatively, all component configuration parameters can be assumed to have no functional effect.

C.2.2. CBML Definition:

In CBML, components can be parametrized using the Parameter metamodel element. To change the value of a component parameter, the Parameter.value is updated, so $changeable(g) = \{Parameter.value\}$. The possible values have to be defined manually for a system at hand. No selection rules and interaction constraints are needed and no elements are added.

C.3. Passive Resources Multiplicity

C.3.1. PCM Definition:

In the PCM, PassiveResources are entities referenced by BasicComponents. The capacity of a PassiveResource is determined by the property PassiveResource.capacity, which is a PCMRandomVariable. Only integer values are allowed. Thus, the set of properties whose instances can be changed is $changeable(g) = \{PassiveResource.capacity\}$ and the value range is $R = \mathbb{N}_+$. R can be restricted on the instance level. No interaction constraints are required.

C.3.2. CBML Definition:

For each Task within a component (i.e. within an LQNSubmodel), the allowed number of parallel executions may be specified in the property

Task.multiplicity. Thus, every Task within a component can be interpreted to be passive resource. If the multiplicity is larger than 1 in the initial model, we can instantiate the degree.

The value range is $R = \mathbb{N}_+$. No additional information is needed.

C.4. Priorities

C.4.1. CBML Definition:

Because priorities are not supported in the PCM metamodel and the PCM analyses, we describe this degree of freedom only for CBML.

For each Task within a component (i.e. within an LQNSubmodel), the priority can be specified in the property Task.priority as a non-negative integer priority value with a priority of zero being the highest. Thus, for every Task within a component, a separate degree can be instantiated.

Thus, the metamodel property whose instances can be changed is $changeable(g) = \{\text{Task.priority}\}$ with a value range of $R = \mathbb{N}_0$. No interaction constraints are required.

Additionally, processors can be configured to use preemptive scheduling (i.e. as soon as a task with higher priority arrives, other executing task with lower priority are stopped and put back in the queue) or to use head of queue scheduling (i.e. the queue is reordered based on incoming request priorities, but tasks that have started execution are not preempted), which could be instantiated as an additional, CBML-specific degree of freedom.

C.5. Allocation

C.5.1. PCM Definition:

AllocationContexts map component instances (i.e. AssemblyContexts) to servers (i.e. ResourceContainers). The metamodel property responsible for the mapping is $changeable(g) = \{\text{AllocationContext.resource-Container}\}$.

Thus, to determine the value rules, we need to determine the servers that provide the required resources. The required resource types of a component can be determined by collecting the resource types (ProcessingResource-Type in the PCM) of all internal resource demands.

Value Rules: The *valueRule*(AllocationContext.resourceContainer) to select the available servers *C* may be allocated to is shown below. It is checked whether the required resources are provided by the candidate server using the helper method getResourceTypes defined on a component.

```
context AllocationContext
def : getPossibleServers : Set ( ResourceContainer ) =

self. allocation . targetResourceEnvironment . resourceContainer –>select ( rc |
    — has the required resources
    self . assemblyContext . encapsulatedComponent . getResourceTypes
        –>forAll ( rt | rc . activeResourceSpecifications –> includes ( rt ))
)
```

The following OCL queries are helper methods to determine the resource types required by a component. If a component is a BasicComponent, the required resources can be queried from the component's RDSEFF (by calling the helper method getResourceTypes defined for ResourceDemand-ingBehaviours). If a component is a composed structure, all its child components are queried recursively.

```
— collect all resource types used by a Repository component.
— Main two options:
—    Component is a BasicComponent, descend into behaviour description
—    Component is a ComposedStructure, descend into parts
context RepositoryComponent
def : getResourceTypes : Set ( ProcessingResourceType ) =
if self . oclIsKindOf ( BasicComponent )
then
    self . oclAsType ( BasicComponent ). serviceEffectSpecifications
        –>select ( rdseff | rdseff . oclIsKindOf ( ResourceDemandingSEFF ))
        . getResourceTypes ()

        — an RDSEFF can contain InternalBehaviours that can be called in
        — multiple places of this SEFF
        –>union ( self . oclAsType ( BasicComponent ). serviceEffectSpecifications
```

```
    ->select(rdseff | rdseff.oclIsKindOf(ResourceDemandingSEFF))
        .resourceDemandingInternalBehaviours.getResourceTypes())

else if self.oclIsKindOf( ComposedProvidingRequiringEntity )
    -- both Subsystems and ComposedComponents
    then
        -- recursively call this method on all inner RepositoryComponents
        self.oclAsType( ComposedProvidingRequiringEntity ).assemblyContexts
            .encapsulatedComponent.getResourceTypes()
    else
        -- Other component types (ProvidesComponentType or
        -- CompleteComponentType) that have no resource demands
        -- OclVoid is the OCL null element that is also treated as an empty
        -- Bag{} (OCL specification, p. 140 sec 11.2.3)
        OclVoid->asSet()
    endif
endif
```

To retrieve the required resource types from an RDSEFF, all actions that may contain resource demands need to be checked. If an action is a control flow action, such as a loop or a branch, that contains inner behaviour (e.g. the loop body or the branches), the following method is called recursively on these inner behaviours.

```
-- handle all the different typs of actions in a RDSEFF that have
-- resource demands.
context ResourceDemandingBehaviour
    def : getResourceTypes : Set ( ProcessingResourceType ) =
        self.steps->select( icfa |
            icfa.oclIsKindOf(AbstractInternalControlFlowAction))
                .flatten().oclAsType(Set(AbstractInternalControlFlowAction))
                    .resourceDemand.requiredResource
        ->union(
            -- asynchronous forked behaviours
            self.steps->select( fork | fork.oclIsKindOf(ForkAction))
                .flatten().oclAsType(Set(AbstractInternalControlFlowAction))
                    .asynchronousForkedBehaviours.getResourceTypes()
        )->union(
            -- synchronous forked behaviours
            self.steps->select( fork | fork.oclIsKindOf(ForkAction))
                .flatten().oclAsType(Set(AbstractInternalControlFlowAction))
                    .synchronisingBehaviours.synchronousForkedBehaviours
                        .getResourceTypes()
        )->union(
            -- loop behaviours
```

478

```
self.steps −>select( loop |
  loop.oclIsKindOf(AbstractLoopAction))
    .flatten ().oclAsType(Set(AbstractLoopAction))
      .bodyBehaviour.getResourceTypes()
)−>union(
  — branched behaviours
  self.steps −>select( branch | branch.oclIsKindOf(BranchAction))
    .flatten ().oclAsType(Set(BranchAction))
      .branches.branchBehaviour.getResourceTypes()
)−>union(
  — recovery blocks
  self.steps −>select( recover |
  recover.oclIsKindOf(RecoveryBlockAction))
    .flatten ().oclAsType(Set(RecoveryBlockAction))
      .recoveryBlockalternativeBehaviours.getResourceTypes()
)
```

As interaction constraints, the constraint isConnectedToAllSender-sAndReceivers of AllocationContexts (see appendix A.6) additionally restricts the design option sets of combinations of Allocation DoF. Models generated by instances of this DoF may violate this constraint. If the component selection also considered components requiring different resources, another interaction constraint would be added that would ensure that all required resources are provided by a server.

C.5.2. ROBOCOP Definition:

The allocation of components to servers in ROBOCOP uses the Mapping element. Here, the property Mapping.toServer can be varied to allocate the referenced Component to another ProcessingNode. So, $changeable(g) = \{Mapping.toServer\}$.

Components can be allocated to servers that offer the required resource types. CPU and memory are the only resource types in ROBOCOP. Thus, we statically check that (1) if the component requires CPU, the server offers a CPU resource and (2) if the component requires memory, whether the server offers a memory resource. Thus, in OCL, the *valueRule*(Mapping.toServer) below describes the allowed servers (c.resources.ior stands for an implemented operation resource usage of a component c and n.blocks refers to the hardware resources, called IP blocks, of a server node n cf. Section 2.6.2 and Bondarev and Chaudron (2006)):

```
context Mapping
  def : getPossibleServers : Set ( ProcessingNode ) =
  self.toServer.resEnv.nodes->select( n |
    self.component.resources.ior->exists(ior | ior.cpu <> OclVoid)
      implies n.blocks->exists(b | b.isOclTypeOf(CPUPerfModel))
    and
    self.component.resources.ior->exists(ior | ior.memory <> OclVoid)
      implies n.blocks->exists(b | b.isOclTypeOf(MemoryPerfModel))
  )
```

No additional interaction constraints are required and no elements are added.

C.6. Allocation with Replication

C.6.1. PCM Definition:

Currently, the PCM only supports the allocation of a component to one server, because the semantics of a 1:n mapping of AssemblyContexts to AllocationContexts which would allow component replication on the allocation level have not been defined yet because several sensible but conflicting semantics exist (e.g. load balancing or replication). Additional metamodel elements to configure an 1:n mapping and define the semantics would be required. Thus, this degree of freedom is not supported yet.

To nonetheless illustrate the degree of freedom, let us consider the following small extension to the PCM with simple semantics, illustrated in Figure C.10: We enable component replications by allowing several AllocationContexts per AssemblyContext. Let the semantics be that the load is balanced to the multiple AllocationContexts of one Assembly-Context and that for every request to the replicated component instance, the AllocationContext to load a server is chosen randomly.

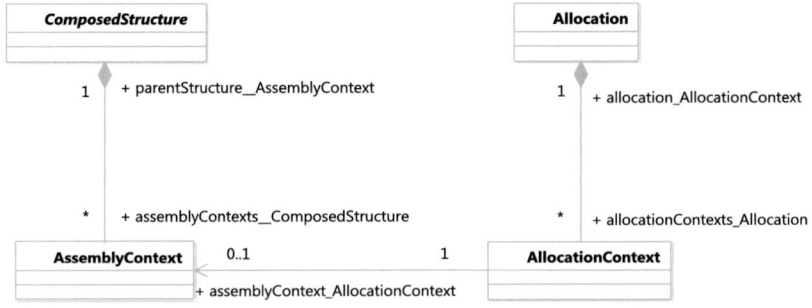

Figure C.10.: Extended PCM to Enable Replication of Components

Then, the metamodel property responsible for the mapping is again

$$changeable(g) = \{\text{AllocationContext.resourceContainer}\}$$

The *valueRule*(AllocationContext.resourceContainer) builds the power set of available servers by using the OCL definitions of the simple "allocation" degree. The value rule uses all queries of the simple "allocation" degree.

```
context AllocationContext
  def : getPossibleServersAsPower : Set ( ResourceContainer ) =
    self.powerSet(self.getPossibleServers)->excluding(Set{})
```

To calculate the power set, we implemented the following recursive algorithm in OCL based on the recursive algorithm presented in (Cameron, 1994, p.40). The power set for a set $\{1,...,n\}$ is the empty set of "$n = 0$ and is determined with the following recursive algorithm for $n > 0$: $\mathscr{P}(\{1,...,n\}) =$

- generate the power set $\mathscr{P}(\{1,...,n-1\})$ and store the result in the set P
- make a new copy of each subset in P resulting in the set P'
- add the element n to every subset in P'
- return the set of all sets created $P \cup P'$.

In OCL, this is implemented in the following query:

```
context AllocationContext
def : powerSet(input : Set( ResourceContainer ))
  : Set ( Set ( ResourceContainer ) ) =

  if input ->isEmpty
then
  let initialPowerSet : Set ( Set () ) = Set{} in
        initialPowerSet ->include(Set{})
else
  let element : ResourceContainer
    = input ->asOrderedSet ->first in
      powerSet(input ->excluding(element))
              ->union(addElementToEachSet(
                 powerSet(input ->excluding(element))))
endif

def : addElementToEachSet(powerSet : Set ( Set (ResourceContainer) ),
  element : ResourceContainer) : Set ( Set ( ResourceContainer ) ) =
powerSet ->iterate( containedSet : Set (ResourceContainer),
  result : Set ( Set (ResourceContainer) ) = Set{}
  result ->include(containedSet ->union(element))
)
```

Additionally, the interaction constraint isConnectedToAllSendersAnd-Receivers defined in Section 7.3.1 needs to be fulfilled for all selected servers in the result model after having applied all changes.

C.6.2. Other Metamodel Definition:

Definition in other CBA models: Allocation with replication is neither supported in CBML nor in ROBOCOP. Thus, we do not give an example here.

C.7. Server Replication

C.7.1. PCM Definition:

This degree of freedom is currently not supported in the PCM, because no metamodel element describes the multiplicity of servers. To nonetheless illustrate the degree of freedom, let us consider to add such a multiplicity element to a PCM resource container as an extension: We model the multiplicity as the metamodel element ResourceContainer.multiplicity of type integer. Let the semantics be that the load is balanced to the multiple server instances and that for every request to the replicated component instance, the server to load is chosen randomly. Then, the set of metamodel properties whose instances are changed is $changeable(g) = \{$ResourceContainer.multiplicity$\}$.

The value range of ResourceContainer.multiplicity is any integer larger than zero on the metamodel level: $R = \mathbb{N}_+$. This set has to be restricted on the model level to account for system-specific restrictions here: There is always a maximum number of servers allowed for a given setting. No interaction constraints are required.

C.7.2. CBML Definition:

Each Processor in CBML can be assigned a multiplicity, which corresponds to the server replication described in this degree. The multiplicity is described with the propertyProcessor.replication, which can take any positive integer value. Thus, for every Processor in the assembly model (the main LQNModel), a separate degree can be instantiated. For the Processors inside components, the degree cannot be instantiated, because these processors will be mapped to Processor in the assembly model when transforming the model to LQNs.

Thus, $changeable(g) = \{$Processor.replication$\}$. The selection rule selects instances of Processor from the main LQNModel only:

```
context LQNModel
    def : getreplicatableServers : Set ( Processor ) =
    self.processors
```

The value range is $R = \mathbb{N}_+$. No interaction constraints are required and no elements are added.

C.8. Resource Selection

C.8.1. PCM Definition:

Resources are contained in servers, i.e., ResourceContainers. A Resource-Container may contain one or several ProcessingResourceSpecifications, referred to by the property ResourceContainer.activeResourceSpecifications.

ProcessingResourceSpecification are not first class entities in the PCM; they are contained in a server and do not have their own identifier. Thus, they are considered a data type here, and the primary changeable element is ResourceContainer.activeResourceSpecifications. A concrete ProcessingResourceSpecification to be changed is identified by its ResourceType (cf. discussion in Section 6.3.3). Then, when appliying a change, the template ProcessingResourceSpecification can be copied from the ResourceRepository to the ResourceContainer.activeResourceSpecification list.

ProcessingResourceSpecification can be annotated with costs in the PCM costs model. A cost model element FixedProcessingResourceCost defines the cost of ProcessingResourceSpecifications in the ResourceEnvironment and in the ResourceRepository. If no costs are defined for a ProcessingResourceSpecification, it is assumed to be free. When a ProcessingResourceSpecification is replaced by a copy of another template ProcessingResourceSpecification, its costs need to updated as well: The FixedProcessingResourceCost of the template ProcessingResourceSpecification needs to be copied and the old FixedProcessingResourceCost needs to be removed. Thus, CostModel.cost is a changeable element. Its value can be derived from the primary change.

Together, we get *changeable*(*g*) = {ResourceContainer.active-ResourceSpecifications, CostModel.cost}.

The available resources to use are located in a ResourceDescription-Repository model. An available resource is described by a ResourceDescription, which combines the ProcessingRateSpecification information and the costs of the resource as FixedProcessingResourceCost (cf. Figure A.8 in Section A.5).

When changing a resource along this degree of freedom, the resource instances in the repository cannot be referenced directly in the system, because one instance of ProcessingRateSpecification can only be contained in one server (or resource description) at a time due to the containment relationship. Thus, the ProcessingRateSpecifications need to be copied when assigned to servers. This is similar to the handling of primitive data types, which are also not referenced, but newly instantiated.

A second particularity of the resource degree is that the ResourceContainer.activeResourceSpecifications property contains one ProcessingRateSpecification per used resource type and that the single specifications are changed independently. This means that for each instance of ResourceContainer.activeResourceSpecifications, there may be several degree of freedom instances, one for each resource type in the set of ProcessingRateSpecification (this number is equal to the number of ProcessingRateSpecifications in the list, as only one ProcessingRateSpecification per resource type is allowed in the PCM).

Let the variable resourceRepository denote the available resource repository in the following OCL queries. For simplicity, we assume one resource repository in the following. The repository could be split into several resource repository models as well. One ProcessingResourceSpecification is chosen to be varied. Then, the cost of the resource to vary with the resource is selected with the following *selectionRule*(CostModel.cost), assuming that the variable costModel allows to navigate to the cost model.

```
—  select  the  right  cost  element  to  change  with  this
—  ProcessingResourceSpecification
context  ProcessingResourceSpecification
  costModel.cost—>select(c  |  c.oclIsKindOf(FixedProcessingResourceCost)
    and  c.oclAsType(FixedProcessingResourceCost)
      .processingresourcespecification  =  self)
```

Then, assuming that a software architect has specified the available resources in the resource repository, the *valueRule*(ResourceContainer.activeResourceSpecifications) is:

Rule to select the available ProcessingResourceSpecification from the resource repository:

```
—  select  available  other  ProcessingResourceSpecification
context  ProcessingResourceSpecification
  resourceRepository.availableProcessingResources—>select(rd  |
    rd.processingResourceSpecification.resourcespecification
      =  self.resourcespecification)
```

As described above, the ProcessingResourceSpecifications have no identity and are contained in their server, thus, they need to be copied here like primitive data types.

The new value of the cost element is determined by *valueRule*(CostModel.cost). In the value rule, we refer to the changed instance of ProcessingResourceSpecifications in the resource repository by the variable prs:

```
context  CostModel
  self.cost—>select(c  |  c.oclIsKindOf(FixedProcessingResourceCost)  and
    c.oclAsType(FixedProcessingResourceCost)
      .processingresourcespecification  =  prs)
```

Again, this selected cost element has to be copied and is used to replace the cost element selected above in the cost model.

No interaction constraints and added elements are required.

C.8.2. ROBOCOP Definition:

In ROBOCOP, the properties of resource can be varied by defining alternative HWIPBlockPerfModels, which can be CPU, memory, or bus models.

Figure C.11.: Resource Repository for ROBOCOP

Similarly to the PCM, an additional resource repository is required for this degree to define the possible available resources. Figure C.11 shows the resource repository.

Then, any resource used in the system (i.e. referenced by a Mapping) can be varied. The metamodel element to change is *changeable(g)* = {*ProcessingNode.blocks*}. Similarly to the PCM, HW IP block performance models in ProcessingNode.blocks can be replaced by copies of the blocks from the resource repository.

The allowed HWIPBlockPerfModels to be copied to ProcessingNode-.blocks are selected by the following value rule *valueRule*(Processing-Node.blocks), which is executed in the context of the HWIPBlockPerf-Models to be replaced. The value rule selects all HWIPBlockPerfModels that have the same type (i.e. CPU or memory) than the currently used HWIPBlockPerfModels. In the query, let the variable resourceRepository denote the available resource repository.

```
context HWIPBlockPerfModels
  resourceRepository.availableHardware −>select(h |
    h.oclIsKindOf(self.oclType))
```

No interaction rules are required and no elements are added.

C.9. Resource Property Change

C.9.1. PCM Definition:

In the PCM, we have included a continuous change of the processing rate as one realisation of this degree. The cost of a resource can be defined as a function of the processing rate (cf. Section 2.5.5) and thus are adjusted automatically when changing the processing rate. We chose to model the MTTF of a server as scaling linearly with the processing rate so that faster servers are also more reliable, because we assume that the more expensive servers are more reliable. The opposite interpretation is just as well justified, so that it would be beneficial to make the relation of MTTF and processing rate configurable in this degree in future work.

The processing rate of a resource is modelled by the property ProcessingResourceSpecification.processingRate, while the MTTF of a resource is modelled by the property ProcessingResourceSpecification.MTTF.

Together, we get *changeable*$(g) = \{$ ProcessingResourceSpecification.processingRate, ProcessingResourceSpecification.MTTF $\}$.

Like in the "Resource Selection Degree", one ProcessingResourceSpecification is chosen to be varied. No additional selection rules are required. Any positive value of the data type of the processing rate specification is allowed, so the value rules return the positive values of the data type's domain. This range should be limited for a specific system at hand because usually, the optimization should not explore arbitrarily fast servers.

To scale the MTTF, we need the initial processing rate and the initial MTTF. Let the variables initialProcRate and initialMTTF denote these values for this ProcessingResourceSpecification. Then, the value rule for the MTTF (in our current interpretation that the MTTF scales linearly with the rate) is

```
— get the value for the MTTF of this ProcessingResourceSpecification
context ProcessingResourceSpecification
   initialMTTF * self.processingRate / initialProcRate
```

No interaction constraints and added elements are needed.

C.9.2. ROBOCOP Definition:

In ROBOCOP, the frequency of CPUs can be varied. It is modelled with the property frequency of a CPUPerfModel that is defined for a server.

Thus, the metamodel element to change is $changeable(g) = \{$ CPUPerf-Model.frequency $\}$. The other rules are analogous to the PCM rules.

C.10. Quality Completion Configuration

C.10.1. PCM Definition:

In the PCM, feature models and feature configuration are used to model completion configuration, as described in Section 2.4.4. To do so, feature models and feature configuration have been described using EMOF. All valid feature combinations are described by the respective feature model, which may contain constraints among features of different subtrees.

For the combined modelling of all features of a feature tree, the design option set is the set of all possible feature configurations. Then, the changeable element is the complete feature configuration, which is references by the root element FeatureConfig.configNode for the PCM. Thus, $changeable(g) = \{$FeatureConfig.configNode$\}$.

For the separate modelling of each feature as a degree of freedom, the choice for each feature configuration is changed. For optional features, each ConfigNode has a configuration state, which is either selected or not selected. Thus, the changeable element is $changeable(g) = \{$ConfigNode.configState$\}$. For exclusive-or choices, the configuration state of all included features have to be considered as one degree of freedom. However, although only one feature of an exclusive-or can be selected at a time, the current feature model in the PCM considers the selection of each contained feature separately. Thus, no primary changeable element can be identified at the moment and a virtual configuration (cf. Section 6.3.1.8) has to be introduced. At the same time, the model is difficult to use by human modellers, because they may easily produce invalid models by selecting several options of an exclusive-or. Here, a more concise metamodel would capture the exclusive-or choice in a dedicated metamodel element.

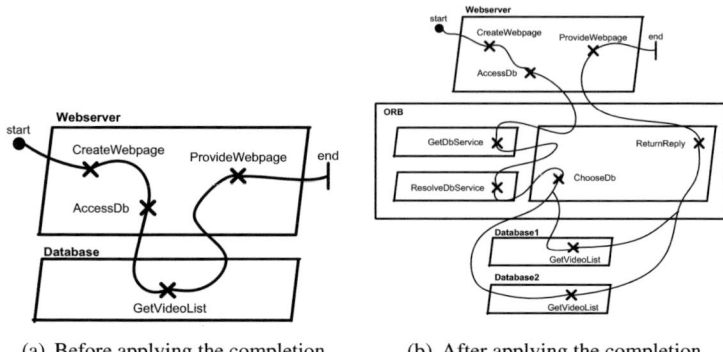

(a) Before applying the completion   (b) After applying the completion

Figure C.12.: Performance Completions for a Web Server from (Woodside et al., 2002), Shown as a Use Case Map

For the modelling of feature model subtrees as separate degrees of freedom, the feature model has to be extended to mark such feature groups of features that belong together. Then, the degrees of freedom can refer to this feature group model.

C.10.2. CBML Definition:

Woodside et al. (2002) present an example for a video server system. Here, the system model in LQN (i.e. in CBML) abstractly models that a web server accesses a database (see Figure 11.12(a)). However, in the system implementation, the database access is realised using an object request broker (ORB) and accesses one of two available database server choices, either an Oracle database or a MySQL database (see Figure 11.12(b), both options are modelled in the figure). The choice of database server selection and its configuration can be varied here and explored by the automated improvement.

C.11. Subsystem Selection in the PCM

In addition to the changeable elements of the component selection degree, we additionally need to change Allocation.allocationContexts. Allocation.allocationContexts is at the same time the primary changeable element, as there is only one possible value for the AssemblyContexts and the connectors resulting in a complete valid SubSystem replacement.

Thus, the changeable elements here is $changeable(g) = \{$ Allocation-.allocationContexts, AssemblyContext.encapsulatedComponent, AssemblyConnector.providedRole, AssemblyConnector.required-Role, ComposedStructure.assemblyConnectors $\}$.

By adding AllocationContexts, the SubSystem Selection degree may open up new Allocation Degrees. We can instantiate Allocation Degrees for each added AllocationContext, and deactivate existing Allocation Degrees for the removed Allocation Contexts. Thus, the values of Allocation-Context.resourceContainer of the newly added AllocationContexts does not have to be defined in the value rules for this degree.

The degree of freedom can be instantiated once per subsystem whose inner components are separately allocated. Thus, we create a selection rule that selects sets of AllocationContexts, one set for each SubSystem that can be replaced. To simplify identifying the SubSystem to replace, we add it to the selection rule *selectionRule*(Allocation.allocationContexts) below and define a new Tuple with the SubSystem and all its AllocationContexts.

```
context Allocation
def : getChangeableAllocationSets
    : Set (TupleType{subsystem: AssemblyContext,
        allocationcontexts : Set (AllocationContext)) =

self.system.getAllInnerSubsystems –>collect( s |
  Tuple {
  subsystem : AssemblyContext = s,
  –– the allocation contexts of the currently used subsystem
  allocationcontexts : Set (AllocationContext) =
    s.getInnerAllocationContext(self)
  })
```

```
context ComposedStructure
def : getAllInnerSubsystems : Set ( AssemblyContext ) =

self . assemblyContexts
  ->select ( c | c . encapsulatedComponent . oclIsKindOf ( SubSystem ))
->union ( self . assemblyContexts
  ->select ( c | c . encapsulatedComponents . oclIsKindOf ( SubSystem ))
  . oclAsType ( Set ( AssemblyContext )). getAllInnerSubsystems )->flatten ()

context AssemblyContext
def : getInnerAllocationContext ( allocation : Allocation )
  : Set ( Allocation ) =

if allocation . allocationContexts ->includes ( self )
then
  allocation . allocationContexts ->select ( a | a = self )
else
  -- otherwise , if inner is SubSystem , descend into it recursively
  if ( self . encapsulatedComponent . oclIsKindOf ( SubSystem ))
  then
    result ->including (
      self . encapsulatedComponent . oclAsType ( SubSystem ). assemblyContexts .
      . getInnerAllocationContext ( allocation )
    )
  else
    -- If inner is not a SubSystem , return null . This can only happen
    -- if this SubSystem is not used at all in the system , so that no
    -- allocation exist , because otherwise , non-SubSystems have to be
    -- allocated by constraint .
    OclVoid
  endif
endif
```

The remaining selection rules are the same as for the component selection degree, just that they need to be called on self.subsystem for the chosen result tuple.

Additionally, the values are defined as follows. Let tuple denote the chosen tuple of the subsystem to change. The following query reuses the query getCompatibleComponents defined for AssemblyContexts in Section 7.2.1. As described above, the values of AllocationContext.resourceContainer of the newly added AllocationContexts do not have to be defined in the value rules for this degree, because new Allocation Degrees are instantiated for them.

valueRule(Allocation.allocationContexts) is:

```
context Allocation
def : getPossibleAllocations : Set ( Set ( AllocationContext ) ) =

— determine the alternative subsystems, including the current one
— collectNested does not flatten the result
tuple . subsystem . getAllocationContextsForSubSystemAlternatives ( self ,
   tuple . allocationcontexts )


context SubSystem
def : getAllocationContextsForSubSystemAlternatives (
   allocation : Allocation ,
   allocationContextSet : Set ( AllocationContext ))
   : Set ( Set ( AllocationContext ) ) =

self . getCompatibleComponents —>select ( oclIsKindOf ( SubSystem ))
   — s is an alternative subsystem to the changed subsystem
   —>collectNested ( s |
      — create new AllocationContexts for all basic components in s
      s . getAllComponentsToAllocate —>collect ( component |
         — take the existing allocation if the component is from the
         — initial subsystem.
         let existingAllocationContexts : Set ( AllocationContext )
            = allocation . allocationContexts —>select ( a | allocationContextSet
            —>includes ( a ))
         if ( existingAllocationContext —>size > 0)
            then
               — can only be one as every component in a subsystem can
               — only be allocated once
               existingAllocationContext
            else
            — create new allocation context
            AllocationContext {
               assemblyContext : AssemblyContext = component ;
               resourceContainer : ResourceContainer = OclVoid ;
            }
         endif
      )—>union (
         — all AllocationContexts that are not for the old SubSystem stay
         — the same
         allocation . allocationContexts —>select ( a |
            not allocationContextSet —>includes ( a )))
   )
```

```
context SubSystem
— gets all inner components of the subsystem that need to be allocated.
— Descends into inner subsystems.
def : getAllComponentsToAllocate : Set (AssemblyContext) =

self.assemblyContexts.encapsulatedComponent—>select(c |
  c.oclIsKindOf(SubSystem)).oclAsType(SubSystem)
    .getAllComponentsToAllocate
    —>union(self.assemblyContexts—>select(a |
      not a.encapsulatedComponent.oclIsKindOf(SubSystem)))
```

valueRule(AssemblyContext.encapsulatedComponent) is:

```
context AssemblyContext
def : getNewSubSystemValue (allocation : Allocation) : SubSystem =

tuple.subsystem.getCompatibleComponents—>select( s |
  s.oclIsKindOf(SubSystem) and
    — if all inner components are allocated, then this is the right one
  s.getAllComponentsToAllocate—>forall( c |
    allocation.allocationContexts
      .assemblyContexts.encapsulatedComponents—>includes(c)))
    — only one such SubSystem is found because each subsystem can only be
    — used once in the system.
```

The value rules for the connectors are the same as for the component selection degree.

As the component selection degree, Subsystem selection may open up additional component selection degrees of freedom. Additionally, it may open up additional Subsystem degrees.

The added and removed elements are as follows. These queries can be executed on the initial architecture model to determine the AllocationContexts that could be added, or on every other candidate model to determine the AllocationContexts that could be added relative to it. Added elements:

```
context Allocation

tuple.subsystem.getAllocationContextsForSubSystemAlternatives(self,
  tuple.allocationContexts)—>flatten()
    —>reject(a | self.allocationContexts.includes(a))
```

Removed elements are all AllocationContexts that are in the set of Allocation-Contexts to be varied with an instance of this degree of freedom and at the same time are currently used in the system:

```
context Allocation

-- select all allocation contexts that allocate any content of the
-- currently used subsystem
self.allocationContexts ->select( a |
  tuple.subsystem.getAllAllocatableComponents
    ->includes(a.assemblyContext)
)
```

```
context SubSystem
-- gets all inner components of the subsystem that could be allocated,
-- including inner subsystem.
def : getAllAllocatableComponents : Set (AssemblyContext) =

self.assemblyContexts.encapsulatedComponent ->select(c |
  c.oclIsKindOf(SubSystem)).oclAsType(SubSystem)
    .getAllAllocatableComponents
      ->union(self.assemblyContexts)
```

D. Quality of Service Modelling Language QML

This section introduces the Quality of Service Modelling Language QML (Frølund and Koistinen, 1998) and presents our extended EMOF model for it. QMl is a language to express quality of service requirements. The original language has been defined using an Extended Backus-Naur Form grammar in Frølund and Koistinen (1998). For the use in our model-based approach, we migrated the language to EMOF. The resulting models are shown in Figure D.13 to D.16. Our extensions to be able to express object-ives are marked with ⊛.

QML is structured in three levels. The first two levels of contract types and contract define quality metrics. *Contract types* (Figure D.16) define observations that can be made for a system as *dimensions*, for example that the response time of a service call can be observed. Dimensions can be grouped into *categories*, which correspond to quality attributes. Optionally,

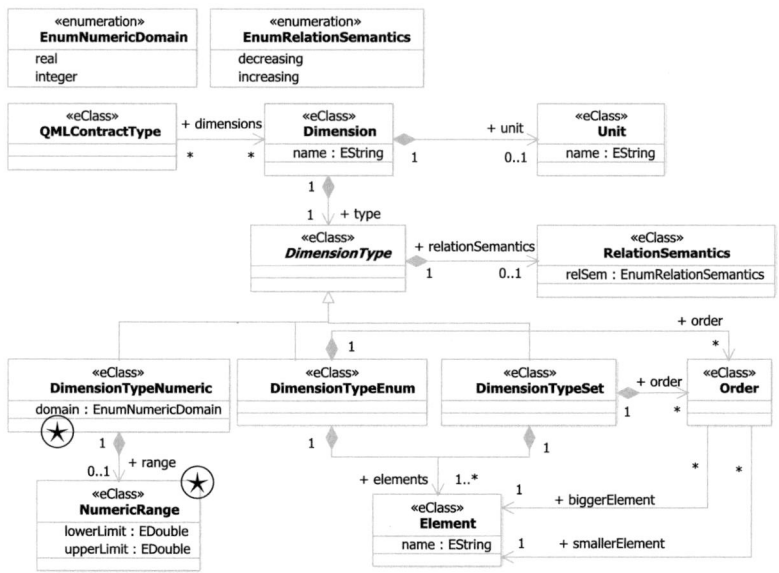

Figure D.13.: QML Contract Type Metamodel with our Extensions (marked ⋆), from (Noorshams, 2010) based on (Frølund and Koistinen, 1998)

an order on the dimension can be defined as *relation semantics*. While the original QML already allowed to define numeric dimensions, we extended these and added the possibility to define numeric ranges. For example, POFOD values can only range between 0 and 1.

QML *contracts* (Figure D.14) define how a dimension is evaluated as *evaluation aspects*. For example, when measuring the response time, it can be defined whether the mean response time or other point estimators are considered as the quality metric. Thus, evaluation aspects define the domain $\mathcal{V}^*_{qm}$ of a quality metric *qm*. The order $\leq_{qm}$ of a quality metric is defined on the contract type level as relation semantics (see above). We extended the metamodel to be able to distinguish between constraints (i.e. quality requirements, which additionally define a value to achieve) and objectives (i.e. quality criteria that are to be optimized). This distinction is currently made at the contract level, however, in accordance with our quality terms, in should be made at the profile level.

QML thus modularizes the quality metric definition: If two metrics "mean response time" and "90% quantile response time" are to be defined, they can both refer to a shared response time dimension.

QML *profiles* (Figure D.15 finally bind quality metrics to artefacts in the system, thus defining quality criteria. To bind the concepts to a concrete CBA metamodel, the Requirements class has to be extended by CBA-metamodel-specific classes, in our case for the PCM UsageScenarioRequirement and EntryLevelSystemRequirement, which define the place in the system where the metric is collected. Addtionally, the scenario is defined by referencing a UsageModel and an Allocation for the PCM.

Finally, QML declarations (Figure D.16) define the root elements to create QML models.

E. OCL in EMOF

EMOF does not provide model elements to specify constraints. UML (and so CMOF) have a specific class Constraint to model such (Object Management Group (OMG), 2006d, p.40 Sec.9.6). Thus, we assume that a constraint is modelled as an EMOF::Operation where the OCL rule is written as an annotation using EMOF::Tag. The name is fixed to be OCL, the value contains the OCL query including one or several context statement (several for the helper methods) as defined by the grammar rule 12.12.1 packageDeclarationCS in the OCL specification (Object Management Group (OMG), 2006b, p.167). The first context statement is the main statement, the others are used for helper OCL statements (cf. OCL queries for the Allocation Degree in Section 7.3.1, for example).

Example: The value of the tag for the value rule *valueRule*(AllocationContext.resourceContainer) to select the available servers (from the Allocation Degree in Section 7.3.1) is the following String:

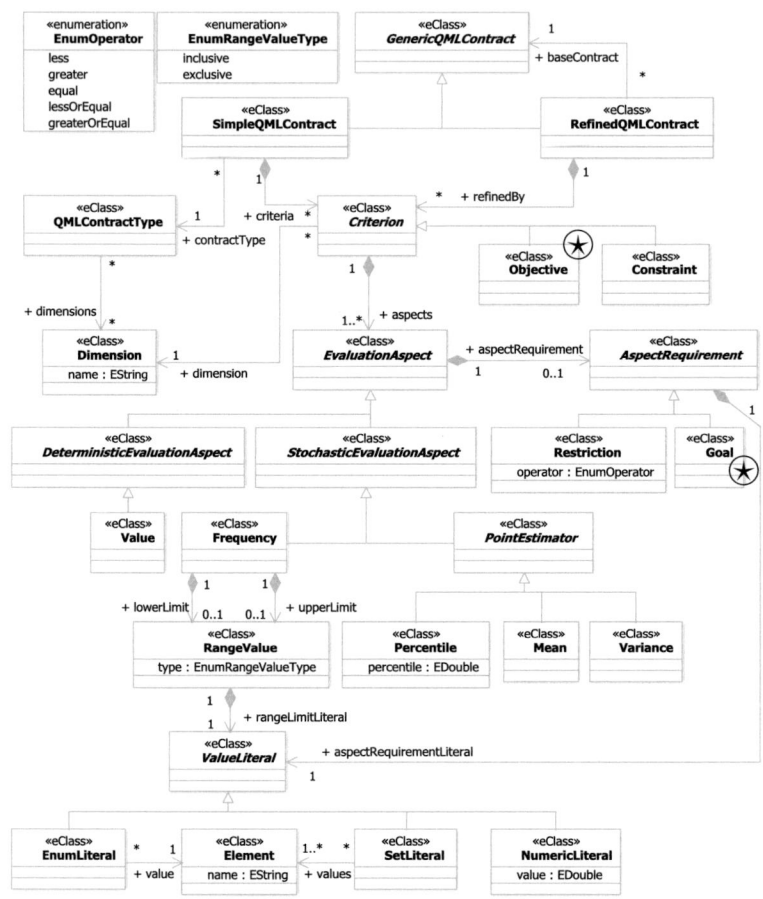

Figure D.14.: QML Contract Metamodel with our Extensions (marked ⋆), from (Noorshams, 2010) based on (Frølund and Koistinen, 1998)

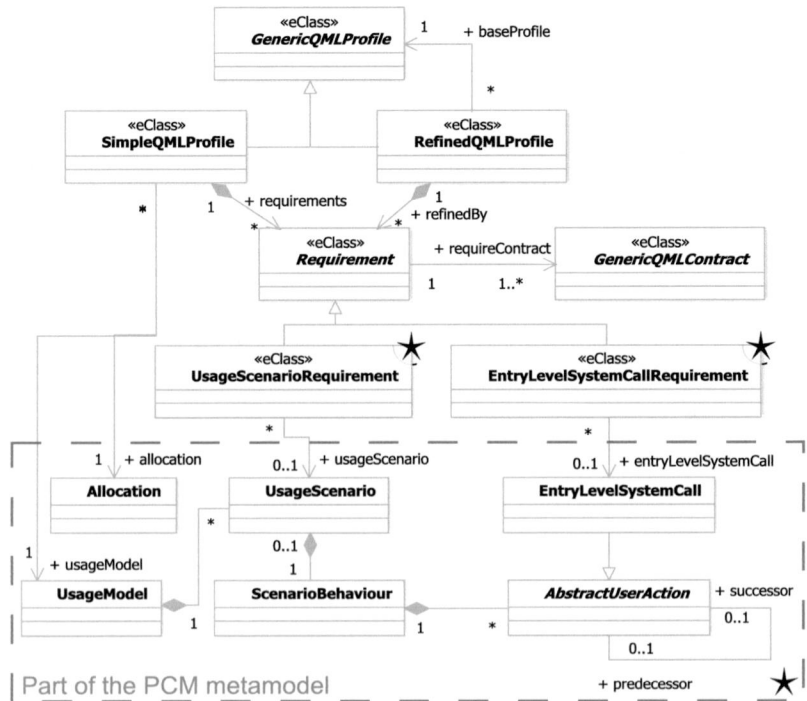

Figure D.15.: QML Profile Metamodel with our Extensions (marked ⋆), from (Noorshams, 2010) based on (Frølund and Koistinen, 1998)

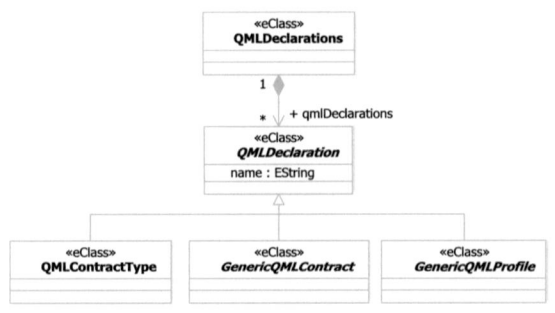

Figure D.16.: QML Declaration Metamodel, from (Noorshams, 2010) based on (Frølund and Koistinen, 1998)

```
context AllocationContext
def : getPossibleServers : Set ( ResourceContainer ) =

self . allocation . targetResourceEnvironment . resourceContainer –>select ( rc  |
  — has the required resources
  self . assemblyContext . encapsulatedComponent . getResourceTypes
    –>forAll ( rt | rc . activeResourceSpecifications –> includes ( rt ))
)


— collect all resource types used by a Repository component.
— Main two options:
—    Component is a BasicComponent, descend into behaviour description
—    Component is a ComposedStructure, descend into parts
context RepositoryComponent
def : getResourceTypes : Set ( ProcessingResourceType ) =

if self . oclIsKindOf ( BasicComponent )
then
  self . oclAsType ( BasicComponent ) . serviceEffectSpecifications
    –>select ( rdseff | rdseff . oclIsKindOf ( ResourceDemandingSEFF ))
      . getResourceTypes ()

    — an RDSEFF can contain InternalBehaviours that can be
    — called in multiple places of this SEFF
    –>union ( self . oclAsType ( BasicComponent ) . serviceEffectSpecifications
      –>select ( rdseff | rdseff . oclIsKindOf ( ResourceDemandingSEFF ))
        . resourceDemandingInternalBehaviours . getResourceTypes ())


else if self . oclIsKindOf ( ComposedProvidingRequiringEntity )
— both Subystems and ComposedComponents
then
    — recursively call this method on all inner RepositoryComponents
    self . oclAsType ( ComposedProvidingRequiringEntity ) . assemblyContexts
      . encapsulatedComponent . getResourceTypes ()
else
    — Other component types ( ProvidesComponentType or
    — CompleteComponentType ) that have no resource demands
    — OclVoid is the OCL null element that is also treated as an empty
    — Bag{} ( OCL specification, p. 140 sec 11.2.3 )
    OclVoid –>asSet ()
endif
endif


— handle all the different typs of actions in a RDSEFF that have
— resource demands.
context ResourceDemandingBehaviour
```

```
def : getResourceTypes : Set ( ProcessingResourceType ) =

self.steps ->select( icfa |
  icfa.oclIsKindOf(AbstractInternalControlFlowAction))
    .flatten().oclAsType(Set(AbstractInternalControlFlowAction))
      .resourceDemand.requiredResource
  ->union(
    — asynchronous forked behaviours
    self.steps ->select( fork | fork.oclIsKindOf(ForkAction))
      .flatten().oclAsType(Set(AbstractInternalControlFlowAction))
        .asynchronousForkedBehaviours.getResourceTypes()
  )->union(
    — synchronous forked behaviours
    self.steps ->select( fork | fork.oclIsKindOf(ForkAction))
      .flatten().oclAsType(Set(AbstractInternalControlFlowAction))
        .synchronisingBehaviours.synchronousForkedBehaviours
          .getResourceTypes()
  )->union(
    — loop behaviours
    self.steps ->select( loop | loop.oclIsKindOf(AbstractLoopAction))
      .flatten().oclAsType(Set(AbstractLoopAction))
        .bodyBehaviour.getResourceTypes()
  )->union(
    — branched behaviours
    self.steps ->select( branch | branch.oclIsKindOf(BranchAction))
      .flatten().oclAsType(Set(BranchAction))
        .branches.branchBehaviour.getResourceTypes()
  )->union(
    — recovery blocks
    self.steps ->select( recover |
      recover.oclIsKindOf(RecoveryBlockAction))
        .flatten().oclAsType(Set(RecoveryBlockAction))
          .recoveryBlockalternativeBehaviours.getResourceTypes()
  )
```

The parameters of the operation are ignored, so this matches EMF model objects where the parameters are used to pass the diagnostic chain to evaluate OCL statements.

F. Notational Conventions

For logic, I use the following convention to avoid the use of parentheses:

- $\neg$ is evaluated first

- $\wedge$ is evaluated next

- $\vee$ is evaluated next

- Quantifiers are evaluated next

- $\rightarrow$ is evaluated last.

Thus, $\forall x : A \wedge B$ is equivalent to $\forall x : (A \wedge B)$, whereas $(\forall x : A) \wedge B$ needs to be bracketed explicitly.

$A \subset B$ means $A \subsetneq B$. If $A = B$ is allowed, I write $A \subseteq B$. This notation fits the common notation of $<$ and $\leq$.

List of Figures

1.1. Traditional Model-based Quality Prediction Process (adapted from (H. Koziolek, 2008)) 6

1.2. Model-based Architecture Improvement Process with Feedback into Requirements Engineering 11

2.1. Main CBA Concepts 29

2.2. Component-based Development Process (from Cheesman and Daniels (2000)) 31

2.3. Software Quality Terms 38

2.4. Relationship between Real World, Model, and Metamodel from (Stahl and Völter, 2006, p.86) 44

2.5. General Modelling Schemata 45

2.6. Excerpt from EMOF 46

2.7. Excerpt of PCM: Allocation 47

2.8. Allocation Excerpt of PCM shown as an Instance of EMOF 47

2.9. Model-based Quantitative Quality Prediction 50

2.10. Example Feature Model for Messaging Configuration from (Happe et al., 2010) 57

2.11. Quality-driven Component-based Development Process by H. Koziolek and Happe, 2006 58

2.12. Quality Analysis Step by H. Koziolek and Happe, 2006 . 59

2.13. Simple Example PCM Model: Business Trip Booking System 61

2.14. Examples for Arbitrary Distribution Functions (Gouvêa et al., 2011) 63

2.15. Excerpt of the PCM Metamodel 65

2.16. Example LQN and CBML Models 71

2.17. Excerpt of the CBML Metamodel, Extracted from the
XML Schema 71

2.18. Excerpt of the ROBOCOP Metamodel, Extracted from
Natural Language Description and Graphics (Bondarev
et al., 2004; Bondarev and Chaudron, 2006) as well as the
ROBOCOP IDL (ROBOCOP consortium, 2003) 73

3.1. Example for Pareto Optimal Solutions 81

3.2. Basic Evolutionary Algorithm 87

3.3. Different Crossover Operators (adapted from (Luke, 2009)) 91

3.4. Hyper-volume Examples 99

5.1. Component-based Development Process with Quality
Exploration (based on (H. Koziolek and Happe, 2006)) . . 147

5.2. Quality Analysis Step in Component-based Development
Process (based on (H. Koziolek and Happe, 2006)) 148

5.3. Automated Architecture Exploration Workflow 150

5.4. Value Chart Example by Rohrberg (2010) for Result
Analysis and Decision Making Workflow (The bars in the
upper part reflect the utility of achieved quality properties
as defined in a utility function. The width of each column
in the upper part can be changed interactively by the user
to reflect the weights of objectives, and the ranking in the
lower part of the figure changes accordingly.) 153

5.5. Model-based Software Architecture Optimization 155

6.1. Alternative Implementation of the IBooking interface . . 170

6.2. Visualization of the Seven-dimensional Design Space of
the Example 176

6.3. A Architectural Candidate Model in the Example 177

6.4. An Additional Server with only Hard Disc Drive 194

6.5. Simple Example with Partially Connected Servers 196

6.6. Degree of Freedom and Change Concepts 205

6.7. Simple Example Metamodel Describing Allocation to
      Illustrate DoFs. 208

6.8. Degrees of Freedom in EMOF 211

6.9. Degree of Freedom Instance Metamodel for Models in
      EMOF 212

6.10. Outline of Design Space Section (Section 6.4) 214

7.1. Component Selection Example for Example Model from
      Figures 2.13 and 6.1. The bold properties in part (a) show
      the Properties to be updated. The bold Properties in
      part (b) show the updated values. Note that the figures
      only show the necessary parts from the model, all other
      Properties have been omitted. 238

7.2. Extended Example System with Component Parameter
      and Passive Resource 241

7.3. Example for Changed Allocation 249

7.4. Example for Changed Allocation with Replication 253

7.5. Example for Server Replication 255

7.6. Examples for Software Stacks 261

7.7. Example of an Explicit Modelling of Infrastructure
      Components by Hauck et al. (2009) 264

7.8. QuickConfirm Cache for the Example of a
      System-Specific Degree of Freedom 271

7.9. System Using the QuickConfirm Cache for the Example
      of a System-Specific Degree of Freedom 271

8.1. Evolutionary Optimization Process 287

8.2. The Beginning of an Exemplary Optimization Run 288

8.3. Resulting Candidates after 2 Iterations (Pareto-optimal
      Candidates: $\Diamond$, Initial Candidate: $\triangle$, Others $\times$) 289
8.4. Example PCM Model for Pareto-optimal Candidate c_6 . . 291
8.5. Metamodel for Candidate Vectors in EMOF 294
8.6. Quality Property Model in EMOF 297
8.7. Candidate Evaluation Steps 298
8.8. Metamodel for Evaluated Candidate Vectors in EMOF . . 299
8.9. Example System for Tactics 313
8.10. Integration of Tactics in the Reproduction Step. Cf.
      Fig 8.1 for an Overview of the Complete Process. 326
8.11. Hybrid Optimization Analytically Providing a Starting
      Population (Martens et al., 2010) 330
8.12. Allocation Scheme Starting Population (by Beyer (2010)) 331
8.13. Architecture of Generic CBA Optimization Framework . 333
8.14. CBA Optimization Framework using PCM and Opt4J . . 335
8.15. Example Search Landscape 339

9.1. PerOpteryx Tool 366
9.2. Degrees of Freedom in PerOpteryx 367
9.3. Business Reporting System: PCM Instance of the Case
      Study System 370
9.4. Usage Scenario for the BRS System 371
9.5. PCM Model of the Industrial Control System (by H.
      Koziolek et al., 2011c 375
9.6. Scatter-plots for the Overall Pareto Front 388
9.7. Costs-performance-trade-off in the Overall Pareto Front
      for Varying Number of Servers 389
9.8. Response Time Histogram for BRS Run (light grey
      histogram: all evaluated candidates, dark blue histogram:
      optimal candidates) 394

9.9. Costs Histogram for BRS Run (light grey histogram: all evaluated candidates, dark blue histogram: optimal candidates) 395

9.10. POFOD Histogram for BRS Run (light grey histogram: all evaluated candidates, dark blue histogram: optimal candidates) 395

9.11. Example: A Pareto-optimal BRS Candidate 396

9.12. Example: Another Pareto-optimal BRS candidate with Longer Response Time and Lower Costs 396

9.13. Scatter-plots for the Resulting Pareto Front 398

9.14. Surface Visualization of the resulting Pareto front 399

9.15. Sample Pareto Front of an Optimization Run for the ABB PCS (Units Obfuscated) 400

9.16. Potential Problem of the Coverage Indicator (by Noorshams (2010), Original Source (Zitzler, 1999)) in a Maximization Problem 406

9.17. Results for M.1: Pareto Front Coverage $C^*(P(T_r^i), P(R_r^i))$ of Runs Using Tactics T over Random Search Runs R for $r \in 0, ..., 9$ (Business Reporting System) 411

9.18. Results for M.1: Pareto Front Coverage $C^*(P(T_r^i), P(B_r^i))$ of Runs Using Tactics T over Standard Evolutionary Optimization B for $r \in 0, ..., 9$ (Business Reporting System) 411

9.19. Results for M.1: Hyper-volume Indicator $S^*(P(T_r^i), P(R_r^i))$ of Runs Using Tactics T over Random Search Runs R for $r \in 0, ..., 9$ (Business Reporting System) 412

9.20. Results for M.1: Hyper-volume Indicator $S^*(P(T_r^i), P(B_r^i))$ of Runs Using Tactics T over Standard Evolutionary Optimization B for $r \in 0, ..., 9$ (Business Reporting System) 412

9.21. Time Savings for BRS. The Label TS_c Denotes the Time Savings Metric $\mathscr{T}_c$. 414

9.22. Results for M.1: Pareto Front Coverage $C^*(P(T_r^i), P(B_r^i))$ of Runs Using Tactics T over Unguided Runs B for $r \in 0, ..., 9$ (ABB system) 417

9.23. Results for M.1: Hyper-volume Indicator $S^*(P(T_r^i), P(B_r^i))$ of Runs Using Tactics T over Unguided Runs B for $r \in 0, ..., 9$ (ABB system) 417

9.24. Result of an Optimization Run MC_0 with medium requirements $scen = M$ and the Constrained Tournament Method $c = C$. 423

9.25. Coverage Measure $\mathscr{C}^*(Wc_r^i, B_r^i)$ in Scenario W, Aggregated over Runs r, for Both Methods $c \in \{C, G\}$ . . 424

9.26. Size of the Dominated Space $\mathscr{S}^*(Wc_r^i)$ in Scenario M, Compared to the Basic Scenario $\mathscr{S}(B_r^i)$, Aggregated over Runs r, for Both Methods $c \in \{C, G\}$ 424

9.27. Coverage Measure $\mathscr{C}^*(Mc_r^i, B_r^i)$ in Scenario M, Aggregated over Runs r, for Both Methods $c \in \{C, G\}$ . . 425

9.28. Size of the Dominated Space $\mathscr{S}^*(Mc_r^i)$ in Scenario M, Compared to the Basic Scenario $\mathscr{S}(B_r^i)$, Aggregated over Runs r, for Both Methods $c \in \{C, G\}$ 425

9.29. Coverage Measure $\mathscr{C}^*(Sc_r^i, B_r^i)$ in Scenario S, Aggregated over Runs r, for Both Methods $c \in \{C, G\}$ 425

9.30. Size of the Dominated Space $\mathscr{S}^*(Sc_r^i)$ in Scenario S, Compared to the Basic Scenario $\mathscr{S}(B_r^i)$, Aggregated over Runs r, for Both Methods $c \in \{C, G\}$ 426

9.31. Coverage Measure $\mathscr{C}^*(Oc_r^i, B_r^i)$ in Scenario O, Aggregated over Runs r, for Both Methods $c \in \{C, G\}$ . . 426

9.32. Size of the Dominated Space $\mathscr{S}^*(Oc_r^i)$ in Scenario O, Compared to the Basic Scenario $\mathscr{S}(B_r^i)$, Aggregated over Runs r, for Both Methods $c \in \{C, G\}$ 426

9.33. Time Savings 427

A.1. Key for RDSEFF Diagram 449

A.2. Key for Combined System and Allocation Diagram . . . 450

A.3. PCM Composition 452

A.4. PCM Core Entity Overview 453

A.5. PCM Delegation 453

A.6. PCM Behaviour Overview 454

A.7. PCM Action Hierarchy 454

A.8. Resource Repository 455

A.9. Three Cases of Navigation when Determining
Communication Partners. Here: Current Component is
the Receiver (Situation in getSenders() method) 457

C.10. Extended PCM to Enable Replication of Components . . 481

C.11. Resource Repository for ROBOCOP 487

C.12. Performance Completions for a Web Server from
(Woodside et al., 2002), Shown as a Use Case Map 490

D.13. QML Contract Type Metamodel with our Extensions
(marked ⋆), from (Noorshams, 2010) based on (Frølund
and Koistinen, 1998) 496

D.14. QML Contract Metamodel with our Extensions (marked
⋆), from (Noorshams, 2010) based on (Frølund and
Koistinen, 1998) 498

D.15. QML Profile Metamodel with our Extensions (marked ⋆),
from (Noorshams, 2010) based on (Frølund and
Koistinen, 1998) 499

D.16. QML Declaration Metamodel, from (Noorshams, 2010)
based on (Frølund and Koistinen, 1998) 499

List of Tables

2.1. Example Quality Metrics 39
2.2. Quality Property Prediction Results 64

4.1. Problem Criteria for Performance Improvement Methods . 112
4.2. Solution Criteria for Performance Improvement Methods . 113
4.3. Flexibility Criteria for Performance Improvement Methods 113
4.4. Problem Criteria for Improvement Methods for Multiple
      Quality Attributes 121
4.5. Solution Criteria for Improvement Methods for Multiple
      Quality Attributes 122
4.6. Flexibility Criteria for Improvement Methods for Multiple
      Quality Attributes 123

6.1. Degrees of Freedom in the Example 175
6.2. Choices for two Architectural Candidate Models 177
6.3. Required Information to Produce Changes 198
6.4. Example DoF 200
6.5. DoFI Definitions for the Example Model 219

7.1. Software and Deployment Degrees of Freedom for CBA
      Overview, with Examples for Primary Changeable
      Elements in the PCM (Default) or Another Metamodel
      (Indicated) 233

7.2. Custom Degrees of Freedom for CBA Overview, with
Examples for Primary Changeable Elements in the PCM
(Default) or Another Metamodel (Indicated) 234

7.3. Evaluation of the PCM Example with Changed
Processing Rates (Columns "P. speed") (Costs in units,
mean response time (column "Mean RT") in seconds. . . . 258

8.1. Performance Improvement Tactics (Koziolek et al., 2011a) 311

8.2. Performance Improvement Tactics (continued) (Koziolek
et al., 2011a) 312

8.3. Reliability Improvement Tactics (Brosch et al., 2011b) . . 321

9.1. Component Selection in BRS: Changes to Initially Used
Component (dem. = demand, failure prob. = failure
probability) 372

9.2. Component Selection in ABB PCS: Relative Changes to
Initially Used Component 376

9.3. Configuration of Tactics in Allocation Study 384

9.4. Allocation Validation Study: Initial Candidate no. 0 and
Chosen Candidates no. 1–3 384

9.5. Measurement vs Predictions for Selected Candidates . . . 385

9.6. CPU Resource Demand in BRS System 390

9.7. Descriptive Statistics for Quality Properties in BRS Run . 394

9.8. Statistical Significance and Time Savings Average 413

9.9. Intensification Phase Results (sig. = significant) 420

9.10. Quality Bound Scenarios 422

A.1. Mapping of PCM Concepts to General CBA Concepts . . 451

Bibliography

Aguirre, H. and Tanaka, K. (2005). Selection, Drift, Recombination, and Mutation in Multiobjective Evolutionary Algorithms on Scalable MNK-Landscapes. In Coello Coello, C. A., Hernández Aguirre, A., and Zitzler, E., editors, *Evolutionary Multi-Criterion Optimization. Third International Conference, EMO 2005*, volume 3410 of *Lecture Notes in Computer Science*, pages 355–369, Guanajuato, México. Springer-Verlag, Berlin, Germany.

Aleti, A., Björnander, S., Grunske, L., and Meedeniya, I. (2009a). Archeopterix: An extendable tool for architecture optimization of AADL models. In *Proceedings of the 2009 ICSE Workshop on Model-Based Methodologies for Pervasive and Embedded Software (MOMPES 2009)*, pages 61–71. IEEE Computer Society.

Aleti, A., Buhnova, B., Grunske, L., Koziolek, A., and Meedeniya, I. (2013). Software architecture optimization methods: A systematic literature review. *IEEE Transactions on Software Engineering*, 39(5):658–683.

Aleti, A., Grunske, L., Meedeniya, I., and Moser, I. (2009b). Let the ants deploy your software - an ACO based deployment optimisation strategy. In *ASE 2009, 24th IEEE/ACM International Conference on Automated Software Engineering, Auckland, New Zealand, November 16-20, 2009*, pages 505–509. IEEE Computer Society.

Arns, M., Buchholz, P., and Müller, D. (2009). OPEDo: a tool for the optimization of performance and dependability models. *SIGMETRICS Performance Evaluation Review*, 36(4):22–27.

Bachmann, F., Bass, L., and Klein, M. (2003). Deriving architectural tactics: A step toward methodical architectural design. Technical Report CMU/SEI-2003-TR-004, CarnegieMellon SEI, Pittsburgh, PA.

Bachmann, F., Bass, L., Klein, M., and Shelton, C. (2005). Designing software architectures to achieve quality attribute requirements. *IEE Proceedings - Software*, 152(4):153–165.

Balsamo, S., Di Marco, A., Inverardi, P., and Simeoni, M. (2004). Model-Based Performance Prediction in Software Development: A Survey. *IEEE Transactions on Software Engineering*, 30(5):295–310.

Bass, L., Clements, P., and Kazman, R. (2003). *Software Architecture in Practice, Second Edition*. Addison-Wesley, Reading, MA, USA.

Becker, S. (2008a). Coupled Model Transformations. In *WOSP '08: Proceedings of the 7th International Workshop on Software and performance*, pages 103–114, New York, NY, USA. ACM.

Becker, S. (2008b). *Coupled Model Transformations for QoS Enabled Component-Based Software Design*, volume 1 of *Karlsruhe Series on Software Quality*. Universitätsverlag Karlsruhe.

Becker, S., Grunske, L., Mirandola, R., and Overhage, S. (2006). Performance Prediction of Component-Based Systems: A Survey from an Engineering Perspective. In Reussner, R., Stafford, J., and Szyperski, C., editors, *Architecting Systems with Trustworthy Components*, volume 3938 of *Lecture Notes in Computer Science*, pages 169–192. Springer-Verlag Berlin Heidelberg.

Becker, S., Koziolek, H., and Reussner, R. (2009). The Palladio component model for model-driven performance prediction. *Journal of Systems and Software*, 82:3–22.

Belton, V. and Stewart, T. J. (2002). *Multiple criteria decision analysis - an integrated approach*. Springer.

Bernardo, M. and Hillston, J., editors (2007). *Formal Methods for Performance Evaluation (7th International School on Formal Methods for the Design of Computer, Communication, and Software Systems, SFM2007)*, volume 4486 of *Lecture Notes in Computer Science*. Springer-Verlag, Berlin, Germany.

Berntsson Svensson, R., Gorschek, T., Regnell, B., Torkar, R., Shahrokni, A., and Feldt, R. (2011). Quality requirements in industrial practice – an extended interview study at eleven companies. *IEEE Transactions on Software Engineering*, preprint:1.

Bertoli, M., Casale, G., and Serazzi, G. (2009). JMT: performance engineering tools for system modeling. *SIGMETRICS Performance Evaluation Review*, 36(4):10–15.

Beume, N., Naujoks, B., and Emmerich, M. (2007). SMS-EMOA: Multiobjective selection based on dominated hypervolume. *European Journal of Operational Research*, 181(3):1653–1669.

Beyer, T. (2010). Domain-specific heuristics for automated improvement of pcm-based architectures. Karlsruhe Institute of Technology. Studienarbeit, Advisors: Ralf Reussner, Anne Martens. http://sdqweb.ipd.kit.edu/publications/pdfs/beyer2010a.pdf.

Bleuler, S., Laumanns, M., Thiele, L., and Zitzler, E. (2003). PISA — a platform and programming language independent interface for search algorithms. In Fonseca, C. M., Fleming, P. J., Zitzler, E., Deb, K., and

Thiele, L., editors, *Evolutionary Multi-Criterion Optimization Second International Conference, EMO 2003*, Lecture Notes in Computer Science, pages 494 – 508, Berlin. Springer.

Blum, C. and Roli, A. (2003). Metaheuristics in combinatorial optimization: Overview and conceptual comparison. *ACM Computing Surveys*, 35(3):268–308.

Boehm, B. W., Abts, C., Brown, A. W., Chulani, S., Clark, B. K., Horowitz, E., Madachy, R., Reifer, D. J., and Steece, B. (2000). *Software Cost Estimation with Cocomo II*. Prentice Hall PTR, Upper Saddle River, NJ, USA.

Boehm, B. W., Brown, J. R., and Lipow, M. (1976). Quantitative evaluation of software quality. In *Proceedings: 2nd International Conference on Software Engineering*, pages 592–605. IEEE Computer Society Press.

Boehm, B. W. and Valerdi, R. (2008). Achievements and challenges in cocomo-based software resource estimation. *IEEE Software*, 25(5):74–83.

Böhme, R. and Reussner, R. (2008a). On metrics and measurements. In *Dependability Metrics*, volume 4909 of *Lecture Notes in Computer Science*, chapter 2, pages 7–13. Springer-Verlag Berlin Heidelberg.

Böhme, R. and Reussner, R. (2008b). Validation of Predictions with Measurements. In *Dependability Metrics*, volume 4909 of *Lecture Notes in Computer Science*, chapter 3, pages 14–18. Springer-Verlag Berlin Heidelberg.

Bohner, S. A. and Arnold, R. S. (1996). *Software change impact analysis*. IEEE Computer Society Press.

Bondarev, E. and Chaudron, M. (2006). Compositional Performance Analysis of Component-Based Systems on Heterogeneous Multiprocessor

Platforms. In *Software Engineering and Advanced Applications, 2006. SEAA'06. 32nd EUROMICRO Conference on*, pages 81–91. IEEE.

Bondarev, E., Chaudron, M., Zhang, J., and Klomp, A. (2006). Quality-Oriented Design Space Exploration for Component-Based Architectures. Technical report, TU Eindhoven Department of Mathematics and Computer Science. Computer Science Report.

Bondarev, E., Chaudron, M. R. V., and de Kock, E. A. (2007). Exploring performance trade-offs of a JPEG decoder using the DeepCompass framework. In *WOSP '07: Proceedings of the 6th international workshop on Software and performance*, pages 153–163, New York, NY, USA. ACM Press.

Bondarev, E., de With, P., Chaudron, M., and Musken, J. (2005). Modelling of Input-Parameter Dependency for Performance Predictions of Component-Based Embedded Systems. In *Proceedings of the 31th EUROMICRO Conference (EUROMICRO'05)*.

Bondarev, E., Muskens, J., With, P. d., Chaudron, M., and Lukkien, J. (2004). Predicting real-time properties of component assemblies: A scenario-simulation approach. In *Proceedings of the 30th EUROMICRO Conference (EUROMICRO'04)*, pages 40–47, Washington, DC, USA. IEEE Computer Society.

Branke, J., Deb, K., Miettinen, K., and Slowinski, R., editors (2008). *Multiobjective Optimization. Interactive and Evolutionary Approaches*. Springer. Lecture Notes in Computer Science Vol. 5252, Berlin, Germany.

Briand, L. C., Emam, K. E., Surmann, D., Wieczorek, I., and Maxwell, K. (1999). An assessment and comparison of common software cost estimation modeling techniques. In *21st International Conference on Software Engineering (ICSE'99)*, pages 313–322.

Briegleb, V. (2007). Bericht: Probleme bei SAPs neuer Mittelstandssoftware. Heise online. 2007-04-16. URL: http://heise.de/-167703.

Briegleb, V. (2008). SAP soll für den Mittelstand attraktiver werden. Heise online. 2007-01-17. URL: http://heise.de/-135709.

Brosch, F., Buhnova, B., Koziolek, H., and Reussner, R. (2011a). Reliability Prediction for Fault-Tolerant Software Architectures. In *International ACM Sigsoft Conference on the Quality of Software Architectures (QoSA)*, pages 75–84, New York, NY, USA. ACM.

Brosch, F., Koziolek, H., Buhnova, B., and Reussner, R. (2010). Parameterized Reliability Prediction for Component-based Software Architectures. In *International Conference on the Quality of Software Architectures (QoSA)*, volume 6093 of *LNCS*, pages 36–51. Springer.

Brosch, F., Koziolek, H., Buhnova, B., and Reussner, R. (2011b). Architecture-based reliability prediction with the palladio component model. *Transactions on Software Engineering*, 38(6).

Buchholz, P. and Kemper, P. (2006). Optimization of markov models with evolutionary strategies based on exact and approximate analysis techniques. In *Third International Conference on the Quantitative Evaluation of Systems (QEST 2006), 11-14 September 2006, Riverside, California, USA*, pages 233–242. IEEE Computer Society.

Bures, T., Hnetynka, P., and Plasil, F. (2006). Sofa 2.0: Balancing advanced features in a hierarchical componentmodel. In *SERA '06: Proceedings of the Fourth International Conference on SoftwareEngineering Research, Management and Applications*, pages 40–48, Washington, DC, USA. IEEE Computer Society.

Cameron, P. J. (1994). *Combinatorics: Topics, Techniques, Algorithms*. Cambridge University Press, Cambridge, England.

Canfora, G., Penta, M. D., Esposito, R., and Villani, M. L. (2005). An approach for QoS-aware service composition based on genetic algorithms. In Beyer, H.-G. and O'Reilly, U.-M., editors, *Proc. of Genetic and Evolutionary Computation Conference (GECCO)*, pages 1069–1075. ACM.

Canfora, G., Penta, M. D., Esposito, R., and Villani, M. L. (2008). A framework for qos-aware binding and re-binding of composite web services. *Journal of Systems and Software*, 81(10):1754–1769.

Carenini, G. and Loyd, J. (2004). ValueCharts: Analyzing Linear Models Expressing Preferences and Evaluations. In *AVI '04: Proceedings of the Working Conference on Advanced Visual Interfaces*, pages 150–157, New York, NY, USA. ACM.

Charette, R. (2008). The software issues behind heathrow's t5 meltdown. IEEE Spectrum Blog The Risk Factor. 2008-05-12. URL: http://spectrum.ieee.org/riskfactor/computing/it/the_software_issues_behind_hea.

Cheesman, J. and Daniels, J. (2000). *UML Components: A Simple Process for Specifying Component-based Software*. Addison-Wesley, Reading, MA, USA.

Chen, S., Gorton, I., Liu, A., and Liu, Y. (2002). Performance Prediction of COTS Component-based Enterprise Applications. In Crnkovic, I., Schmidt, H., Stafford, J., and Wallnau, K., editors, *Proceeding of the 5th ICSE Workshop on Component-Based Software Engineering: Benchmarks for Predictable Assembly*, Orlando, Florida.

Cheng, B., de Lemos, R., Giese, H., Inverardi, P., Magee, J., Cheng, B., de Lemos, R., Giese, H., Inverardi, P., Magee, J., Andersson, J., Becker, B., Bencomo, N., Brun, Y., Cukic, B., Di Marzo Serugendo, G., Dustdar, S., Finkelstein, A., Gacek, C., Geihs, K., Grassi, V., Karsai, G., Kienle, H., Kramer, J., Litoiu, M., Malek, S., Mirandola, R., Müller, H., Park,

S., Shaw, M., Tichy, M., Tivoli, M., Weyns, D., and Whittle, J. (2009). Software engineering for self-adaptive systems: A research roadmap. In *Software Engineering for Self-Adaptive Systems*, volume 5525 of *Lecture Notes in Computer Science*, pages 1–26. Springer-Verlag, Berlin, Germany. 10.1007/978-3-642-02161-9_1.

Cheng, R., Gen, M., and Tsujimura, Y. (1999). A tutorial survey of job-shop scheduling problems using genetic algorithms. II. Hybrid genetic search strategies. *Computers & Industrial Eng.*, 37(1-2):51–55.

CIO Wirtschaftsnachrichten (2011). SAP enttäuscht trotz Umsatz- und Gewinnplus Erwartungen. CIO. 2011-04-28. URL: http://www.cio. de/news/wirtschaftsnachrichten/2273391/index2.html. Accessed, (Archived by WebCite at http://www.webcitation.org/ 5yZiceiaJ).

Clements, P. C., Kazman, R., and Klein, M. (2001). *Evaluating Software Architectures*. SEI Series in Software Engineering. Addison-Wesley, Boston, Mass.

Coello Coello, C. A. (1999). A comprehensive survey of evolutionary-based multiobjective optimization techniques. *Knowledge and Information Systems*, 1:269–308.

Coello Coello, C. A. (2002). Theoretical and numerical constraint-handling techniques used with evolutionary algorithms: A survey of the state of the art. *Computer Methods in Applied Mechanics and Engineering*, 191(11–12):1245–1287.

Coello Coello, C. A., Dhaenens, C., and Jourdan, L. (2010). Multi-objective combinatorial optimization: Problematic and context. In Coello, C. A. C., Dhaenens, C., and Jourdan, L., editors, *Advances in Multi-Objective Nature Inspired Computing*, volume 272 of *Studies in Computational Intelligence*, pages 1–21. Springer.

Coello Coello, C. A., Lamont, G. B., and Van Veldhuizen, D. A. (2007). *Evolutionary algorithms for solving multi-objective problems.* Genetic and evolutionary computation series. Springer-Verlag, New York, USA, New York, 2. edition.

Coello Coello, C. A. and Salazar Lechuga, M. (2002). MOPSO: A Proposal for Multiple Objective Particle Swarm Optimization. In Fogel, D. B., El-Sharkawi, M. A., Yao, X., Greenwood, G., Iba, H., Marrow, P., and Shackleton, M., editors, *Congress on Evolutionary Computation (CEC'2002)*, volume 2, pages 1051–1056, Piscataway, New Jersey. IEEE Service Center.

Coffman, Garey, and Johnson (1978). An application of bin-packing to multiprocessor scheduling. *SICOMP: SIAM Journal on Computing*, 7.

Corner, J. L. and Buchanan, J. T. (1997). Capturing decision maker preference: Experimental comparison of decision analysis and mcdm techniques. *European Journal of Operational Research*, 98(1):85 – 97.

Cortellessa, V., Di Marco, A., Eramo, R., Pierantonio, A., and Trubiani, C. (2010a). Digging into uml models to remove performance antipatterns. In *Proceedings of the 2010 ICSE Workshop on Quantitative Stochastic Models in the Verification and Design of Software Systems*, QUOVADIS '10, pages 9–16, New York, NY, USA. ACM.

Cortellessa, V. and Frittella, L. (2007). A framework for automated generation of architectural feedback from software performance analysis. In Wolter, K., editor, *Formal Methods and Stochastic Models for Performance Evaluation, Fourth European Performance Engineering Workshop, EPEW 2007, Berlin, Germany, September 27-28, 2007, Proceedings*, volume 4748 of *Lecture Notes in Computer Science*, pages 171–185. Springer.

Cortellessa, V., Marco, A. D., Eramo, R., Pierantonio, A., and Trubiani, C. (2009). Approaching the model-driven generation of feedback to remove software performance flaws. In *EUROMICRO-SEAA*, pages 162–169. IEEE Computer Society.

Cortellessa, V., Marinelli, F., and Potena, P. (2008). An optimization framework for 'build-or-buy' decisions in software architecture. *Computers & Operations Research*, 35(10):3090 – 3106. Part Special Issue: Search-based Software Engineering.

Cortellessa, V., Martens, A., Reussner, R., and Trubiani, C. (2010b). A process to effectively identify guilty performance antipatterns. In Rosenblum, D. and Taentzer, G., editors, *Fundamental Approaches to Software Engineering, 13th International Conference, FASE 2010*, pages 368–382. Springer-Verlag Berlin Heidelberg.

Crnković, I., Sentilles, S., Vulgarakis, A., and Chaudron, M. R. V. (2010). A classification framework for software component models. *IEEE Transactions on Software Engineering*. preprint.

Czarnecki, K. and Eisenecker, U. W. (2000). *Generative Programming*. Addison-Wesley, Reading, MA, USA.

Dakin, R. (1965). A tree search algorithm for mixed integer programming problems. *Computer Journal*, 8:250–255.

Deb, K. (2001). *Multi-Objective Optimization using Evolutionary Algorithms*. John Wiley & Sons, Chichester, UK.

Deb, K. (2005). Multi-Objective Optimization. In Burke, E. K. and Kendall, G., editors, *Search Methodologies. Introductory Tutorials in Optimization and Decision Support Techniques*, pages 273–316. Springer.

Deb, K. (2008). Introduction to evolutionary multiobjective optimization. In Branke, J., Deb, K., Miettinen, K., and Slowinski, R., editors, *Mul-*

tiobjective Optimization, volume 5252 of *Lecture Notes in Computer Science*, pages 59–96. Springer Berlin / Heidelberg.

Deb, K., Agrawal, S., Pratap, A., and Meyarivan, T. (2000). A fast elitist non-dominated sorting genetic algorithm for multi-objective optimization: NSGA-II. In *Parallel Problem Solving from Nature PPSN VI*, volume 1917/2000, pages 849–858. Springer-Verlag, Berlin, Germany.

Deb, K. and Goyal, M. (1996). A combined genetic adaptive search (GeneAS) for engineering design. *Computer Science and Informatics*, 26:30–45.

Deb, K., Mohan, M., and Mishra, S. (2003). Towards a quick computation of well-spread pareto-optimal solutions. In Fonseca, C., Fleming, P., Zitzler, E., Thiele, L., and Deb, K., editors, *Evolutionary Multi-Criterion Optimization*, volume 2632 of *Lecture Notes in Computer Science*, pages 68–68. Springer Berlin / Heidelberg. 10.1007/3-540-36970-8_16.

Deep, K. and Thakur, M. (2007). A new mutation operator for real coded genetic algorithms. *Applied Mathematics and Computation*, 193(1):211 – 230.

Díaz Pace, A., Kim, H., Bass, L., Bianco, P., and Bachmann, F. (2008). Integrating quality-attribute reasoning frameworks in the archE design assistant. In Becker, S., Plasil, F., and Reussner, R., editors, *Proceedings of the 4th International Conference on the Quality of Software-Architectures (QoSA 2008)*, volume 5281 of *Lecture Notes in Computer Science*, pages 171–188. Springer-Verlag, Berlin, Germany.

Dimitrov, A. (2010). Termination criteria for multi-objective optimization of software architectures. Karlsruhe Institute of Technology. Studienarbeit, Advisors: Ralf Reussner, Anne Martens. http://sdqweb.ipd.kit.edu/publications/pdfs/dimitrov2010a.pdf.

Dobrica, L. and Niemelä, E. (2002). A survey on software architecture analysis methods. *IEEE Trans. Software Eng*, 28(7):638–653.

Doerner, K., Gutjahr, W. J., Hartl, R. F., Strauss, C., and Stummer, C. (2004). Pareto Ant Colony Optimization: A Metaheuristic Approach to Multiobjective Portfolio Selection. *Annals of Operations Research*, 131(1–4):79–99.

Durillo, J. J., Nebro, A. J., and Alba, E. (2010). The jMetal framework for multi-objective optimization: Design and architecture. In *IEEE Congress on Evolutionary Computation*, pages 1–8. IEEE.

Efftinge, S., Friese, P., Haase, A., Hübner, D., Kadura, C., Kolb, B., Köhnlein, J., Moroff, D., Thoms, K., Völter, M., Schönbach, P., and Eysholdt, M. (2008). openArchitectureWare User Guide. `http://www.openarchitectureware.org/pub/documentation/4.3/openArchitectureWare-4.3-Reference.pdf`. Version 4.3.

Ehrgott, M. (2005). *Multicriteria Optimization*. Springer-Verlag, Berlin, Germany.

Ehrgott, M. and Gandibleux, X. (2004). Approximative solution methods for multiobjective combinatorial optimization. *TOP*, 12:1–63.

Eiben, A. E., Hinterding, R., and Michalewicz, Z. (1999). Parameter control in Evolutionary Algorithms. *IEEE Transactions on Evolutionary Computation*, 3(2):124.

El-Sayed, H., Cameron, D., and Woodside, M. (2001). Automation support for software performance engineering. In *SIGMETRICS '01: Proceedings of the 2001 ACM SIGMETRICS international conference on Measurement and modeling of computer systems*, pages 301–311, New York, NY, USA. ACM.

Eriksdotter, H. (2010). SAP-Projekt abgeschlossen – Business by Design eingeführt. CIO, 2010-06-29, URL: http://www.cio.de/saas/it-anwender/2238157/.

Fairbanks, G. (2010). *Just Enough Software Architecture: A Risk-Driven Approach.* Marshall & Brainerd, Boulder, CO, USA.

Falcone, G. (2010). *Hierachy-aware Software Metrics in Component Composition Hierarchies.* PhD thesis, Universität Mannheim.

Feiler, P. H., Gluch, D. P., and Hudak, J. J. (2006). The architecture analysis & design language (aadl): An introduction. Cmu/sei-2006-tn-011, Carnegie Mellon University, Software Engineering Institute.

Fonseca, C. M. and Fleming, P. J. (1993). Genetic algorithms for multiobjective optimization: Formulation, discussion and generalization. In Forrest, S., editor, *Proceedings of the 5th International Conference on Genetic Algorithms (ICGA'93)*, pages 416–423. Morgan Kaufmann.

Fonseca, C. M., Paquete, L., and López-Ibáñez, M. (2006). An Improved Dimension-Sweep Algorithm for the Hypervolume Indicator. In *2006 IEEE Congress on Evolutionary Computation (CEC'2006)*, pages 3973–3979, Vancouver, BC, Canada. IEEE.

Franks, G. (1999). *Performance Analysis of Distributed Server Systems.* PhD thesis, Department of Systems and Computer Engineering, Carleton University,Ottawa, Ontario, Canada.

Franks, G., Maly, P., Woodside, M., Petriu, D. C., and Hubbard, A. (2008). Layered queueing network solver and simulator user manual. Revision 7586 for LQN Solver Tools version 4.3. 7586.

Franks, G., Omari, T., Woodside, C. M., Das, O., and Derisavi, S. (2009). Enhanced modeling and solution of layered queueing networks. *IEEE Trans. on Software Engineering*, 35(2):148–161.

Frølund, S. and Koistinen, J. (1998). Quality-of-Service Specification in Distributed Object Systems. Technical Report HPL-98-159, Hewlett Packard, Software Technology Laboratory.

Garlan, D. and Shaw, M. (1994). An introduction to software architecture. Technical Report CS-94-166, Carnegie Mellon University, School of Computer Science.

Glass, R. L. (1998). *Software Runaways: Monumental Software Disasters.* Prentice Hall, Englewood Cliffs, NJ, USA.

Gokhale, S. S. (2007). Architecture-based software reliability analysis: Overview and limitations. *IEEE Trans. on Dependable and Secure Computing*, 4(1):32–40.

Goldberg, D. E. (1989). *Genetic Algorithms in Search, Optimization and Machine Learning.* Addison-Wesley Publishing Company, Reading, Massachusetts.

Goseva-Popstojanova, K. and Trivedi, K. S. (2001). Architecture-based approach to reliability assessment of software systems. *Performance Evaluation*, 45(2-3):179–204.

Gouvêa, D. D., Muniz, C., Pinto, G., Avritzer, A., Leão, R. M. M., de Souza e Silva, E., Diniz, M. C., Berardinelli, L., Leite, J. C. B., Mossé, D., Cai, Y., Dalton, M., Kapova, L., and Koziolek, A. (2011). Experience building non-functional requirement models of a complex industrial architecture. In Kounev, S., Cortellessa, V., Mirandola, R., and Lilja, D. J., editors, *Proceedings of the second joint WOSP/SIPEW international conference on Performance engineering (ICPE 2011)*, pages 43–54, New York, NY, USA. ACM.

Gray, J., Lin, Y., and Zhang, J. (2006). Automating change evolution in model-driven engineering. *Computer*, 39(2):51–58.

Grefenstette, J. J. (1987). Incorporating problem specific knowledge into genetic algorithms. In Davis, L., editor, *Genetic Algorithms and Simulated Annealing*, Research Notes in Artificial Intelligence, pages 42–60, London. Pitman Publishing.

Gries, M. (2003). Methods for evaluating and covering the design space during early design development. Technical Report UCB/ERL M03/32, Electronics Research Lab, University of California at Berkeley.

Grunske, L. (2006). Identifying "good" architectural design alternatives with multi-objective optimization strategies. In Osterweil, L. J., Rombach, H. D., and Soffa, M. L., editors, *28th International Conference on Software Engineering (ICSE 2006)*, pages 849–852. ACM.

Grunske, L. and Joyce, D. (2008). Quantitative risk-based security prediction for component-based systems with explicitly modeled attack profiles. *Journal of Systems and Software*, 81(8):1327–1345.

Grunske, L., Lindsay, P. A., Bondarev, E., Papadopoulos, Y., and Parker, D. (2006). An outline of an architecture-based method for optimizing dependability attributes of software-intensive systems. In de Lemos, R., Gacek, C., and Romanovsky, A. B., editors, *Architecting Dependable Systems IV*, volume 4615 of *Lecture Notes in Computer Science*, pages 188–209. Springer-Verlag, Berlin, Germany.

Happe, J. (2008). *Predicting Software Performance in Symmetric Multicore and Multiprocessor Environments*. Dissertation, University of Oldenburg, Germany.

Happe, J., Becker, S., Rathfelder, C., Friedrich, H., and Reussner, R. H. (2010). Parametric Performance Completions for Model-Driven Performance Prediction. *Performance Evaluation (PE)*, 67(8):694–716.

Happe, J., Koziolek, H., and Reussner, R. H. (2006). Parametric Performance Contracts for Software Components with Concurrent Behaviour.

In de Boer, F. S. and Mencl, V., editors, *Proceedings of the 3rd International Workshop on Formal Aspects of Component Software (FACS)*, volume 182 of *Electronic Notes in Theoretical Computer Science*, pages 91–106.

Harman, M. (2007). The current state and future of search based software engineering. In Briand, L. C. and Wolf, A. L., editors, *International Conference on Software Engineering, ISCE 2007, Workshop on the Future of Software Engineering, FOSE 2007*, pages 342–357. IEEE.

Harman, M., Mansouri, S., and Zhang, Y. (2009). Search based software engineering: A comprehensive analysis and review of trends techniques and applications. Technical Report TR-09-03, Department of Computer Science, King's College London.

Hauck, M., Happe, J., and Reussner, R. (2011). Towards Performance Prediction for Cloud Computing Environments Based on Goal-oriented Measurements. In *Proceedings of the 1st International Conference on Cloud Computing and Services Science (CLOSER 2011)*, pages 616–622. SciTePress.

Hauck, M., Kuperberg, M., Krogmann, K., and Reussner, R. (2009). Modelling Layered Component Execution Environments for Performance Prediction. In *Proceedings of the 12th International Symposium on Component Based Software Engineering (CBSE 2009)*, number 5582 in LNCS, pages 191–208. Springer.

Holland, J. H. (1975). *Adaption in Natural and Artificial Systems*. University of Michigan Press, Ann Arbor, Michigan.

Huber, N., Becker, S., Rathfelder, C., Schweflinghaus, J., and Reussner, R. (2010). Performance Modeling in Industry: A Case Study on Storage Virtualization. In *ACM/IEEE 32nd International Conference on Software*

Engineering, Software Engineering in Practice Track, pages 1–10, New York, NY, USA. ACM.

IEEE Std. 1471-2000 (2000). *IEEE Recommended Practice for Architectural Description of Software-intensive Systems.* IEEE Standards Board, New York, NY, USA.

IEEE Std 610.12-1990 (1990). *IEEE Standard Glossary of Software Engineering Terminology.* IEEE Standards Board, New York, NY, USA.

Immonen, A. and Niemelä, E. (2008). Survey of reliability and availability prediction methods from the viewpoint of software architecture. *Software and System Modeling*, 7(1):49–65.

Intel Corporation (2010). Intel®processor price list, effective feb 8th, 2010. `http://www.intc.com/priceList.cfm`. last visit March 10th, 2010.

ISO/IEC 9126-1:2001(E) (2001). *Software engineering – Product quality – Part 1: Quality model.* International Organization for Standardization, Geneva, Switzerland.

Jain, R. (1991). *The Art of Computer Systems Performance Analysis : Techniques forExperimental Design, Measurement, Simulation, and Modeling.* Wiley.

Jin, Y. and Branke, J. (2005). Evolutionary optimization in uncertain environments - a survey. *IEEE Transactions on Evolutionary Computation*, 9(3):303–318.

Jørgensen, M. (2007). Forecasting of software development work effort: Evidence on expert judgement and formal models. *International Journal of Forecasting*, 23(3):449 – 462.

Kapova, L. (2011). *Configurable Software Performance Completions through Higher-Order Model Transformations.* PhD thesis, Institut für

Programmstrukturen und Datenorganisation (IPD), Karlsruher Institut für Technologie, Karlsruhe, Germany.

Kapova, L. and Becker, S. (2010). Systematic refinement of performance models for concurrent component-based systems. In *7th International Workshop on Formal Engineering approaches to Software Components and Architectures (FESCA)*, Electronic Notes in Theoretical Computer Science. Elsevier.

Kapova, L. and Reussner, R. (2010). Application of advanced model-driven techniques in performance engineering. In Aldini, A., Bernardo, M., Bononi, L., and Cortellessa, V., editors, *Computer Performance Engineering*, volume 6342 of *Lecture Notes in Computer Science*, pages 17–36. Springer Berlin / Heidelberg. 10.1007/978-3-642-15784-4_2.

Keeney, Ralph L. ; Raiffa, H. (2003). *Decisions with multiple objectives : preferences and value tradeoffs*. Cambridge University Press, Cambridge [u.a.], [reprinted] edition.

Kienzle, J. (2003). Software fault tolerance: An overview. In *Proc. of Ada-Europe*, volume 2655 of *LNCS*, pages 45–67. Springer.

Klein, M. H., Ralya, T., Pollak, B., Obenza, R., Gonza, M., and Harbour, L. (1993). *A Practitioners Handbook for Real-Time Analysis: Guide to Rate Monotonic Analysis for Real Time Systems*. Kluwer Academic Publishers,.

Knowles, J. (2006). ParEGO: a hybrid algorithm with on-line landscape approximation for expensive multiobjective optimization problems. *IEEE Trans. Evolutionary Computation*, 10(1):50–66.

Knowles, J., Thiele, L., and Zitzler, E. (2006). A tutorial on the performance assessment of stochastic multiobjective optimizers. 214, Computer Engineering and Networks Laboratory (TIK), ETH Zurich, Switzerland. revised version.

Knowles, J. D. and Corne, D. (2002). Towards landscape analyses to inform the design of hybrid local search for the multiobjective quadratic assignment problem. In Abraham, A., del Solar, J. R., and Köppen, M., editors, *HIS*, volume 87 of *Frontiers in Artificial Intelligence and Applications*, pages 271–279. IOS Press.

Knowles, J. D. and Corne, D. W. (2000). Approximating the Nondominated Front Using the Pareto Archived Evolution Strategy. *Evolutionary Computation*, 8(2):149–172.

Koziolek, A., Koziolek, H., and Reussner, R. (2011a). Peropteryx: automated application of tactics in multi-objective software architecture optimization. In Crnkovic, I., Stafford, J. A., Petriu, D. C., Happe, J., and Inverardi, P., editors, *Joint proceedings of the Seventh International ACM SIGSOFT Conference on the Quality of Software Architectures and the 2nd ACM SIGSOFT International Symposium on Architecting Critical Systems (QoSA-ISARCS 2011)*, pages 33–42. ACM, New York, NY, USA.

Koziolek, A., Noorshams, Q., and Reussner, R. (2011b). Focussing multi-objective software architecture optimization using quality of service bounds. In Dingel, J. and Solberg, A., editors, *Models in Software Engineering, Workshops and Symposia at MODELS 2010, Oslo, Norway, October 3-8, 2010, Reports and Revised Selected Papers*, volume 6627 of *Lecture Notes in Computer Science*, pages 384–399. Springer-Verlag Berlin Heidelberg.

Koziolek, A. and Reussner, R. (2011). Towards a generic quality optimisation framework for component-based system models. In Crnkovic, I., Stafford, J. A., Bertolino, A., and Cooper, K. M. L., editors, *Proceedings of the 14th international ACM Sigsoft symposium on Component based software engineering*, CBSE '11, pages 103–108, New York, NY, USA. ACM, New York, NY, USA.

Koziolek, H. (2008). *Parameter Dependencies for Reusable Performance Specifications of Software Components*, volume 2 of *The Karlsruhe Series on Software Design and Quality*. Universitätsverlag Karlsruhe.

Koziolek, H. (2010). Performance evaluation of component-based software systems: A survey. *Performance Evaluation*, 67(8):634–658. Special Issue on Software and Performance.

Koziolek, H. (2011). Sustainability evaluation of software architectures: A systematic review. In *Proc. 7th Int. ACM/SIGSOFT Conf. on the Quality of Software Architectures (QoSA'11)*. ACM.

Koziolek, H., Becker, S., and Happe, J. (2007). Predicting the Performance of Component-based Software Architectures with different Usage Profiles. In *Proc. 3rd International Conference on the Quality of Software Architectures (QoSA'07)*, volume 4880 of *Lecture Notes in Computer Science*, pages 145–163. Springer-Verlag Berlin Heidelberg.

Koziolek, H. and Brosch, F. (2009). Parameter dependencies for component reliability specifications. In *Proceedings of the 6th International Workshop on Formal Engineering approaches to Software Components and Architectures (FESCA)*, volume 253(1) of *ENTCS*, pages 23 – 38. Elsevier.

Koziolek, H. and Firus, V. (2005). Empirical Evaluation of Model-based Performance Predictions Methods in Software Development. In Reussner, R. H., Mayer, J., Stafford, J. A., Overhage, S., Becker, S., and Schroeder, P. J., editors, *Proceeding of the first International Conference on the Quality of Software Architectures (QoSA'05)*, volume 3712 of *Lecture Notes in Computer Science*, pages 188–202. Springer-Verlag Berlin Heidelberg.

Koziolek, H. and Firus, V. (2006). Parametric Performance Contracts: Non-Markovian Loop Modelling and an Experimental Evaluation. In Kuester-

Filipe, J., Poernomo, I. H., and Reussner, R. H., editors, *Proc. of the 5th Int. Workshop on Formal Foundations of Embedded Software and Component-Based Software Architectures (FESCA'06)*, volume 176(2) of *ENTCS*, pages 69–87. Elsevier Science Inc.

Koziolek, H. and Happe, J. (2006). A QoS Driven Development Process Model for Component-Based Software Systems. In Gorton, I., Heineman, G. T., Crnkovic, I., Schmidt, H. W., Stafford, J. A., Szyperski, C. A., and Wallnau, K. C., editors, *Proc. 9th Int. Symposium on Component-Based Software Engineering (CBSE'06)*, volume 4063 of *Lecture Notes in Computer Science*, pages 336–343. Springer-Verlag Berlin Heidelberg.

Koziolek, H., Happe, J., and Becker, S. (2006). Parameter Dependent Performance Specification of Software Components. In Hofmeister, C., Crnkovic, I., Reussner, R. H., and Becker, S., editors, *Proc. 2nd Int. Conf. on the Quality of Software Architectures (QoSA'06)*, volume 4214 of *Lecture Notes in Computer Science*, pages 163–179. Springer-Verlag Berlin Heidelberg.

Koziolek, H. and Reussner, R. (2008). A Model Transformation from the Palladio Component Model to Layered Queueing Networks. In *Performance Evaluation: Metrics, Models and Benchmarks, SIPEW 2008*, volume 5119 of *Lecture Notes in Computer Science*, pages 58–78. Springer-Verlag Berlin Heidelberg.

Koziolek, H., Schlich, B., Bilich, C., Weiss, R., Becker, S., Krogmann, K., Trifu, M., Mirandola, R., and Koziolek, A. (2011c). An industrial case study on quality impact prediction for evolving service-oriented software. In Taylor, R. N., Gall, H., and Medvidovic, N., editors, *Proceeding of the 33rd international conference on Software engineering (ICSE 2011), Software Engineering in Practice Track*, pages 776–785. ACM, New York, NY, USA. Acceptance Rate: 18% (18/100).

Krogmann, K. (2010). *Reconstruction of Software Component Architectures and Behaviour Models using Static and Dynamic Analysis.* PhD thesis, Karlsruhe Institute of Technology (KIT), Karlsruhe, Germany.

Krogmann, K., Kuperberg, M., and Reussner, R. (2010). Using Genetic Search for Reverse Engineering of Parametric Behaviour Models for Performance Prediction. *IEEE Transactions on Software Engineering*, 36(6):865–877.

Krogmann, K., Schweda, C. M., Buckl, S., Kuperberg, M., Martens, A., and Matthes, F. (2009). Improved Feedback for Architectural Performance Prediction using Software Cartography Visualizations. In Mirandola, R., Gorton, I., and Hofmeister, C., editors, *Architectures for Adaptive Systems (Proceedings of QoSA 2009)*, volume 5581 of *Lecture Notes in Computer Science*, pages 52–69. Springer.

Kruchten, P. (2004). An ontology of architectural design decisions. In Bosch, J., editor, *2nd Groningen Workshop on Software Variability Management*, Groningen, NL. Rijksuniversiteit Groningen.

Künzli, S. (2006). *Efficient Design Space Exploration for Embedded Systems.* PhD thesis, Swiss Federal Institute of Technology, Zürich, Switzerland.

Künzli, S., Thiele, L., and Zitzler, E. (2005). Modular design space exploration framework for embedded systems. *IEE Proceedings Computers and Digital Techniques*, 152(2):183–192.

Kuo, W. and Wan, R. (2007). Recent advances in optimal reliability allocation. In Levitin, G., editor, *Computational Intelligence in Reliability Engineering*, volume 39 of *Studies in Computational Intelligence*, pages 1–36. Springer-Verlag, Berlin, Germany.

Kuperberg, M., Krogmann, K., and Reussner, R. (2008). Performance Prediction for Black-Box Components using Reengineered Parametric Behaviour Models. In *Proceedings of the 11th International Symposium on Component Based Software Engineering (CBSE 2008), Karlsruhe, Germany, 14th-17th October 2008*, volume 5282 of *Lecture Notes in Computer Science*, pages 48–63. Springer-Verlag Berlin Heidelberg.

Laumanns, M., Zitzler, E., and Thiele, L. (2001). On the effects of archiving, elitism, and density based selection in evolutionary multi-objective optimization. In Zitzler, E., Thiele, L., Deb, K., Coello Coello, C., and Corne, D., editors, *Evolutionary Multi-Criterion Optimization*, volume 1993 of *Lecture Notes in Computer Science*, pages 181–196. Springer-Verlag, Berlin, Germany. 10.1007/3-540-44719-9_13.

L'Ecuyer, P. and Buist, E. (2005). Simulation in Java with SSJ. In *WSC '05: Proceedings of the 37th conference on Winter simulation*, pages 611–620. Winter Simulation Conference.

Li, H., Casale, G., and Ellahi, T. (2010a). Sla-driven planning and optimization of enterprise applications. In *Proceedings of the first joint WOSP/SIPEW international conference on Performance engineering*, pages 117–128, New York, NY, USA. ACM.

Li, J. Z., Chinneck, J. W., Woodside, C. M., and Litoiu, M. (2009). Fast scalable optimization to configure service systems having cost and quality of service constraints. In Dobson, S. A., Strassner, J., Parashar, M., and Shehory, O., editors, *ICAC*, pages 159–168. ACM.

Li, R., Chaudron, M. R. V., and Ladan, R. C. (2010b). Towards automated software architectures design using model transformations and evolutionary algorithms. In *Genetic and Evolutionary Computation Conference, GECCO 2010, Proceedings, Portland, Oregon, USA, July 7-11, 2010, Companion Material*, pages 2097–2098.

Litoiu, M., Woodside, C. M., Wong, J., Ng, J., and Iszlai, G. (2010). A business driven cloud optimization architecture. In Shin, S. Y., Ossowski, S.,

Schumacher, M., Palakal, M. J., and Hung, C.-C., editors, *Proceedings of the 2010 ACM Symposium on Applied Computing (SAC), Sierre, Switzerland, March 22-26, 2010*, pages 380–385. ACM.

López-Ibáñez, M., Knowles, J. D., and Laumanns, M. (2011). On sequential online archiving of objective vectors. In Takahashi, R. H. C. et al., editors, *Evolutionary Multi-Criterion Optimization. 6th International Conference, EMO 2011*, volume 6576 of *Lecture Notes in Computer Science*, pages 46–60. Springer-Verlag, Berlin, Germany.

Luckham, D. C., Kenney, J. L., Augustin, L. M., Vera, J., Bryan, D., and Mann, W. (1995). Specification and analysis of system architecture using Rapide. *IEEE Transactions on Software Engineering*, 21(4):336–355.

Lukasiewycz, M., Glaß, M., Reimann, F., and Helwig, S. (2010). Opt4J - The Optimization Framework for Java. `http://www.opt4j.org`.

Luke, S. (2009). *Essentials of Metaheuristics*. Lulu. Available at `http://cs.gmu.edu/~sean/book/metaheuristics`.

Malavolta, I., Muccini, H., Pelliccione, P., and Tamburri, D. A. (2010). Providing architectural languages and tools interoperability through model transformation technologies. *IEEE Transactions of Software Engineering*, 36(1):119–140.

Martens, A., Ardagna, D., Koziolek, H., Mirandola, R., and Reussner, R. (2010). A Hybrid Approach for Multi-Attribute QoS Optimisation in Component Based Software Systems. In Heineman, G., Kofron, J., and Plasil, F., editors, *Research into Practice - Reality and Gaps (Proceedings of the 6th International Conference on the Quality of Software Architectures, QoSA 2010)*, volume 6093 of *Lecture Notes in Computer Science*, pages 84–101. Springer-Verlag Berlin Heidelberg.

Martens, A., Koziolek, H., Prechelt, L., and Reussner, R. (2011). From monolithic to component-based performance evaluation of software architectures. *Empirical Software Engineering*, 16(5):587–622.

Maswar, F., Chaudron, M. R. V., Radovanovic, I., and Bondarev, E. (2007). Improving architectural quality properties through model transformations. In *Proceedings of the 2007 International Conference on Software Engineering Research & Practice, SERP 2007, Volume II, June 25-28, 2007, Las Vegas Nevada, USA*, pages 687–693. CSREA Press.

McCall, J. A., Richards, P. K., and Walters, G. F. (1977). Factors in software quality, volume I, II, and III. Technical Report RADC-TR-77-369, Rome Air Development Center, Griffiss AFB, Rome, NY 13441-5700. Available from Defense Technical Information Center, Cameron Station, Alexandria, VA 22304-6145, order number ADA049014, ADA049015, and ADA049055.

McGregor, J. D., Bachmann, F., Bass, L., Bianco, P., and Klein, M. (2007). Using arche in the classroom: One experience. Technical Report CMU/SEI-2007-TN-001, Software Engineering Institute, Carnegie Mellon University.

Meedeniya, I., Buhnova, B., Aleti, A., and Grunske, L. (2010). Architecture-driven reliability and energy optimization for complex embedded systems. In *6th International Conference on the Quality of Software Architectures, QoSA 2010*, volume 6093 of *Lecture Notes in Computer Science*, pages 52–67. Springer.

Meedeniya, I., Buhnova, B., Aleti, A., and Grunske, L. (2011a). Reliability-driven deployment optimization for embedded systems. *Journal of Systems and Software*, 84(5):835 – 846.

Meedeniya, I., Moser, I., Aleti, A., and Grunske, L. (2011b). Software architecture evaluation under uncertainty. In *Proceedings of the Seventh*

International ACM Sigsoft Conference on the Quality of Software Architectures (QoSA 2011), Boulder, Colorado, USA. Association of Computing Machinery. to appear.

Menascé, D. A., Almeida, V. A. F., and Dowdy, L. W. (2004). *Performance by Design*. Prentice Hall.

Menascé, D. A., Casalicchio, E., and Dubey, V. (2008). A heuristic approach to optimal service selection in service oriented architectures. In Avritzer, A., Weyuker, E. J., and Woodside, C. M., editors, *Proceedings of the 7th Workshop on Software and Performance, WOSP 2008*, pages 13–24. ACM.

Menascé, D. A., Casalicchio, E., and Dubey, V. (2010a). On optimal service selection in service oriented architectures. *Performance Evaluation*, 67(8):659–675. Special Issue on Software and Performance.

Menascé, D. A., Ewing, J. M., Gomaa, H., Malex, S., and Sousa, J. a. P. (2010b). A framework for utility-based service oriented design in SASSY. In *Proc. of Proceedings of the first joint WOSP/SIPEW International Conference on Performance Engineering (WOSP/SIPEW)*, pages 27–36. ACM.

Merks, E. (2007). Is EMF going to replace MOF? `http://ed-merks.blogspot.com/2007/10/is-emf-going-to-replace-mof.html` (archived at `http://www.webcitation.org/5yKfkaro9`).

Microsoft Cooperation (2004). *Improving .NET Application Performance and Scalability (Patterns and Practices)*. Microsoft Press.

Miettinen, K. (2008). Introduction to multiobjective optimization: Noninteractive approaches. In Branke, J., Deb, K., Miettinen, K., and Slowinski, R., editors, *Multiobjective Optimization*, volume 5252 of *Lecture Notes in Computer Science*, pages 1–26. Springer.

Miettinen, K., Deb, K., Jahn, J., Ogryczak, W., Shimoyama, K., and Vetschera, R. (2008a). Future challenges. In Branke, J., Deb, K., Miettinen, K., and Slowinski, R., editors, *Multiobjective Optimization*, volume 5252 of *Lecture Notes in Computer Science*, pages 435–461. Springer-Verlag, Berlin, Germany.

Miettinen, K., Ruiz, F., and Wierzbicki, A. (2008b). Introduction to multiobjective optimization: Interactive approaches. In Branke, J., Deb, K., Miettinen, K., and Slowinski, R., editors, *Multiobjective Optimization*, volume 5252 of *Lecture Notes in Computer Science*, pages 27–57. Springer-Verlag, Berlin, Germany.

Montealegre, R. and Keil, M. (2000). De-escalating Information Technology Projects: Lessons from the Denver International Airport. *MIS Quarterly*, 3:417–447.

Musa, J. D., Iannino, A., and Okumoto, K. (1987). *Software Reliability – Measurement, prediction, application*. McGraw-Hill, New York.

Nannen, V., Smit, S. K., and Eiben, A. E. (2008). Costs and benefits of tuning parameters of evolutionary algorithms. In Rudolph, G., Jansen, T., Lucas, S. M., Poloni, C., and Beume, N., editors, *Parallel Problem Solving from Nature – (10th PPSN'08)*, volume 5199 of *Lecture Notes in Computer Science*, pages 528–538. Springer-Verlag, Berlin, Germany, Dortmund, Germany.

Noorshams, Q. (2010). Focusing the optimization of software architecture models using non-functional requirements. Master's thesis, Karlsruhe Institute of Technology, Germany. Advisors: Ralf Reussner, Anne Martens, Zoya Durdik, Johannes Stammel.

Noorshams, Q., Martens, A., and Reussner, R. (2010). Using quality of service bounds for effective multi-objective software architecture optimization. In *Proceedings of the 2nd International Workshop on the Quality of Service-Oriented Software Systems (QUASOSS '10), Oslo, Norway, October 4, 2010*, pages 1:1–1:6. ACM, New York, NY, USA.

Object Management Group (OMG) (2005). Unified Modeling Language Specification: Version 2, Revised Final Adopted Specification (ptc/05-07-04).

Object Management Group (OMG) (2006a). Meta Object Facility (MOF) Core Specification – Version 2.0.

Object Management Group (OMG) (2006b). Object Constraint Language – Version 2.0.

Object Management Group (OMG) (2006c). UML Profile for Modeling and Analysis of Real-Time and Embedded systems (MARTE) RFP (realtime/05-02-06).

Object Management Group (OMG) (2006d). Unified Modeling Language: Infrastructure – Version 2 (formal/05-07-05).

Object Management Group (OMG) (2009). Meta Object Facility (MOF) 2.0 Query/View/Transformation Specification – Version 1.1 Beta 2.

Paech, B., Oberweis, A., and Reussner, R. (2009). Qualität von Geschäftsprozessen und Unternehmenssoftware - Eine Thesensammlung. In Münch, J. and Liggesmeyer, P., editors, *Software Engineering (Workshops)*, volume 150 of *LNI*, pages 223–228. GI.

Pareto, V. (1896). *Cours D'Économie Politique*, volume I and II. F. Rouge, Lausanne.

Parsons, T. and Murphy, J. (2008). Detecting performance antipatterns in component based enterprise systems. *Journal of Object Technology*, 7(3):55–90.

Parsopoulos, K. E. and Vrahatis, M. N. (2002). Particle swarm optimization method in multiobjective problems. In *Proceedings of the 2002 ACM Symposium on Applied Computing (SAC), March 10-14, 2002, Madrid, Spain*, pages 603–607.

Pelikan, M., Goldberg, D. E., and Lobo, F. G. (2002). A survey of optimization by building and using probabilistic models. *Computational Optimization and Applications*, 21:5–20.

Perry, D. E. and Wolf, A. L. (1992). Foundations for the study of software architecture. *ACM SIGSOFT Software Engineering Notes*, 17(4):40–52.

Pillay, N. and Banzhaf, W. (2010). An informed genetic algorithm for the examination timetabling problem. *Applied Soft Computing*, 10(2):457 – 467.

Posch, T., Birken, K., and Gerdom, M. (2004). *Basiswissen Softwarearchitektur: Verstehen, entwerfen, wiederverwenden*. Dpunkt Verlag, 1 edition.

Pullum, L. L. (2001). *Software Fault Tolerance Techniques and Implementation*. Artech House Publishers.

R Development Core Team (2007). *R: A Language and Environment for Statistical Computing*. R Foundation for Statistical Computing, Vienna, Austria. ISBN 3-900051-07-0, Last retrieved 2008-01-06.

Reiser, M. and Lavenberg, S. S. (1980). Mean-value analysis of closed multichain queuing networks. *J. ACM*, 27:313–322.

Reussner, R., Becker, S., Burger, E., Happe, J., Hauck, M., Koziolek, A., Koziolek, H., Krogmann, K., and Kuperberg, M. (2011). The Palladio Component Model. Technical report, KIT, Fakultät für Informatik, Karlsruhe.

Reussner, R. H., Poernomo, I. H., and Schmidt, H. W. (2003). Reasoning on Software Architectures with Contractually Specified Components. In Cechich, A., Piattini, M., and Vallecillo, A., editors, *Component-Based Software Quality: Methods and Techniques*, volume 2693 of *Lecture Notes in Computer Science*, pages 287–325. Springer-Verlag Berlin Heidelberg.

Robertson, D. (2008). Ba loses 220,000 passengers following t5 debacle. Times Online. 2008-05-06. URL: `http://business.timesonline.co.uk/tol/business/industry_sectors/transport/article3881109.ece` (Archived by WebCite at `http://www.webcitation.org/5yZu6cxWM`).

ROBOCOP consortium (2003). ITEA Project ROBOCOP: Deliverable 1.5 - revised specification of framework and models. `http://www.hitech-projects.com/euprojects/robocop/deliverables_public/robocop_wp1_deliverable15_18july2003.pdf`.

Rohrberg, T. (2010). Result visualization and design decision support for the PCM. Master's thesis, Karlsruher Institut für Technologie. Advisors: Ralf Reussner, Anne Martens, Klaus Krogmann.

Rozanski, N. and Woods, E. (2005). *Software Systems Architecture: Working With Stakeholders Using Viewpoints and Perspectives*. Addison-Wesley.

Rudolph, G. (2001). Evolutionary search under partially ordered fitness sets. In Sebaaly, M., editor, *Proceedings of the International NAISO Congress on Information Science Innovations (ISI 2001)*, pages 818–822, Millet/Sliedrecht. ICSC Academic Press.

Rudolph, G. and Agapie, A. (2000). Convergence properties of some multi-objective evolutionary algorithms. In et al., A. Z., editor, *Proceedings of the 2000 Congress on Evolutionary Computation (CEC 2000)*, volume 2, pages 1010–1016, Piscataway (NJ). IEEE Press.

Saaty, T. L. (1980). *The Analytic Hierarchy Process, Planning, Piority Setting, Resource Allocation*. McGraw-Hill, New york.

Saxena, D. K., Ray, T., Deb, K., and Tiwari, A. (2009). Constrained many-objective optimization: A way forward. In *IEEE Congress on Evolutionary Computation*, pages 545–552. IEEE.

Saxena, T. and Karsai, G. (2010a). MDE-based approach for generalizing design space exploration. In *Model Driven Engineering Languages and Systems - 13th International Conference, MODELS 2010*, volume 6394 of *LNCS*, pages 46–60. Springer.

Saxena, T. and Karsai, G. (2010b). Towards a generic design space exploration framework. In *Proceedings of the 2010 10th IEEE International Conference on Computer and Information Technology*, CIT '10, pages 1940–1947, Washington, DC, USA. IEEE Computer Society.

Schaefer, C. A., Prankratius, V., and Tichy, W. F. (2010). Engineering parallel applications with tunable architectures. In *Proceedings of the 32nd ACM/IEEE International Conference on Software Engineering*, volume 1, pages 405–414. Association of Computing Machinery.

Schmidt, C. (2007). *Evolutionary computation in stochastic environments*. PhD thesis, Universität Karlsruhe.

Schmidt, D., Stal, M., Rohnert, H., and Buschmann, F. (2000). *Pattern-Oriented Software Architecture – Volume 2 – Patterns for Concurrent and Networked Objects*. Wiley & Sons, New York, NY, USA.

Schmietendorf, A. and Scholz, A. (2001). Aspects of Performance Engineering - an Overview. In Dumke, R., editor, *Performance Engineering: State of the art and current trends*, volume 2047 of *Lecture Notes in Computer Science*. Springer-Verlag, Berlin, Germany.

Sharma, V. S. and Jalote, P. (2008). Deploying software components for performance. In Chaudron, M. R. V., Szyperski, C. A., and Reussner, R., editors, *CBSE*, volume 5282 of *Lecture Notes in Computer Science*, pages 32–47. Springer.

Siegel, S. and Castellan, N. J. (1988). *Nonparametric Statistics for the Behavioral Sciences*. McGraw-Hill, 2 edition.

Smith, C. U. (1990). *Performance Engineering of Software Systems*. Addison-Wesley, Reading, MA, USA.

Smith, C. U. and Williams, L. G. (2000). Software performance antipatterns. In *Workshop on Software and Performance*, pages 127–136.

Smith, C. U. and Williams, L. G. (2002a). New software performance antipatterns: More ways to shoot yourself in the foot. In *Int. CMG Conference*, pages 667–674. Computer Measurement Group.

Smith, C. U. and Williams, L. G. (2002b). *Performance Solutions: A Practical Guide to Creating Responsive, Scalable Software*. Addison-Wesley, Boston, Mass.

Smith, C. U. and Williams, L. G. (2003). More new software antipatterns: Even more ways to shoot yourself in the foot. In *Int. CMG Conference*, pages 717–725. Computer Measurement Group.

Sommerville, I. (2004). *Software Engineering*. Pearson Education/Addison-Wesley, 7th edition.

Spears, W. M. and DeJong, K. A. (1991). On the virtues of parametrized uniform crossover. In Belew, R. K. and Booker, L. B., editors, *Proceedings of the Fourth International Conference on Genetic Algorithms (ICGA'91)*, pages 230–236, San Mateo, California. Morgan Kaufmann Publishers.

Srinivas, N. and Deb, K. (1994). Multiobjective Optimization Using Non-dominated Sorting in Genetic Algorithms. *Evolutionary Computation*, 2(3):221–248.

Stachowiak, H. (1973). *Allgemeine Modelltheorie*. Springer Verlag, Wien.

Stahl, T. and Völter, M. (2006). *Model-Driven Software Development*. John Wiley & Sons.

Steinberg, D., Budinsky, F., Paternostro, M., and Merks, E. (2008). *EMF: Eclipse Modeling Framework*. Eclipse series. Addison-Wesley Longman, Amsterdam, second revised edition.

Storm, I. T. (2008). SAP-Co Léo Apotheker räumt Fehler ein. Heise resale. 2009-05-16. URL: http://heise.de/-219358.

Suman, B. and Kumar, P. (2006). A survey of simulated annealing as a tool for single and multiobjective optimization. *Journal of the Operational Research Society*, 57(10):1143–1160.

Sywerda, G. (1989). Uniform crossover in genetic algorithms. In *Proceedings of the third international conference on Genetic algorithms*, pages 2–9, San Francisco, CA, USA. Morgan Kaufmann Publishers Inc.

Szyperski, C., Gruntz, D., and Murer, S. (2002). *Component Software: Beyond Object-Oriented Programming*. ACM Press and Addison-Wesley, New York, NY, 2 edition.

Taylor, R. N., Medvidovic, N., and Dashofy, E. M. (2009). *Software Architecture: Foundations, Theory, and Practice*. Wiley.

Thomson, R. (2008). Update: lack of software testing to blame for terminal 5 fiasco, ba executive tells mps. ComputerWeekly.com. 2008-03-05. URL: http://www.computerweekly.com/Articles/2008/05/09/230629/Update-lack-of-software-testing-to-blame-for-Terminal-5-fiasco-BA-executive-tells.htm.

Trautmann, H., Wagner, T., Naujoks, B., Preuß, M., and Mehnen, J. (2009). Statistical methods for convergence detection of multi-objective evolutionary algorithms. *Evolutionary Computation*, 17(4):493–509.

Trubiani, C. (2011). *A Model-based Framework for Software Performance Feedback*. PhD thesis, Università degli Studi dell'Aquila.

Trubiani, C. and Koziolek, A. (2011). Detection and solution of software performance antipatterns in palladio architectural models. In Kounev, S., Cortellessa, V., Mirandola, R., and Lilja, D. J., editors, *Proceeding of the second joint WOSP/SIPEW international conference on Performance engineering*, ICPE '11, pages 19–30. ACM, New York, NY, USA. ICPE best paper award.

van Veldhuizen, D. A. (1999). *Multiobjective Evolutionary Algorithms: Classifications, Analyses, and New Innovations*. PhD thesis, Department of Electrical and Computer Engineering. Graduate School of Engineering. Air Force Institute of Technology, Wright-Patterson AFB, Ohio. Technical report No. AFIT/DS/ENG/99-01.

van Veldhuizen, D. A. and Lamont, G. B. (1998). Multiobjective Evolutionary Algorithm Research: A History and Analysis. Technical Report TR-98-03, Department of Electrical and Computer Engineering, Graduate School of Engineering, Air Force Institute of Technology, Wright-Patterson AFB, Ohio.

van Veldhuizen, D. A. and Lamont, G. B. (2000). Multiobjective evolutionary algorithms: Analyzing the state-of-the-art. *Evolutionary Computation*, 8(2):125–147.

Varga, A. and Hornig, R. (2008). An overview of the OMNeT++ simulation environment. In Molnár, S., Heath, J. R., Dalle, O., and Wainer, G. A., editors, *SimuTools*, page 60. ICST.

Weise, T., Niemczyk, S., Skubch, H., Reichle, R., and Geihs, K. (2008). A tunable model for multi-objective, epistatic, rugged, and neutral fitness landscapes. In *2008 Genetic and Evolutionary Computation Conference (GECCO'2008)*, pages 795–802, Atlanta, USA. ACM Press. ISBN 978-1-60558-131-6.

Westermann, D. and Happe, J. (2010). Towards performance prediction of large enterprise applications based on systematic measurements. In Bühnová, B., Reussner, R. H., Szyperski, C., and Weck, W., editors, *Proceedings of the Fifteenth International Workshop on Component-Oriented Programming (WCOP) 2010*, volume 2010-14 of *Interne Berichte*, pages 71–78, Karlsruhe, Germany. Karlsruhe Institue of Technology, Faculty of Informatics.

Williams, L. G. and Smith, C. U. (2003). Making the Business Case for Software Performance Engineering. In *Proceedings of the 29th International Computer Measurement Group Conference, December 7-12, 2003, Dallas, Texas, USA*, pages 349–358. Computer Measurement Group.

Wolpert, D. H. and Macready, W. G. (1997). No free lunch theorem for optimization. *IEEE Transactions on Evolutionary Computation*, 1(1):67–82.

Woodside, C. M. and Monforton, G. G. (1993). Fast allocation of processes in distributed and parallel systems. *IEEE Trans. Parallel Distrib. Syst*, 4(2):164–174.

Woodside, M., Franks, G., and Petriu, D. C. (2007). The Future of Software Performance Engineering. In *Proceedings of ICSE 2007, Future of SE*, pages 171–187. IEEE Computer Society, Washington, DC, USA.

Woodside, M., Petriu, D. C., and Siddiqui, K. H. (2002). Performance-related Completions for Software Specifications. In *Proceedings of the*

22rd International Conference on Software Engineering, ICSE 2002, 19-25 May 2002, Orlando, Florida, USA, pages 22–32. ACM.

Wu, X. (2003). An Approach to Predicting Performance for Component Based Systems. Master's thesis, Carleton University.

Wu, X. and Woodside, C. M. (2004a). Performance modeling from software components. In Dujmovic, J. J., Almeida, V. A. F., and Lea, D., editors, *WOSP*, pages 290–301. ACM.

Wu, X. and Woodside, C. M. (2008). A calibration framework for capturing and calibrating software performance models. In Thomas, N. and Juiz, C., editors, *EPEW*, volume 5261 of *Lecture Notes in Computer Science*, pages 32–47. Springer-Verlag, Berlin, Germany.

Wu, X. and Woodside, M. (2004b). Performance Modeling from Software Components. *SIGSOFT Softw. Eng. Notes*, 29(1):290–301.

Xu, J. (2008). Rule-based automatic software performance diagnosis and improvement. In *WOSP '08: Proceedings of the 7th international workshop on Software and performance*, pages 1–12, New York, NY, USA. ACM.

Xu, J. (2010). Rule-based automatic software performance diagnosis and improvement. *Performance Evaluation*, 67(8):585–611. Special Issue on Software and Performance.

Yagiura, M. and Ibaraki, T. (2001). On metaheuristic algorithms for combinatorial optimization problems. *Systems and Computers in Japan*, 32(3):33–55.

Zeng, L., Benatallah, B., Dumas, M., Kalagnanam, J., and Sheng, Q. Z. (2003). Quality driven web services composition. In *WWW*, pages 411–421.

Zeng, L., Benatallah, B., Ngu, A. H. H., Dumas, M., Kalagnanam, J., and Chang, H. (2004). QoS-aware middleware for web services composition. *IEEE Trans. Software Eng*, 30(5):311–327.

Zeng, L., Ngu, A., Benatallah, B., Podorozhny, R., and Lei, H. (2008). Dynamic composition and optimization of web services. *Distributed and Parallel Databases*, 24:45–72. 10.1007/s10619-008-7030-7.

Zheng, T. and Woodside, C. M. (2003). Heuristic optimization of scheduling and allocation for distributed systems with soft deadlines. In Kemper, P. and Sanders, W. H., editors, *Computer Performance Evaluation / TOOLS*, volume 2794 of *Lecture Notes in Computer Science*, pages 169–181. Springer.

Zhu, L., Aurum, A., Gorton, I., and Jeffery, D. R. (2005). Tradeoff and sensitivity analysis in software architecture evaluation using analytic hierarchy process. *Software Quality Journal*, 13(4):357–375.

Zitzler, E. (1999). *Evolutionary Algorithms for Multiobjective Optimization: Methods and Applications*. PhD thesis, ETH Zürich, Switzerland.

Zitzler, E., Deb, K., and Thiele, L. (2000). Comparison of Multiobjective Evolutionary Algorithms: Empirical Results. *Evolutionary Computation*, 8(2):173–195.

Zitzler, E., Knowles, J., and Thiele, L. (2008). *Quality Assessment of Pareto Set Approximations*, volume 5252 of *LNCS*, pages 373–404. Springer-Verlag, Berlin.

Zitzler, E. and Künzli, S. (2004). Indicator-based selection in multiobjective search. In Yao, X., Burke, E., Lozano, J. A., Smith, J., Merelo-Guervós, J. J., Bullinaria, J. A., Rowe, J., Kabán, P. T. A., and Schwefel, H.-P., editors, *Parallel Problem Solving from Nature - PPSN VIII*, volume 3242 of *LNCS*, pages 832–842, Birmingham, UK. Springer-Verlag.

Zitzler, E., Laumanns, M., and Thiele, L. (2002a). SPEA2: Improving the Strength Pareto Evolutionary Algorithm. In Giannakoglou, K., Tsahalis, D., Periaux, J., Papailou, P., and Fogarty, T., editors, *EUROGEN 2001. Evolutionary Methods for Design, Optimization and Control with Applications to Industrial Problems*, pages 95–100, Athens, Greece.

Zitzler, E. and Thiele, L. (1999). Multiobjective evolutionary algorithms: a comparative case study and the strength pareto approach. *IEEE Trans. Evolutionary Computation*, 3(4):257–271.

Zitzler, E., Thiele, L., and Bader, J. (2010). On set-based multiobjective optimization. *IEEE Transactions on Evolutionary Computation*, 14:58–79.

Zitzler, E., Thiele, L., Laumanns, M., Fonseca, C. M., and da Fonseca, V. G. (2002b). Performance assessment of multiobjective optimizers: An analysis and review. *IEEE Trans. on Evolutionary Computation*, 7:117–132.

Index

$M(p \leftarrow v)$, *see* Change value of property

$P(S_r^i)$, *see* Pareto front, Of run r at iteration i

T, *see* Candidate transformation function

Φ, *see* Candidate evaluation function

Φ^*, *see* Quality evaluation function

Φ_Q, *see* Multi-objective candidate evaluation function

$M \blacktriangleleft MM$, *see* Conforms-to relationship

$M \vartriangleleft MM$, *see* Structurally-conforms-to relationship

changeable(ct), *see* Changeable element

ct, *see* Change Type

designOptions(d), *see* Design option set

hvolume(P, z), *see* Hyper-volume

primaryChangeable(ct), *see* Primary changeable element

primaryChanged(d), *see* Primary changed model element

updated(c), *see* Change

e instanceOf *mc*, *see* Instance-of relationship for model elements

$\leq_{qm}$, *see* Order on a quality metric domain

$\mathscr{C}^*$, *see* Coverage indicator

$\mathscr{D}$, *see* Design Space, Unconstrained Design Space

$\mathscr{F}$, *see* Design Space, Feasible Design Space

$\mathscr{O}$, *see* Decision space

$\mathscr{S}^*$, *see* Hyper-volume indicator

$\mathscr{T}_q$, *see* Time savings metric

$\prec$, *see* Pareto dominance

$\preceq$, *see* Weak Pareto dominance

$c_1 \circ c_2$, *see* Sequence of changes

d, *see* Degree of Freedom Instance

$e \in M$, *see* Model element

g, *see* Degree of Freedom

q, *see* Quality criterion

qm, *see* Quality metric

x, *see* Candidate vector or decision vector

$z_{F,Q,R}$, *see* Reference point for hyper-volume indicator

$m(q)$, *see* Quality metric

Allocation, 245

Architectural Candidate Model, 220

Architecture Trade-off Analysis Method, 36

ATAM, *see* Architecture Trade-off Analysis Method

Business quality attributes, 35

Candidate evaluation, 294

Candidate evaluation function, 275

Candidate Model, *see* Architectural Candidate Model

Candidate representation, 291

Candidate reproduction, 299

Candidate selection, 302

Candidate transformation function, 222

Candidate vector, 221

CBA, *see* Component-based software architecture

CBA model, *see* Component-based architecture model

CBAM, *see* Costs Benefit Analysis Method

CBML, *see* Component-Based Modeling Language

Change, 179

   Change with conforming models, 180

   Valid Change, 181

Change Group, 191

Change Type, 182

   Change Type that Affects a Quality Attribute, 184

   Functionally Equivalent Change Type, 183

   Indivisible Change Type, 187

Change value of property, 203

Changeable element, 182, 198

Component, *see* Software component

Component allocation, *see* Allocation

Component assembly, 26

Component composition, 26

Component selection, *see* Selection of components

Component-based architecture, *see* Component-based software architecture

Component-Based Modeling Language, 70

Component-based software architecture, 5, 27

Component-based architecture model, 28

Composed structure, 26

Conforms-to relationship, 44

Costs, 35, 39

Costs Benefit Analysis Method, 36

Coverage indicator, 404

Crossover operator, 89, 301

Decision space, 75, 221

Decision vector, 75

Degree of Freedom, 198

Degree of Freedom Instance, 201

Degrees of freedom for CBA, 233, 234

Design option set, 201

Design Space
  Feasible Design Space, 225
  Unconstrained Design Space, 221

Design space constraints, 224, 301

DoF, *see* Degree of Freedom

DoFI, *see* Degree of freedom instance

EMOF, *see* Essential Meta Object Facility

Essential Meta Object Facility, 46

Formal model, 43

Hyper-volume, 100

Hyper-volume indicator, 405

Instance-of relationship for model elements, 44

Instance-of relationship for models, 44

Intensification, 328

Interaction constraints, 196

Interaction of changes, 196

Layered Queueing Network, 70

LQN, *see* Layered Queueing Network

Metamodel, 43

Model, 43

Model element, 44

Model-based quality prediction, 49

Modifiability, 34
Monetary benefit, 35
Multi-criteria optimization, 77
Multi-objective candidate evaluation function, 277
Multi-objective optimization, 76, 77
Mutation operator, 88, 300

Objective space, 76
Optimization, 75
Optimization framework, 332
Optimization problem, 76, 277
Order on a quality metric domain, 275

Palladio Component Model, 59
Pareto dominance, 81
Pareto dominance ranking, 97
Pareto front, 82
    Of run *r* at iteration *i*, 403
Pareto optimality, 82
Pareto-optimal candidates, 277
PCM, *see* Palladio Component Model
Performance, 33
Performance of an optimization technique, 360
POFOD, *see* Probability of failure on demand
Primary Changeable Element, 189

Primary changeable element, 198
Primary changed model element, 201
Probability of failure on demand, 39

Quality attribute, 35
Quality bound, 42
Quality criterion, 39, 40
Quality effects, 232
Quality evaluation function, 51
Quality metric, 38
Quality of an optimization technique, 360
Quality property, 42
Quality requirement, 41

Reference point for hypervolume indicator, 404
Reliability, 33
Resource selection, 256
Response time, 39

Security, 34
Selection of components, 235
Selection rules, 195
Sequence of changes, 186
Single-objective optimization, 75
Software component, 25
Software quality attributes, 33

Starting population, 329

Stop criteria, 307

Structurally-conforms-to rela-
        tionship, 44

Structurally-conforms-to rela-
        tionship, 44

Tactics, 308

Tactics operators, 324

Testability, 34

Time savings metric, 407

Time-to-market, 35

Valid model instance, 44

Value rules, 195

Weak Pareto dominance, 82